# *WAFFEN-SS* ARMOUR IN NORMANDY

## THE COMBAT HISTORY OF *SS-PANZER REGIMENT 12* AND *SS-PANZERJÄGER ABTEILUNG 12*, NORMANDY 1944, BASED ON THEIR ORIGINAL WAR DIARIES

### Norbert Számvéber

Translated by Blanka Gálné Bíró
Additional translation by Dr Frederick P. Steinhardt, MS, PhD.

## Helion & Company Ltd

Helion & Company Limited
26 Willow Road
Solihull
West Midlands
B91 1UE
England
Tel. 0121 705 3393
Fax 0121 711 4075
Email: info@helion.co.uk
Website: www.helion.co.uk

Published by Helion & Company 2012

Designed and typeset by Farr out Publications, Wokingham, Berkshire
Cover designed by Farr out Publications, Wokingham, Berkshire
Printed by Gutenberg Press Limited, Tarxien, Malta

ISBN 978 1 907677 24 3

British Library Cataloguing-in-Publication Data.
A catalogue record for this book is available from the British Library.

For details of other military history titles published by Helion & Company Limited contact the above address, or visit our website: http://www.helion.co.uk.

We always welcome receiving book proposals from prospective authors.

# Contents

---

\*      This Appendix also includes biographical data relating to several award holders who were not officers.

---

†     This Appendix also includes biographical data relating to several award holders who were not officers.

# List of Illustrations

The images of individuals that follow include not only personnel of *SS-Panzer Regiment 12* and *SS-Panzerjäger Abteilung 12*, but others relevant to both formations from *"Hitlerjugend"* as well as other units. As a component of the *I.SS-Panzer Korps*, both units considered in this volume often fought in conjunction with other elements of *"Hitlerjugend"* along with other units subordinated to the *Korps*. In the latter case these were primarily parts of the *1.SS-Panzer Division "Leibstandarte"* and the Tiger-equipped *schwere SS-Panzer Abteilung 101*. In instances where notations direct the reader to either Appendix II or Appendix XVIII, these include both biographical data as well as the surviving recommendations for the awards in question. Combined, *SS-Panzer Abteilung 12* and *SS-Panzerjäger Abteilung 12* were awarded one Oakleaves to the Knight's Cross, seven awards of the Knight's Cross, and nine awards of the German Cross in Gold for combats during the Normandy campaign. Other captions direct the reader to biographical footnotes for personnel specifically outside the two primary units under study, aside from those individuals also being mentioned in the primary text.

# List of Maps

## Black and white maps

All the above maps are used with the permission of the Vojenský Historický Archiv, Praha.

## Colour maps (in colour section)

Colour map 1 © Barbara Taylor, colour maps 2-8 used with the permission of Hubert Meyer and J.J. Fedorowicz Publishing Inc.

# Glossary

| | |
|---|---|
| *Abteilung* | detachment/battalion (dependent upon context) |
| *Abteilungskommandeur* | detachment/battalion commander |
| *Abteilungsarzt* | detachment/battalion doctor |
| *Armeekorps* | Army Corps |
| *Artillerie* | artillery |
| *Arzt* | doctor |
| *Aufklärung* | reconnaissance |
| *Aufklärungsabteilung* | reconnaissance detachment |
| *Aufklärungszug* | reconnaissance platoon |
| *Aufstellungsstab* | formation staff |
| *Ausbildungs* | training |
| *Ausbildungs und Ersatz* | training and replacement |
| *Bataillon* | battalion |
| *Bataillonsarzt* | battalion doctor |
| *Batterie* | battery |
| *Befehlshaber* | senior area commander |
| *Chefsarzt* | head surgeon |
| *d.R. (der Reserve)* | reserve grade officer |
| *Divisionsarzt (IVb)* | divisional doctor |
| *Divisionsbegleitkompanie* | divisional escort company |
| *Divisionsstab* | divisional staff |
| *Einheit* | unit, could be a generic term, or refer to a specific, often temporary unit, e.g. *Einheit "Krause"* |
| *Einsatzstab* | operational staff |
| *Ersatz* | replacement |
| *Feldbrückekolonne* | field bridging column |
| *Feldlazarett* | field hospital |
| *Flak* | anti-aircraft |
| *Generalstabsoffizier* | General Staff Officer |
| *Gruppe* | squad |
| *Gruppenführer* | squad leader, also an SS General officer rank |
| *Halbzugführer* | half platoon leader |
| *Hauptmann beim Stabe* | battalion staff head |
| *Heeresgruppe* | Army Group |
| *Hilfsarzt* | assistant doctor |
| *Ia* | first staff officer (*1.Generalstabsoffizier*) |
| *Ib* | supply officer |
| *Ic* | intelligence officer |
| *IIa* | adjutant |

11

| | |
|---|---|
| *IVa* | administrative officer |
| *IVb* | doctor |
| *V* | engineer |
| *Infanterie* | infantry |
| *Inspekteur* | Inspector |
| *Instandsetzungsabteilung* | maintenance detachment |
| *Kampfgruppe* | battle group (temporarily assembled) |
| *Kommandeur* | commander |
| *Kompanie* | company |
| *Kompanie Chef* | company commander (permanent) |
| *Kompanie Führer* | company leader (not permanently designated, although they often were later) |
| *Korps* | corps |
| *Kraderkundungszug* | motorcycle reconnaissance platoon |
| *Kradmelderzug* | motorcycle dispatch rider platoon |
| *Kradschützen* | motorcycle riflemen |
| *Kradschützenzug* | motorcycle platoon |
| *Krankenkraftwagenkolonne* | ambulance column |
| *Lehrgruppe* | teaching group |
| *leichte* | light |
| *Major beim Stabe* | regimental staff head |
| MLR | main line of resistance (in German, *HKL, Hauptkampflinie*) |
| *Nachschubdienst* | supply service |
| *Nachschubtruppen* | supply troops |
| *Nachrichten* | signals/communications |
| *Nachrichtenoffizier* | signals officer |
| *Nachrichtenzug* | signals platoon |
| *Nachrichtenabteilung* | signals detachment |
| *NPEA* | *Nationalpolitische Erziehungsansalt*, National Political Education Institute |
| *O1* | ordnance officer, assigned to Ia |
| *O2* | ordnance officer, assigned to Ib |
| *Offizier* | Officer |
| *Ordnungspolizei* | Order Police (uniformed) |
| *Ordonnanz Offizier* | ordnance officer |
| *O.U.* | lit. *Ortsunterkunft*, a designation which means the entry was written at the present location of the unit, ie. location on that date |
| *Panzer* | armour/tank |
| *Panzer Grenadier* | armoured infantry |
| *Panzergrenadierschule* | armoured infantry school |
| *Panzerjäger* | tank hunter |
| *Panzerjägerzug* | tank hunter platoon |
| *Panzerjäger Abteilung* | tank hunter detachment |
| *Panzerkorps* | armoured corps |

| | |
|---|---|
| *Pionier* | engineer |
| *Pionier Bataillon* | engineer battalion |
| *Regimentsarzt* | regimental doctor |
| *Regimentskommandeur* | regimental commander |
| *Sanitäts* | medical |
| *Sanitätsabteilung* | medical detachment |
| *Sanitätskompanie* | medical company |
| *Sanitäts Staffel* | medical group |
| *Scheinwerfer* | searchlight |
| *Schirrmeister* | NCO for motor vehicles |
| *Stab* | staff/HQ |
| *Stabsbatterie* | staff battery |
| *Stabschef* | Chief of Staff |
| *Stabskompanie* | staff company |
| *Stabsscharführer* | senior designated NCO |
| *Sturmgeschütz* | assault gun (limited traverse armoured vehicle) |
| *TFK* | Technical Officer for Vehicles |
| *TFW* | Technical Officer for Weapons |
| *Truppführer* | squad leader |
| *Truppenübungsplatz* | troop training area |
| *Unterführeranwärter Lehrgang* | non-commissioned officer-candidate instruction course |
| *Versorgungskompanie* | supply company |
| *Verwaltungsführer* | officer responsible for administration |
| *Verwaltungsoffizier* | administrative officer |
| *Werfer* | rocket projector |
| *Werkmeister* | maintenance foreman |
| *Werkstattkompanie* | repair company |
| *Werkstattzug* | repair platoon |
| *Wirtschafts Abteilung* | administrative detachment |
| *Zahnarzt* | dentist |
| *Zug* | platoon |
| *Zugführer* | platoon leader |
| *II.Zugführer* | 2nd platoon leader |
| *2./SS-Panzer-Grenadier-Regiment 25* | 2nd Company of SS-Armoured Infantry Regiment 25 (same for a Panzer Regiment) |
| *III./ SS-Panzer-Grenadier-Regiment 25* | 3rd Battalion of SS-Armoured Infantry Regiment 25 |
| *I./Artillerie Regiment* | 1st Detachment of the Artillery Regiment (same for Panzer Regiment) |
| *3./Artillerie Regiment* | 3rd Battery of the Artillery Regiment |
| *2./Panzerjäger Abteilung* | 2nd Company of Tank Hunter Detachment |

# Introduction

In recent years a number of books, articles and other publications have been issued regarding the fighting in Normandy during 1944. These works discuss in great detail the operations, including the equipment, armament, tactics, command practice and tactical operational decisions of both sides.[1] Why, then, another book about the German troops in Normandy? Is there anything that we don't already know about these operations?

Most of the documentation of the German operational and strategic command and control levels has survived and is available to military historians. However, the contemporary unit documentation of the German troops deployed in Normandy is mostly unavailable in military archives today. Such documents were mainly compiled from the official war diaries of the different units with attachments and appendices (reports, accounts, telegrams, map drafts, etc.). The majority of these documents were, either deliberately or accidentally, eradicated in the hell of the Falaise Cauldron in August 1944 or during the chaotic withdrawal. This is why it is so significant that almost the complete unit documentation of the *12.SS-Panzer Division "Hitlerjugend"*, the main German unit involved in the fighting around Caen and Falaise, survives in the Military History Archives of the Czech Army in Prague.

I would like to thank both Colonel Mgr. Josef Žikeš, director of the Vojenský Ústřední Archiv in Prague and PhDr. Július Baláž, CSc., director of the Vojenský Historický Archiv, for their help. Without them this book could never have been completed.

The majority of these contemporary documents, of which there are a massive amount, have never been published, thus it is hoped military historians will find it useful to be able to access the almost full-length original documents in English. These documents were written during the summer of 1944 by *SS-Panzer Regiment 12* and *SS-Panzerjäger Abteilung 12*. The former unit was equipped with Panther and Panzer IV tanks, and was often used as the iron fist of the division.

The war diary entries and the attachments of both *SS-Panzer Abteilung* are given in chronological order. The numerous military abbreviations used have been simplified in the translation in order to aid understanding. Where it was necessary we have included additions in brackets to help understand the text, due to the omission of many verbs and nouns in the original German documents. At the same time we have striven to keep the contemporary military style of the war diaries, which was often quite laconic. Footnotes have been added for explanation, and to help interpret and contextualise the text. Typing errors in the original German text have been corrected without indication. Appendix numbers appearing in Arabic numerals refer to original war diary appendices that are, where possible, reproduced within the main text; appendices with Roman numerals direct readers to appendices at the end of this book. Due to the repeated occurrence of

---

1   One of the most detailed summaries of the German battle for Normandy is Niklas Zetterling, *Normandy 1944: German Military Organization, Combat Power and Organizational Effectiveness,* Winnipeg: J.J. Fedorowicz, 2000.

SS ranks, the prefix *SS-* before each, e.g. *SS-Unterscharführer*, has been omitted to avoid constant repetition and to save space; however, this prefix is present throughout the original documents.

*Waffen-SS* numerical designations generally followed the Army system utilized in the prewar *SS-Verfügungstruppe*. Roman numerals designated a platoon (*Zug*), battalion (Bataillon), detachment (*Abteilung*), and a corps (*Korps*). Arabic numbers designated a company (*Kompanie*), battery (*Batterie*), and Division (*Division*). Thus, the *I./3./SS-Panzer-Grenadier-Regiment 26* was the 1st Platoon of the 3rd Company of *SS-Panzer-Grenadier-Regiment 26*. The *3./III./SS-Panzer-Grenadier-Regiment 26* was the 3rd Company, 3rd Battalion of *SS-Panzer-Grenadier-Regiment 26*. In most instances only a single number identified the sub-unit in question, such as the *3./SS-Panzer-Artillerie-Regiment 12* designating the 3rd Battery of the artillery contingent or the *4./SS-Panzer Regiment 12* denoting the 4th Company of *SS-Panzer Regiment 12*. German artillery and tank units were designated detachments, along with some smaller divisional elements, while American forces of the period used the term battalions for similar units.

The *12.SS-Panzer Division* not only had tanks; it also had Jagdpanzer IVs within *SS-Panzerjäger Abteilung 12*. The second half of the book outlines the history of this unit in Normandy, based on their war diaries and other documents from the *Abteilung*.

The book is thus a unique composition of primary sources based on the war diaries of *SS-Panzer Regiment 12* and *SS-Panzerjäger Abteilung 12*, together with explanations and original research. A section about combat history in Normandy, paralleling the unit history of the *12.SS-Panzer Division*,[2] has also been included.

Those who are interested will find a number of supplementary tables in the appendices section. The data in these tables are partly derived directly from the contemporary documents, and are partly our summaries of the original data.

I would like to thank Mr. Duncan Rogers for opening the door to publishing this book in English.

I am also thankful for Péter Illésfalvi, my colleague and friend, who helped me select photographs from the collection belonging to the HM Museum and Institute of Military History (HM Hadtörténeti Intézet és Múzeum).

The publishers and myself would like to thank Mr. Mark C. Yerger for contributing so much to this book. He readily helped proofread and added much information relating to the *12.SS-Panzer Division* generally, and its officers in particular. He also was very generous with sending us photographs and documents which have enhanced this book greatly. We would also like to thank M. Charles Trang for assisting with some of the photographs.

I hope that the data provided in this book will serve as a helpful addition to existing accounts of the combat fought in Normandy in 1944, especially that of the tank battles which raged on the frontline.

My family has had to put up with me while I was working on this book. Not only did they have to live without me for a while, but as I worked I listened mostly to the German thrash metal band Kreator to help keep my thoughts on appropriate Germanic culture!

---

2    See Hubert Meyer, *Kriegsgeschichte der 12. SS-Panzerdivision "Hitlerjugend"*, Band I, Osnabrück: Biblio Verlag, 1999, 4th edition.

My lovely wife was endlessly patient, and kindly proofread the manuscript for me. I am extremely grateful to her.

Norbert Számvéber

# Part I

# The Combat History of *SS-Panzer Regiment 12* in Normandy

# 1

# Organization and Training of *SS-Panzer Regiment 12* (29 June 1943–6 June 1944)

Initial negotiations concerning an *SS Division* to be composed of young members of the *Hitlerjugend* commenced in February 1943 between the representatives of the Waffen-SS and the National Socialist youth organization. On their recommendation on 24 June 1943 Adolf Hitler issued an order for the division to be set up in the Beverloo training facility north of Brussels.

The officers and NCOs of the new unit were reassigned from its patron division the *1.SS-Panzer-Grenadier-Division "Leibstandarte SS Adolf Hitler"*[1]. The enlisted were mainly German young men born in the first half of 1926 who had already received paramilitary training.

*SS-Panzer Regiment 12* had been in formation since 29 June 1943 in the Mailly-le-Camp training facility northeast of Paris. Approximately 200 soldiers were transferred to the new regiment from the patron division's *SS-Panzer Regiment 1*. At the end of 1943 the *I./SS-Panzer Regiment 12* was still far from being operational. The chronology of the organization, training and equipment of the unit in 1944 is as follows:[2]

| | |
|---|---|
| 1 January 1944 | *SS-Panzer Regiment 12*, which at the time was stationed at the Mailly-le-Camp training facility in France, received an order from the *Oberbefehlshaber "West"* (Senior Area Commander "West") to relocate to the training facility near Beverloo in Belgium to join the other units of the division being trained there. |
| 4 January 1944 | Distribution of the tactical identification (turret) numbers. The tactical identification number system applied in *SS-Panzer Regiment 12* was different from the principles followed by the Army and the armoured units within the *Waffen-SS*. |
| | Turret number 055 was assigned to the tank of the *Regimentskommandeur*, turret number 054 to the *Regimentsadjutant*, and turret number 053 to the *Regiment Ordonnanz Offizier*. Numbers 055–060 were assigned to the tanks of the regimental (Panzer IV) *Panzer Aufklärungszug*. The commander of the *I./SS-Panzer Regiment 12* received the number 155 for his tank, the number 154 was assigned |

---

1   The name of the division was usually abbreviated as *"LAH"* or *"LSSAH"*. In wartime as a brigade and later division its standard title was *"Leibstandarte,"* the lengthier title was more from its *SS-Verfügungstruppe* period and earlier when a bodyguard unit.

2   Unless indicated otherwise, data has been taken from the activity report of *SS-Panzer Regiment 12* between 1 January and 4 June 1944. See Vojenský Historický Archiv, Praha (Military History Archives, Prague), Tätigkeitsbericht des *SS-Panzer Regiments 12*, 1 Januar–4 Juni 1944.

The first commander of the *12.SS-Panzer Division "Hitlerjugend"*, Fritz Witt is shown as an *Obersturmbannführer* in a signed photo (see Chapter 2 Footnote 5). (Mark C. Yerger)

Josef "Sepp" Dietrich commanded the *I.SS-Panzer Korps* in Normandy (see Chapter 2 Footnote 23). (Mark C. Yerger)

to the *Abteilungsadjutant* and the *Nachrichtenoffizier* was given turret number 153. The five (Panther) tanks of the *Panzer Aufklärungszug* of *I./SS-Panzer Regiment 12* were given the numbers 156–160. The commander of the *II./SS-Panzer Regiment 12* received turret number 555, number 554 was assigned to his *Adjutant* and number 553 was handed out to the *Nachrichtenoffizier*. Turret numbers 556–560 were assigned to the (Panzer IV) *Panzer Aufklärungszug* of the *II./SS-Panzer Regiment 12*.[3]

The 35cm high, 22cm wide numbers with 1cm border had to be painted in black, on the back of the tanks, and on the sides of their turrets, which were painted in camouflage colours. Between the numbers a 4cm wide clear stripe had to be left.[4]

---

3   See Appendix III for the original order. The numbering system of the tanks of the *Kompanie Chef* was as follows: the number of their *Kompanie* + 05 (for example 105 for the *Chef* of the *1.Kompanie* and 505 for the *Chef* of the *5.Kompanie*), the reserve tank (which at the same time served as the tank of the deputy *Kompanie Chef*) received its number according to the *Kompanie* number + 04 (for example 104 for *1.Kompanie* and 504 for *5.Kompanie*). Within the platoon the first tank (of the *Zugführer*) received the number made up from the *Kompanie* number, that of the platoon, and + 5 (for example the *Zugführer* of the *I./1.Kompanie* received turret number 115). Further tanks of the platoon were given the numbers 6, 7, 8 and 9 following the number of their *Kompanie* and *Zug* number, for example, the five tanks of the *I./1.Kompanie* were designated by the numbers 115, 116, 117, 118 and 119. The last tank of the *III./8. Kompanie* received number 839. See Anlage II/4 zum Tätigkeitsbericht *SS-Panzer Regiment 12*.

4   See Appendix III for the original order. According to original photographs, some of which can be seen in this book, the numbers were painted with black numbers in a white border on the Panzer IVs, and with red numbers in a white border on the Panthers. The size and system of the numbers remained as described above.

An excellent close-up of a Panzer IV from *II./SS-Panzer Regiment 12* on exercises in Belgium, winter 1943/44. (Bundesarchiv, Bild 101I-297-1722-27, photo: Kurth)

Panzer IV from *6.Kompanie II./SS-Panzer Regiment 12*, Belgium, winter 1943/44. This image gives a good impression of the application of the tactical numbers to the tanks. (Bundesarchiv, Bild 101I-297-1725-09, photo: Kurth)

A frontal view of the same Panzer IV. (Bundesarchiv, Bild 101I-297-1725-11, photo: Kurth)

*Generalfeldmarschall* Gerd von Rundstedt observing exercises conducted by *SS-
Panzer Regiment 12*, March 1944. From left to right: von Rundstedt (*Oberbefehlshaber
West*), *Standartenführer* Kurt Meyer (commander *SS-Panzer-Grenadier-Regiment
25*, later commander *12.SS-Panzer Division*), *Brigadeführer* Fritz Witt (commander,
*12.SS-Panzer Division*), *Obergruppenführer* Joseph Dietrich (commander, *I.SS-
Panzer Korps*). (Bundesarchiv, Bild 101I-297-1739-16A, photo: Kurth)

Panzer IV tanks from *5.Kompanie, II./SS-Panzer Regiment 12* parade
before *Generalfeldmarschall* Gerd von Rundstedt, March 1944.
(Bundesarchiv, Bild 101I-297-1740-19A, photo: Kurth)

| | |
|---|---|
| 7 January 1944 | Arrival of a new Panther tank for the *I./SS-Panzer Regiment 12*. |
| 10 January 1944 | Beginning of the train loading in Mailly-le-Camp. |
| 16 January 1944 | *SS-Panzer Regiment 12* arrived at the training facility near Beverloo. |
| 29 January 1944 | Regrouping of the *I./SS-Panzer Regiment 12* and the regimental units to Hasselt and the northern region. |
| 31 January 1944 | The training of the *I./SS-Panzer Regiment 12* in January proceeded as ordered, although the shortage of fuel and training ammunition hindered the work. One NCO and three enlisted men were killed this month. |
| 6 February 1944 | *Generaloberst* Heinz Guderian, General Inspector for the *Panzertruppen*, inspected the drill of the *3./SS-Panzer Regiment 12* with the theme, "attack in motion against enemy in the air". During the first week of February 16 Panther tanks arrived for the *I./SS-Panzer Regiment 12*. |
| 15 February 1944 | Command drill of the *I./SS-Panzer Regiment 12* with the theme: "attack of a Panzer *Abteilung* with limited goals". The regimental *Flak Zug* (one officer, five NCOs and 64 enlisted men), with *Zugführer Untersturmführer* Walter Schaffert were directed to Schwetzingen, in order to receive training with *Panzer-Ausbildungs-und Ersatz Abteilung 204*. |

Max Wünsche as a *Sturmbannführer* with the *"Leibstandarte"* wearing
his Knight's Cross, later the first commander of *SS-Panzer Regiment
12* (see Appendix II and main text). (Mark C. Yerger)

*Obersturmbannführer* Max Wünsche in his Panther command tank (*Pz Bef Wg Panther*)
during an exercise with *SS-Panzer Regiment 12* in Belgium, March 1944. The additional
antennae for the command equipment are clearly visible. (National Archives)

A close-up view of *Obersturmbannführer* Max Wünsche, Belgium, March 1944. Note the *zimmerit* anti-magnetic mine paste on the tank. (National Archives)

Panthers from *2.Kompanie, I./SS-Panzer Regiment 12* on exercise in Belgium, March 1944. (National Archives)

A Panther from *I./SS-Panzer Regiment 12*, Belgium, March 1944. (National Archives)

A rear view of Wünsche's command Panther, Belgium, March 1944. (National Archives)

An iconic view of *Obersturmbannführer* Max Wünsche, commander of *SS-Panzer Regiment 12* during the fighting in Normandy. (National Archives)

17 February 1944   The regimental *Panzer-Pionier-Kompanie* was created from the *Ausbildungskompanie* of *SS-Panzer-Pionier-Bataillon 12* (*Kompanie Chef*: *Oberleutnant* Müller[5]) near Zonhoven.

29 February 1944   Command drill for the *Zugführer* und *Kompanie Chef* at the *Stab* of the *12.SS-Panzer Division* in Turnhout. Theme: "Panzer group combat against panzer group".

During the month, four enlisted men were killed, and one NCO was shot in accordance with the death-sentence of the field court martial.

3 March 1944   Participation of *SS-Panzer Regiment 12* in battle-group training with the armoured personnel vehicles of the *III./SS-Panzer-Grenadier-Regiment 26* and the Wespe and Hummel self-propelled howitzers of the *I./SS-Panzer-Artillerie-Regiment 12*. Themes covered: "attack of armoured *Kampfgruppe* with limited goals" and "cooperation of subordinated units and armament".

12 March 1944   Drill of *SS-Panzer Regiment 12* at full strength. Theme: "*Kampfgruppe* against *Kampfgruppe*".

5   Because of the shortage of trained officers, approximately 50 officers were reassigned from the German Army to the *12.SS-Panzer Division "Hitlerjugend"*. Most of them were former members of the *Hitlerjugend*. They did not wear SS uniforms, but belonged to the division strength in every other sense. See also Hubert Meyer, *Kriegsgeschichte der 12. SS-Panzerdivision "Hitlerjugend"* Band I, Osnabrück: Biblio Verlag, 1999, 4th edition, p.19 (hereafter cited as Meyer).

14-17 March 1944    Command and signal drill within *Panzerkorps 1* in Dieppe. Participants from the *I./SS-Panzer Regiment 12*: *Abteilungsadjutant, Ordonnanz Offizier, Nachrichtenoffizier*, two motorized reporters, one radio station. The theme: "exercise of the forwarding of orders and signals, training of officers".

18 March 1944    *General der Panzertruppe* Heinrich Eberbach, Inspector of the *Panzertruppen des Ersatzheeres*[6] visited the *I./SS-Panzer Regiment 12* and the *2.Kompanie* training in the following areas:
- shooting theory on plotting board;
- lecture in tactics: "the tank in attack";
- gas training of platoon formations;
- aiming practice in the target village;
- lecture on the tank gun, ammunition, electrical equipment, sighting device.

19 March 1944    General Eberbach first inspected the training of the *1./SS-Panzer Regiment 12* completing the following tasks:
- tasks of the tank commander, routine process in case of a reported enemy armoured fighting vehicle;
- decision tasks in platoon formation, routine process in case of reported enemy anti-tank guns and/or running over a mine;
- arrangement of tank-platoon for retreat, routine process in case of breakdown of a tank or armament.

Practices of the *3./SS-Panzer Regiment 12*:
- *Panzer Kompanie* attack with live fire, within that fire strikes and fire concentration;
- cooperation of *Panzer Zug* with *Pionier Zug* (attack with live fire).

Practice of the *Flak Zug* of the *I./SS-Panzer Regiment 12*:
- deployment of the *Flak Zug* against ground and air targets.

22 March 1944    *Oberstgruppenführer und Panzer Generaloberst der Waffen-SS* Sepp Dietrich, commander of the *I.SS-Panzer Korps,* visited *SS-Panzer Regiment 12.*

23-30 March 1944 The *3./SS-Panzer Regiment 12* won the regiment's position building contest.

30 March 1944    The regimental *Panzer-Pionier-Kompanie* was disbanded and its strength was divided into two *Panzer-Pionier-Züge* for the *Stabskompanien* of each *Panzer Abteilung.*

During the month of March, one officer and three enlisted men died.

1 April 1944    Beginning of *SS-Panzer Regiment 12's* relocation to the Evreux–Le Neubourg–Bernay area in France.

2 April 1944    The regiment received its 12 Flak Panzer 38(t) self-propelled anti-aircraft guns, all of which were equipped with 2cm automatic cannon.

---

6    The armoured troops of the Replacement Army.

Max Wünsche giving Hitler the donations of the *I.SS-Panzer Korps*
(see KTB entry for 20 April 1944). (Mark C. Yerger)

| | |
|---|---|
| 12-19 April 1944 | The relocation tasks were completed and training was resumed. Combat post of the *I./SS-Panzer Regiment 12* in Le Neubourg. |
| 20 April 1944 | The *I./SS-Panzer Regiment 12* had 26 Panther tanks that day, 23 of which were operational.[7] Birthday celebrations for the Fuehrer by all units of *SS-Panzer Regiment 12*. *Obersturmbannführer* Max Wünsche, commander of the regiment, as a member of the delegation of the *I.SS-Panzer Korps*, delivered the gift from the *I.SS-Panzer Korps*, two million six thousand *Reichsmarks*.[8] |
| 27-29 April 1944 | Regimental drill in Louviers. The *I./SS-Panzer Regiment 12* participated with *Panzer Group "Blue"* of *Obersturmbannführer* Wünsche. Theme: *"panzer group combat against panzer group"*. The exercise was inspected by *Generaloberst* Heinz Guderian, *General der Panzertruppe* Leo Geyr von Schweppenburg, commander of the *Panzergruppe „West,"* and *Oberstgruppenführer und Panzer Generaloberst der Waffen-SS* Josef Dietrich. |
| 30 April 1944 | The regiment at this time possessed six Panzer II light tanks, one short-barrelled (L/24) Panzer IV tank, three long-barrelled (L/43) Panzer IV tanks, 90 long-barrelled (L/48) Panzer IV tanks, 26 Panther tanks, three quadruple-barrelled 2cm anti-aircraft guns, |

---

7   Kamen Nevenkin, *Fire Brigades – The Panzer Divisions 1943–1945*, Winnipeg: J.J. Fedorowicz, 2008, p.905 (hereafter cited as Nevenkin).

8   For comparison, this amount of money equalled the construction price of eight Tiger B heavy tanks.

18 2cm anti-aircraft machine cannon, 326 machine guns, 249 sub-machine guns, 1650 rifles, 1496 pistols and 919 bayonets.[9]

Further vehicles of the unit: 50 motorcycles, 52 Volkswagen off-road cars, 62 medium cars, one heavy car, 11 vans, two light trucks, 111 heavy trucks, 7 Sd.Kfz. 9 18-ton towing cars, one workshop platoon (four Büssing heavy trucks), one maintenance unit (two medium Opel trucks), two ambulance cars and a captured Italian SPA Radschlepper wheeled prime mover.

| | |
|---|---|
| 8 May 1944 | Of the now seven Panzer II light tanks in the *Aufklärungszug* of the *Regiment*, two were sent to each *Panzer Abteilung*, one to the regimental *Flak Zug* and two to the workshop platoon. |
| 10 May 1944 | The *Flak Zug* of the *II./SS-Panzer Regiment 12* shot down an Allied P-47 Thunderbolt at 1612 hours while aircraft were attacking the bridge on the Seine near Elbeuf. |
| 13 May 1944 | The regimental *Flak Zug* shot down an Allied P-47 Thunderbolt fighter-bomber aircraft at 1130 hours at the railway bridge near Le Manoir. |
| 21 May 1944 | Arrival of eight Panther tanks for the *I./SS-Panzer Regiment 12*. |
| 22 May 1944 | An American B-26 Marauder bomber aircraft crashed down in the quarters area of the *II./SS-Panzer Regiment 12*. Two members of the crew who parachuted were captured. |
| 23 May 1944 | Arrival of further eight Panther tanks for the *I./SS-Panzer Regiment 12*. |
| 25 May 1944 | The regimental *Flak Zug* destroyed another Allied P-47 Thunderbolt fighter-bomber aircraft attacking at low level at 1146 hours at the railway bridge near Le Manoir. |
| | Around the same time, at 1047 hours at Elbeuf, in the area of the bridge on the Seine, the *Flak Zug* of the *II./SS-Panzer Regiment 12* destroyed two attacking Allied P-47 Thunderbolts. |
| 26 May 1944 | The bridge on the Seine at Elbeuf was destroyed by the Allied fighter-bomber aircraft. |
| 27 May 1944 | Forty enemy bomber aircraft attacked the railway bridge at Le Manoir which was secured by the regimental *Flak Zug* with Flak Panzer 38(t) anti-aircraft guns in order to provide a bridge for the heavier tanks to cross the river. The *Flak Zug* did not suffer any losses. |
| 29 May 1944 | The railway bridge in the Orival area, which was suitable for the Panther tanks to cross the Seine, was destroyed by an Allied air raid. The bridge was secured by the *Flak Zug* of the *I./SS-Panzer Regiment 12*. |
| 30 May 1944 | The *Flak Zug* of the *II./SS-Panzer Regiment 12*, between 1650 hours and 1653 hours, that is, within only three minutes, shot down three Allied P-47 Thunderbolt fighter-bomber aircraft attacking the bridge on the Seine near Elbeuf. However the bridge was destroyed by the Allied air force that same day. |

---

9   See Appendix V.

31 May 1944 | Arrival of two shipments (seven and seven, altogether 14) of Panther tanks for the *I./SS-Panzer Regiment 12*. Radio command practice for the *Abteilung*. Theme: "attack against invading enemy forces". The lesson: controlling tanks with morse code is only possible until the attack is launched; further training is needed, because stricter control has to be kept during the broadcasting of messages.

3 June 1944 | *Obersturmführer* Rudolf von Ribbentropp, *Kompanie Chef* of the *3./ SS-Panzer Regiment 12*[10] was wounded during a fighter-bomber raid.

4 June 1944 | Tank training and tank gun fire practice between 0700 and 1100 hours for the officers and NCOs of the *Regimentsstab*, and Panzerfaust training in Louviers.

The theoretical order of battle for the *I./SS-Panzer Regiment 12* within the *Panzer Regiment* of the *12.SS-Panzer Division* on 1 June 1944, five days prior to the invasion of the Allied Forces at Normandy:

*Kompanienstab*;
*Stabskompanie*
    *Nachrichtenzug* (three command Panther tanks);
    *Aufklärungszug* (five Panther tanks and two armoured personnel carriers), terrain reconnaissance platoon and *Panzer-Pionierzug* (Kettenkrads, Schwimmwagens and three armoured personnel carriers),
    *Flak Zug* (three self-propelled 2cm quadruple-barrelled anti-aircraft guns);
four *Panzer-Kompanien* ( 17 Panther tanks in each)
    *Kompanie Chef* unit (two Panther tanks);
    three *Panzer Züge* (each equipped with five Panther tanks);
workshop (*Instandsetzungs*) *Kompanie*
*Versorgungskompanie*.

The *II./SS-Panzer Regiment 12* was organized by a similar order of battle, only the tanks were Panzer IVs instead of Panthers and instead of an workshop *Kompanie* only a workshop platoon was provided. The required strength (*Soll-Stärke*) determined for *SS-Panzer Regiment 12* allocated five Panzer IV tanks and three Panther command tanks for the *Regimentsstab*, 73 Panthers, three Panther command tanks and Bergepanther armoured recovery vehicles for the *I./SS-Panzer Regiment 12* and 93 Panzer IVs and three Panzer IV command tanks for the *II./SS-Panzer Regiment 12*.[11] According to this, the regiment should have been equipped with 2,301 soldiers, four Panzer IIIs, 101 Panzer IVs, and 81 Panther tanks. However, this was far from the case in reality. Out of the four Panzer IIIs only two were present on 1 June 1944 (both of them operational), besides at least one Panzer II.

Altogether 66 Panther tanks were allotted for *SS-Panzer Regiment 12* until 1 June 1944.[12] According to the data above however, only 56 of these had reached the troops by

---

10  Oldest of the five sons of Joachim von Ribbentropp, the German Foreign Minister. See Appendix II.
11  See document number SS-FHA Amt II Org.Abt. Ib Tgb. Nr. II/2534/44 geh., an attachment without number to the activity report of the regiment.
12  Nevenkin, p.905.

the day of departure to the frontline. A further 10 Panthers were still en route via railway transport. Of the already arrived tanks 48 Panthers were in operational condition on 1 June 1944. Two were repaired within the first two weeks, and it took far longer to repair another six. Only two of the three command Panthers in the *Regimentsstab* were operational.[13] On the basis of this data 46 of the 53 Panther tanks that arrived for the *I./ SS-Panzer Regiment 12* were in operational condition at the beginning of June 1944. The three command Panther tanks were still missing from the force of the *Stabskompanie* as well as the five tanks of the *Aufklärungszug*.

The *Flak Zug* of the *I./SS-Panzer Regiment 12* is sort of a 'mystery'. According to the exceptionally detailed history of the Division[14] the *Abteilung* did not have such a unit at all on 1 June 1944 – as opposed to the three 2cm quadruple-barrelled anti-aircraft guns depicted in the appendix of the order of battle drawing from the report for that day. At the same time the contemporary documents of the *I./SS-Panzer Regiment 12* reveal that the unit had already been in existence in March 1944. The unit also participated in the battles in Normandy.

The *Flak Zug* of the *II./SS-Panzer Regiment 12* was also different than that described in the theoretical order of battle. Instead of the six 2cm anti-aircraft machine guns indicated in the report on 1 June 1944 there were three self-produced self-propelled 2cm quadruple-barrelled anti-aircraft guns mounted on Panzer IV tank chassis.[15] There was also a *Flak Zug* in the *Stabskompanie* of *SS-Panzer Regiment 12*, with 12 Flak-Panzer 38(t) self-propelled anti-aircraft guns.[16] When comparing the data we would assume that the *Flak Zug* of the *I./SS-Panzer Regiment 12* received three to six anti-aircraft guns of the latter.

On 1 June 1944 the *1.* and *2.Kompanien* of *SS-Panzer Regiment 12* had 17 Panthers each, the *3./SS-Panzer Regiment 12* had 10 Panther tanks, the *4.Kompanie* of the *Abteilung* however did not have any operational tanks.[17] The *I./SS-Panzer Regiment 12* received less vehicles than originally prescribed, and the workshop *Kompanie* did not have its Bergepanther armoured recovery vehicles yet.[18] On 1 June 1944, 91 of the 98 Panzer IV tanks of *SS-Panzer Regiment 12* were operational. The primary officers of *SS-Panzer Regiment 12* on 6 June 1944 was as follows:

*Stab, SS-Panzer Regiment 12*
- *Regimentskommandeur*: *Obersturmbannführer* Max Wünsche
  - *Adjutant*: *Hauptsturmführer* Georg Isecke
  - *Ordonnanz Offizier*: *Untersturmführer* Rudolf Nerlich
  - *Nachrichtenoffizier*: *Hauptsturmführer* Helmut Schlauß
  - *Regimentsarzt*: *Hauptsturmführer* Dr. Rudolf Stiawa

*I./SS-Panzer Regiment 12* (Panther)
- *Abteilungskommandeur*: *Sturmbannführer* Arnold Jürgensen
  - *Adjutant*: *Untersturmführer* Heinz Hubertus Schröder

---

13  See the monthly report of the *12.SS-Panzer Division* dated 1 June 1944 in Meyer, pp.757–760.
14  Meyer, p.14.
15  These became the "prototypes" for the mass production of an anti-aircraft gun called "Wirbelwind".
16  2cm anti-aircraft automatic cannons mounted on the chassis of the Panzer 38(t) light tank.
17  Meyer, p.757.
18  Meyer, p.760.

- ◆ *Ordonnanz Offizier*: *Untersturmführer* Hans Hogrefe
- ◆ *Nachrichtenoffizier*: *Untersturmführer* Rolf Jauch
- ◆ *Abteilungsarzt*: *Obersturmführer* Dr. Wilhelm Daniel
- *Chef* of the *1.Kompanie*: *Hauptsturmführer* Kurt-Anton Berlin
- *Chef* of the *2.Kompanie*: *Obersturmführer* Helmut Gaede
- *Chef* of the *3.Kompanie*: *Obersturmführer* Rudolf von Ribbentrop
- *Chef* of the *4.Kompanie*: Haupsturmführer Hans Pfeiffer
- Workshop *Kompanie*: *Untersturmführer* Robert Maier

*II./SS-Panzer Regiment 12* (Panzer IV)
- *Abteilungskommandeur*: *Sturmbannführer* Karl-Heinz Prinz
  - ◆ *Adjutant*: *Obersturmführer* Friedrich Hartmann
  - ◆ *Ordonnanz Offizier*: *Untersturmführer* Herbert Walther
  - ◆ *Nachrichtenoffizier*: *Untersturmführer* Hermann Komadina
  - ◆ *Abteilungsarzt*: *Hauptsturmführer* Dr. Oskar Jordan
- *Chef* of the *5.Kompanie* : *Obersturmführer* Helmut Bando
- *Chef* of the *6.Kompanie* : *Hauptsturmführer* Ludwig Ruckdeschel
- *Chef* of the *7.Kompanie* : *Hauptsturmführer* Heinrich Bräcker
- *Chef* of the *8.Kompanie*: *Obersturmführer* Hans Siegel
- *Chef* of the *9.Kompanie*[19]: *Hauptsturmführer* Wolf Buettner
- Workshop platoon: *Obersturmführer* Dieter Müller

Order of Battle for the *12.SS-Panzer Division* apart from *SS-Panzer Regiment 12* was as follows:

- *Divisionsstab* with ordnance surveyor group, *Divisionsbegleitkompanie* and four *Feldgendarmerie-Züge*;
- *SS-Panzer-Grenadier-Regiment 25*:
  - ◆ *I–III. SS-Panzer-Grenadier-Bataillone*: *1–4., 5–8., 9–12. Kompanien*[20]
  - ◆ *13.* SS- (towed heavy infantry gun) *Kompanie*
  - ◆ *14.* SS- (towed anti-aircraft gun) *Kompanie*
  - ◆ *15.* SS- (motorcycle) *Kompanie*
  - ◆ *16.* SS- (armoured pioneer) *Kompanie*
- *SS-Panzer-Grenadier-Regiment 26*:
  - ◆ *I–III. SS-Panzer-Grenadier-Bataillone*: *1–4., 5–8., 9–12.Kompanie*[21], the *III./SS-Panzer-Grenadier-Regiment 26* was equipped with armoured personnel carriers
  - ◆ *13.* SS- (towed heavy infantry gun) *Kompanie*
  - ◆ *14.* SS- (towed anti-aircraft gun) *Kompanie*
  - ◆ *15.* SS- (motorcycle) *Kompanie*
  - ◆ *16.* SS- (armoured pioneer) *Kompanie*

19  Five *Kompanien* instead of four were organized in the *II./SS-Panzer Regiment 12.* There were fewer tanks provided for the *5-8.Kompanien* than the originally planned 17 tanks, and the remaining tanks were allotted to form the strength of the *9. Kompanie.* The *Kompanien* with lesser strength were presumably deemed by the Germans to be more controllable in combat.
20  The *4., 8.* and *12.Kompanien* were *schwere* (heavy weapons) *Kompanien*.
21  The *4., 8.* and *12.Kompanien* were *schwere* (heavy weapons) *Kompanien*.

- *SS-Panzer-Artillerie-Regiment 12*:
  - (self-propelled) *I./SS-Panzer-Artillerie-Abteilung* (*1–2. Batterien* with 10.5cm Wespes, *3. Batterie* with 15cm Hummel self-propelled artillery guns)
  - *II./SS-Panzer-Artillerie-Abteilung* (three *Batterien* with 10.5cm towed light field howizers)
  - *III./SS-Panzer-Artillerie-Abteilung* (three *Batterien* with 15cm towed heavy field howizers and a *Batterie* with 10.5cm guns)
  - *IV(Werfer)./SS-Panzer-Artillerie-Abteilung* (four *Batterien* with 15cm launchers)
- *SS-Panzer-Aufklärungs-Abteilung 12*:
  - *Stabskompanie* with armoured cars
  - *1.* (wheeled armoured car), *2.* (half-tracked armoured car) *Kompanie*, *3-4.* (armoured personnel carrier) *Kompanie*, *5.* (armoured heavy weapons) *Kompanie*, 1 *Versorgungskompanie*
- *SS-Panzerjäger Abteilung 12*:
  - *1.* (Jagdpanzer), *2.* (Jagdpanzer), *3.* (towed heavy anti-tank gun) *Kompanien*
- *SS-Panzer-Pionier-Bataillon 12*:
  - *1–3.Kompanie* (*1.Kompanie* armoured personnel carriers), *"B" Feldbrückekolonne, leichte Pionierkolonne*
- *SS-Panzer-Nachrichten-Abteilung 12*:
  - *1.*(telephone), *2.*(radio) *Kompanie*
- *SS-Panzer-Flak-Abteilung 12*:
  - *1–3.* (8.8cm), *4.* (3.7cm), *5. Scheinwerfer Batterien*
- *SS-Panzer-Feldersatz-Bataillon 12*
- *12.SS-Panzer Division Nachschub-Truppen*
- *SS-Panzer-Instandsetzungs-Abteilung 12*
- *SS-Wirtschafts Abteilung 12*
- *SS-Sanitätsabteilung 12*

The units of the division – apart from the *IV.(Werfer) Abteilung* of *SS-Panzer-Artillerie-Regiment 12* and *SS-Panzerjäger Abteilung 12* still in formation – were qualified as of 1 June 1944 as fit for carrying out any assault tasks on the Western frontline.

# 2

# The First Battle for Caen, 6–10 June 1944

## 6 June 1944

### *I./SS-Panzer Regiment 12*[1] (Le Neubourg):

Level II Luftwaffe alarm at 0235 hours. Level I alarm for the remaining *Kompanien* of the *Abteilung* at 0250 hours. The commander[2], who went to St. André with the new tanks for training with *SS-Panzer-Grenadier-Regiment 25*, is notified by the *Adjutant*.[3] The alarm-word "Blücher" is given at 0615 hours by the regiment. The beginning of the march from Le Neubourg is scheduled for 1300 hours by the order of the regiment. *Kompanien* are drawn forward to the departure point. *Hauptsturmführer* Waldemar Schütz, as *Kompanieführer*, is responsible for the remaining *Kompanien*.

March of the *Kompanien* via Epreville–La Riviere–Thibouville–Fontaine la S. to Boissy, where the *Stab* and the *Stabskompanie* establishes itself from 1500 hours. Position of the other *Kompanien*: *1.Kompanie* Berthouville, *2.Kompanie* Borsan, *3.Kompanie* Le Theil-Nolent, *4.Kompanie* St. Claire, *Versorgungskompanie* Le Mitaterie, workshop *Kompanie* on the Evreux–Liseux road, in the mansion in front of Boissy. The immobile vehicles remain in the former quarters area with most of the workshop *Kompanie*. They concentrate on the armoured fighting vehicle quarters area, south of Le Neubourg. The pack column remains in Le Neubourg until further order.

One truck of the *3.Kompanie* is counted as a loss because of an accident. At 1810 hours British air raid of fighter–bombers near Boissy on the advance route. No material losses or casualties.

The *Abteilung* was again set to march via Thiberville– Orbec– Monnai towards Gace in order to join the main strength of the *Abteilung*.

### *II./SS-Panzer Regiment 12*[4] (Vimoutiers):

0330 hours: alarm of the forces of the *II./SS-Panzer Regiment 12* directed to *SS-Panzer-Grenadier-Regiment 25* for eight days training. The following are sent:

- command and control staff
- *7., 8.* and *9.Kompanien* with 10-10 Panzer IVs
- *5.* and *6.Kompanien* 14-14 Panzer IVs

---

1  Unless indicated otherwise, data has been taken from Kriegstagebuch (War Diary, hereafter abbreviated KTB) no.1. of the *I./SS-Panzer Regiment 12* concerning the period 6 June–29 August 1944. See Vojenský Historický Archiv, Praha (Military History Archives, Prague).

2  *Sturmbannführer* Arnold Jürgensen, commander of the *I./SS-Panzer Regiment 12.* See Appendix II.

3  *Untersturmführer* Heinz Hubertus Schröder, *Abteilungsadjutant* of the *I./SS-Panzer Regiment 12.*

4  Unless indicated otherwise, data have been taken from KTB no.3 of the *II./SS-Panzer Regiment 12* concerning the period 6 June-30 August 1944. See Vojenský Historický Archiv, Praha (Military History Archives, Prague).

The basis of German infantry tactics in the Second World War rested on the general-purpose machine gun. This photograph shows German *Panzergrenadiers* using a 7.92 mm MG 34 machine gun, which was also used by the forces of the *12. SS-Panzer Division "Hitlerjugend"* in Normandy. (Hungarian Institute and Museum of Military History 41294)

- *Werkstatt Kompanie* (without 1 *Zug*) with the *Schlepper Zug*
- *Stabskompanie* with 6 supply and 3 ammunition trucks

0415 hours: the *Abteilung* is ready for departure.

0530 hours: notice from *SS-Panzer Regiment 12* by telephone. As ordered by the regiment, the parts of the *Abteilung* mentioned above are to remain by *SS-Panzer-Grenadier-Regiment 25*, and are ordered to cooperate. The parts that remain in the quarters area are to stay there until ordered otherwise.

1015 hours: Order of *Standartenführer* Meyer[5] for the commander of the *II./SS-Panzer Regiment 12*. The parts of the *II./SS-Panzer Regiment 12* being positioned in the quarters area of *SS-Panzer-Grenadier-Regiment 25* are subordinated to *SS-Panzer-Grenadier-Regiment 25*, and march with the battalions where they are positioned like so:

---

5   *Standartenführer* Kurt Meyer was commander of *SS-Panzer-Grenadier-Regiment 25* until 14 June 1944. Command of the division passed to him after *Brigadeführer und Generalmajor der Waffen-SS* Fritz Witt was killed that day by Allied naval gunfire that struck the divisional command post. A early member of the *„Leibstandarte"* in 1933, Witt won the Knight's Cross commanding the *I./Deutschland* on 4 September 1940. Awarded the German Cross in Gold as an *Obersturmbannführer* with the *„Leibstandarte"* on 8 February 1942, he was promoted to *Standartenführer* on 30 January 1943. Witt then won the Oakleaves on 1 March 1943 as commander of *SS-Panzer-Grenadier-Regiment 1* with the *„Leibstandarte"*. He was appointed the first divisional commander of *„Hitlerjugend,"* becoming an *Oberführer* on 1 July 1943 and a *Brigadeführer und Generalmajor der Waffen-SS* on 20 April 1944.

A Panzer IV Ausf J from *II./SS-Panzer Regiment 12* moving to the front,
June 1944. (Bundesarchiv, Bild 101I-493-3355-10, photo: Siedel)

- *7.* and *8.Kompanien* with the *I. Bataillon*;
- *9.Kompanie* with the *II. Bataillon*;
- *5.* and *6.Kompanien* with the *III. Bataillon*.

*I.Bataillon* marches from Vimoutiers via Livarot and Le Mesnil-Eudes to St. Pierre des Ifs. The command and control staff, the *7.* and *8.Kompanien* join the column of the *I.Bataillon* in the following marching order:

- *8.Kompanie* at the head
- command and control staff with the reconnaissance platoon;
- *7.Kompanie*
- remaining parts of the *Stabskompanie* and the train.[6]

1230 hours: departure from Vimoutiers. Column order as described above. No notable events at the *II.Abteilung*.

1600 hours: new command post between St. Pierre des Ifs and the Lisieux–St. Pierre sur Dives road.

No engagement with the enemy. Enemy activity: fighter aircraft and battle noise from the north. Vehicle losses: none.

Weather: cloudy and rainy with sunny intervals.

During the march the drivers and the escort proved to be well-trained. However, the lack of battle experience was apparent. Instead of staying 100 metres apart as was ordered, this distance was reduced when enemy aircraft appeared. The training of the

6    In this context, train in its traditional military sense, meaning baggage.

From left to right: *Standartenführer* Kurt Meyer (commander, *SS-Panzer-Grenadier-Regiment 25*), *Brigadeführer* Fritz Witt (commander, *12.SS-Panzer Division*) and *Obersturmbannführer* Max Wünsche (commander, *SS-Panzer Regiment 12*), Ardenne Abbey, the command post of the division, early June 1944. (Cody Images)

drivers of out of service vehicles with the *SS-Panzer-Grenadier-Bataillone* will be more intensive. One man shall be placed by the side of the out of service vehicle to notify the approaching column, otherwise there is a danger that the units coming behind them would find their advance interrupted.

## 7 June 1944
### *I./SS-Panzer Regiment 12* (on the march):
At 0030 hours the first soldier of the *1.Kompanie* was killed in a low-level air raid. Most of the *Abteilung* was in march on the St. André–Damville–Breteuil–La Ferté Frênel road, joining the other *Kompanien* at 0600 hours.

   March of the whole *Abteilung* via Trun–Falaise–Ussy–Thury Harcourt, then on the western bank of the Orne towards Amayé. From Maizet the *Kompanien* took positions along the route of the march. One fuel truck of the *Kompanie* was destroyed in a fighter-bomber raid. One truck of the *Versorgungskompanie*, loaded with armour-piercing shells, was blown up in a low-level air-raid. The supply truck of the workshop *Kompanie* was burnt out in a low-level air-raid. One anti-aircraft vehicle[7] burnt out, the vehicle of the maintenance unit was destroyed, and two trucks were temporarily unfit for deployment due to a raid against the column of the *Stabskompanie*.

---

7    Presumably a Flak-Panzer 38(t) self-propelled anti-aircraft gun of the *Flak Zug* of the *Abteilung*.

A formal portrait of Max Wünsche in black Panzer uniform after being awarded the Knight's Cross (see Appendix II and main text). (Mark C. Yerger)

Daily losses: Six trucks lost as a consequence of enemy engagement, eight trucks damaged.

Briefing at 2300 hours for the *Kompanie Chefs*.

### *II./SS-Panzer Regiment 12*:

General situation: the enemy succeeded in invading the shoreline between Le Havre and Cherbourg in the early morning hours of 6 June 1944. Large numbers of airborne troops were reported to have landed in the area northwest of Caen[8].

Task of the *12.SS-Panzer Division "Hitlerjugend"*: departure from the quarters area, attack the enemy in Caen, destroy them and push them back into the sea.

For this, SS-*Panzer-Grenadier-Regiment 25* with the units of the *II./SS-Panzer Regiment 12* prepare north of the Caen–St. Germain–Bretteville road.

The *II./SS-Panzer Regiment 12* occupies the attack position in the following battle order: *8.Kompanie* on the right, the *5.* and *6.Kompanien* on the side, and the *9.* and *7.Kompanien* behind them as reserves. Order for the *II.Abteilung*: attack and destroy the enemy. Launch attack on the orders of the *Abteilungskommandeur*. Pack at Etterville on the Venoix-Evrecy road. The workshop *Kompanie* remains in Meulles on the Orbec–Vimoutiers road until further [orders].

1330 hours: the *II.Abteilung* occupies the allocated attack position.

1400 hours: appearance of enemy tanks at Franqueville and Authie. The *5.* and *6.Kompanien* instantly engaged the enemy and destroyed a number of Sherman tanks[9]. The enemy retreated. Ammunition expenditure: 300 high explosive shells, 235 armour-piercing shells, 800 steel core [machine-gun ammunition].

1730 hours: the *II.Abteilung* departs against the enemy, which advances towards Caen from the northwest. The *Abteilung* marches through the positions of the SS-*Panzer-Grenadier-Bataillone* lying under enemy fire, and attacks the enemy tanks and anti-tank guns. Scores:

- the *5.Kompanie* knocked out 9 Shermans at Franqueville and Authie
- the *6.Kompanie* knocked out 14 Shermans, 3 armoured personnel carriers and 4 anti-tank guns at Authie
- the *7.Kompanie* knocked out 5 Shermans at Bouron
- the *8.Kompanie* knocked out 1 Sherman at la Folie[10]

---

8  Roads from the east and southeast leading to the Allied beachheads occupied on 6 June 1944 ran through this city in Normandy. As most of the German armoured reserves were stationed north of the Seine on the day of the invasion of Normandy, they had to march through Caen in order to strike back. According to the Allied plans, the city was to be occupied on the day following the invasion (D-Day + 1).

9  The Shermans were presumably tanks of the Canadian 27th Armoured Regiment (The Sherbrooke Fusiliers).

10  The battalion-sized 27th Armoured Regiment, from the Canadian 2nd Armoured Brigade, lost 60 soldiers (of them, 26 were killed) and 28 tanks (of these, 21 were destroyed and only seven remained, albeit damaged). See Michael Reynolds, *Acélpokol. Az I. SS-páncéloshadtest Normandiában* (English edition – *Steel Inferno. I SS Panzer Corps in Normandy*), Debrecen: Hajja és Fiai Könyvkiadó, 1999, p.90 (hereafter cited as Reynolds).

The 5. and 6.*Kompanien* took 450 prisoners of war[11] altogether, who were taken back by the soldiers of the *SS-Panzer-Grenadier-Bataillone*. Our own losses that day:

- 3 Panzer IVs of the 5.*Kompanie*
- 4 Panzer IVs of the 6.*Kompanie*
- 4 Panzer IVs of the 7.*Kompanie*
- 1 Panzer IV of the 8.*Kompanie*

|  | **Officers** | **NCOs** | **Enlisted Men** |
|---|---|---|---|
| Killed | – | 1 | 12 |
| Severely wounded | 1 | 1 | 5 |
| Lightly wounded | 2 | – | 13 |
| Total | 3 | 2 | 30 |

The *Flak Zug* of the *II.Abteilung* advanced with the attack, and shot down five enemy fighter-bomber aircraft.

With this success the *II.Abteilung* managed to stop the American [sic.] [12] attack against Caen, take the towns northwest of Caen into German control, and carry out the counterstroke.

Weather: dry and warm.

Ammunition expenditure: 944 high explosive shells, 721 armour-piercing shells, 1500 rounds of 2cm anti-aircraft ammunition.

The Panzergrenadiers must not remain lying in their positions, but should follow the attack of the armoured fighting vehicles. Otherwise their offensive force will not be utilised.

## 8 June 1944
### I./SS-Panzer Regiment 12 (Maizet):
At 0200 hours order was given to march into the attack positions. This order could not be carried out because the fuel supply did not arrive in time. The columns departed at 0930 hours towards the attack positions assigned north of Caen; the 1.*Kompanie* was at the head. Arrival around 1600 hours.

Around 2000 hours the *1., 3.* and *4.Kompanien* departed against Bretteville [l'Orgueilleuse]. The *3.Kompanie*[13] took over the securing of Gruchy[14] with the support

---

11  Mainly from the ranks of the Canadian 7th, 8th and 9th Infantry Brigades. According to the data collected by the Allies after the war, it can be confirmed that the *SS-Panzergrenadiers* leading them back executed at least 41 of them on 7 June 1944. For this, see Reynolds, p.115.

12  There were British and Canadian troops fighting around the Caen area, not Americans.

13  Originally the *Kompanie Chef* of the *3./SS-Panzer Regiment 12* was *Hauptsturmführer* Rudolf von Ribbentrop, but he was wounded on 3 June 1944 in an Allied fighter-bomber raid (see Appendix II). The *Kompanie* was then commanded by *Hauptmann* Lüdemann.

14  In the case of most securing tasks, German tank formations fought the enemy forces attacking the first lines of the defence with local fire control from previously surveyed positions (even from tanks covered up to their turrets, but always allowing for the possibility of withdrawal). After a few rounds vehicles had to change positions according to plan to avoid a counterstroke by the enemy. A Panzer *Zug* could secure a frontline of at least 200 meters (with 50 meters distance between the vehicles). A Panzer *Kompanie* could secure at least a 1000–1500 metres-long and 500 metres-deep frontline. For more

of an infantry unit. Heavy artillery fire, no losses. Movement of armoured fighting vehicles was discovered within 7000 metres.

Task of the *4.Kompanie*: fight against the enemy armoured fighting vehicles in the Le Bourg–Rots area, and against enemy gunners withdrawn into Bretteville.

The *Kompanie* followed the enemy. Machine gun fire from 100–200 metres away 1 km west of Rots. Fire was returned, destroying the crew of six small American [sic.] tracked vehicles.[15] Most of their infantry mounted on the tanks were shot down. The Panthers advanced further towards Bretteville [l'Orgueilleuse]. 150 metres from the village heavy anti-tank gun fire; four British [sic.][16] anti-tank guns were disabled, and one or two small tracked vehicles were destroyed. Heavy anti-tank gun, tank and machine gun fire. The tanks returned the fire and stopped the enemy fire. Tank no. 427 was damaged by anti-tank gun hit (by hitting the gun mantlet) and was burnt out.

Reorganization of the *Kompanie*. Tank no. 418 leading the column was damaged by a direct hit of an anti-tank gun and was knocked out. The burning and exploding leading tank prevented the leading platoon from resuming their advance as the road was thus blocked. The village was bypassed from the left. Heavy anti-tank gun and tank gun fire from its southern parts. The village was set ablaze by gunfire. After suppressing the enemy's preventive fire, the *Kompanie* attacked and reached the north-western exit of Bretteville [l'Orgueilleuse]. Following the given orders, they advanced through the next village. After this no enemy activity was detected, hence the *Kompanie* withdrew as ordered. On the way back, machine gun, pistol and rifle fire from the burning Bretteville [l'Orgueilleuse] and anti-tank gun fire again. Anti-tank gun hit tank no. 425, piercing the turret. The enemy infantry tried to approach the armoured fighting vehicles under the cover of the fog. The *Kompanie* was hurriedly withdrawn and following orders is withdrawn into the area south and west of Le Bourg–Rots for securing tasks.

Due to the descending darkness, the *1.Kompanie* aborted its attack around 2100 hours. The *Kompanie* assembled on the Caen–Bayeux main road then renewed its attack. Tank no. 116 counts as total loss due to anti-tank gun hit, the turret of tank no. 115 was damaged by an anti-tank gun hit. Securing the road together with the mounted infantry. [Next day] morning at 0700 hours turned to the new securing position west of Rots.

## War Diary Appendix no.3.

*12.SS-Panzer Division "Hitlerjugend"*                    O.U., 15 July 1944
*4.[Kompanie]/SS-Panzer Regiment 12*
Attack against Rots–Le Bourg–Bretteville [l'Orgueilleuse] on 06. 08. 1944[17]

Situation:
The *Abteilung* prepared to attack north of the Caen–St. Germain road in the direction of St. Aubin-sur-Mur. The enemy dominated the air. The launch of an enemy assault with

---

information, see Wolfgang Schneider, *Panzertaktik. German Small-Unit Armour Tactics*, Winnipeg: J.J. Fedorowicz, 2000, p.91.

15  In the original: *Karetten*. These were not American vehicles but presumably British-made Universal (or Bren Gun) carriers; small, open-top tracked fighting vehicles.

16  On that day there were no British troops in the area of Rots, only elements of the Canadian Regina Rifles Infantry Regiment and the anti-tank guns of the 2nd Royal Canadian Artillery Regiment.

17  In the original document 06. 11. 1944 can be seen as the date of attack, presumably because of a typing error.

armoured fighting vehicles in the direction of Caen airfield, towards our southern flank, meant that the direction of our planned assault was altered and set to the westn in order to reach the enemy's left flank.

Task:
The *4.Kompanie* to attack the villages of Le Bourg and Bretteville [l'Orgueilleuse] right of the Caen–Bayeux road, and secure the hills north and northwest of Bretteville [l'Orgueilleuse].

Course of battle:
The *Kompanie* prepared to carry out the ordered attack with the *II.Zug* on the left, the *I.Zug* on the right, between them the *Kompanie Chef*'s unit, and behind it the *III. Zug*. The Grenadiers mounted the Panthers. The *Kompanie* reached Le Bourg with a swift advance and without contacting the enemy. The *Kompanie* formed a column with *Hauptsturmführer* Hans Pfeiffer at the head, then the *II.Zug* , the *I.* and *III. Züge*. After reaching the western exit of Le Bourg, close contact was made with the enemy infantry. Fire was returned by machine guns and the Panzergrenadiers. When asked, the inhabitants told us that the enemy retreated in the direction of Bretteville [l'Orgueilleuse]. Radio message to the *Kompanie*: "The *Kompanie* is to follow them with utmost speed!" Between Le Bourg and Bretteville [l'Orgueilleuse] heavy enemy anti-tank and machine gun fire from six armoured personnel carriers (small tracked vehicles) between Le Bourg and Bretteville [l'Orgueilleuse]. The Grenadiers suffered losses and dismounted the Panthers. The *Kompanie* advanced without delay to the entrance of Bretteville [l'Orgueilleuse], where they again met heavy enemy tank, anti-tank and machine gun fire from the perimetres of Bretteville [l'Orgueilleuse]. Panther no. 404 discovered an enemy tank at the entrance of the village, opened fire and knocked out a Sherman. Order for the *Kompanie* on the radio: "The *II.Zug* left of the road, the *I.Zug* right of the road are to draw up in firing line and engage the enemy armoured fighting vehicles and anti-tank guns!" Meanwhile the no. 427 tank of *Unterscharführer* Hartmann was put out of action because of a hit on its turret. The commander, the gunner and the loader were wounded. The *Regiments-* and *Abteilungskommandeur* reached the *Kompanie*. Order of the *Regimentskommandeur*: "The *Kompanie* – with a *Zug* at the head, followed by the others in column – will advance through Bretteville [l'Orgueilleuse] and reach the assigned aim of attack!"

With the *I.Zug* at the head, the first vehicle – *Unterscharführer* Mühlhausen's tank no. 418 – departed at 2400 hours. The first tank had reached the centre of the village when its turret was hit by an anti-tank gun from 50 metres away. After three more hits tank no. 418 burnt out. The commander, the driver and the gunner were killed, the loader wounded. New order of the *Regimentskommandeur*: "The *Kompanie* retreats and flanks the village from the left!"

The *III.Zug* was at the head, followed by the *II.* and the *I. Züge*, and the *Kompanie Chef* was behind the *III.Zug*. The *III.Zug* formed a firing line and fired at Bretteville [l'Orgueilleuse] from all sides. Bretteville [l'Orgueilleuse] was on fire. The enemy resistance was weakening. At around 0100 hours the *Kompanie* reached the hill north of Bretteville [l'Orgueilleuse] and secured the position. Heavy firing by the enemy artillery prevented the Grenadiers' advance. New order of the *Regiment* on radio: "The *Kompanie*

Field Marshal Bernard Law Montgomery, supreme commander of the British-Canadian 21st Army Group. His command, though suffering severely, successfully contained most of the German armoured divisions deployed against the Allied beachheads in Normandy. However, he also launched a number of unsuccessful attacks in order to capture Caen leading to severe British-Canadian armoured losses. (Hungarian Institute and Museum of Military History 26797)

retreats to the western exit of Le Bourg and secures in the direction of Bretteville towards Norrey!" The enemy resistance revived itself upon the disengagement. *Untersturmführer* Johannes Hillig was wounded by an anti-tank gun hit; *Unterscharführer* Unglaub received a wound in the head from a machine-gun round. The *Kompanie* reached the area west of Le Bourg to be secured, as ordered.

Pohl
*Leutnant* and *Kompanieführer*

**II./SS-Panzer Regiment 12:**
The *Kompanien* of the *II.Abteilung* remained in the positions they occupied the day before. No combat activity. Heavy artillery harassing fire on all securing positions of the *Abteilung*. The tanks left at the previous quarters area near Elbeuf only arrived that day. The following list contains the tank strength of the deployed units of the *II.Abteilung* on the evening of 08. 08. 1944.

**War Diary Appendix no. 1.**
Tank strength on the evening of 08.06.1944.
Available strength on 08.06.1944 – 87 Panzerkampfwagen IVs (long-barrelled)

| Total losses until 08. 06. 1944 | | Operational on 08. 06. 1944 |
| --- | --- | --- |
| Staff | – | 3 Panzerkampfwagen IVs |
| 5.Kompanie | 3 Panzerkampfwagen IVs | 6 Panzerkampfwagen IVs |
| 6.Kompanie | 4 Panzerkampfwagen IVs | 6 Panzerkampfwagen IVs |
| 7.Kompanie | 4 Panzerkampfwagen IVs | – |
| 8.Kompanie | 1 Panzerkampfwagen IV | 5 Panzerkampfwagen IVs |
| 9.Kompanie | – | 10 Panzerkampfwagen IVs |

En route, or under repair:
Staff:             –
5.Kompanie :   –
6.Kompanie :   7 Panzerkampfwagen IVs
7.Kompanie :   13 Panzerkampfwagen IVs
8.Kompanie :   11 Panzerkampfwagen IVs
9.Kompanie :   6 Panzerkampfwagen IVs

# 9 June 1944
## I./SS-Panzer Regiment 12 (command post: Le Bourg):
Attack of the *1.Kompanie* towards Norrey [-en-Bessin] at 1200 hours. From a position hidden behind a slope, all tank guns opened fire at the church steeple, because it was probable that an artillery spotter was placed there. They had driven with the utmost speed towards Norrey [-en-Bessin]. Two anti-tank guns and infantry positions were destroyed. By the order of the *Chef*, the *Kompanie* returned to its departure position.

At the same time the *3.Kompanie* also launched an attack and advanced well. Anti-tank gun fire from around the church and the wooded area to the right of it. Fire was returned, 2 anti-tank guns were destroyed. Tank nos. 325, 328, 335, 336 and 337 were hit by anti-tank gun fire and became total losses within five minutes (the enemy anti-tank guns or tanks could not be seen). Tank nos. 327 and 329 were damaged by anti-tank gun hits; these retreated to the repair station. The *Kompanie* retreated on order.

They resumed the fight from the position behind the slope. Repeated withdrawal and establishing positions behind the *1.Kompanie*.

Task of the *4.Kompanie*: securing, defence of the flanks of the attacking *1.* and *3.Kompanien*, providing supporting fire from the positions. Sudden anti-tank gun fire from Bretteville [l'Orgueilleuse]. Tank no. 471 was burnt out due to the direct hit of an anti-tank gun. The *Kompanie* occupied new positions while securing the road, opened fire and destroyed the discovered anti-tank gun.

The hull of tank no. 404 was hit by an anti-tank gun, and was towed to the repair station. Firing on the presumed anti-tank guns. At the same time, the enemy infantry launched an attack on both sides of the road towards Rots. The attack was repulsed by units of the *15./SS-Panzer-Grenadier-Regiment 25*.[18]

---

18  This was the *Kradschützen Kompanie* of *SS-Panzer-Grenadier-Regiment 25* carrying out reconnaissance tasks.

Position of the *2.Kompanien* northwest of Fontenay [-le-Pesnel], where they knocked out 3 Shermans.[19] In the evening, the *3* and *4.Kompanien* knocked out one Sherman each.

From 2300 hours the *Abteilung* relocated to Fontenay [-le-Pesnel].

**War Diary Appendix no. 4.**

*12.SS-Panzer Division "Hitlerjugend"*                                    O.U., 26 September 1944
*4. [Kompanie]/SS-Panzer Regiment 12*


Attack against Norrey [-en-Bessin] on 09. 06. 1944


Situation:
The enemy firmly held the villages of Bretteville [l'Orgueilleuse] and Norrey [-en-Bessin] again and tried to advance on the Bretteville [l'Orgueilleuse]–Caen road. The *1.* and *3.Kompanien* attacked Norrey [-en-Bessin].


Task:
The *4.Kompanie* took over the task of securing the right flank and oversaw the advance of the two *Kompanien*.


Course of battle:
The sector of the attack position was under heavy enemy artillery fire. At 1440 hours departure of the *1.* and *3.Kompanien* towards Norrey [-en-Bessin]. The Grenadiers followed them. The *4.Kompanie* covered the right flank by fire towards Norrey [-en-Bessin] and Bretteville [l'Orgueilleuse]. The *1.* and *3.Kompanien* retreated into their original positions because of the extremely heavy enemy defence. Constant heavy artillery fire. The *4.Kompanie* established firing-line in the direction of Bretteville [l'Orgueilleuse]. In the meantime tank no. 416[20] of *Unterscharführer* Voss was knocked out by anti-tank gun fire. The tank was burnt out, and the commander, the gunner and the loader were killed. The driver and the radio operator were severely burnt. The enemy advanced on the road leading to Le Bourg, and the *Kompanie* opened fire on them. In the meantime, tank no. 404 of *Oberscharführer* Heinz Lehmann was hit three times by anti-tank guns and was knocked out. The driver, *Rottenführer* Heckl, managed to drive the tank to a position behind a slope and save it, despite his serious wounds. Then he got out of the tank and was carried to the dressing-station. The radio operator, *Schütze* Finke, was killed. The *Kompanie* repulsed the attack of the enemy launched in the direction of Le Bourg, and secured the direction as ordered. During this further heavy enemy fire *Unterscharführer* Karst, tank driver of the *Kompanie Chef*, was killed.

Pohl
*Leutnant* and *Kompanieführer*

---

19  Written as "Cherman" in the original document. In the two *Abteilung* KTB of *SS-Panzer Regiment 12* the Sherman tanks are often referred to as "Cherman". The tanks knocked out were presumably duplex drive amphibious DD Shermans, and probably belonged to the 24th Lancers of the British 8th Armoured Brigade.

20  According to the KTB of the *I./SS-Panzer Regiment 12*, Panther no. 417 was damaged here and became a total loss.

*II./SS-Panzer Regiment 12:*
Regrouping of the *Abteilung*:

- the *7.Kompanie* occupied position directly north of Gruchy with 4 tanks
- the *5.Kompanie* north of Buron with 8 tanks
- the *6.Kompanie* northwest of Authie with 9 tanks
- the *8.* and *9.Kompanien* remained in their positions occupied the day before south of Cambes and northeast of St. Contest

1100 hours: the *5.Kompanie* discovered 13 enemy tanks advancing from northeast to southwest. From appropriate firing positions we knocked out five tanks. During the morning, the *5.Kompanie* also knocked out two anti-tank guns.

In the morning and during the afternoon heavy artillery harassing fire on the positions of the *II.Abteilung*.

One] of the *Zugführer*'s tanks of the *7.Kompanie* received a direct artillery hit (*Untersturmführer* Hartfried Zick and the crew were disabled).

The *8.Kompanie* repulsed an infantry attack supported by tanks, and rendered one enemy tank immobile.

Tank supported infantry attack also in the sector of the *9.Kompanie*. Attack repulsed. The *9.Kompanie* knocked out three Shermans and three anti-tank guns.

2000 hours: preparations of the *Abteilung* for regrouping to Fontenay-le-Pesnel (15 km west of Caen).

## 10 June 1944
*I./SS-Panzer Regiment 12* (**Fontenay-le-Pesnel**):
Occupying the securing positions around 0500 hours.

The *2.Kompanie* remained in the wooded area northwest of Fontenay. The *1.* and *3.Kompanien* established positions north of the road to Caen. The *4.Kompanie* remained in Rots to carry out securing tasks. Both the *2.* and *3.Kompanien* knocked out a Sherman. The *4.Kompanie* damaged a Dreadnought[21] by a hit on its turret. The tank is towed away. Wounded soldiers are observed being pulled out of the tank.

The heaviest bomber, fighter-bomber and artillery activity. Total losses: 3 trucks.

---

21  Presumably a special version of the British Churchill heavy tank, equipped with a large calibre gun.

Knight's Cross holder Wilhelm Beck in a formal portrait (see
Chapter 2 Footnote 22). (Mark C. Yerger)

*Hauptsturmführer d.R.* Wilhelm Beck is killed at the headquarters of the
*Oberbefehlshaber "West"*.[22] Daily order of *Oberstgruppenführer* Josef Dietrich[23] for the
*Division "Hitlerjugend"*.[24]

### II./SS-Panzer Regiment 12:
Until 0600 hours regrouping and establishing securing positions at Fontenay-le-Pesnel.
The *Kompanien* occupied the positions in the following order:

---

22  *Hauptsturmführer d.R.* Wilhelm Beck was previously *Kompanie Chef* of the *2./SS-Panzer Regiment
    12*. At this time he was serving as the liason officer of the *I.SS-Panzer Korps* at the headquarters of
    *Panzergruppe "West"*. That headquaters was raided by Allied fighter-bombers and twin-engine bombers
    on 10 June 1944 at approximately 2030 hours. 32 men were killed from the *Stab* and its subordinated
    control units, one man is missing. Beck had attended *Junkerschule* Braunschweig in 1940 before serving
    as a *Zugführer* in the *"Leibstandarte" Sturmgeschütz Batterie*. He won the Knight's Cross on 28 March
    1943 as *Kompanie Chef* of the *2./SS-Panzer Regiment 1* of the *1.SS-Panzer Division "Leibstandarte"* and
    was promoted to *Hauptsturmführer d.R.* on 19 November 1943.
23  *Oberstgruppenführer und Panzer Generaloberst der Waffen-SS* Joseph (Sepp) Dietrich was then
    commander of the *I.SS-Panzer Korps,* having obtained his unique rank on 20 April 1942. The original
    commander of the *"Leibstandarte,"* he was awarded the Knight's Cross on 4 July 1940 commanding the
    then *SS-Infanterie Regiment (mot.) "Leibstandarte"* and stayed through the unit's development. Awarded
    the Oakleaves on 31 December 1941 commanding the expanded *SS-Division (mot.) "Leibstandarte,"*
    his Swords was won on 14 March 1943 when his command had become *SS-Panzer-Grenadier-Division
    "Leibstandarte"*. Dietrich's Diamonds to the Knight's Cross (one of two awarded the Waffen-SS) came
    on 6 August 1944 as an *Oberstgruppenführer* und Panzer *Generaloberst* commanding the *I.SS-Panzer
    Korps*. He was one of four SS officers to attain the rank of *Oberstgruppenführer* and ended the war in
    command of the *6.SS-Panzerarmee*. Josef Dietrich died in Ludwigsburg on 21 April 1966.
24  The order cannot be found in the Appendices to the KTB.

Wilhelm Mohnke as a *Standartenführer* showing his Knight's
Cross (see Chapter 2 Footnote 25). (Mark C. Yerger)

- *Stab* in Fontenay-le-Pesnel
- 5. and 6.*Kompanien* east of the Fontenay [-le-Pesnel]–Rauray road
- 8. and 9.*Kompanien* directly north of the Fontenay [-le-Pesnel]–Tilly

The remaining tanks of the 7.*Kompanie* were allocated to the 6.*Kompanie*. Nothing notable occurred during the regrouping.

0900 hours: heavy artillery harassing fire in the new quarters area of the *II.Abteilung*.

1200 hours: relocation of the *Abteilung* command post. New command post 2.5 km south of [Fontenay-le-Pesnel] on the [Fontenay-le-Pesnel]–Rauray road.

1515 hours: *Obersturmbannführer* Wilhelm Mohnke (*SS-Panzer-Grenadier-Regiment 26*) requests tank support against enemy tanks which were advancing from the northwest.[25] The 8. and the 9.*Kompanien* immediately launched a flank attack against these enemy tanks. The 5. and 6.*Kompanien* , on alert, remained in their positions.

The enemy turned to the north even before our tanks appeared; therefore engagement with the enemy did not occur. However, the 8. and 9.*Kompanien* remained on the

---

25  Wilhelm Mohnke was among the earliest „*Leibstandarte*" officers, as a *Hauptsturmführer* commanding the 5/*LSSAH* in 1934. As a *Sturmbannführer* he led the *II./LSSAH* into Russia and won the German Cross in Gold on 26 December 1941. Mohnke then commanded the *Ersatz Bataillon* of the „*Leibstandarte*". Promoted to *Obersturmbannführer* on 21 June 1943, he became commander of *SS-Panzer-Grenadier-Regiment 26* with „*Hitlerjugend*" in mid-September 1943 and won the Knight's Cross as its commander on 11 July 1944. Promoted to *Oberführer* on 9 November 1944 and to *Brigadeführer und Generalmajor der Waffen-SS* on 30 January 1945, Mohnke commanded the *1.SS-Panzer Division „Leibstandarte*" from 20 August 1944 to 6 February 1945. He ended the war leading the *ad-hoc* units defending the Reich Chancellery in Berlin and spent 10 years as a POW in Russia. Wilhelm Mohnke died in Barsbüttel on 6 August 2001.

benchmark points 1 km northwest and northeast of Hill 102 and occupied securing positions there. Late afternoon the *9.Kompanie* captured two soldiers.

1730 hours: the command tank no. 553 burnt out. Cause unknown. Heavy enemy harassing fire all day, and heavy (fighter-bomber) aircraft activity over the sector of the *II.Abteilung*. The battle casualties and vehicle losses of the *Abteilung* are summarized in Appendix 2.

**War Diary Appendix no. 2.**
Battle casualties and vehicle losses between 6 and 10 June 1944

Battle casualties[26]:

| *Kompanie* | Killed | | | Seriously wounded | | | Lightly wounded | | | Wounded, remained with their units | | |
|---|---|---|---|---|---|---|---|---|---|---|---|---|
| | O | NCO | M | O | NCO | M | O | NCO | M | O | NCO | M |
| *Stabskompanie* | – | – | 2 | – | – | 1 | – | 1 | – | – | – | – |
| *5.Kompanie* | – | 1 | 1 | – | – | 2 | – | – | 3 | 1 | 1 | 1 |
| *6.Kompanie* | – | 1 | 6 | – | 1 | 1 | – | 2 | 6 | – | – | – |
| *7.Kompanie* | 2 | – | 8 | 1 | – | 1 | – | – | 1 | 1 | 1 | 1 |
| *8.Kompanie* | – | 1 | 5 | – | 1 | 1 | – | – | 2 | 1 | – | 1 |
| *9.Kompanie* | – | 2 | 2 | – | – | 2 | – | – | – | – | – | 2 |
| Total | 2 | 5 | 24 | 1 | 2 | 8 | - | 3 | 12 | 3 | 2 | 5 |

Key: O = Officers; NCO = NCOs; M = Enlisted Men.

Vehicle losses:
One medium motorcycle, two light cars, two medium cars, one prime mover, one heavy truck, one heavy motorcycle, 18 Panzerkampfwagen IVs (long barrelled).

---

26  In the 'battle casualties' chart, a key to the division of casualties between the three tiers of rank and a totals row have been added for this book.

# 3

# The Second Battle for Caen, 11–18 June 1944

## 11 June 1944
### I./SS-Panzer Regiment 12:

The *Kompanien* were in securing positions. Around 14:00 12 enemy armoured fighting vehicles attacked Reitzenstein's unit with mounted infantry.[1] The *1.Kompanie* took over the securing tasks.

At 1430 hours the *3.Kompanie* was hit by heavy tank and artillery fire. The Caen–Fontenay [-le-Pesnel] road was battered by smoke and high explosive shells. Both the *1.* and *2.Kompanien* knocked out one Sherman each, the *Pionier Zug* destroyed two anti-tank guns, and rendered one Sherman immobile. *Untersturmführer* Fritz Fiala was wounded on his right forearm.

The *4.Kompanie* repulsed a reconnaissance unit of 12 soldiers. A British vehicle with two radio operators ran into the line held by the *4.Kompanie*. The vehicle was taken into safety and the British[2] were shot down because they attempted resistance. The *Ordonnanz Offizier* immediately took the documents to the division. The *4.Kompanie* knocked out 16 Shermans during the attack against Rots. *Hauptsturmführer* Hans Pfeiffer was killed during the attack.[3]

Heavy artillery activity occurred during the whole day. Losses due to shell fragments (wounded soldiers).

## War Diary Appendix no. 5.

*12.SS-Panzer Division "Hitlerjugend"*           *O.U.*, 15. 06. 1944
*4. [Kompanie]/SS-Panzer Regiment 12*

Prevention of enemy tank attack against Rots and Le Bourg on 11. 06. 1944

Situation:
Heavy enemy pressure towards Rots and Le Bourg. The reconnaissance sweeps of the enemy towards Rots and Le Bourg were repulsed on 10. 6. 10.

---

1   *Hauptsturmführer* Gerd *Freiherr* von Reitzenstein was the the *Kompanie Chef* of the *5.(schwere) Kompanie* of *SS-Panzer Aufklärungsabteilung 12*. He had won the German Cross in Gold on 9 April 1943, as *Kompanie Chef* of the *7./Der Führer* with „*Das Reich*".
2   It is more likely that these soldiers were English-speaking Canadians.
3   *Hauptsturmführer* Hans Pfeiffer was *Kompanie Chef* of the *4./SS-Panzer Regiment 12*. A prewar *Zugführer* of the *Panzerspäh Zug* of the *"Leibstandarte,"* he came to *"Hitlerjugend"* having served as *Kompanie Chef* of the *6./SS-Panzer Regiment 1*.

*Hauptsturmführer* Gerd *Freiherr* von Reitzenstein being awarded his German Cross
in Gold by Walter Krüger (see Chapter 3 Footnote 1). (Mark C. Yerger)

Task:
Secure the Rots–Le Bourg line together with the Grenadiers, that is, on the left flank
at Le Bourg with 5 tanks of the *Kompanie*, and on the right flank on the western side of
Rots with 2 tanks; securing in the south-western, western and north-western direction.

Course of battle:
On 11. 06. constant heavy artillery fire on the securing positions of the *Kompanie* until
the evening. 15–45 enemy tanks were observed from Rots moving northwards on
the Bretteville road. 16 enemy armoured fighting vehicles provided constant security
towards Le Bourg on the northern outskirts of Bretteville [l'Orgueilleuse]. Heightened
vigilance was ordered to be kept on the right flank. Tank no. 425 was damaged in
an enemy artillery fire strike, and the radio operator, *Schütze* Testor was killed. The
observed enemy armoured fighting vehicles were immediately reported to the *Kompanie
Chef*, who then went to the right flank and saw them for himself. The damaged tank was
withdrawn from the securing line and was taken to the maintenance unit for repairs.

At 1830 hours the *Kompanie* received the following report: "490 from the direction
of (Villons [-les-Buissons]) 71 towards (Rots) 46 enemy tanks. Achtung! Achtung!"[4] Our
own force on the threatened flank consisted of three tanks.

The *Kompanie Chef* and the *Zugführer* of the *III.Zug*, *Untersturmführer* Günther
Deutscher, fell back from the left flank at Le Bourg and took over the securing of the

---

4   These tanks were presumably vehicles of the Canadian 10th Armoured Regiment (The Fort Garry
Horse). Squadrons B and C of the battalion-sized regiment were equipped with duplex drive (DD,
amphibious) Shermans. Each tank platoon included one Sherman Firefly with increased firepower.

A command conference at the divisional command post, Caen-Venoix, 13 or 14 June 1944 – left to right are *Obersturmbannführer* Max Wünsche (commander, *SS-Panzer Regiment 12*), *Brigadeführer* Fritz Witt (commander, *12.SS-Panzer Division*) and *Standartenführer* Kurt Meyer (commander, *SS-Panzer-Grenadier-Regiment 25*). (Bundesarchiv, Bild 146-1988-028-25A)

northern perimetres of Rots. Around 1900 hours enemy tank sweeps began on the Bretteville road towards Le Bourg. *Unterscharführer* Hanitsch's tank no. 438 knocked out a Churchill from 900 metres away.

Shortly afterwards tank no. 415 of *Leutnant* Erich Pohl knocked out a Sherman from a distance of 70 metres and another one from 10 metres. The other tanks turned to the west.

Around 1930 hours repeated attacks followed heavy artillery preparation. In a fierce battle *Oberscharführer* Heinz Lehmann's tank no. 426 knocked out four of the attacking 12 enemy tanks, hit a further three, upon which the enemy tanks retreated (four Shermans knocked out, two Shermans and one Churchill hit). Panther no. 426 received an order from the *Kompanie Chef* to relocate to the northern outskirts of Rots, where the damage done by artillery fire (on the running gear, on the tracks and the wheels) could be repaired by the maintenance unit. Around 2130 hours heavy artillery fire introduced an enemy tank attack against Rots, and the enemy succeeded in entering the village with infantry and tanks.

*Hauptsturmführer* Hans Pfeiffer decided to carry out a rush forward with three tanks and the Grenadiers. *Untersturmführer* Deutscher's tank no. 435 entered Rots on the Le Bourg road, reached the church and knocked out three tanks (Shermans) in a streetfight. Panthers no. 405 and 426 also attempted to reach the church from the east, but upon

A knocked out British Humber Mk. IV armoured reconnaissance car near Caen in June 1944. The armament of this 6.5 ton vehicle consisted of a 37 mm gun and a co-axial machine gun. Its crew of three was protected by a maximum 15mm armour. The vehicle was mainly used by the reconnaissance regiments of the British infantry divisions. (Hungarian Institute and Museum of Military History 52809)

reaching the eastern outskirts of the village they met enemy tanks, out of which three Shermans were knocked out by the tank of the *Kompanie Chef*. These burning tanks could not be rounded on the narrow road. The two tanks occupied an ambush position on the outskirts of the village behind the hedges, and with high explosive shells and machine gun fire repulsed the enemy infantry advancing through the village. *Untersturmführer* Deutscher's tank no. 435 could not be contacted on radio, and as it later turned out, was knocked out. One of the enemy tanks that had broken through was set aflame by a hit from *Unterscharführer* Schlehuber's tank no. 425. The enemy succeeded in defeating the right flank and forced the remains of the *Kompanie* with two tanks to retreat to the Caen–Le Bourg road.

Meanwhile the tank of the *Kompanie Chef* was hit on its hatch, *Hauptsturmführer* Hans Pfeiffer was killed.

There was no radio connection anymore with the left flank of the *Kompanie*, therefore they could not be informed about the current situation, and there was apparent danger that they could be cut off. *Leutnant* Pohl gathered the remains of the *Kompanie*, three tanks altogether, and until noon, defended the previous position. After the Grenadiers

*Sturmbannführer* Bernhard Krause (see Chapter 3 Footnote 5). (Mark C. Yerger)

retreated 1 km, the *Kompanie* also retreated knocking out four armoured personnel carriers en route.

Pohl<br>
*Leutnant* and *Kompanieführer*

### II./SS-Panzer Regiment 12:

In the morning up until noon, nothing notable happened except for artillery and aircraft activity.

1645 hours: report of *SS-Panzer-Grenadier-Regiment 26*, according to which the enemy tanks had broken into the positions of the *Regiment 26* (at *Einheit "Krause"*[5]).

1700 hours: the *II.Abteilung* moved against the enemy armoured fighting vehicles at Bretteville [l'Orgueilleuse] and Norrey [-en-Bessin]. The *8.* and *9.Kompanien* launched attack from the west, the *5.* and *6.Kompanien* from southwest. The enemy was repulsed. *SS-Panzer-Grenadier-Regiment 26* could now occupy its former positions. We knocked out:

- 10 Shermans and 4 General Lees[6] at le Mesnil-Patry by the *8.Kompanie*;

---

5   *Sturmbannführer* Bernhard Krause was commander of the *I./SS-Panzer-Grenadier-Regiment 26* and won the German Cross in Gold for command of that *Bataillon* on 7 August 1944. He'd graduated with the first cadet class at *Junkerschule* Bad Tölz and became a *Hauptsturmführer* on 1 June 1940. Krause commanded the *Flak Abteilung* of the *"Leibstandarte"* when Russia was invaded and became a *Sturmbannführer* on 1 September 1941. Promoted to *Obersturmbannführer* on 1 September 1944, Krause won the Knight's Cross for his command of *SS-Panzer-Grenadier-Regiment 26* on 18 November 1944. He was killed commanding that regiment on 19 February 1945.

6   This tank was brought into service as the M3 Grant in the British Army. Only the version called "Canal Defence Light" was used in Normandy, which provided illumination of roads and targets during night

Knocked out British Cromwell IV medium tanks in the Caen sector, June 1944. The armament of the tank consisted of a 75 mm gun and two machine guns. The crew of five was protected by armour a maximum of 76mm thick. The Cromwell was used by the British, Canadian, Polish armoured reconnaissance regiments and the armoured regiments of the British 7th Armoured Division in Normandy. (Hungarian Institute and Museum of Military History 55505-36)

- 7 Shermans at le Mesnil-Patry by the *9.Kompanie.*[7]

20:30: all armoured *Kompanien* return to their initial positions. Our total losses:

- 5 tanks of the *8.Kompanie*
- 1 tank of the *9.Kompanie*

According to the score report of the *II.Abteilung* found in Appendix 3, our scores so far amount to 63 tanks, 9 anti-tank guns and more than 450 prisoners of war.

---

raids with its high-performance searchlight. The type was deployed in the 11th, 42nd and 49th Royal Tank Regiment battalions of the British 79th Armoured Division.

7   On that day the battalion-sized 6th Armoured Regiment (1st Hussars) of Canadian 2nd Armoured Brigade lost 34 (mainly duplex drive, that is, DD) Shermans and 3 Sherman Firefly tanks altogether in the battle against the Panzergrenadiers and Panzer *Pioniers* of the *12.SS-Panzer Division* equipped with hand-held anti-tank rocket launchers (*Panzerfäuste*) and magnetic hollow charges, and against the Panzer IV tanks of the *II./SS-Panzer Regiment 12.* The Germans waited for the Canadians in ambush positions, after the upcoming attack was discovered by the radio reconnaissance of *SS-Panzer-Nachrichten-Abteilung 12* with the help of a code book found in a Sherman knocked out on 09. 06. 1944.

Another view of knocked out British Cromwell IV tanks near Caen, June 1944. (Hungarian Institute and Museum of Military History)

## War Diary Appendix no. 3.

Score report

| Unit | Amount | Type | Location | Date (month/day/year) |
|---|---|---|---|---|
| 5.Kompanie | 9 | Sherman | Authie | 06. 07. 1944 |
| | 5 | Sherman | Buron NW | 06. 09. 1944 |
| | 2 | anti-tank gun | Buron NW | 06. 09. 1944 |
| some 150 prisoners of war (the infantry had taken charge of them) | | | | |
| 6.Kompanie | 14 | Sherman | Authie | 06. 07. 1944 |
| | 3 | armoured personnel carrier | Authie | 06. 07. 1944 |
| | 4 | anti-tank gun | Authie | 06. 07. 1944 |
| some 300 prisoners of war (the infantry had taken charge of them) | | | | |
| 7.Kompanie | 5 | Sherman | Buron | 06. 07. 1944 |
| | 1 | Sherman | Franqueville | 06. 09. 1944 |
| 8.Kompanie | 1 | Sherman | La Folie | 06. 07. 1944 |
| | 2 | Sherman | La Folie | 06. 08. 1944 |
| | 1 | Sherman immobile | La Folie | 06. 08. 1944 |

| | 1 | Sherman | La Folie | 06. 09. 1944 |
|---|---|---|---|---|
| | \multicolumn: 2 prisoners of war | | | |
| | 10 | Sherman | Le Mesnil-Patry | 06. 11. 1944 |
| | 4 | General Lee | Le Mesnil-Patry | 06. 11. 1944 |
| *9.Kompanie* | 3 | Sherman | St. Contest | 06. 09. 1944 |
| | 3 | anti-tank gun | St. Contest | 06. 09. 1944 |
| | 7 | Sherman | Le Mesnil-Patry | 06. 11. 1944 |

Total: 63 tanks, 9 anti-tank guns, more than 450 prisoners of war.

## 12 June 1944
### *I./SS-Panzer Regiment 12*:
The *Kompanien* remained in their securing positions. As a result of heavy artillery fire all day, one prime mover, one Kfz.1[8] and a radio car were total losses, and around 1030 hours a tank hit the gun mantlet of tank no. 305.

### *II./SS-Panzer Regiment 12*:
No combat activity. The *Kompanien* remained in their securing positions. Heavy artillery harassing fire, heavy aircraft activity. Based on the previous days spent in battle, five Iron Crosses 1st Class, and 45 Iron Crosses 2nd Class were awarded to the *Abteilung*. The *Abteilung* commander bestowed them as follows:

Iron Cross 1st Class:
- *Obersturmführer* Hans Siegel
- *Untersturmführer* Rudolf Walther
- *Untersturmführer* Helmut Kasemiresch
- *Unterscharführer* Rudolf Weber
- *Unterscharführer* Storck

Iron Cross 2nd Class:
- *5.Kompanie*:: 15
- *6.Kompanie*: 13
- *7., 8.* and *9.Kompanien*: 5-5.

## 13 June 1944
### *I./SS-Panzer Regiment 12*:
At 1300 hours disengagement of the *1.* and *3.Kompanien* and the three command tanks via Rauray–Noyers towards Monts [d'Eraines], to repulse enemy armoured fighting vehicles which had burst into the positions there. 1 km north of Monts the *Abteilung* was ordered back to its previous position, because the enemy armoured fighting vehicles were beaten by that time. The *1.Kompanie* relocated its positions to the hills directly southeast of Tilly-sur-Seulles, in order to cover the frontline towards the west that was expanded at the *Regiment 902*[9] (on the western flank of the *Abteilung*).

---

8   Kubelwagen, the German equivalent of the US jeep utility vehicle.
9   *Panzergrenadier-Lehr-Regiment 902* of the *Panzer-Lehr-Division*.

Kurt Meyer in a portrait as a *Standartenführer* and Oakleaves holder. He
succeeded Fritz Witt as *"Hitlerjugend"* division commander on 14 June 1944
(see Chapter 2 Footnote 5 and Chapter 8 Footnote 26). (Mark C. Yerger)

Kurt Meyer being presented his Oakleaves by Adolf Hitler (see
Chapter 8 Footnote 26). (Mark C. Yerger)

The *4.Kompanie* was ordered to cooperate with *SS-Panzer-Grenadier-Regiment 26*, and was in Marcelet.

The *2.Kompanie* was ordered to cooperate with *SS-Aufklärungsabteilung 12*.

At the *4.Kompanie*, a reconnaissance aircraft that had to carry out an emergency landing in between the enemy positions[10], was destroyed by armour-piercing shells and its crew was killed by machine gun fire whilst crawling out of the plane.

Three Iron Crosses 1st Class and 30 Iron Crosses 2nd Class were awarded to soldiers of the *Abteilung*.

### II./SS-Panzer Regiment 12:

No combat activity. The *Kompanien* remained in their securing positions. Heavy artillery and rocket-launcher harassing fire meant losses for the *5.Kompanie* and the *Stabskompanie*.

In the evening heavy aircraft activity over the sector of the *II.Abteilung*. Here the quadruple-barrelled anti-aircraft guns of the *II.Abteilung* shot down the following aircraft:

- one Hurricane at 1858 hours ✓
- one Thunderbolt at 2136 hours ✓
- one Thunderbolt at 2156 hours ✓

The commander instructed *Obersturmführer* Albert Gasch to re-establish the *7.Kompanie* in Saussaye.

## 14 June 1944

### I./SS-Panzer Regiment 12:

At 1200 hours the *Flak Zug* of the *Stabskompanie* shot down a Thunderbolt[11] arriving over the positions with a thin streak of smoke; the aircraft crashed 3 km due south of Vendes. Confirmed by *Oberleutnant* Burckhardt (field post number 00954).

The *3.Kompanie* handed three tanks over to the *1.Kompanie*, three to the *Stabskompanie* (to the *Aufklärungszug*), and two to the *4.Kompanie*. The officers, NCOs and the enlisted men of the *3.Kompanie* were ordered back to Le Neubourg to fill up the ranks.

Otherwise the day was calm. Occasional artillery harassing fire and light aircraft activity.

Daily order of *Oberstgruppenführer* Dietrich: "Acknowledgements for the *Korps* for the defensive combat on the invasion frontline".

### II./SS-Panzer Regiment 12:

There was no close contact with the enemy today. Artillery fire strikes on positions in front of us and to our left. *Unterscharführer* Zschage was severely wounded by a shot, and was taken into hospital.

---

10  This was an Allied observation aircraft carrying out an emergency landing behind their own lines.
11  P-47 Thunderbolt, an American single-seat dual-purpose fighter and fighter-bomber aircraft.

## 15 June 1944
*I./SS-Panzer Regiment 12*:
During the day heavy fire strikes on the combat posts.

Around 1500 hours the *2.Kompanie* knocked out a tank (its type could not be identified because only its turret was visible), which was blown up after a hit. Furthermore, six armoured personnel carriers were also destroyed. The *1.Kompanie*, around 1900 hours, destroyed three armoured personnel carriers with their mounted infantry.

*II./SS-Panzer Regiment 12*:
There was no particular combat activity or other events during the day. The *Kompanien* remained in their securing positions. Heavy artillery harassing fire on both sides.

## 16 June 1944
*I./SS-Panzer Regiment 12* (Bas des Forges):
From 0000 hours relocation of the *Abteilung* to its new quarters area at Bas des Forges, without any notable events. Before the relocation of the *Abteilung* command post heavy low-level air-raid by 15 aircraft. [Fontenay-le-Pesnel] was attacked with bombs and aircraft weapons. There were no battle casualties or material losses.

The new quarters area of the battalion was clear of artillery fire. Considerably lighter aircraft activity than on the previous day.

Around 1927 hours the *Flak Zug* shot down a Thunderbolt. At 2130 hours one further aircraft was shot down. Losses: one Kfz.1 and a truck due to deterioration.

*II./SS-Panzer Regiment 12*:
During the straightening of the frontline the armoured *Kompanien* followed the retreat of the Panzergrenadiers. Due to this position changes occurred regarding the middle *Kompanien* and the *Abteilung* command post.

From 0100 hours new command post 400 metres northeast of Rauray. The *6.* and *5.Kompanien* remained in their previous positions. The *8.Kompanie* relocated its position to the previous battalion command post. The *9.Kompanie* established positions at Mercelet and was ordered to cooperate with *Einheit "Krause"*.

From 1100 hours unusually heavy enemy bombardment of the positions abandoned yesterday. From the heavy bombardment we presumed the intention of the enemy to launch an attack.

The units of the *II.Abteilung* prepared to receive the attack and to carry out a possible repulse of it.

At 1945 hours the quadruple-barrelled anti-aircraft gun of the *II.Abteilung* shot down a Typhoon[12]. In Appendix 4 we summarize the aircraft shot down by the *Flak Zug* of the *II.Abteilung* from the beginning of the mission.[13] *Schütze* Stanieck (*5.Kompanie*) was wounded by a shell fragment.

---

12  Hawker Typhoon IB British single-seat fighter-bomber. Among the best Allied ground attack aircraft, its accurate rocket firing capabilities wrecked havoc on the German ground troops during the Normandy fighting.

13  Unfortunately this appendix was lost.

## 17 June 1944
### *I./SS-Panzer Regiment 12*:
At 1100 hours a Typhoon was shot down at the *Flak Zug*. Otherwise, no notable events.

### *II./SS-Panzer Regiment 12*:
Today, after heavy artillery preparation the enemy succeeded in breaking into the positions of *SS-Panzer-Grenadier-Regiment 26* (Siebken's unit[14]) north of the small wooded area of Park de Boislonde and controlling the latter.

At 1330 hours our Grenadiers launched a counterattack. The *8./SS-Panzer Regiment 12* controlled and supported this counterattack from the southwest.

1430 hours: in order to be able to provide further support for the counterattack, the *6./SS-Panzer Regiment 12* launched an attack from its securing positions at 1430 hours and reached the positions behind the slope southeast of Hill 102. We were not able to drive the enemy out of the Park de Boislonde. During this attack the armoured *Kompanien* achieved the following scores:

- The *6.Kompanie* knocked out three Sherman and one Churchill tanks, five anti-tank guns
- The *8.Kompanie* knocked out two Sherman tanks.

At 2330 hours withdrawal of both *Kompanien*: the *6.Kompanie* to its departure positions 1 km north of Rauray, the *8.Kompanie* to the positions 1.5 km northwest of Point no. 75[15]. Total loss of one tank per *Kompanie*:

- tank no. 645 at the *6.Kompanie*
- tank no. 816 at the *8.Kompanie*

Losses:

|          | Officer | NCOs | Enlisted men |
|----------|---------|------|--------------|
| Killed   | –       | 1    | 1            |
| Wounded  | 1       | 2    | 10           |
| Missing  | –       | 1    | 4            |

The quadruple-barrelled anti-aircraft gun of the *Flak Zug* of the *II./SS-Panzer Regiment 12* succeeded in shooting down a Typhoon at 1130 hours. The victory was unambiguously confirmed by the crew of the quadruple-barrelled anti-aircraft gun of the *Flak Zug*.

---

14  A member of the *"Leibstandarte"* since March 1933, *Sturmbannführer* Bernhard Siebken was commander of the *II./SS-Panzer-Grenadier-Regiment 26* from late September 1943 and became an *Obersturmbannführer* on 20 June 1944. He took command of the *Ersatz Brigade* of the *I.SS-Panzer Korps* in December 1944 and won the Knight's Cross as an *Obersturmbannführer* commanding *SS-Panzer-Grenadier-Regiment 2* of the *"Leibstandarte"* on 17 April 1945. Siebken was hanged by the British in Hameln on 20 January 1949.

15  Point 57 is written in the original document, presumably because of a writing mistake.

## 18 June 1944
### I./SS-Panzer Regiment 12:
No notable events.

### II./SS-Panzer Regiment 12:
Apart from the light artillery activity on both sides the morning of 18. 06. 1944 was spent without any notable events.

1235 hours: heavy fire strike by our artillery on the Park de Boislonde small wooded area. After the fire strike two armoured personnel carrier *Kompanien*[16] launched an attack (on foot) with the tank support of the *6.* and *8.Kompanien*. We did not manage to control the small wooded area.

At 1335 hours the quadruple-barrelled anti-aircraft gun of Großedirkschmalz, attacking with the *6.Kompanie*, shot down a British artillery observation aircraft (Auster IV). The aircraft crashed on Hill 102. Its two-man crew was killed.

1645 hours: another artillery fire strike on the small wooded area.

1700 hours: repeated infantry attacks with tank support against the Park de Boislonde. We failed again to control the small wooded area and to help the infantry get back to their previous positions with this attack. Our right flank succeeded in entering the small wooded area. Further advance was, however, repulsed by heavy preventive fire. During this combat the *6.Kompanie* successfully knocked out 4 Shermans, despite heavy artillery fire. There were no losses on our side.

*Oberscharführer* Kastner was severely wounded by shell fragments. In the *6.Kompanie* a number of tanks were damaged during the heavy artillery fire which need repairing at the workshop *Kompanie*.

Ammunition expenditure: 100 high explosive shells, 50 armour-piercing shells, 1,000 anti-aircraft rounds, 1,200 steel-core [machine-gun ammunition], 680 steel-core tracer [machine-gun ammunition], 450 submachine gun [ammunition], 36 pistol [ammunition]. Hand grenades: 2 *Stielhandgranate*, 20 egg hand grenades (*Eierhandgranate*), 18 smoke candles.

---

16  Two *SS-Panzergrenadier Kompanien* equipped with armoured personnel carriers.

# 4

# Operational Interval, 19–24 June 1944

**19 June 1944**
*I./SS-Panzer Regiment 12*:
Reconnaissance mission of the *4.Kompanie* to estimate the condition of tank no. 438 which had been left behind in Rots. One man was wounded during the mission.

*II./SS-Panzer Regiment 12*:
The day was spent without close contact with the enemy. Light artillery activity on both sides. Three enlisted men from the *9.Kompanie* were battle casualties due to artillery fire, of whom one was killed, one severely wounded and one lightly wounded.

Appendix no.5 summarizes the operational tanks of the *II.Abteilung* on 19. 06. 1944, 1930 hours.

Appendix no.6 summarizes the total tank losses of the *II.Abteilung* until 2400 hours, 19. 06. 1944.

**War Diary Appendix no. 5.**
Operational tanks with turret-numbers at 1930 hours on 19 June 1944

| *Stab* | 555 | 554 | 552 | and two anti-aircraft vehicles | |
|---|---|---|---|---|---|
| | Total | 5 tanks | | | |
| *5.Kompanie* | 505 | 504 | | | |
| | 515 | 525 | 526 | 527 | |
| | 536 | 537 | 538 | 546 | |
| | 547 | 735 | | | |
| | Total | 12 tanks | | | |
| *6.Kompanie* | 605 | 604 | | | |
| | 617 | 625 | 626 | 627 | |
| | 635 | 636 | 637 | 646 | |
| | 738 | | | | |
| | Total | 11 tanks | | | |
| *8.Kompanie* | 804 | | | | |
| | 818 | 826 | 828 | 835 | |
| | 837 | 845 | 717 | 745 | |
| | Total | 9 tanks | | | |
| *9.Kompanie* | 904 | | | | |
| | 916 | 917 | 918 | 925 | |
| | 926 | 927 | 935 | 936 | |

| Stab | 555 | 554 | 552 | and two anti-aircraft vehicles | |
|---|---|---|---|---|---|
| | 937 | 946 | 715 | | |
| | Total | 12 tanks | | | |
| | Total number of operational tanks of the *Abteilung* 49 tanks | | | | |

**War Diary Appendix no. 6.**
Total losses in Panzerkampfwagen IVs in the period between 06.–19. 06. 1944, 2400 hours

| Stab | 553 | | | | | |
|---|---|---|---|---|---|---|
| 5.Kompanie | 516 | 517 | 528 | 535 | | |
| 6.Kompanie | 615 | 616 | 618 | 628 | 645 | |
| 7.Kompanie | 705 | 704 | 716 | 726 | 736 | 746 |
| 8.Kompanie | 805 | 816 | 825 | 826 | 827 | 847 |
| 9.Kompanie | 915 | | | | | |
| Total losses until 19. 06. 1944 2400 hours: 23 Panzerkampfwagen IVs | | | | | | |

# 20 June 1944
## I./SS-Panzer Regiment 12:
A new reconnaissance unit of the *4.Kompanie* was commanded by *Unterscharführer* Mais. The position and condition of the tank no.438 was accurately estimated. Around 0430 hours, despite the machine gun fire, the tank was pulled out with the help of two prime movers and a captured armoured fighting vehicle and was towed to the repairs station. One of the prime movers was hit a few times, but there were no other losses. The *Regimentskommandeur* awarded the Iron Cross 1st Class to the commander of the reconnaissance unit, and the Iron Cross 2nd Class to the soldiers taking part in the mission.

## II./SS-Panzer Regiment 12:
The combat units of the *II.Abteilung* remained in their securing positions of the previous day. There was no close contact with the enemy during the day. Only light aircraft activity.

Heavy enemy artillery harassing fire was laid on all positions of the *II.Abteilung*. Due to this, there was one loss (killed) from the enlisted men. *Hauptsturmführer* Dr. Oskar Jordan [1] was injured by a fall (probable broken shin-bone). At the onset of darkness the *8.Kompanie* was recalled into its departure positions (to the former *Abteilung* command post), 2.5 km south of Fontenay-le-Pesnel.

# 21 June 1944
## I./SS-Panzer Regiment 12:
No notable events during the day.

---

1   *Hauptsturmführer* Dr. Oskar Jordan was *Abteilungsarzt* of the *II./SS-Panzer Regiment 12*.

Rudolf von Ribbentrop as an *Obersturmführer* (see Appendix II). (Mark C. Yerger)

Both wounded in Normandy, Rudolf von Ribbentrop (left) is driven by Panzer Regiment commander Max Wünsche, June 1944 (see Appendix II and throughout text). (Mark C. Yerger)

*Obersturmbannführer* Herbert Kuhlmann while with the *"Leibstandarte"* (see Appendix II). He later commanded *SS-Panzer Regiment 12*. (Mark C. Yerger)

### II./SS-Panzer Regiment 12:
The *II.Abteilung* had no contact with the enemy during the day. In the early morning hours heavy artillery fire on the positions of the *Abteilung*. Due to this, three killed, five wounded and one car lost by the *6.Kompanie*. Occasional artillery strikes during the day on both sides. Otherwise, no particular events.

## 22 June 1944
### I./SS-Panzer Regiment 12:
No notable events during the day.

### II./SS-Panzer Regiment 12:
The *II.Abteilung* had no contact with the enemy today. Positions of the *Kompanien* and the command post of the *Abteilung* as before. Intensive artillery harassing fire on both sides during the day; otherwise no notable events.

## 23 June 1944
### I./SS-Panzer Regiment 12:
Nothing notable.

### II./SS-Panzer Regiment 12:
There was no particular contact with the enemy during the day. Artillery harassing fire on both sides all day.

Aircraft activity was scarce; in spite of this, the loss of four vehicles due to bombs and machine gun rounds.

Ammunition usage: 600 2cm anti-aircraft shells.

## 24 June 1944
### *I./SS-Panzer Regiment 12*:
The *1.Kompanie* received orders to secure at St. Germain [-la Blanche-Herbe], northwest of Caen. Otherwise, no notable events.

### *II./SS-Panzer Regiment 12*:
The *Kompanien* of the *II.Abteilung* remained in their securing positions of the previous day. Artillery harassing fire on both sides all day. Due to this, loss of a vehicle and an enlisted man.

Scarce aircraft activity. No change in the *Abteilung* command post. Ammunition usage: 100 2cm anti-aircraft shells.

# 5

# The Third Battle for Caen, 25–30 June 1944

## 25 June 1944[1]
### I./SS-Panzer Regiment 12:
At 1300 hours two platoons from each of the *2.* and *4.Kompanien* departed for Fontenay [-le-Pesnel]. The attack had to be aborted because the enemy proved to be too strong. Tank no. 217 was total loss. The *Adjutant, Untersturmführer* Heinz Schröder, was missing.[2] Tank no. 438[3] was a total loss due to a hit from an anti-tank gun. Tanks no. 236 and 427 had to be abandoned because of anti-tank gun hits on the lateral countershaft and the running gear.

Regrouping of the *Abteilung* to Tessel-Bretteville. The new attack in the direction of Fontenay [-le-Pesnel] had to be suspended. The *Abteilung* was encircled and stood in a circular defence. The remaining tanks of the *2.* and *4.Kompanien* were drawn forward to Tessel-Bretteville and occupied securing positions. The *1.Kompanie* was also withdrawn from its securing positions at St. Germain [-la Blanche-Herbe] in order to carry out securing tasks north and northwest of Tessel-Bretteville. The *2.Kompanie* destroyed a Sherman.

## War Diary Appendix no. 6.
*12.SS-Panzer Division "Hitlerjugend"*                    *O.U.*, 15. 07. 1944
*4. [Kompanie]/SS-Panzer Regiment 12*

Attack towards Fontenay [-le-Pesnel] on 25. 06. 44

Situation:
The enemy succeeded in occupying Fontenay [-le-Pesnel] on the Caen–St. Lô main road with tanks and closing the road.

---

1   Operation Epsom of the British–Canadian 21st Army Group commenced on this day and lasted until 30 June 1944. During the operation the task of the strengthened VIII Corps was to cross the Odon river, take the hills behind the river in control (especially Hills 112 and 113), and penetrate into the Orne valley. With this, the British–Canadian troops would separate Caen from the south, forcing the Germans to abandon the city. The VIII Corps consisted of the 15th (Scottish) and the 43rd (Wessex) Infantry Divisions, the 11th Armoured Division, the 4th Armoured Brigade, the 31st Tank Brigade and a special tank battalion, with more than 600 armoured fighting vehicles and 900 guns. The Shermans of the 4th Armoured Brigade supported the 43rd Infantry Division, while the Churchill heavy tanks of the 31st Tank Brigade supported the 15th Infantry Division. In case of a successful breakthrough the 11th Armoured Division was to develop the attack towards the Orne valley. The VIII Corps was further supported by three navy cruisers and the fighter–bomber group of the 2nd Tactical Air Force.
2   *Untersturmführer* Schröder was killed when getting out of his tank. See Meyer, p.176.
3   This was the Panther tank which was successfully towed out of Rots by the Germans a few days earlier.

Grenadiers near a Panther from *I./SS-Panzer Regiment 12*, 25 June 1944. (Ullstein Bilderdienst)

Task:
The *4.Kompanie*, within the force of the *Abteilung*, was to follow the *2.Kompanie*, attack the village, then occupy and control the hill northwest of the village.

Course of battle:
The *Kompanie*, following the *2.Kompanie*, advanced from the start position on the road leading to Fontenay [-le-Pesnel] through Rauray. Heavy fire from enemy artillery while passing the hill south of Fontenay [-le-Pesnel]. *Unterscharführer* Hanitsch's tank no. 429 was out of order because of a hit on the running gear; the tank had to be towed away. Upon reaching the outskirts of Fontenay [-le-Pesnel], order of the *Regiment* on radio: "Outflank and attack the village from the left and reach the target of the attack!" *Untersturmführer* Helmut Flämmig's *II.Zug* fanned out to the left, behind them the *I.Zug* occupied the southern perimetres of Fontenay [-le-Pesnel] and received heavy anti-tank gun fire from the direction of the church, which knocked out tank no. 427 of *Unterscharführer* Sedat. *Untersturmführer* Flämmig's tank no. 425 destroyed the anti-tank gun, but reported by radio: "A sunken road is in front of me, cannot get in the village". Tank no. 427 of *Unterscharführer* Sedat was already stuck in the sunken road. In addition to this, a watercourse was stretching athwart the direction of attack, which also

formed an anti-tank obstacle. The new order of the *Regiment*: "The *Kompanie* crosses the brook in Tessel-Bretteville, and again attacks Fontenay and the hills north of the village left of this brook!"

The *Kompanie* effected communication with the *Wehrmacht* units of the *Lehr-Division*[4] in Tessel [-Bretteville] and immediately launched the attack. The enemy entrenched and camouflaged itself well in terrain broken up with hedges and ditches; due to this, the attack made real progress only in the area of the *II.Zug*. The *I.Zug* on the left flank of the *Kompanie* had fallen across the small wooded area heavily controlled by the enemy, and faced heavy artillery, anti-tank gun and tank fire. *Zugführer Oberscharführer* Heinz Lehmann's tank no. 415 had its radio disabled. *Zugführer Oberscharführer* Lehmann got into Panther no. 416 and reported by radio that the engineers of the *Lehr-Division* would not follow up the attack as they could not get through this small wooded area alone because of a heavy enemy presence there.

The *Kompanieführer*, *Leutnant* Erich Pohl's order on the radio: "The *I.Zug* is to follow the *II.Zug* in the area of the latter!" The *Kompanieführer* reached the target of the attack with the *II.Zug* and secured the hill. The *I.Zug* established communication with the Grenadiers, came round the small wooded area and also attacked the hill behind the small wooded area. While mounting a hedge Panther no. 417 of *Unterscharführer* Ratka was hit three times by enemy armoured fighting vehicles which opened fire from well-camouflaged positions, and when the platoon resumed its way they hit and knocked out the *Unterscharführer* Meiss's tank no. 438. The tank was burnt out. *Oberscharführer* Heinz Lehmann, *I.Zugführer*, got out, established communication on foot with *Leutnant* Pohl, and around 0200 hours the *I.Zug* with its two tanks reached the *Kompanie*.

The *Kompanie* within the force of the *Abteilung* established circular defensive positions. The enemy attacked the village of Tessel-Bretteville on 26. 06. with major armoured forces and cut the *I.Abteilung* off. According to the order of the regiment received by radio, the hill was to be kept at all costs until communication was re-established. The enemy secured itself with tanks and anti-tank guns against our breakout from the circular defence, and with a direct hit *Untersturmführer* Flammig's tank no. 425 was rendered disabled; the commander, the gunner and the loader were wounded. The anti-tank gun was destroyed.

Around 1400 hours the *Abteilung* received an order to break through to the lines running at Rauray and reconnect with our own forces. After thorough reconnaissance a spot was discovered in the riverbed that allowed the crossing of the armoured fighting vehicles. The *2.Kompanie* headed the column, followed by the *Aufklärungszug*, the *Abteilungsstab*; the rearguard securing task was taken over by the *4.Kompanie* at 0600 hours[5].

With skilled command, despite extremely difficult conditions, they succeeded in crossing the riverbed and reached the hills beyond it. The enemy discovered the breakthrough attempt and placed artillery covering fire on the breakthrough point. The *Kompanie* with the mounted Grenadiers succeeded in breaking through the enemy lines and in reconnecting with the regiment; this was possible with skilled and determined

---

4   Units of the *Panzer-Lehr-Division* of the Army.
5   For tanks the direction is specified clockwise, and '1200 hours' always shows the direction square to the glacis plate. In the case of '0600 hours' direction the gun of the tank looks backwards, over the rear hull armour, parallel to the hull.

movement. Following this, the *Kompanie* was deployed between Vendes and Tessel-Bretteville for securing tasks, to be relieved later by the *2.Kompanie;* the *Kompanie* was sent to its previous quarters area for ammunition and fuel supplementation.

Pohl
*Leutnant* and *Kompanieführer*

### II./SS-Panzer Regiment 12:
The *II.Abteilung* remained in its previous combat sector with securing tasks. Hours of heavy artillery fire was laid on the positions of the *II.Abteilung* which caused battle casualties and material losses.

During the day intensive aircraft activity over the positions. At 0805 hours the four tanks of the *8.Kompanie* were drawn forward to Fontenay-le-Pesnel. Ammunition usage: 800 2cm anti-aircraft shells.

## 26 June 1944
### I./SS-Panzer Regiment 12:
In the morning the *1.* and *2.Kompanien* stood in circular defence northwest of Tessel-Bretteville. The northern and north-western borders of Tessel-Bretteville were secured and held by the remaining tanks of the *2.* and *4.Kompanien*, the *1.Kompanie* and the *Aufklärungszug.* The sweep forward of the Tiger tanks, intended to relieve the encircled *Abteilung*, was unsuccessful.

At 1500 hours the encircled *Abteilung* received an order to break out from the enemy encirclement independently. The manoeuvre was successful. In the afternoon the *Abteilung* was sent into action in the Tessel-Bretteville–Vendes sector to create a new main battle line. We knocked out 7 Shermans during this fighting. Total losses: tanks number 236, 438, 204, 419 and 427.

### II./SS-Panzer Regiment 12:
At 0500 hours the *II.Abteilung* (without the *8.* and *9.Kompanien*) launched an attack on the wooded area west of Tessel-Bretteville against the enemy armoured fighting vehicles and infantry units that penetrated through Fontenay-le-Pesnel. Heavy artillery fire from the enemy at the onset of the manoeuvre.

0830 hours: attack of enemy tanks from the direction of Fontenay [-le-Pesnel] towards Rauray and on the area east of this road.

The *Abteilung* command post held until now had to be abandoned in the face of heavy artillery and tank gun fire. The withdrawal of all units of the command and control staff proceeded in order. Losses of the motorcycle dispatch rider unit due to artillery fire: two heavy motorcycles with sidecars, three medium motorcycles. The *Abteilung* commander's vehicle (Kfz. 15) was severely damaged, but was able to retreat on its own.

The *5.* and *6.Kompanien* and the *Kampfstaffel* of the *Stab* were recalled before the assault on the wooded area west of Tessel-Bretteville, because there were only weak enemy forces on said wooded area, and they were sent into action against the enemy armoured fighting vehicles approaching from the north. Although facing extremely heavy resistance the *5.* and *6.Kompanien* succeeded in retaking their former positions, in order to be able to provide gunfire support for the *Infanterie* to gather and regroup.

The terrain in Normandy was especially suitable for establishing ambush positions. This photograph shows a heavily camouflaged towed 7.5 cm Pak 40 anti-tank guns of the German Army (*Heer*). It was barely possible for armoured vehicles moving through the dense vegetation of the Normandy *bocage* to spot and combat hidden anti-tank weapons before the first shots were fired. (Hungarian Institute and Museum of Military History 52835)

The Panzergrenadiers in Fontenay-le-Pesnel retreated southwards in the direction of Rauray to avoid artillery fire and the heavy pressure of the enemy. The 8.*Kompanie* covered their disengagement and slowly followed this retreat until the Rauray area. The 5. and 6.*Kompanien* held their former positions even in the face of the heaviest enemy pressure.

During the afternoon preparations for a counter-attack in cooperation with the *Tiger Abteilung*[6] of the *Korps*. However this counter-attack was called off and the Tigers were withdrawn to be redeployed at another section of the division.

According to the reports of the adjoining troops on the right[7] increasing enemy pressure is apparent towards Cheux, in the direction of Grainville [sur-Odon]. During the morning engagements *Hauptsturmführer* Ludwig Ruckdeschel (6.*Kompanie Chef*) was severely wounded. The command of the *Kompanie* was transferred to *Untersturmführer* Buchwald.[8]

2300 hours: new command post of the *Abteilung* 600 metres south of Rauray on the Rauray–Grainville [sur-Odon] road. Ammunition expenditure: 680 high explosive

---

6    Namely *schwere SS-Panzer Abteilung 101* fighting as *Korps Truppen* of the *I.SS-Panzer Korps.*
7    On the right flank of *SS-Panzer Regiment 12* fought units of *SS-Panzer-Grenadier-Regiment 26* and *SS-Panzer-Pionier-Bataillon 12.*
8    *Untersturmführer* Helmut Buchwald was killed in action on 28 June 1944.

Grenadiers from *12.SS-Panzer Division* near Caen, June 1944. (Cody Images)

shells, 320 armour-piercing shells, 1,000 2cm anti-aircraft shells, 1,100 steel core [machine-gun ammunition], 14 smoke candles.

## 27 June 1944

### *I./SS-Panzer Regiment 12:*

The *1.Kompanie* secured in its positions directly south of Tessel-Bretteville. By order of the regiment the *2.Kompanie* was withdrawn from the securing sector of the *Abteilung*, in order to repulse the enemy tanks that broke through in the area of Grainville [sur-Odon].[9] The *4.Kompanie* was subordinated to the *II.Abteilung*, and secured directly southeast of Rauray.[10]

During the battle we destroyed 25 Shermans, two Churchills and one tank of unknown type. *Unterscharführer* Wolf destroyed one further Sherman with a

---

9    The Panthers of the *2./SS-Panzer Regiment 12* might have been deployed against the Churchill heavy tanks of the 7th Royal Tank Regiment (a battalion-sized unit) supporting the Scottish 9th Cameronians (Scottish Rifles). The British lost three tanks there that day. See Reynolds, p.156.

10   Rauray was attacked by the 11th Durham Light Infantry Infantry of the British 70th Infantry Brigade, and was occupied that day with the support of the duplex drive (DD) Sherman tanks of the British 8th Independent Armoured Brigade.

*Faustpatrone*.[11] Two small armoured vehicles[12] with machine guns were destroyed; three of our tanks are counted as total losses. Three tanks have to be sent to the repairs station because of anti-tank gun and artillery hits.

**War Diary Appendix no. 7.**
*12.SS-Panzer Division "Hitlerjugend"*                                    O.U., 15. 07. 1944
*4. [Kompanie]/SS-Panzer Regiment 12*

Prevention of enemy tank attack against Rauray on 27. 06. 44

Situation
The enemy tried to push its attack opened in the direction of Fontenay [-le-Pesnel] and Tessel-Bretteville forward towards Rauray and exerted heavy pressure on the *II.Abteilung* securing positions there.

Task:
The *Kompanie* did not occupy positions in the former quarters area but returned immediately and was subordinated to the *II.Abteilung*. The *Kompaniefuhrer* immediately went forward for briefing.

Course of battle:
The *Kompanie* was led by *Oberscharfuhrer* Heinz Lehmann to the crossroad specified in the order and the *Kompaniefuhrer, Leutnant* Pohl immediately directed them towards the sector to be secured. Securing began at around 0200 hours. In order to assess the circumstances, the *Kompaniefuhrer* and the two *Zugfuhrers* remained ahead by the Grenadiers[13] to draw the tanks forward into the area of the Grenadiers and take over the securing tasks there. At this moment, around 0600 hours, the enemy was already attacking Rauray with heavy armoured forces, that is, 16 tanks. The *Kompaniefuhrer* directed the tanks himself into the different positions, while the commander's tank no. 405 became unusable because of engine failure. Tank no. 415 of *Oberscharfuhrer* Lehmann knocked out a Churchill soon after the events described above. The Grenadiers abandoned the village and retreated into the *Kompanie* lines, meanwhile securing the exits of the village. *Unterscharfuhrers* Sedat and Gerlinger knocked out two more enemy tanks. The enemy assault was halted in front of our positions. The infantry entrenched itself among the hedges 100 metres in front of our own positions; we barraged them with machine gun fire and high explosive shells.

Three short enemy artillery engagements followed in rapid succession, after which the enemy renewed their assault. The enemy attack was again repulsed, while *Leutnant* Pohl and *Unterscharfuhrer* Burkert knocked out two armoured fighting vehicles. The enemy again answered by firing heavily until late at night, during which *Unterscharfuhrer*

---

11  The *Faustpatrone* was a recoilless shaped charge anti-tank projectile fired from an 80cm long 3.2kg launch tube. On impact the projectile produced a cumulative gas jet which could penetrate armour up to 140mm. It was accurate up to approximately 30 metres. The first *Faustpatronen* were sent to the troops in August 1943.
12  Presumably British Universal (or Bren Gun) carriers.
13  These were presumably units of *SS-Panzer-Aufklärungs-Abteilung 12*.

Knight's Cross holder *Hauptsturmführer* Hans Siegel, *Kompanie Chef* of the *8./SS-Panzer Regiment 12* (see Appendix II and throughout text). (Mark C. Yerger)

Eiserloh, the radio operator of the *Kompanie Chef* was wounded. We destroyed an anti-tank gun from 15 metres away whilst it was directed into position. In the morning of 28. 06. we received the order to retreat together with the Grenadiers which we completed with great success, remaining hidden from the enemy.

Pohl
*Leutnant* and *Kompanieführer*

**II./SS-Panzer Regiment 12:**
The night of 26 June was spent relatively calmly. Apart from the heavy artillery fire no particular combat activity. In the morning hours a new enemy attack against the positions of the *II.Abteilung* and *SS-Panzer-Grenadier-Regiment 26*. The armoured *Kompanien* held their positions even in the face of the intensified enemy pressure and their own losses. The *8.Kompanie* with its remaining three tanks and with some Panzer V tanks were deployed against the enemy coming from the direction of Cheux. Positions of the *8.Kompanie* north of the railway, between Grainville [sur-Odon] and the overcrossing 600 metres west of Grainville [sur-Odon]. The fighting today indicated that the enemy attacks in the north-south direction, where three obvious directions of attack can be defined:

1.   through Fontenay-le-Pesnel towards Rauray;
2.   through Cheux towards Grainville [sur-Odon];
3.   through Mouen towards Tourville.

The continuity of the frontline was secured by the *II.Abteilung* in the sector of *SS-Panzer Regiment 12*. There was communication with both the left and right side neighbours. The positions of the *II.Abteilung* were strengthened with the subordination of seven Panthers of the *4.Kompanie*.

The *Kompanien* had the following operational tanks at 2100 hours, 27. 06. 1944:

- the *5.Kompanie*: 7 tanks
- the *6.Kompanie*: 6 tanks
- the *8.Kompanie*: 4 tanks
- the *9.Kompanie*: 8 tanks
- *Stab*: 3 tanks
- total: 28 tanks

During the heavy fighting today *Obersturmführer* Helmut Bando, *5.Kompanie Chef*, was killed. The temporary command of the *5.Kompanie* was assigned to *Obersturmführer* Karl-Heinz Porsch. *Hauptsturmführer* Hans Siegel, *8.Kompanie Chef*, was seriously wounded.

Ammunition expenditure: 480 high explosive shells, 260 armour-piercing shells, 1,500 steel core [machine-gun ammunition]. The losses of 26–27. 06. 1944 are summarized in Appendix 7.

**War Diary Appendix no. 7.**
Losses on 26–27. 06. 1944

Total losses of Panzerkampfwagen IVs:
tanks with tactical numbers 505, 515, 518, 605, 616, 618, 835, 836, 715, 527 and 626.

Panzerkampfwagen IVs to be repaired: 21 Panzerkampfwagen IVs

Vehicle losses:
Two medium motorcycles with sidecars, two medium motorcycles, two cars (these are total losses); four cars (under repair).
Battle casualties:

| | **Officer** | **NCO** | **Enlisted** |
|---|---|---|---|
| Killed | 3 | 2 | 10 |
| Wounded | 3 | 4 | 23 |
| Of this, remained with their units | – | 2 | 5 |
| Missing | – | – | 3 |

## 28 June 1944
### I./SS-Panzer Regiment 12:
At 0600 hours the *Abteilung* with all its *Kompanien* was regrouped to the area of Esquay with securing tasks, in order to block the road from the direction of Esquay northwards.

*Sturmbannführer* Erich Olboeter, commander of the *III./SS-Panzer-Grenadier-Regiment 26* during the Normandy fighting (see Chapter 5 Footnote 20). (Mark C. Yerger)

The *Kompanien* were in securing positions north and northwest of Esquay. In the afternoon the *2.Kompanie* was subordinated[14] to the *II.Abteilung*[15] and deployed south of Hill 112 in order to eliminate a local breakthrough. The *1./Panzer Regiment 3*[16], which has knocked out 8 Shermans[17] at Mondrainville, was subordinated to the *Abteilung*; the said tanks are immediately burnt out. One tank is a total loss, one tank goes to the repairs station.

### War Diary Appendix no. 8.
*12.SS-Panzer Division "Hitlerjugend"*　　　　　　　　　　　　　　　O.U., 15. 09. 1944
*4. [Kompanie]/SS-Panzer Regiment 12*

Prevention of enemy tank attack at Esquay on 28–29. 06. 1944

---

14　The *2./SS-Panzer Regiment 12* knocked out a Churchill heavy tank that day. This was the 21st Allied tank defeated by the *2.Kompanie*. See Meyer, p.217.

15　To the *II./SS-Panzer Regiment 12* equipped with Panzer IV tanks.

16　The *1./Panzer Regiment 3 (2.Panzer Division)* of the Army was temporarily subordinated to the *I./SS-Panzer Regiment 12*. The unit was also equipped with Panther tanks and its *Kompanie Chef* was *Hauptmann* Gottfried Jährig, who was killed on 29 June 1944 at Fervaches. From 27 June 1944 the other *Kompanien* of the *I./Panzer Regiment 3* also fought subordinated to the *12.SS-Panzer Division "Hitlerjugend"*. The Panthers of the *I./Panzer Regiment 3* reported knocking out a total of 14 Allied tanks on 27 June 1944, as well as 53 tanks and 15 anti-tank guns on 28 June 1944. See also Strauß, Franz Josef, *Geschichte der 2. (Wiener) Panzer-Division*, Eggolsheim, p.166.

17　These tanks fought within the ranks of the battalion-sized 23rd Hussars armoured regiment of the 29th Armoured Brigade in the British 11th Armoured Division.

Grenadiers move forwards near Tilly, Normandy, 28 June 1944. In support
are Panthers from *I./SS-Panzer Regiment 12*. (Ullstein Bilderdienst)

Situation:
The enemy had succeeded in breaking through in the south and occupied Gavrus, Baron
and Maltot; the enemy tried to gain further ground in a southerly direction.

Task:
The *4.Kompanie* reached Esquay at speed, arriving from the direction of Rauray, via
Noyers–Evrecy, and secured the north-eastern perimetres of Esquay.

Course of battle:
The *Kompanie* reached the southern entrance to Esquay, the commander of the *I.Abteilung*
held a briefing, and the head of the echelon reached the church of Esquay. There the tank
commanders were ordered forward for briefing by the *Kompanieführer*. Directly after
this the village was hit by heavy enemy artillery fire. The enemy already occupied the hill
north of Esquay and stood with its tanks in positions behind the slope, so they were able
to detect any movement. The Grenadiers suffered losses due to the artillery attacks. With
skilful exploitation of the short intervals between the artillery fire strikes the *Kompanie*
succeeded in occupying its observed securing positions, although the slightest movement
or noise provided a reason to launch a new fire strike.

    The enemy tried to enter the village with its tanks from the north, but we repulsed the
attempt. During this *Unterscharführer* Sedat knocked out four enemy tanks (Shermans)
in short succession and *Unterscharführer* Hellwig a further two. Artillery activity was
heightened hour by hour, and went on all day and night. Because of this, the fire strikes

took *Sturmmann* Seher unaware and he was seriously wounded while trying to have a tactical discussion with the other tanks, as was ordered. The heavy and constant artillery fire forced the whole *Kompanie* to remain in their tanks all day and night, until the units of the *10.SS-Panzer Division "Frundsberg"* took back the hills on 29. 06., and with this, the securing tasks of the *Kompanie* also ended. [18] During the days of securing we knocked out nine enemy tanks in Esquay.

Pohl<br>
*Leutnant* and *Kompanieführer*

### II./SS-Panzer Regiment 12:

On the night of 27. 06. 1944 no combat activity apart from enemy harassing fire.

At 0500 hours the *Abteilung* received an order to withdraw all tanks, gather and direct them to a new frontline sector. The frontline sector held by the *II.Abteilung* until this time was taken over by a *bataillon* of the *Regiment "Der Führer".*[19] The relieving of the *II.Abteilung* by the *Bataillon* of *Regiment "Der Führer"* and the withdrawal of the tanks proceeded smoothly.

At the same time, the infantry from *Einheit "Olboeter"*[20] withdrew and mounted on the tanks of the *II.Abteilung*. The following route was given to the *II.Abteilung*: Noyers–Vacognes–Avenay–Vieux. The route of the *Abteilung* was disturbed by the attacks of British fighter–bomber aircraft, although without any effect. Already the head of the marching echelon discovered a significant number of enemy tanks[21] on the hills in front of the village of Baron. This meant that the enemy had succeeded in advancing with its tanks until reaching these areas.

The tanks of the *II.Abteilung* immediately occupied positions northwest of Vieux in front of the enemy-occupied Hill 112, in order to prevent them advancing further.

The 5. and 6.*Kompanien* had launched a counterattack by 1300 hours, although they had to retreat following a short engagement.

The 8.*Kompanie*, that occupied positions behind the 5.*Kompanie*, was deployed on the right flank of the 6.*Kompanie*, and around 1630 hours again launched an attack against Hill 112. *Einheit "Gaede"*[22] of the *I.Battalion* was also involved in this attack with 6 Panzer Vs. The *Kompanie* of *Obersturmführer* Helmut Gaede was placed on the right flank of the 8.*Kompanie*, and advanced from the east against the enemy behind Hill 112. Within a short time this attack was also stuck, and the armoured *Kompanien* had to retreat into their previous positions.

---

18  The *10.SS-Panzer Division "Frundsberg"* was under the command of *Brigadeführer* Heinz Harmel who won the Swords to the Knight's Cross for his leadership of the division on 15 November 1944.

19  *I./SS-Panzer-Grenadier Regiment 4 "Der Führer"* of the *2.SS-Panzer Division "Das Reich"*.

20  *Sturmbannführer* Erich Olboeter was commander of the *III./SS-Panzer-Grenadier-Regiment 26* equipped with armoured personnel carriers. The soldiers were forced to use the tanks as vehicles presumably due to the heavy losses in armoured personnel carriers. Attending *Junkerschule* Braunschweig from April 1937 to the end of January 1938, he became a *Sturmbannführer* on 30 January 1944. Olboeter won the Knight's Cross for his command of that Bataillon on 27 July 1944 per his approved recommendation. Having been awarded the German Cross in Gold with the *4./Aufklärungsabteilung* of the *"Leibstandarte"* on 21 March 1943, after being wounded he died in a Belgian hospital on 2 September 1944.

21  These were parts of the British 11th Armoured Division.

22  The *2./SS-Panzer Regiment 12*.

At 2030 hours a new attack was launched with the support of a Hummel[23] and a Wespe[24]-*Batterie*. At 2045 hours, following artillery preparation the *5., 6.* and *8.Kompanien* launched a new attack towards the square-shaped forest in front of and towards Hill 112. The latter was reached though not taken. The extremely heavy enemy artillery fire forced our *Kompanien* to retreat. By order of the regiment they retreated into their departure positions. The success of this day lies in the fact that we stopped the forceful attacks of the enemy in the southern and south-eastern directions with the heavy counterattacks of the *II.Abteilung*. During these counterattacks the following were scored: 14 enemy tanks and 10 heavy prime movers knocked out. *Abteilung* command post in Vieux.

## 29 June 1944
### *I./SS-Panzer Regiment 12:*
The *Abteilung* was in securing positions with the assigned *Kompanien* of the Army (one *Kompanie* of Panzer Vs and a *Kompanie* of Panzer IVs)[25] north and west of Esquay. During the day the *1.Kompanie* knocked out a Sherman on the hill northwest of Esquay. The tank of the *Nachrichtenoffizier*[26] knocked out a further Sherman. The tank was damaged due to a hit to the lateral countershaft. During the night a tank of the *2.Kompanie* was deployed in the securing sector of the *4.Kompanie*; the tank knocked out a Sherman northeast of Esquay.

In the evening hours heavy battle noise on the left flank, at the assigned Army unit. The *1.Kompanie* knocked out a Sherman. The *1./Panzer Regiment 3* destroyed 14 Shermans during the day, all of which are burnt out. An ammunition carrier truck was also destroyed.

### *II./SS-Panzer Regiment 12:*
After the ceasing of the fighting of the previous day around 2300 hours the remaining hours of the night were spent without any notable events or close contact with the enemy.

On 29. 06. 1944 the *Kompanien* remained in their securing positions as occupied the day before. There was no combat activity. Anti-tank gun, tank gun and artillery fire laid on the positions all day. One tank was lost due to a direct hit. *Untersturmführer* Helmut Buchwald was killed by a hit to its escape hatch.

## 30 June 1944
### *I./SS-Panzer Regiment 12:*
The day was spent without any particular events except the artillery fire strikes. During a reconnaissance mission the reconnaissance platoon captured two anti-tank guns and three small tracked vehicles that were abandoned by the British. Three prisoners of war were taken. The subordinated Army unit, the *1./Panzer Regiment 3*, knocked out

---

23  The name of the 15cm self-propelled artillery gun used by the self-propelled *Artillerie Abteilung* of a German *Panzer-Artillerie-Regiment*.

24  The name of the 10.5cm self-propelled artillery gun used by the self-propelled *Artillerie Abteilung* of a German *Panzer-Artillerie-Regiment*.

25  These two units might have been the *1./Panzer Regiment 3 (2.Panzer Division)* equipped with Panthers and a *Kompanie of Panzer Regiment 22 (21.Panzer Division)* equipped with Panzer IVs.

26  The *Nachrichtenoffizier* of the *I./SS-Panzer-Regiment 12* was *Untersturmführer* Rolf Jausch.

three Shermans[27]. Three Shermans were destroyed by the *4.Kompanie*, and one by the *2.Kompanie*.[28]

At 2300 hours regrouping of the *Abteilung* to the area east of Maltot.

### *II./SS-Panzer Regiment 12:*
[No entry.][29]

---

27  According to the KTB of *Panzergruppe "West,"* the Panthers of the *1./Panzer Regiment 3* had knocked out 89 Allied armoured fighting vehicles by 15 July 1944 while subordinated to the *I.SS-Panzer Korps*.

28  *SS-Panzer Regiment 12* reported knocking out a total of 219 enemy tanks in the period of 7–30 June 1944, during the battles fought in the Caen area. See also Meyer, p.231.

29  In the surviving KTB of the *II./SS-Panzer Regiment 12* there are no entries for the days from 30 June to 7 July 1944. The KTB was probably kept on these days, but for unknown reasons the entries are missing.

# 6

# Another Operational Interval and the Fourth Battle for Caen, 1–10 July 1944

**1 July 1944**
*I./SS-Panzer Regiment 12:*
At 0745 hours the *Kompanien* occupied positions in the willow groves. The *2.Kompanie* took over the securing task north of Maltot. The day was spent without any notable events.

*II./SS-Panzer Regiment 12:*
[No entry.]

**2 July 1944**
*I./SS-Panzer Regiment 12*:
The day was spent without any notable events.

*II./SS-Panzer Regiment 12*:
[No entry.]

**3 July 1944**[1]
*I./SS-Panzer Regiment 12*:
The day was spent without any notable events.

*II./SS-Panzer Regiment 12*:
[No entry.]

**4 July 1944**
*I./SS-Panzer Regiment 12:*
The *Abteilung* with three *Kompanien* was sent to provide defence for the airfield of Caen[2]. The *2.Kompanie* was deployed at the Venoix main road in the northern direction, the

---

1   According to a report written on 3 July 1944, from the 144 Allied tanks knocked out by the *12.SS-Panzer Division "Hitlerjugend,"* 105 were destroyed by the tanks of *SS-Panzer Regiment 12*, 16 by towed anti-tank and anti-aircraft guns, and 23 by handheld anti-tank weapons (Panzerfaust, Panzerschreck). In the evening of 3 July 1944, the British battleship HMS *Rodney* fired 15 shells from its 40.6cm guns at the buildings of the Carpiquet airfield, where they anticipated finding the hidden tanks of *SS-Panzer Regiment 12*. See also Werner Kortenhaus, *21. Panzerdivision, 1943–1945*, Uelzen: Schneider Armour Research, 2007, p.221.
2   An airfield west of Caen and north of Carpiquet.

An SdKfz 222 armoured car from *SS-Panzeraufklärungsabteilung 12*, Caen, July 1944. (Cody Images)

*4.Kompanie* at the Venoix–St. Germain [-la Blanche-Herbe] road in the western and north-western directions. The *1.* and *2.Kompanien* received heavy artillery fire.

During the afternoon hours the *2.Kompanie,* adjacent to the *9.Kompanie*[3], was shifted northwards, in the direction of the aircraft hangars, as far as the 'Krause bunker'.[4]

The *1.Kompanie* knocked out eight Shermans, the *2.Kompanie* four Shermans.[5] Three tanks (no. 117, 228 and 237) were damaged due to artillery hits and were towed to the repairs station.

**II./SS-Panzer Regiment 12:**
[No entry.]

## 5 July 1944
**I./SS-Panzer Regiment 12:**
The defence of Caen airfield continued. The *4.Kompanie* launched a night attack towards Carpiquet in a task force with the Grenadiers of the *1./SS-Panzer-Grenadier-Regiment 1*

---

3   The *9./SS-Panzer Regiment 12.*
4   *Sturmbannführer* Bernhard Krause was commander of the *I./SS-Panzer-Grenadier-Regiment 26.*
5   The Allied tanks knocked out were presumably the Shermans of the Canadian 10th Armoured Regiment (The Fort Garry Horse).

of the *"Leibstandarte"*.[6] The task of the *Kompanie* was to engage Carpiquet from the north and help the infantry penetrating the village. Following two introductory fire strikes by the artillery the enemy replied with heavy infantry and artillery fire. During the attack the enemy retreated to the western sector of the village, although they advanced again because the Grenadiers did not push forward into the village in time.

The enemy planted a number of batteries and heavy anti-tank guns west of Carpiquet and prevented the Grenadiers from advancing further with the heavy concentrated fire of its heavy weapons. The *4.Kompanie* stood in its positions on the main road, south of Franqueville, and supported the advance of the Grenadiers with high explosive shells, the fire of its machine guns and with fire strikes. Meanwhile it destroyed an enemy battery position with three (10.5cm) guns. At dawn the armoured fighting vehicles were engaged in targeted fire by enemy anti-tank guns. This way tank no. 418 was destroyed and *Untersturmführer* Günther Deutscher was not able to get out of the tank and was killed in action. A number of other tanks received anti-tank gun hits although these were to little effect. The disadvantageous, twisted position and the heavy enemy defence forced the tanks to retreat. They occupied the previous securing positions again.

Before the attack of the *4.Kompanie*, the *1.Kompanie*, commanded by *Hauptsturmführer* Kurt-Anton Berlin, carried out a distracting attack and destroyed five enemy tanks and two anti-tank guns. Furthermore, the *1.Kompanie* captured 14 Canadians who belonged to the French–Canadian "de la Chaudiére"[7] Regiment. Tank no. 138 from the *1.Kompanie* was knocked out and burnt out.

**War Diary Appendix no. 10.**

*12.SS-Panzer Division "Hitlerjugend"*　　　　　　　　　　　O.U., 26. 09. 1944
*4. [Kompanie]/SS-Panzer Regiment 12*

Night attack towards Carpiquet on 05. 07. '44

Situation:
Following four hours of heavy, thunderstorm-like artillery fire on Carpiquet, Caen airfield and the hills south of the airfield, the enemy had succeeded in occupying Carpiquet village and with this, threatening our right flank, that is, the *I./SS-Panzer-Grenadier-Regiment 26*.

Task:
The *Kompanie* as swift as it could, reached the Fontenay [-le-Pesnel]–St. Germain [-la Blanche-Herbe] road and was to secure in the western direction towards Carpiquet and the airfield.

Course of battle:
Around 0800 hours in the morning the *Kompanie* took over the sector to be secured given in the order. At 2230 hours the *Kompanie* received the order to attack Carpiquet from the north and support the attack and the penetration of the Grenadiers into the village. Around 2300 hours the *Kompanie* detached from the secured sector and coming through

---

6    *1./SS-Panzer-Grenadier-Regiment 1* of the *1.SS-Panzer Division "Leibstandarte"*.
7    The Regiment was a unit of the Canadian 8th Infantry Brigade.

Caen reached the abbey 2 km north of St. Germain [-la Blanche-Herbe]. A short briefing about the situation was held there for the tank commanders. The *Kompanie* attacked at 0200 hours, with the *I.Zug* on the left and the *II.Zug* on the right. The rolling attack soon reached its aim, the Caen–Bretteville [l'Orgueilleuse] road 800 metres north of Carpiquet. Following three heavy fire strikes by the Nebelwerfers[8] and the artillery, the Grenadiers launched the attack. The *Kompanie* supported this attack with the firepower of all of its guns. The Grenadiers first reached the railway embankment, then the northern outskirts of Carpiquet. The enemy pulled itself together and responded with heavy machine gun fire. After this, the enemy artillery covered the *Kompanie* positions in heavy fire. The *Kompanieführer* identified enemy artillery fire at a distance of 1,200 metres. By the order of the *Kompanieführer*, the fire of the *I.Zug* destroyed six guns. The covered batteries that were unseen by the *Kompanie* repeated their fire with intensified force. Our Grenadiers suffered heavy losses and could not advance into Carpiquet on their own. The order of the *Abteilung* was then received: "The *Kompanie* is to advance as far as the railway embankment!"

The *II.Zug* attacked the railway embankment with the fire support of the *I.Zug*, and received heavy anti-tank gun fire. One enemy tank was knocked out. Tanks no. 405, 415 and 426 received anti-tank gun hits although without effect.

*Leutnant* and *Kompanieführer* Erich Pohl ordered the *Kompanie* to retreat along the road to Caen. During the retreat *Untersturmführer* Günther Deutscher's tank no. 418 was hit on the right side of its turret, and shortly after on the right side of the hull. The tank was burnt out. *Untersturmführer* Deutscher and the gunner, *Sturmmann* Rausch were killed. The *Kompanie* then took over its own sector again to be secured. We destroyed a number of machine gun nests and infantry gun positions.

Pohl

*Leutnant* and *Kompanieführer*

**II./SS-Panzer Regiment 12:**
[No entry.][9]

# 6 July 1944
**I./SS-Panzer Regiment 12:**
The securing of the airfield continued. The *1.* and *2.Kompanien* stood all day under heavy enemy artillery harassing fire and fire strikes. The *2.Kompanie* fired continuously at the vehicles moving in the direction of Moner. The hit and abandoned vehicles were rescued by the enemy during the night.

The *4.Kompanie* gave over its tanks to the *Aufklärungszug* and the *3.Kompanie*, and left for St. Aubin for reorganization. The *3.Kompanie* that was stationed in Harcourt for reorganization reached the *Abteilung* with 14 tanks and occupied positions east of Maltot, in the orchards.

---

8  Towed or self-propelled half-tracked German multiple rocket launchers in one *Abteilung* of the Army's *Werfer Regiment 83*.

9  According to the KTB of *Panzergruppe "West"* (later *5.Panzerarmee*) *SS-Panzer Regiment 12* lost a total of 44 Panzer IVs and 21 Panthers between 6 June and 5 July 1944, that is, during approximately one month of combat activity.

*II./SS-Panzer Regiment 12:*
[No entry.]

## 7 July 1944
*I./SS-Panzer Regiment 12:*
The securing continued under heavy harassing fire and fire strikes, especially against the *1.* and *2. Kompanien.* In the late night hours the enemy air force carried out a heavy bombing attack[10] against Caen and St. Germain. Approximately 800 four-engine bombers took part in the mission, dropping shell and phosphorus bombs. The *Abteilung* survived this attack without losses. The *3.Kompanie* reached the area of Louvigny at night and established positions there.

*II./SS-Panzer Regiment 12:*
[No entry.]

## 8 July 1944[11]
*I./SS-Panzer Regiment 12:*
The *Abteilung* secured the airfield of Carpiquet. At 0000 hours the enemy started to barrage our positions like thunder. The firing lasted almost ceaselessly until 1100 hours. At 1100 hours the *3.Kompanie* was deployed towards Buron[12], supported by the Panzergrenadiers[13]. The confident attack soon gained ground. In these engagements we destroyed 22 Sherman-type enemy tanks and 6 small armoured fighting vehicles with machine-guns.[14] During the advance into the village we knocked out a further five Sherman tanks. The anti-tank guns knocked out five of our tanks because the Grenadiers followed them only very cautiously, and the tanks were left alone on the obstructed terrain. Following the securing of Cussy village the *3.Kompanie* retreated to the hill of the Ardenne abbey. During this action the enemy anti-tank guns and tanks destroyed a further two of our tanks.[15]

The enemy pressure towards the Ardenne abbey was intensified. At 1500 hours the artillery fire grew into thunder-like noise coming from all calibres and from naval

---

10  The Allied attack began at 2150 hours and lasted until 2230 hours. The mission was carried out by 467 Halifax and Lancaster heavy bombers as well as a number of fighter-bombers, dropping 2,500 tons of bombs. The German military losses were minimal, but hundreds of French civilians died.

11  Operation Charnwood of the British–Canadian 21st Army Group began that day, northwest of Caen, and lasted until 11 July 1944. The main effort came from I Corps. Subordinated to I Corps fought the British 3rd and 59th (Staffordshire) Infantry Divisions, the Canadian 3rd Infantry Division, the British 27th Armoured Brigade equipped with duplex drive (DD) Shermans, the British 33rd Armoured Brigade and the Canadian 2nd Armoured Brigade. The operation was supported by the units of the 79th Armoured Division equipped with special tanks, the 51st (Highland) Infantry Division and the artillery of two armies and four battleships.

12  Buron was attacked that day by the Canadian 9th Infantry Brigade and the 27th Armoured Regiment (The Sherbrooke Fusiliers), and these troops encircled parts of the *III./SS-Panzer-Grenadier-Regiment 25*.

13  Presumably parts of *SS-Panzer-Grenadier-Regiment 25*.

14  Presumably British Universal (or Bren Gun) carriers.

15  Most of the German armoured vehicle losses around Buron were caused by British M10 tank destroyers, which are reported to have destroyed 13 German armoured vehicles that day. See also John Buckley, *British Armour in the Normandy Campaign*. London: Frank Cass, 2004, p.31.

guns. The artillery reconnaissance aircraft of the enemy (similar to our Storches[16]) were constantly circling in low levels and thus were able to control fire perfectly without the slightest possibility for us to counter them.

The enemy attacked with major infantry and tank forces. During these engagements a further five of our armoured fighting vehicles were damaged due to artillery fire and were put out of action. The *2.Kompanie* secured south of the airfield and destroyed a lone Sherman thrusting forward in the southern direction. The *Kompanie* stood all day in heavy enemy fire.

At 1300 hours the *1.Kompanie*, commanded by *Hauptsturmführer* Kurt-Anton Berlin, and the *Aufklärungszug*, commanded by *Untersturmführer* Fritz Fiala, with six and four tanks respectively, as well as the remains of the *3.Kompanie* with two tanks, were deployed in securing the Ardenne abbey. In the artillery fire that lasted for hours, two of the tanks of the *1.Kompanie* became total losses due to direct hits, and three more tanks were seriously damaged. One of the tanks of the *Aufklärungszug* was hit in the fuel tank, and the track of another was hit. The tank of the *Zugführer* was hit by an anti-tank gun, though without any particular effect: the optics were damaged and the turret-machine gun broke down because of the hit. During these engagements the *1.Kompanie* knocked out four Shermans, the *Aufklärungszug* five Shermans, an anti-tank gun and 1–2 *Kompanien* of enemy infantry, partly in close combat. In the evening hours the remains of the *Abteilung*, abandoned the abbey, because our infantry was not there, and established new securing positions on the northern outskirts of St. Germain [-la Blanche-Herbe].

### II./SS-Panzer Regiment 12:

[ … ] heavily on the right flank of the division from the back and sides due to flanking fire.[17]

Because a new breakthrough between Buron and Galmanche was reported, the *Aufklärungszug* of the regiment with the *Pak Zug* of the *II.Abteilung* [18] and the command tank, led by the *Kommandant*, were detached forward to La Folie. The breakthrough by armoured fighting vehicles reported by the regiment did not prove to be real and the tanks reached Mâlon without enemy engagement; there they secured the infantry and with elements of them covered themselves east of La Folie, towards Hill 64.

The *5.Kompanie* was hard-pressed at Franqueville; they repulsed two enemy attacks together with the infantry, upon which the enemy retreated. Due to another heavy attack launched there, a further 4 Panthers were deployed.

Around 1800 hours the left flank of the *5.Kompanie* withdrew as far as the regimental command post at Ardenne, due to the retreat of the infantry under heavy artillery fire.

Following the repulse of a new enemy attack at Ardenne and Cussy, the enemy moved again, following heavy artillery fire, and occupied Ardenne. The tanks, in close

---

16 Fieseler Fi 156 Storch (Stork) light reconnaissance and liaison aircraft. The Allied aircraft in question would almost certainly have been Auster IV observation planes.

17 The KTB of the *II./SS-Panzer Regiment 12* continues on 8 July 1944, but the entry of that day is half missing.

18 *"Pak Zug"* in the original. The *II./SS-Panzer Regiment 12* did not have an anti-tank gun platoon. Most probably due to a typing error, this was written in the KTB instead of *"Flak Zug"* (anti-aircraft platoon), or, it was meant to be the anti-tank gun platoon of the *II.Bataillon* (not the *II.Abteilung*) of *SS-Panzer-Grenadier-Regiment 25*.

Albert Frey as an *Obersturmbannführer* and Oakleaves holder
(see Chapter 6 Footnote 21). (Mark C. Yerger)

contact with the infantry, retreated until 300 metres south of Ardenne; at 2300 hours the right flank, together with the infantry, went back from Mâlon, La Folie and St. Contest to the quarry on the north-western outskirts of Caen.

The tanks of the *II.Abteilung* established blocking positions for the infantry, strengthened by an 8.8cm battery with some infantry from *II.Bataillon* of *Einheit "Olboeter"* and the *Sicherungskompanie* of the division.[19] On the left flank at St. Germain [-la Blanche-Herbe] stood five Panthers of the *I.Abteilung* with the infantry of *SS-Panzer-Grenadier-Regiment 25* and the *II. Bataillon/LSSAH*[20], though small in number.

Ammunition expenditure: 160 high explosive shells, 190 armour-piercing shells; 2,000 high explosive and 2,800 armour-piercing anti-aircraft rounds.

## 9 July 1944
### I./SS-Panzer Regiment 12:
After the *Abteilung* established new securing positions during the night hours, it was ordered to take over the securing of Hill 65. Apart from the *2.Kompanie,* assigned to *Regiment "Frey"*[21], the *Kompanien* departed at 0700 hours, and the *Abteilung* also

---

19  This was presumably the *Division Begleitkompanie* of the *12.SS-Panzer Division*. The *Begleitkompanie* was the defensive unit of the *Divisionsstab*, defending it from surprise attacks launched by advancing enemy spearheads. Usually it consisted of a *Panzergrenadier Zug*, a *Kradschützen Zug*, a self-propelled anti-aircraft gun platoon, and probably a number of mortars, anti-tank guns and infantry guns. Such units of the Panzer divisions were equipped with armoured personnel carriers.

20  This is presumably the *II./SS-Panzer-Grenadier-Regiment 1* of the *1.SS-Panzer Division "Leibstandarte"*.

21  *SS-Panzer-Grenadier Regiment 1* of the *1.SS-Panzer Division "Leibstandarte"* commanded by *Obersturmbannführer* Albert Frey. Highly decorated, Frey won the German Cross in Gold on 17 November 1941 leading the *III./Leibstandarte* and the Knight's Cross on 3 March 1943 as commander of

relocated its command post from Venoix to the eastern bank of the Orne. We crossed the Orne at Athis without any incidents. On Hill 65 the tanks at first occupied advantageous positions on the front-facing slopes, but the enemy immediately discovered it and launched harassing fire. The *2.Kompanie,* which arrived from the subordination around noon, went into positions south of Ifs. *Abteilung* command post 500 metres south of Hill 65.

The *2.Kompanie,* assigned to *Regiment "Frey"* of the *1.SS-Panzer Division "LSSAH,"* received the task of a special mission to secure the airfield until the withdrawal was completed. During this, the *2.Kompanie* knocked out four Shermans.

### II./SS-Panzer Regiment 12:

The infantry of the *I.* and *II. Bataillone* retreated without pause. At night an order was received that the tanks of the *II.Abteilung* were to hold the hill positions northwest of Caen town until the next [occurrence of] heavy enemy pressure, then to retreat to the outskirts of the town, but this was cancelled at 0345 hours. This was followed by a new order from the division, according to which retreat would be effected into the southern area of Caen in one step, together with *SS-Panzer-Grenadier-Regiment 25* and other elements, securing positions with the tanks of the *II.Abteilung* in the sector of Eterville, Athis and the Orne crossing.

Two tanks of the *9.Kompanie* (the remains of the *9.Kompanie*) were assigned to *Kompanie "Gaede"* to cover the retreat at Bretteville [sur-Odon]. When the tanks had to withdraw from the hills north of Ardenne at 0445 hours, the infantry securing there had already retreated approximately 0.5 km behind the tanks, although they were not ordered to do so. The enemy did not follow them, therefore they managed to abandon the positions unseen, without any notable events and the leaving behind of any material or people.

On 8 July the *II.Abteilung* destroyed a total of:

- *5.Kompanie*: 22 tanks, 6 armoured personnel carriers and an anti-tank gun
- *8.* and *6.Kompanien*: 14 tanks, a number of anti-tank guns
- *9.Kompanie*: 5 tanks
- *Regiment Aufklärungszug*: 2 tanks

Our losses:

- *5.Kompanie* : two tanks as total losses
- *9.Kompanie*: one tank
- one tank had to be blown up during the retreat of the *5.Kompanie* because it was totally immobile and could not be towed away
- one tank of the *Aufklärungszug* ran onto one of our own mines during the night retreat

---

the *I./SS-Panzer-Grenadier-Regiment 1*. As regimental commander of *SS-Panzer-Grenadier-Regiment 1* he was awarded the Oakleaves on 29 December 1943 and ended the war as a *Standartenführer*. He died on 1 September 2003.

The wreckage of an American P–47D Thunderbolt fighter-bomber plane shot down by the Germans (although not soldiers from *SS-Panzer Regiment 12*) in the sector of Argentan on 14 August 1944. The self-propelled 2 cm anti-aircraft guns of *SS-Panzer Regiment 12* shot down eight such aircraft before the invasion and at least five more during the fighting in Normandy. (Hungarian Institute and Museum of Military History 55577-13)

The command of the *Regiment Aufklärungszug* by an *Oberscharführer* did not fulfil expectations, because, not having radio connections, the *Aufklärungszug* was driving to and fro in the area. It was only stopped at night and subordinated to the *8.Kompanie* for the securing of the hill. However, the unit retreated from this position also, without orders, in an unknown direction.

The *Abteilung* command post in Athis from 07. 09. 1944, in the afternoon at Etavaux by the Orne. At the command post in Athis a driver and a radio operator were seriously wounded in a fighter–bomber aircraft attack. Upon reaching the securing positions between Eterville and Athis the *II.Abteilung* had the following operational vehicles:

- 3 command tanks
- 2 anti-aircraft tanks
- *5.Kompanie*: 5 tanks
- *8.* and *6.Kompanien*: 6 tanks
- *9.Kompanie*: 2 tanks

Arnold Jürgensen as a *Sturmbannführer* displaying his Knight's
Cross (see Appendix II). (Mark C. Yerger)

Apart from the constant artillery fired on our securing positions the day was spent
relatively calmly. Ammunition usage: 1,000 high explosive and 500 armour-piercing
2cm anti-aircraft shells.

## 10 July 1944[22]
### I./SS-Panzer Regiment 12:
The *Abteilung* secured on the eastern bank of the Orne, through Hill 65, in the direction
of Ifs. At times harassing fire and fire strikes hit us. *Untersturmführer* Richard Kulke
died in the hospital (paraplegia); *Hauptscharführer* Pohl also died, due to a shell lodged
in his head.

### II./SS-Panzer Regiment 12:
The *Abteilung*, with 17 Panzer IVs and 2 anti-aircraft vehicles, was ordered to cooperate
with *SS-Panzer-Grenadier-Regiment 1 "Leibstandarte"*. In order to carry out the order, it
established communication with *Obersturmbannführer* Albert Frey in the early morning
hours of 10. 07. 1944. At night and in the early morning hours the enemy thrust forward
in the sector of the *10.SS-Panzer Division"Frundsberg"* from Fontaine [-Etoupefour]

---

22  Operation Jupiter of the British VIII Corps began that day, west of Caen, and lasted until 11 July 1944.
    The operation was launched to exploit the retreat of the Germans from the town. The task of the Corps
    was to occupy Hill 112 and Maltot, then penetrate with its tanks into the Orne Valley. Subordinated to
    the VIII Corps were the 43rd (Wessex) Infantry Division and the 46th (Highland) Infantry Brigade of
    the 15th (Scottish) Infantry Division which was supported by the Churchills of the 31st Tank Brigade.
    In case of a successful breakthrough the Shermans of the 4th Armoured Brigade were to penetrate the
    Orne valley.

*Hauptsturmführer* Erich Grätz, commander of the *III./SS-Panzer-Grenadier-Regiment 1* of the *"Leibstandarte"* (see Chapter 6 Footnote 23). (Mark C. Yerger)

towards Eterville and Maltot, and this way, succeeded in breaking through at more than one point calling for the recall of the infantry at Eterville.

The tanks of the *8.* and *5.Kompanien* occupied securing positions from the crossroad northeast of Maltot to the road leading to Hill 400 being north of Athis, with the frontline towards the west and northwest. Three tanks were temporarily relocated to *Hauptsturmführer* Erich Grätz's command post[23], the château east of Maltot.

Some Tigers (approximately four) from the Tiger *Abteilung* of the *Korps*[24] went into positions south of the crossroad northeast of Maltot.

During the repulse of the enemy attacks launched with tank support, and during the counterstroke carried out north of Maltot towards Maltot and Eterville, the *II.Abteilung* destroyed:

- 19 Churchills
- 12 Shermans
- 1 Cromwell
- 1 flamethrower tank
- 15 armoured personnel carriers
- 1 self-propelled gun

23  A *Hauptsturmführer* since 20 April 1942, Erich Grätz was commander of the *III./SS-Panzer-Grenadier-Regiment 1* of the „*Leibstandarte*" from early July 1944. He won the German Cross in Gold on 20 September 1943 with the *18./SS-Panzer-Grenadier-Regiment 1* of the *"Leibstandarte"* and the Knight's Cross commanding the same *Kompanie* on 14 May 1944.

24  This is *schwere SS-Panzer Abteilung 101* of the *I.SS-Panzer Korps*, although by this time *schwere SS-Panzer Abteilung 102* of the *II.SS-Panzer Korps* was also fighting in the area.

- 1 anti-tank gun

During the fighting *Untersturmführer* Willi Kändler showed outstanding capacities when he alone, knocked out 8 Churchills in the valley north of Maltot with his tank. *Untersturmführer* Porsch destroyed five enemy armoured fighting vehicles with his tank. *Sturmmann* Haase showed outstanding bravery when he continued to fire although his tank, no. 946, was hit several times, until the tank caught fire due to further hits. He himself knocked out three enemy tanks here.

As for our tanks, tank no. 552 received a direct artillery hit and thus was rendered immobile, and one of the tanks of the *9.Kompanie*, assigned to the *5.Kompanie*, was also rendered immobile because of a hit from an anti-tank gun.

In the late evening hours we ventured to carry out a counterstroke towards Eterville with some tanks of the *I.Abteilung* and the infantry of *Regiment "Frey"*[25], after occupying Maltot again[26]. In the north-eastern area of Eterville the infantry succeeded in breaking through, however, after the enemy strengthened its positions in the western part of the village and received reinforcements, the occupied parts of Eterville had to be abandoned.

During the night we secured westwards on the general line crossroads 48–Hill 400.

At night the assault guns of *SS-Sturmgeschütz Abteilung 1* of the *"Leibstandarte"*[27] (approx. 40 armoured fighting vehicles) arrived at the positions of the *I* and *II.Abteilung*. This way, these could carry out regrouping into the Le Mesnil-Robert area via the bridge at St. André-sur-Orne Ferrières and could gather their forces.

During the afternoon and in the night hours heavy bombardment was laid on the command post at Etavaux, during which *Hauptsturmführer* Hermann Tirschler was wounded. The command post was temporarily west of Hill 67, north of St. André-sur-Orne.

## 11 July 1944
### *I./SS-Panzer Regiment 12:*
The *Abteilung* secured with 12 tanks at the same place as yesterday. The constantly intensified harassing artillery fire did not cause any losses to the *Abteilung*. Around 2100 hours the *Abteilung* received orders from *Obersturmbannführer* Wünsche to occupy Maltot via the Orne. The bridge at Amayé–St. André [sur-Orne] was reconstructed as ordered, in order to allow the crossing of tracked vehicles.

The task of the *Abteilung* was to thrust forward via Maltot towards Eterville. At dusk the *Abteilung* departed with 10 tanks from the area of Maltot under heavy artillery fire, then after travelling 100 metres, flanking fire from anti-tank guns completely destroyed two tanks. The enemy defended itself harder and offered more resistance than was expected; therefore the tanks were recalled to the outskirts of Maltot. The continuing heavy artillery fire completely destroyed another one of our tanks with a direct hit. The securing continued during the early morning hours, during which we knocked out one

---

25  This was *SS-Panzer-Grenadier-Regiment 1* of the *"Leibstandarte"*.
26  Maltot itself was presumably taken back from the 4th Dorsetshires, 43rd (Wessex) Infantry Division, supported by a company of the 9th Royal Tank Regiment (a battalion-sized unit), 31st Tank Brigade, equipped with Churchills, by parts of *SS-Panzer Regiment 12*, the Tigers of *schwere SS-Panzer Abteilung 102*, and portions of *SS-Panzer-Grenadier-Regiment 2 (10.SS-Panzer Division "Frundsberg")*.
27  *SS-Sturmgeschütz Abteilung 1* was equipped with Sturmgeschütz IV assault guns.

Sherman, three anti-tank guns, and a small armoured vehicle[28]. In the morning hours the *Abteilung* was replaced by the assault guns of the *1.SS-Panzer Division "Leibstandarte"*. The *Abteilung* was withdrawn, and relocated to the area of St. Aignan-de-Cramesnil. *Abteilung* command post at the church at Cintheaux.

### II./SS-Panzer Regiment 12:

On 11. 07. 1944 carrying out assembly in the area of Le Mesnil-Robert. Meanwhile *Untersturmführer* Herbert Walther, the *Ordonnanz Offizier*, was wounded in his Panzer II. The tank was a total loss. Otherwise no notable events on 11.07.1944.

---

28  Presumably British Universal (or Bren Gun) carriers.

# 7

# Replacement and Reorganization, 12–17 July 1944

## 12 July 1944
### I./SS-Panzer Regiment 12:
The *2.Kompanie* of the *Abteilung* bivouacked, that is, took up positions at St. Aignan-de-Cramesnil; the *3.Kompanie* was in Cintheaux in the open. The *1.Kompanie* handed over its tanks to the *2.* and *3.Kompanien* and has left with the strength of 2/14/48 to Le Neubourg for reorganization.[1] The *Aufklärungszug*, following the illness and assignment to hospital of its *Zugführer*, *Untersturmführer* Fritz Fiala, was included in the *3.Kompanie*.

### II./SS-Panzer Regiment 12:
In the early morning hours of 12. 07. 1944 the replacement of the *II.Abteilung* by the assault gun unit of the *9.SS-Panzer Division "Hohenstaufen"*. The *II.Abteilung* received a quarters area assigned to them southeast of St. Aignan-de-Cramesnil. The *Kompanien* are located as follows:

- *6.* and *8.Kompanien* in Conteville
- *5.* and *9.Kompanien* in Poussy
- *Abteilung* command post in Daumesrol
- *Stabskompanie* west of Bretteville-sur-Laize

The *Kompanien* are ordered to use the resting time for engineering and maintenance work. The *Abteilung* has, on this day, 31 tanks, of which only 10 are operational. 21 tanks have to undergo repairs partly by the workshop *Kompanie*, partly by the maintenance units.

## 13 July 1944
### I./SS-Panzer Regiment 12:
The *Abteilung* was stationed in the same sector. Engineering service and maintenance works.

### II./SS-Panzer Regiment 12:
The *Abteilung* remained in the quarters area occupied the day before. This day was special because the commander of the *II.Abteilung*, *Sturmbannführer* Karl-Heinz Prinz, was awarded the Knight's Cross of the Iron Cross.

---

1   2 officers, 14 NCOs, and 48 enlisted men.

The reorganization of the division was carried out on 13. 07. 1944. The division formed a *Kampfgruppe*, commanded by *Obersturmbannführer* Max Wünsche[2], with the following order of battle:

- a *Panzer Abteilung* commanded by *Sturmbannführer* Arnold Jürgensen
- an armoured personnel carrier *Bataillon* commanded by *Sturmbannführer* Erich Olboeter
- and a *Panzerjäger Kompanie* commanded by *Obersturmführer* Georg Hurdelbrink

Order of battle for the *Panzer-Abteilung* is as follows:

- 2 Panther *Kompanien* (*2.* and *3.Kompanien*)
- 2 Panzer IV *Kompanien* (8. and *9.Kompanien*)

The 8. and *9.Kompanien* were complemented by the remnants of the *II.Abteilung*. The *8.Kompanie* had, on the evening of 13. 07. 1944, 14 tanks commanded by *Obersturmführer* Herbert Höfler, and the *9.Kompanie* had 15 tanks commanded by *Obersturmführer* Wolf Buettner.

The remaining elements of the *II.Abteilung*, the *Stabskompanie,* and the command and control staff, received the order to march to La Saussaye during the night of 13 July 1944. The commander of the *II./SS-Panzer Regiment 12* received orders to form a *Panzer Abteilung*, consisting of two Panzer IV and two Panther *Kompanien*, from the remaining elements of the *I* and *II.Abteilung* in the earlier quarters area of the regiment.

## 14 July 1944
### I./SS-Panzer Regiment 12:
The *Abteilung* was stationed in the same sector. Engineering service and maintenance works.

### II./SS-Panzer Regiment 12:
During the night of 13. 07. 1944 the disengagement of those elements ordered to La Saussaye was completed. The process occurred without any notable events. Fighter-bomber aircraft attacks destroyed the following vehicles of the *Tragkolonne/5.Kompanie*:

- 1 medium (kitchen) truck
- 1 medium (food carrier) truck
- 1 (Mercedes) car

Battle casualties of the enlisted men:

- 1 killed (*Sturmmann* Pabst)

---

2    On that day *Panzer Kampfgruppe "Wünsche"* was formed from the *12.SS-Panzer Division*. It contained two Panther *Kompanien* (the *2.* and *3.*) and two Panzer IV *Kompanien* (8. and 9.) from *SS-Panzer Regiment 12*, the armoured personnel carriers of the *III./SS-Panzer-Grenadier-Regiment 26,* and the Jagdpanzer IVs of the *1./SS-Panzerjäger Abteilung 12*. On the evening of 16 July 1944 the operational tanks of the mixed *SS-Panzer Abteilung* consisted of 13 Panthers and 18 Panzer IVs.

From left are Karl-Heinz Prinz being given the Knight's Cross by Josef "Sepp" Dietrich while *SS-Panzer Regiment 12* commander Max Wünsche watches at right (see Appendix II and Chapter 2 Footnote 23). (Mark C. Yerger)

- 2 seriously wounded (*Sturmmann* Schwitzky, *Schütze* Hüttner)
- 1 lightly wounded (*Schütze* Wienecke)

The formation of the new *Panzer Abteilung* commenced immediately in La Saussaye. The following quarters areas were assigned to the different *Kompanien*:

- *1.Kompanie*: Villets
- *4.Kompanie*: St. Aubin d'Écrosville
- *6.Kompanie*: Thuit-Anger
- *7.Kompanie*: Le Gros-Theil and Le Haye du Theil
- *Stabskompanie* and *Stab*: La Saussaye

The day of 14. 07. 1944 was spent setting up the quarters area, and engineering service, cleaning and repair works.

## 15 July 1944
### *I./SS-Panzer Regiment 12*:
The *Abteilung* was stationed in the same area. Engineering service and maintenance works.

### *II./SS-Panzer Regiment 12*:
On 07. 15. 1944 at 1200 hours a discussion was held at the officers' quarters, led by *Sturmbannführer* Karl-Heinz Prinz, where the guidelines of the establishment and

Knight's Cross holder Richard Rudolf. Note his sleeve title can
be partly seen (see Appendix II). (Mark C. Yerger)

training of the two Panzer IV and the two Panther *Kompanien* were determined. Furthermore, the *Abteilungskommandeur* ordered an *Unteroffizier* training course and a tank driving school to be set up. The relationship of the two Panzer V *Kompanien* to the *II.Abteilung* was defined and the two *Kompanien* will be subordinated to the *II.Abteilung* in the future. The supply of these two *Kompanien* will be provided by the *II./SS-Panzer Regiment 12*.

During the discussion *Hauptsturmführer* Hermann Tirschler was appointed with the command of the *6.Kompanie*, to be set up anew. At the same time, *Hauptsturmführer* Tirschler was tasked with establishing communications with *SS-Feldersatz Bataillon 12* in connection with the selection of soldiers for the new *Panzer Abteilung*.

Until the arrival of *Hauptsturmführer* Hans Siegel, *Untersturmführer* Herbert Walther was appointed to conduct the *Unteroffizier* training, which, regarding economical and disciplinary matters, is subordinated to the *6.Kompanie*. The trainer officers for this are as follows:

- *Oberscharführer* Olszok, *Abteilungsstab*
- *Unterscharführer* Meinzer, *Stabskompanie*
- *Unterscharführer* Hauck, *Stabskompanie*
- *Unterscharführer* Schieth, *Stabskompanie*
- *Unterscharführer* Jonas, *6.Kompanie*
- *Unterscharführer* Gebauer, *6.Kompanie*

On 15. 07. 1944 the *II./SS-Panzer Regiment 12* was informed by *Obersturmführer* Albert Gasch on the telephone that the 17 Panzer IVs from Linz have arrived at Dreux, and have been dispatched to the *Abteilung*. Their estimated arrival to the quarters area is late afternoon on 16. 07. 1944.

## 16 July 1944
### *I./SS-Panzer Regiment 12:*
The *Abteilung* remained in the same area as before. Engineering service and maintenance works.[3]

### *II./SS-Panzer Regiment 12:*
On 16. 07. 1944, at 1100 hours in the morning, *Hauptsturmführer* Götz Großjohann (former *Regimentsadjutant*) reported from the *SS-Panzer-Ausbildungs-und Ersatz Regiment* in Riga. *Hauptsturmführer* Götz Großjohann had escorted the tanks with *Obersturmführer* Gasch and his personnel from Linz to the quarters area with 61 NCOs and crews, because lately the regulations require the loading of tanks only with their full crew. *Hauptsturmführer* Großjohann drove forward from Dreux to be able to report accurately.

In the late afternoon hours of 16. 07. 1944 the tanks arrived at Le Gros-Theil. The transport from Linz to the quarters area was calm and uneventful. Minor damage incurred during transportation was quickly repaired by the maintenance unit of the *7.Kompanie.*

In the late evening hours, arrival of an officer (*Untersturmführer* Gunnar Johnsson), an *Unteroffizier* and 42 enlisted men from SS-*Feldersatz Bataillon 12*. By the order of the Division, the 61 NCOs and the crew brought by *Hauptsturmführer* Großjohann will remain by *SS-Panzer Regiment 12*, and will be used for complementing the *1., 4., 6.* and *7.Kompanien.*

The commander of the *II./SS-Panzer Regiment 12* personally took over the allocation of the NCOs, and enlisted men arrived from the *SS-Feld-Ersatz-Bataillon* and the *SS-Panzer-Ausbildungs-und Ersatz Regiment*. During the allocation it was taken into consideration that the *4.* and *7.Kompanien* were complemented at first to full strength. *Obersturmführer* Gasch received the task of immediately forming an operational combat unit with his *Kompanie* and 15 tanks which can be launched into combat at any time. The *6.Kompanie* kept only 2 of the 17 tanks for training purposes. The *Kompanien* have the following tanks at their disposal for training purposes:

- *1.Kompanie*: –
- *4.Kompanie*: 2 Panzer Vs
- *6.Kompanie*: 2 Panzer IVs
- *7.Kompanie*: 15 Panzer IVs
- *Stab*: 2 Panzer IVs (command tanks)

## 17 July 1944
### *I./SS-Panzer Regiment 12*:
The *Abteilung* relocated to the north-western area of Manerbe on the night of 16. 07. Relocation without notable events. *Abteilung* command post at Bezin, 6 km northwest of Manerbe. The *Kompanien* settled on both sides of the Manerbe–Valsemé road.

---

3    The *I./SS-Panzer Regiment 12* had 18 operational Panther tanks on this day.

*II.*/SS-Panzer Regiment 12:
[No entry.]

# 8

# Fighting between Falaise and Caen, 18 July–21 August 1944

**18 July 1944**[1]
*I./SS-Panzer Regiment 12:*
The day was spent without notable events. In the morning a march alert was ordered for the *Abteilung* which was cancelled at 1200 hours but was ordered again at 1600 hours.

*II./SS-Panzer Regiment 12:*
Of the anticipated tanks: One tank (a Panzer V) from the workshop *Kompanie*, which arrived at Paris on 18. 07. 1944. This tank, upon arrival, will be given over to the *1.Kompanie*; this way this unit will also have a tank for training purposes.

**19 July 1944**
*I./SS-Panzer Regiment 12:*
The *I./SS-Panzer Regiment 12* was relocated to the area of Vimont on the night of 18. 07. The *3.Kompanie* secure north of the Vimont–Caen road, the *2.Kompanie* south of the road. In order to strengthen the aforementioned securing line, in the morning the 4 Panzer IVs of the *8.Kompanie* were deployed behind the *2.* and *3.Kompanien*, in the sector of the crossroad 1 km west of the Point 162. The infantry observed major tank grouping southwest of Cagny.

The remaining parts of the *8.Kompanie* secured the sector of St. Gabriel, 500 metres north of Point 162. The *9.Kompanie* is at the disposal of the *Abteilung* in the woods 500 metres south of the south-eastern part of Vimont. In the afternoon harassing fire on the securing lines.

*II./SS-Panzer Regiment 12:*
On 07. 19. 1944 30 cubic metres of Otto-fuel was allocated to the *II.Abteilung* which can be transported from Rouen; thus for the present the fuel necessary for training purposes is provided for the *II.Abteilung*.

After the *Kompanien* had been set up based on strength of the officers, *Unteroffiziere* and enlisted men, the *Abteilungskommandeur* summarized in writing the essential necessities for the arrangement and training of the soldiers. This *Abteilung* order no. 401/44. geh. (secret) is attached in the Appendix of this report with the corresponding training directives.[2]

---

1 Operation Goodwood, launched by the British VIII Corps began that day, east of Caen, and lasted until 20 July 1944. Three British Armoured Divisions (7th, 11th and Guards) took part in the operation subordinated to the Corps. The objective was to advance east of the Orne river and reach the Bourguébus ridge from the south, which dominated the road to Falaise.
2 This document is not included in this book.

A destroyed British Sherman Firefly tank lies on its side on the distinctive Normandy terrain. The "52" above the right back fender indicates that the vehicle was probably belonged to the battalion-sized Staffordshire Yeomanry armoured regiment of the independent British 27th Armoured Brigade. In theory, the British, Canadian and Polish tank troops consisted of one Firefly with increased firepower besides three Shermans, but the shortage of Fireflies available frequently prevented this allocation. (Hungarian Institute and Museum of Military History)

In order to be able to register and bring back the wounded soldiers of the *I* and *II.Abteilung* lying in French hospitals, *Obersturmführer* Dr. Claus Müller (deputy *Abteilungsarzt*) has been appointed the task of visiting the hospitals in question and visiting the soldiers. At the same time *Obersturmführer* Dr. Müller has been assigned the task of tending to all of the wounded of the *Abteilung*.

As a result of these visits to hospitals, 25 officers, NCOs and enlisted men will be returning within 14 days.

## 20 July 1944[3]
### I./SS-Panzer Regiment 12:
Reconnaissance sweeps of the enemy with tanks, in front of the line of the *2.* and *3.Kompanien*. The *2.Kompanie* knocked out a Sherman. Early morning the 9 tanks of the *9.Kompanie* were relocated to the south-western sector of Vimont, 5 tanks were in the previous attack position. At times heavy artillery harassing fire.

---

3    Following days of heavy streetfighting the Canadian II Corps occupied the town of Caen that day.

## II./SS-Panzer Regiment 12:

The regimental order attached arrived to the *Abteilung* on 20. 07. 1944. According to the order, the *7.Kompanie* with 15 tanks were to depart immediately and report to the regiment. The prearranged quarters area of the *7.Kompanie* was Ouezy–Cesny. The details can be found in the attached order.

The *7.Kompanie* , commanded by *Obersturmführer* Albert Gasch, departed at 0015 hours. The *Kompanie* reached the assigned aim without any combat activity or any events. The *Kompanie* for the time being serves as *Regimentsreserve*.

Together with the order determining the departure of the *7.Kompanie* , an order (see Attachment [no.10.]) arrived stating that *Hauptsturmführer* Dr. Oskar Jordan is, for the time being, reassigned to the *Divisionsstab* as the *Chef* of the convalescent *Kompanie*[4] of the division that is to be newly set up. As a substitute for him *Stabsarzt* Gustav Busse has been appointed. *Stabsarzt* Busse arrived at the *Abteilung* at 2200 hours on 20. 07. 1944. He was given the task by the commander of tending primarily to the *1.* and *4.Kompanien* and he is to establish his quarters in the quarters area of the *4.Kompanie*.

### War Diary Appendix no. 10.

20. 07. 1944 1600 hours

Arrived at 2110 hours by *Untersturmführer* Horst Borgsmüller, *Ordonnanz Offizier* of *SS-Panzer Regiment 12*

To the commander of the *II./SS-Panzer Regiment 12*

1. By the order of the Division the Panzer IV *Kompanie* is to be directed to the regiment during the night of 20. 07. 1944.

2. The *Kompanie* is to be drawn forward via Mezidon to the Quecy–Cesny area. Its *Chef* is to move forward to the regimental command post at Ingouville/ Moult. The positioning is to be accurately prearranged.

3. The *Regimentskommandeur* has ordered that 15 Panzer IVs shall drive forward. 2 Panzer IVs are to be retained for training purposes.

4. The *Kampfgruppe* is deployed on both sides of the main road west of Bellengreville in order to prevent enemy breakthrough attempts. So far no losses.

5. Major attack is anticipated!

signed Isecke
*Hauptsturmführer* and *Adjutant*

Addendum

By the order of the division *Hauptsturmführer* Dr. Oskar Jordan is, for the time being, reassigned to the *Divisionsstab* as the *Chef* of the convalescent *Kompanie*, that is to be newly created. He is to report on 21. 07. 1944 to Petteville near Laigle (former quarters of the *Sanitätsabteilung*). Briefing held by *Obersturmbannführer* Schulz. For this time *Stabsarzt* Busse is assigned to the *II.Abteilung*.

signed
Isecke

---

4   The *Kompanie* was formed from wounded soldiers who were more or less recovered and already discharged from field hospitals.

Arnold Jürgensen in black Panzer uniform while with the *"Leibstandarte"*. He commanded the *I./SS-Panzer Regiment 12* in Normandy (see Appendix II and throughout text). (Mark C. Yerger)

## 21 July 1944
### *I./SS-Panzer Regiment 12:*
The *Abteilung* was in its previous sector – at times enemy harassing fire, which intensified during the evening and at night.

### *II./SS-Panzer Regiment 12:*
On 21. 07. 1944 the *Unteroffizier* training course (led by *Untersturmführer* Herbert Walther) and the tank driving school (led by *Hauptscharführer* Speuser) starts. Coming from Paris, *Hauptsturmführer* Josef Pezdeuscheg, who had the task of bringing *Hauptsturmführer* Hans Siegel, some NCOs and enlisted men from the hospitals in Paris, had an accident. *Hauptsturmführer* Pezdeuscheg broke his knee-cap and went to hospital. According to medical opinions *Hauptsturmführer* Pezdeuscheg will not be back for at least two months.

At first *Untersturmführer* Freitag was appointed as the *Chef* of the *Stabskompanie*. *Hauptsturmführer* Siegel has returned to his unit and has taken over the leading of the *Unteroffizier* training course. *Obersturmführer* Jürgen Chemnitz from the *I./SS-Panzer Regiment 12* has been assigned to the *Unteroffizier* training course as training officer and tank expert.

## 22 July 1944
### *I./SS-Panzer Regiment 12:*
Engineers laid minefields near our lines. The Sturmpanzer IVs[5] assigned to the *Abteilung*[6] fired 250–270 (15cm) shells over Frénouville. Artillery activity on both sides in the morning light. Around 1000 hours the enemy placed heavy artillery fire and fire strikes on the sector to be secured. *Einheit "Hurdelbrink"*[7] destroyed the turret of an enemy tank in the afternoon; the vehicle was able to retreat.

### *II./SS-Panzer Regiment 12:*
On 22. 07. 1944 *Obersturmführer* Bernhard Meitzel from the command staff of the *12.SS-Panzer Division "Hitlerjugend"*, and *Untersturmführer* Leopold Spranz from *schwere SS-Panzer Abteilung 101* report as being reassigned to the *Abteilung*[8].

During the evening of 22. 07. 1944 those members of the *II.Abteilung* summarized in the annex attached hereto[9] returned from hospital. These wounded soldiers are mostly accommodated in the convalescent quarters of the *II.Abteilung* in La Saussaye for aftercare. Only after regaining their full readiness for service will they be directed to their respective *Kompanien*. No observable enemy aircraft activity over the quarters area of the *II.Abteilung* in the past eight days. Each day some German fighter aircraft fly over the quarters area.

## 23 July 1944
### *I./SS-Panzer Regiment 12:*
Enemy harassing fire. Yesterday the *2.Kompanie* knocked out an enemy tank that appeared at the south-eastern perimetres of Frénouville. The *3.Kompanie* deployed three tanks for the first time on the road east of Château de St. Pierre [Oursin].

### *II./SS-Panzer Regiment 12:*
On the basis of the directives given by the *Abteilungskommandeur* the training at the *Unteroffizier* training course and the tank driving school has started with great enthusiasm from the *Kompanien*. The training focuses on firing with tank guns and machine guns mounted parallel to the tank guns.

As determined by the regimental order, the reorganization of the *II.Abteilung* to the new (1944) combat table of organization and equipment as of 01. 04. 1944 is to be accomplished immediately. According to this, the order of battle of the *II.Abteilung* is formed as follows:
- *Stab*

---

5    Sturmpanzer IV assault tanks, known my their nickname "Brummbär", of the Army's *1./Sturmpanzer Abteilung 217*. These armoured fighting vehicles were designed to combat field fortifications and for direct support of the attacking infantry, and not against armoured forces.

6    The *I./SS-Panzer Regiment 12* had 26 operational Panther tanks that day.

7    The *1./SS-Panzerjäger Abteilung 12* (*Kompanie Chef*: *Obersturmführer* Georg Hurdelbrink) with Jagdpanzer IVs. See Appendix XVIII for data on Hurdelbrink.

8    The *II./SS-Panzer Regiment 12* had 43 operational Panzer IV tanks that day. Meitzel had served as *Ordonnanz Offizier* (O1) on the divisional staff. He survived the war and died on 28 April 1951 in Hamburg. Spranz was killed while still with the *II.Abteilung* on 18 March 1945.

9    Altogether 26 soldiers returned to the *II./SS-Panzer Regiment 12*. The document is not included in this book.

- *Stabskompanie*
- *Versorgungskompanie*
- 4 medium *Kompanien* (*5., 6., 7., 8.Kompanien*)

## 24 July 1944
*I./SS-Panzer Regiment 12:*
Heavy artillery activity on both sides. During the night dummy tanks were placed in the frontline sector. The *7.Kompanie* was subordinated to the *Abteilung* with 14 tanks.

*II./SS-Panzer Regiment 12:*
[No entry.]

## 25 July 1944
*I./SS-Panzer Regiment 12:*
Heavy artillery fire especially during the disengagement of the *3.Kompanie*, the sector of which has been taken over by the *7.Kompanie* . Our own aircraft are dropping bombs on our positions, though no losses have been suffered due to this. At 0900 hours fighter–bombers attacked Waldmüller's[10] frontline sector with bombs, especially the new dummy tank positions. Heavy enemy aircraft and artillery activity all day. At 2200 hours concentrated fire strike with all of our heavy weapons at Krause's [11] frontline sector. The *3.Kompanie* stands in the previous attack positions of the *7.Kompanie* .

*II./SS-Panzer Regiment 12:*
On 25. 07. 1944 arrival of 12 NCOs and 188 enlisted men from the *"LSSAH"*. Distribution of these reserves by the *Abteilungskommandeur* among the *Kompanien* of the *I* and *II.Abteilung* and the *Werkstatt Kompanie*. More than once enemy fighter and fighter–bomber aircraft units crossed the sky over the quarters area of the *II.Abteilung*.

## 26 July 1944
*I./SS-Panzer Regiment 12:*
At times heavy enemy artillery fire. The fighter-bomber aircraft knocked out one of the trucks of the *7.Kompanie* and it burnt out. No notable events.

*II./SS-Panzer Regiment 12:*
[No entry.]

## 27 July 1944
*I./SS-Panzer Regiment 12:*
Heavy enemy artillery activity. Panzerkampfwagen IV no. 537 was hit directly on its turret. Due to this, one man was seriously injured whilst two others were lightly

---

10 *Sturmbannführer* Hans Waldmüller had been commander of the *I./SS-Panzer-Grenadier-Regiment 25* since November 1943. As a *Hauptsturmführer* leading the *I./SS-Panzer-Grenadier-Regiment 1* of the *„Leibstandarte"* he had won the German Cross in Gold on 6 May 1943. Waldmüller was awarded the Knight's Cross for command of the *I./SS-Panzer-Grenadier-Regiment 25* on 27 August 1944 and then killed commanding the same unit on 10 September 1944.

11 *Sturmbannführer* Bernhard Krause was commander of the *I./SS-Panzer-Grenadier-Regiment 26*.

*Sturmbannführer* Hans Waldmüller, commander of the *I./SS-Panzer-Grenadier-Regiment 25* (see Chapter 8 Footnote 10). (Mark C. Yerger)

wounded. The artillery fire goes on in the evening and all night. In the hours before and after midnight intensive aircraft activity near us.

### II./SS-Panzer Regiment 12:
[No entry.]

## 28 July 1944
### I./SS-Panzer Regiment 12:
Due to the heavy artillery fire yesterday, the following tanks were damaged: no. 235 and 335 at the *2.Kompanie,* no. 474 at the *8.Kompanie.* Otherwise the day was spent quietly.

### II./SS-Panzer Regiment 12:
At 0940 hours, 28. 07. 1944 visit of the *Regimentskommandeur.* Inspection of the arrived supplies, the *Kompanien,* the *Unteroffizier* training course, and the tank driving school. Discussion of the reorganization of the *Abteilung* to the new combat table of organization and equipment.

1500 hours: Iron Crosses 1st and 2nd Class were awarded to the soldiers of the *II.Abteilung* by the *Regimentskommandeur.* Around 2230 hours the commander travelled back to the regimental command post.

## 29 July 1944
### I./SS-Panzer Regiment 12:
The artillery fire is going on almost ceaselessly. Due to this, the following tanks[12] have been damaged: 229 and 135[13], and these have been sent to the maintenance unit. At 2200 hours the sector of the *2.Kompanie* was taken over by the *9.Kompanie*; during the manoeuvre, heavy artillery fire on the sector to be secured.

### II./SS-Panzer Regiment 12:
At 1100 hours discussion for the commanders at the officers' quarters. Problems dealt with: reorganization of the *II.Abteilung*[14] according to the combat table of organization and equipment as of 01. 04. 1944. The following will be appointed to commanders of the different units:

- at the *5.Kompanie* (former *9.Kompanie*) *Obersturmführer* Wolf Buettner
- at the *6.Kompanie Hauptsturmführer* Hermann Tirschler
- at the *7.Kompanie Obersturmführer* Albert Gasch
- at the *8.Kompanie Obersturmführer* Herbert Höfler
- at the *Stabskompanie Untersturmführer* Herbert Walther
- at the *Versorgungskompanie Hauptsturmführer* Götz Großjohann

The NCOs and enlisted men arrived from *SS-Feldersatz Bataillon 12* and the *SS Panzer-Ausbildungs-und Ersatz Regiment* are concentrated into an *Ausbildungskompanie* under command of *Hauptsturmführer* Hans Siegel (quarters area: Le Gros-Theil and Le Haye du Theil).

The following are included in the *Ausbildungskompanie*:

- the *Unteroffizier* training course
- the tank driving school

As *Zugführer* the following have been reassigned to the *Kompanie*:

- *Obersturmführer* Gaspard Gillis
- *Obersturmführer* Fritz Eggers
- *Untersturmführer* Hans-Joachim Boske
- *Untersturmführer* Günther Deutscher

*Hauptsturmführer* Götz Großjohann, who travelled to Metz and Berlin on 23. 07. 1944 to ascertain allocation of armoured fighting vehicles, returned at 1400 hours on 29. 07. 1944. No one knows about the new allocations, neither in Metz nor in Berlin.

---

12  That night 22 Panther tanks were in operational condition with the *I./SS-Panzer Regiment 12.*
13  The original document provides the number 153, but this was probably a typing error, as no such number had been allocated in the turret number system of *SS-Panzer Regiment 12.*
14  That night 39 Panzer IV tanks were operational with the *II./SS-Panzer Regiment 12.*

All finished weapons have been sent to the Eastern Front until further arrangements.[15] Berlin will inform us when new tanks are to arrive for the *II.Abteilung*.

**War Diary Appendix no.12.**
*12.SS-Panzer Division "Hitlerjugend"*
*SS-Panzer Regiment 12*                                    Regimental command post, 29. 07. 1944
Ia Is.Schm. 13/44. g. Kdos.

10 copies
2nd copy

Copy
Order on the reorganization of *Kampfgruppe*s
1.  The *I.SS-Panzer Korps "LSSAH"* has ordered an intervention group to be set up from the *Stab* of *SS-Panzer Regiment 12*, from parts of the *12.SS-Panzer Division "Hitlerjugend,"* and the *1.SS-Panzer-Division "LSSAH,"* and from *Korps* units.
2.  Relocation of the *Kampfgruppe* to the area of Conteville–St. Aignan-de-Cramesnil on the night of 30. 07. 1944 to be available for the *I.SS-Panzer Korps "LSSAH."*
3.  The foregoing *Kampfgruppe* has been taken over by the commander of the *II./SS-Panzer Regiment 12* as of 30. 07. 1944 with the following composition:

> *Stab, II./SS-Panzer Regiment 12*
> *II./SS-Panzer Regiment 12*
> *III./SS-Panzer-Grenadier-Regiment 26*
> *1./Sturmpanzer Abteilung 217*

    *Kampfgruppe "Prinz"* is subordinated to the *12.SS-Panzer Division "Hitlerjugend"*.
4.  The *2.Kompanie* is to be replaced in the securing positions by the *9.Kompanie* on the night of 29. 07. 1944.
    The *2.Kompanie* is to be on alert as intervention reserve in the Moult area.
5.  All parts of the *Abteilung* in the La Saussaye–St. Aubin area are immediately subordinated to *Hauptsturmführer* Hermann Tirschler.
6.  Signals connections:
    a.  *Kampfgruppe "Prinz"* will take over the network of *Kampfgruppe "Wünsche"*.
    b.  The network in the previous sector is to be dismantled by the *II./SS-Panzer Regiment 12* except for the most necessary connections.
    c.  The *II./SS-Panzer Regiment 12* is to hand over 8 field telephones and 12 sets of cables to the *Regimentsstab* on 30. 07. 1944.
7.  Providing maintenance stations:
    a.  The maintenance group of the *I./SS-Panzer Regiment 12* is to finish its work and is to relocate to the sector chosen by the *I./SS-Panzer Regiment 12*.
    b.  The workshop *Kompanie* (without one of its *Züge*) is to relocate to the area of St. Pierre. The field research is to be commenced immediately.

---

15  The offensive of the Soviet troops launched on 22 June 1944 had totally disrupted *Heeresgruppe „Mitte"* by the middle of July. Due to this all available reinforcements were deployed to close the enormous gap opened on the Eastern Front.

    c.   The *1./Werkstattkompanie* will relocate to the former sector of the maintenance group of the *I./SS-Panzer Regiment 12* and is available for the *II./SS-Panzer Regiment 12*.

8.  Supply:

    a.   The *Regimentsstabskompanie* will relocate on order to the area of Magny [-le Campagne]–Condé. The field research is to be commenced immediately.

    b.   All supply units of the *I./SS-Panzer Regiment 12* will relocate to the area of Maizières–Soignolles–Le Bû [-sur-Rouvres]. Results of the field research are to be reported!

    c.   The *I./SS-Panzer Regiment 12* will return 10 trucks to the *II./SS-Panzer Regiment 12* of the 15 trucks to be handed over.

9.  On the morning of 30. 07. 1944 the *II./SS-Panzer Regiment 12* will relocate to the regimental command post with its command and control staff. The *Regimentskommandeur* is to go forward.

10.  On the night of 30. 07. 1944 relocation of parts of the *Stabskompanie* of the *II./ SS-Panzer Regiment 12* is necessary for the supply of the *Kampfgruppe*.

11.  Medical treatment:

The *II./SS-Panzer Regiment 12* will leave a field medical officer in its previous sector. *Hauptsturmführer* Jordan is again reassigned to the *II./SS-Panzer Regiment 12*.

12.  The *Unteroffizier* training course is to be continued.

13.  The technical supervision of the tank driving school and the in-service training of the maintenance groups within those elements in the La Saussaye area are assigned to *Untersturmführer* Langreiter.

commander/*SS-Panzer Regiment 12*

        signed

*Obersturmbannführer* Wünsche

## 30 July 1944

### *I./SS-Panzer Regiment 12:*

At 0230 hours order from the regiment for the immediate regrouping of the *Abteilung*[16] with the *2.* and *3.Kompanien* to the Bray-la-Campagne area. Regrouping accomplished with all elements at 0530 hours. The *Kompanien* took positions behind dense bushes. The *7., 8.* and *9.Kompanien* were disengaged from the *I.Abteilung*, and are now subordinated again to the *II.Abteilung*.

### *II./SS-Panzer Regiment 12:*

At 0400 hours order from the regiment to send 12 tank crews to Linz to take over 12 Panzerkampfwagen IVs. This allocation arrives from the *Panzergruppe "West"*[17] via the division.

---

16  The *I./SS-Panzer Regiment 12* had 22 operational Panther tanks that day.

17  This Armee level command was created on 24 January 1944 from the *Stab* of the *General der Panzertruppe* cooperating with the *Oberbefehlshaber "West"* (Senior Area Commander "West"). Its commander was *General der Panzertruppe* Leo *Freiherr* Geyr von Schweppenburg until 2 July 1944, then *General der Panzertruppen* Heinrich Eberbach from 3 July 1944 until 5 August 1944. On 5 August 1944 the command was renamed Staff *Panzerarmee 5*.

*Untersturmführer* Karl Pucher, *Oberscharführer* Seiwert and 60 NCOs and enlisted men with two trucks immediately depart to Linz.

*Hauptsturmführer* Götz Großjohann, who, during his journey to Germany, had precursory discussions with the transport officer (*Transportführer*) of the SS in Paris, reports that 230 NCOs and enlisted men are on their way from Riga to *SS-Panzer Regiment 12* as reinforcements. The transport officer of the SS will inform the *II.Abteilung* when this supply arrives on the Western Front. The following officers are reassigned to the *II.Abteilung*:

- *Obersturmführer* Bernhard Meitzel
- *Obersturmführer* Fritz Eggers
- *Obersturmführer* Gaspard Gillis
- *Untersturmführer* Hans-Joachim Boske
- *Untersturmführer* Leopold Spranz
- *Untersturmführer* Hans Deutsch

During the first half of the week only weak enemy and German aircraft activity. During the second half of the week the enemy aircraft activity increased. No fighter-bomber attacks in the quarters area of *II.Abteilung* are confirmed. Our own aircraft activity in the evening and during the night hours has increased. Twin-engine bombers in the direction of the invasion frontline.

At 0400 hours regimental order according to the attached copy no. 12. The *Stab*, the *Stabskompanie*, and the *Versorgungskompanie* relocated to the sector given in the order during the day and night of 30. 07.

1300 hours: *Sturmbannführer* Karl-Heinz Prinz takes over *Kampfgruppe "Wünsche"*[18]. The force, now named *Kampfgruppe "Prinz"*, consists of the following:

- *Stab, II./SS-Panzer Regiment 12*
- the *II./SS-Panzer Regiment 12*[19]
- the *III./SS-Panzer-Grenadier-Regiment 26*
- the *1./Sturmpanzer Abteilung 217*
- the *12.SS-Panzer Division Sicherungskompanie*.

The *Stab* of the *II.Abteilung* took over the command post of the *Kampfgruppe "Wünsche"*. The subordinated units – apart from the *8.Kompanie* – remained in their previous positions. The *8.Kompanie* received an order to abandon its positions held until then on the night of 30. 07. 1944. The new sector allocated for the *8.Kompanie* is a wooded area 1500 metres west from Valmeray.

The *Vierling Zug* of the *II./SS-Panzer Regiment 12* received an order to carry out a changing of positions. The *Flak Zug* is in a new position 1,000 metres west of the Prinz command post. The change of positions is to commence on the night of 30. 07. 1944.

---

18  *SS-Panzergruppe "Wünsche"* was the reserve for *I.SS-Panzer Korps*. It consisted of the *Stab* of *SS-Panzer Regiment 12* and the operational parts of the *II./SS-Panzer Regiment 12*. The *"Leibstandarte"* provided the *I./SS-Panzer Regiment 1* and the *III./SS-Panzer-Grenadier-Regiment 2* with the *I.SS-Panzer Korps* attaching *schwere SS-Panzer Abteilung 101*.

19  The *II.Abteilung* reported having 39 operational Panzer IV tanks on that day.

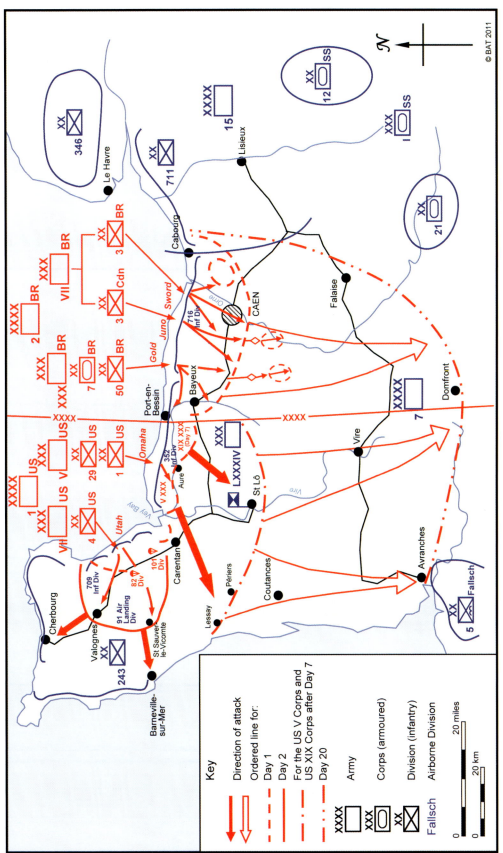

1. The Invasion of Normandy 1944

**Key**

Direction of attack

Ordered line for:
- Day 1
- Day 2
- For the US V Corps and US XIX Corps after Day 7
- Day 20

XXXX Army
XXX Corps (armoured)
XX Division (infantry)
XX Airborne Division

Fallsch = Fallsch

© BAT 2011

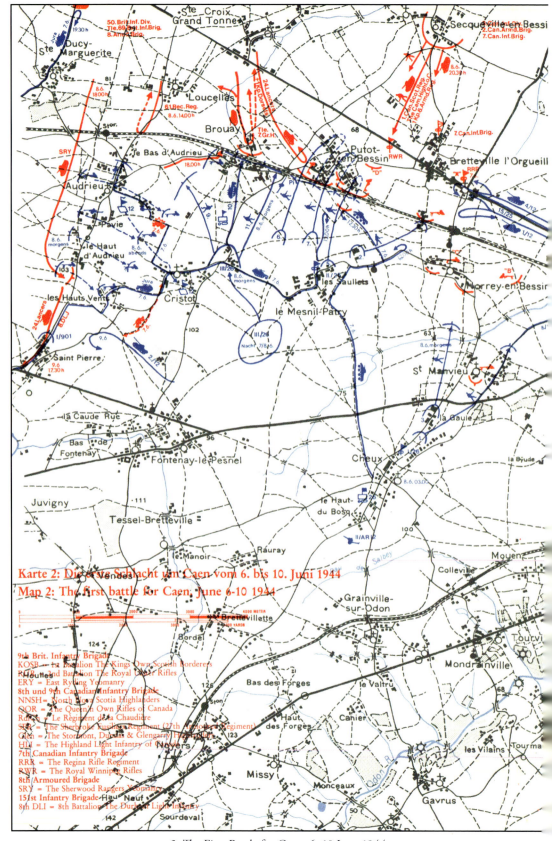

Karte 2: Die erste Schlacht um Caen vom 6. bis 10. Juni 1944
Map 2: The first battle for Caen, June 6–10 1944

9th Brit. Infantry Brigade
KOSB = 1st Battalion The King's Own Scottish Borderers
RUR = 2nd Battalion The Royal Ulster Rifles
ERY = East Riding Yeomanry
8th und 9th Canadian Infantry Brigade
NNSH = North Nova Scotia Highlanders
QOR = The Queen's Own Rifles of Canada
RdeC = Le Régiment de la Chaudière
SRR = The Sherbrooke Fusiliers Regiment (27th Armoured Regiment)
Glen = The Stormont, Dundas & Glengarry Highlanders
HLI = The Highland Light Infantry of Canada
7th Canadian Infantry Brigade
RRR = The Regina Rifle Regiment
RWR = The Royal Winnipeg Rifles
8th Armoured Brigade
SRY = The Sherwood Rangers Yeomanry
151st Infantry Brigade
8th DLI = 8th Battalion The Durham Light Infantry

2. The First Battle for Caen, 6–10 June 1944

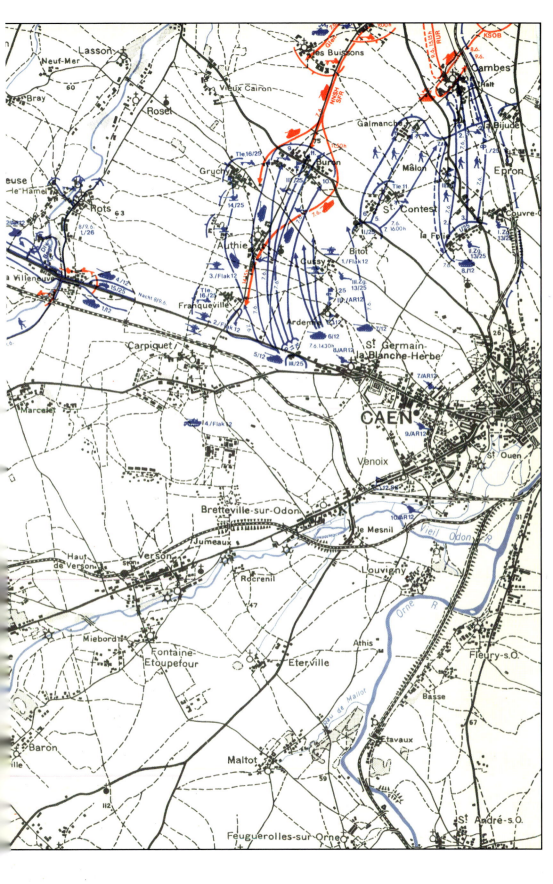

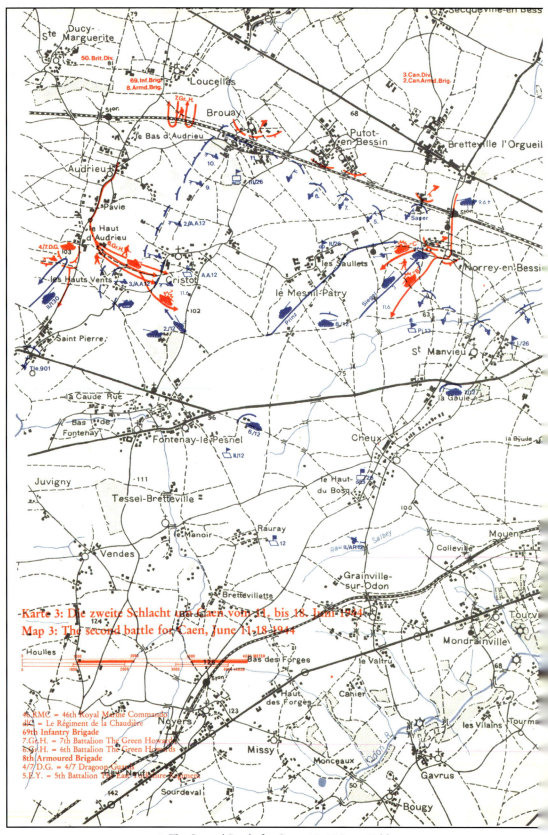

Ste Marguerite · Ducy-Marguerite

79

50. Brit.Div.

69. Inf.Brig.
8. Armd.Brig.

Loucelles

3.Can.Div.
2.Can.Armd.Brig.

7.Gr.H.

Brouay

68

Le Bas d'Audrieu

Putot-en-Bessin

Bretteville l'Orgueil

Audrieu

10.

11/26

9.

6.

7.

Sager

9.6.+

Pavie

2./A.A.12

5.

Le Haut
d'Audrieu

8.Gr.H.

11/26

4/7.D.G.    103

les Saullets

Morrey-en-Bessi

les Hauts Vents

3./A.A.12

Cristot

A.A.12

11.6.

Siege

11/30

2/12

102

le Mesnil-Patry

Prinz

8./12

Pi/12

1/26

Saint Pierre

St Manvieu

Tle 901

75

la Caude Rue

96

la Gaule

II/27

Bas de
Fontenay

Fontenay-le-Pesnel

6/12

Cheux

la Byude

II/12

Juvigny

·111

le Haut-
du Bosq

26

Tessel-Bretteville

100

le Manoir

Rauray

12

Raw II/ART2

Salbey

Mouen

Colleville

Vendes

Grainville-
sur-Odon

Tourv

Brettevillette

**Karte 3: Die zweite Schlacht um Caen vom 11. bis 18. Juni 1944**
**Map 3: The second battle for Caen, June 11–18 1944**

Houlles

124

128

Bas des Forges

le Valtru

68

Mondrainville

Haut
des Forges

Cahier

46.RMC = 46th Royal Marine Commando
dlC = Le Régiment de la Chaudière
**69th Infantry Brigade**
7.Gr.H. = 7th Battalion The Green Howards
6.Gr.H. = 6th Battalion The Green Howards
**8th Armoured Brigade**
4/7.D.G. = 4/7 Dragoon Guards
5.E.Y. = 5th Battalion The East Yorkshire Regiment

123

Noyers

Missy

Monceaux

les Vilains

Tourma

Gavrus

142

Sourdeval

50

Bougy

3. The Second Battle for Caen, 11–18 June 1944

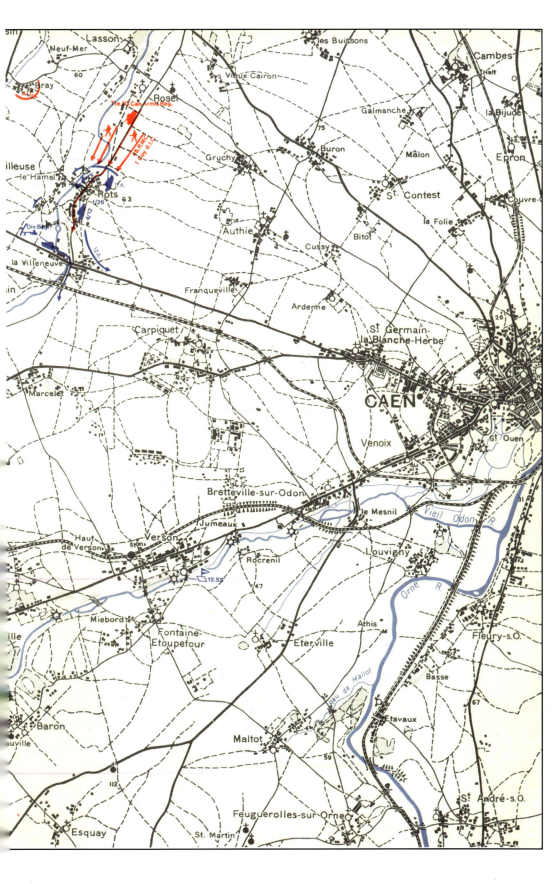

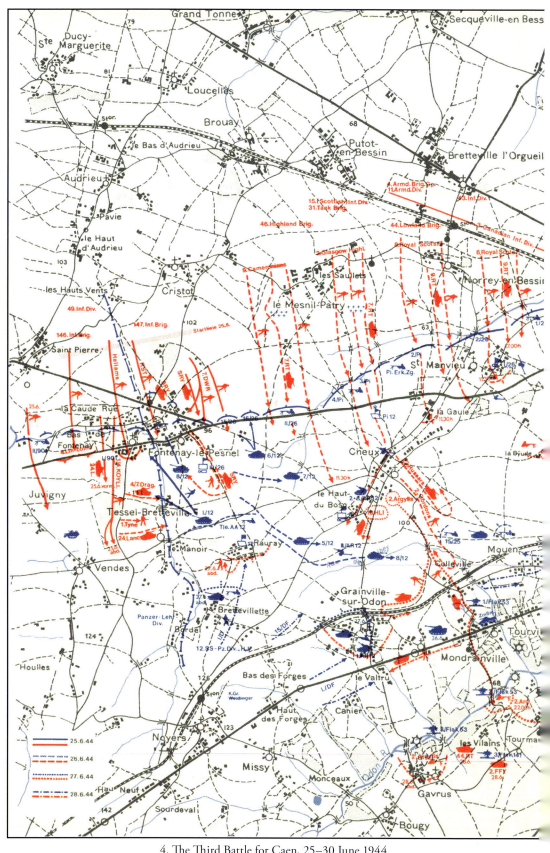

4. The Third Battle for Caen, 25–30 June 1944

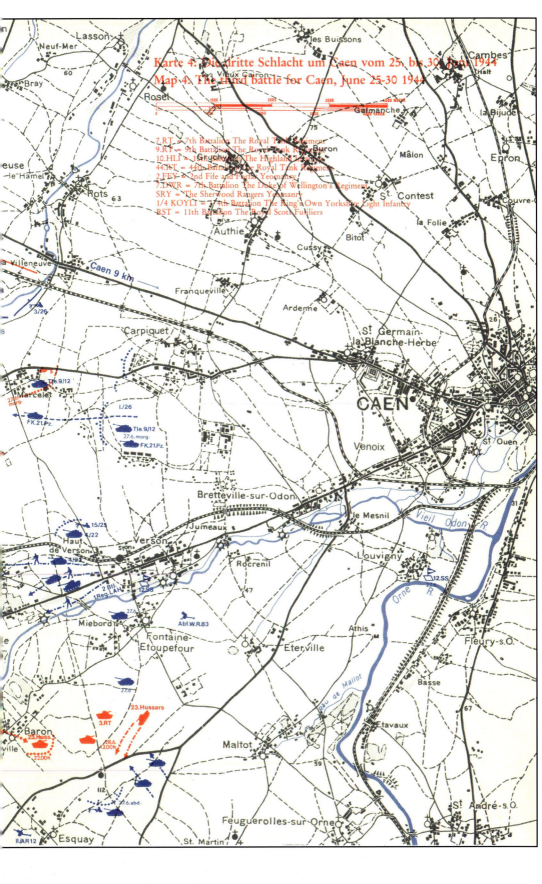

Karte 4: Die dritte Schlacht um Caen vom 25. bis 30. Juni 1944
Map 4: The third battle for Caen, June 25-30 1944

7.RT = 7th Battalion The Royal Tank Regiment
9.RT = 9th Battalion The Royal Tank Regiment
10.HLI = 10th Battalion The Highland Infantry
44.RT = 44th Battalion The Royal Tank Regiment
2.FFY = 2nd Fife and Forfar Yeomanry
7.DWR = 7th Battalion The Duke of Wellington's Regiment
SRY = The Sherwood Rangers Yeomanry
1/4 KOYLI = 1/4th Battalion The King's Own Yorkshire Light Infantry
RST = 11th Battalion The Royal Scots Fusiliers

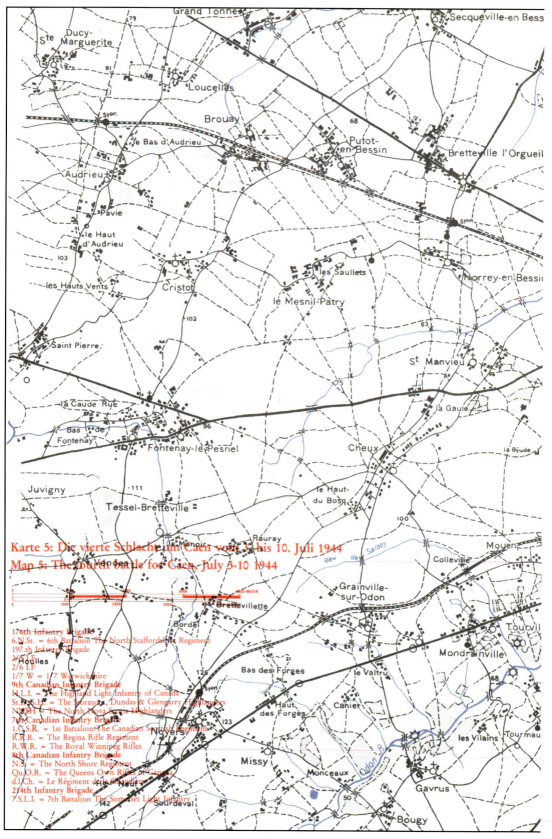

Karte 5: Die vierte Schlacht um Caen vom 3. bis 10. Juli 1944
Map 5: The fourth battle for Caen, July 3-10 1944

176th Infantry Brigade
6.N.St. = 6th Battalion The North Staffordshire Regiment
197th Infantry Brigade
2/5 LF
2/6 LF
1/7 W = 1/7 Warwickshire
9th Canadian Infantry Brigade
H.L.I. = The Highland Light Infantry of Canada
St.D.&G.H. = The Stormont, Dundas & Glengarry Highlanders
N.N.S.H. = The North Nova Scotia Highlanders
7th Canadian Infantry Brigade
1.C.S.R. = 1st Battalion The Canadian Scottish Regiment
R.R.R. = The Regina Rifle Regiment
R.W.R. = The Royal Winnipeg Rifles
8th Canadian Infantry Brigade
N.S. = The North Shore Regiment
Qu.O.R. = The Queens Own Rifles of Canada
d.l.Ch. = Le Régiment de la Chaudière
214th Infantry Brigade
7.S.L.I. = 7th Battalion The Somerset Light Infantry

5. The Fourth Battle for Caen, 3–10 July 1944

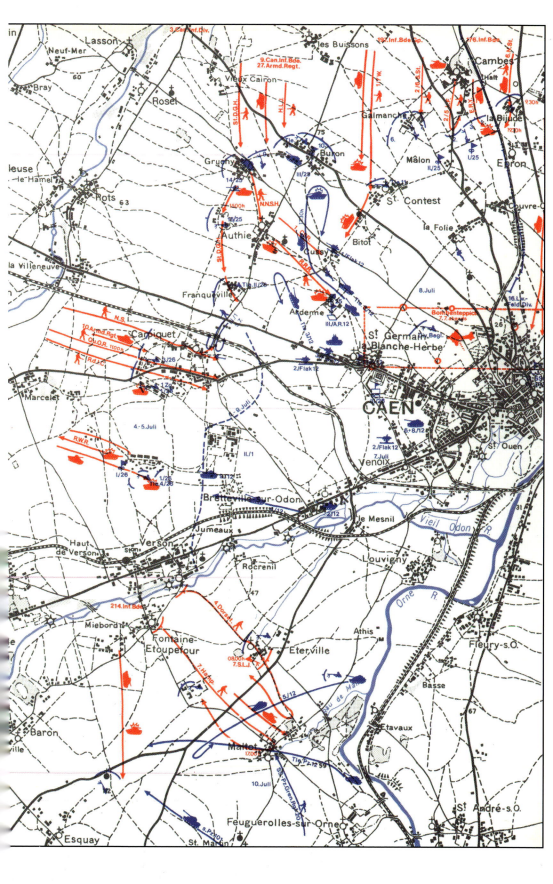

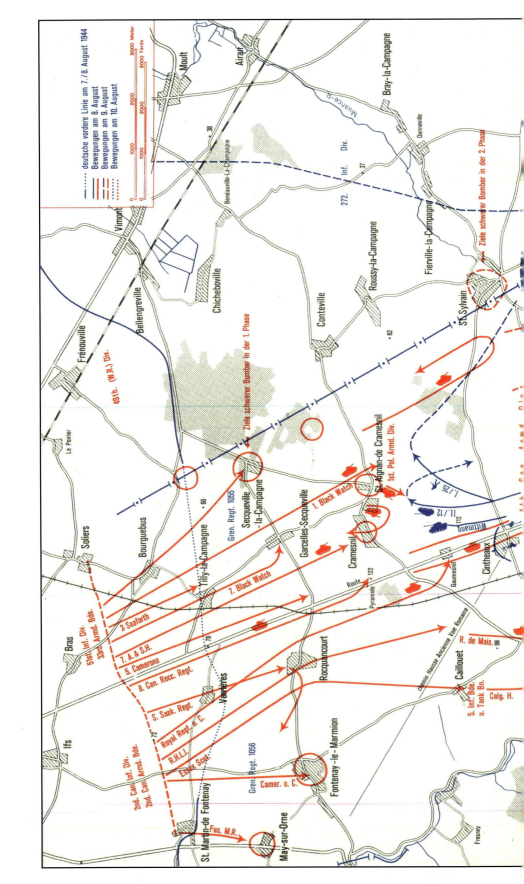

**Legend (top left):**
- — — — — deutsche vordere Linie am 7./8. August 1944
- Bewegungen am 8. August
- Bewegungen am 9. August
- Bewegungen am 10. August

Scale: 0 — 1000 — 2000 — 3000 Meter / 0 — 1000 — 2000 — 3000 Yards

**Place names and labels:**

Moult, Airan, Bray-la-Campagne, Vimont, Bellengreville, Frénouville, Chicheboville, Bénéauville-La-Campagne, Dannevville, 272. Inf. Div., 38, 37, Roussy-la-Campagne, Conteville, Fierville-la-Campagne, St. Sylvain, Ziele schwerer Bomber in der 2. Phase, 62

49th. (W.R.) Div., Le Poirier, Soliers, Bourguebus, Ziele schwerer Bomber in der 1. Phase, 60, Gren. Regt. 1055, Sequeville-la-Campagne, Tilly-la-Campagne, Garcelles-Secqueville, 1. Black Watch, St. Aignan-de-Cramesnil, 1st. Pol. Armd. Div., 11./12, Wittmann, 112, Cramesnil, I./25

Bras, Ifs, 51st. Inf. Div., 33rd. Armd. Bde., 2 Seaforth, 7. A. & S.H., 5. Camerons, 8. Can. Recc. Regt., S. Sask. Regt., Royal Regt. o. C., R.H.L.I., Eslzk. Scot., 2nd. Can. Inf. Div., 2nd. Can. Armd. Bde., 72, 76, 7. Black Watch, Vernères, Rocquancourt, Pyramide, 122, Route, Gaumesnil, Cintheaux

Fontenay-le-Marmion, Gren. Regt. 1056, Camer. o. C., St. Martin-de-Fontenay, Fus. M.R., May-sur-Orne, 5. Inf. Bde. u. Tank Bn., Calg. H., Caillouet, R. de Mais., 98, Chemin Hasse Ancienne Voie Romaine, Fresney

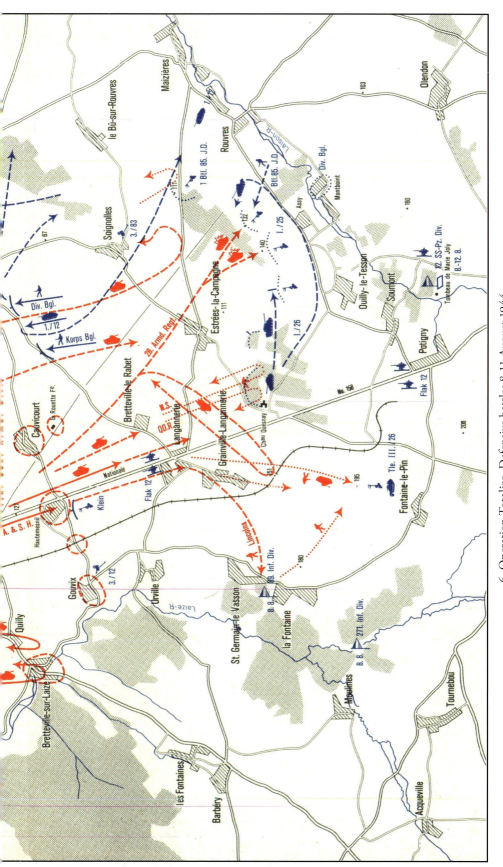

6. Operation Totalize. Defensive battles 8-11 August 1944

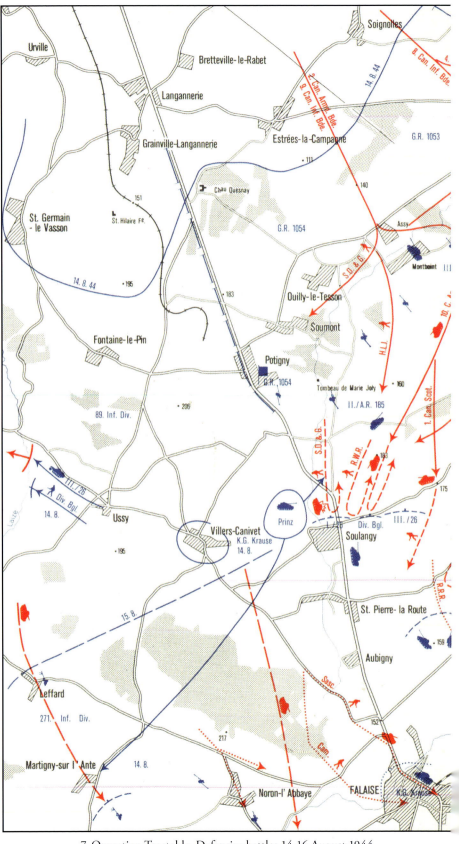

7. Operation Tractable. Defensive battles 14-16 August 1944

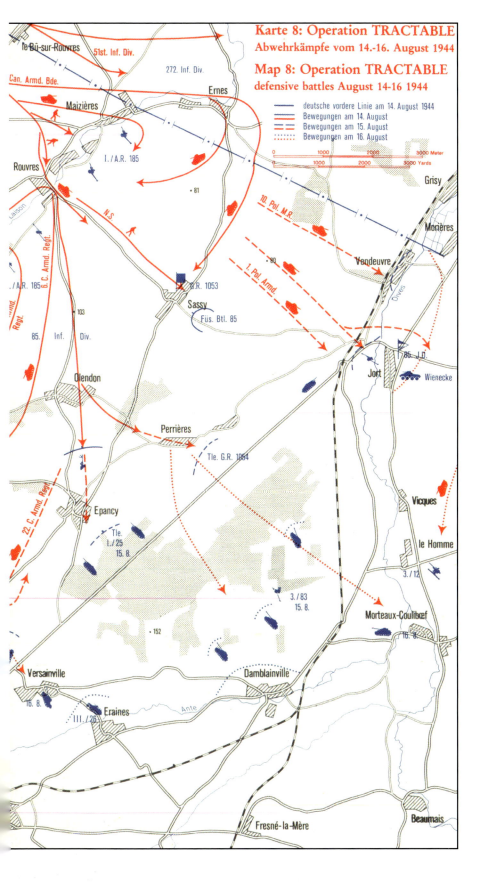

**Karte 8: Operation TRACTABLE**
Abwehrkämpfe vom 14.-16. August 1944

**Map 8: Operation TRACTABLE**
defensive battles August 14-16 1944

| | |
|---|---|
| ——— | deutsche vordere Linie am 14. August 1944 |
| ——— | Bewegungen am 14. August |
| – – – | Bewegungen am 15. August |
| ········· | Bewegungen am 16. August |

0 ......... 1000 ......... 2000 ......... 3000 Meter
0 ......... 1000 ......... 2000 ......... 3000 Yards

le Bû-sur-Rouvres

51st. Inf. Div.

272. Inf. Div.

Can. Armd. Bde.

Ernes

Maizières

Grisy

I. / A.R. 185

Rouvres

· 81

N.S.

10. Pol. M.R.

Morières

Laison

· 80

Vendeuvre

. / A.R. 185

6. C. Armd. Regt.

1. Pol. Armd.

Dives

G.R. 1053

85. J.D.

Sassy

Jort

Wienecke

Füs. Btl. 85

103

85. Inf. Div.

Olendon

Perrières

Tle. G.R. 1054

Vicques

22. C. Armd. Regt.

Epancy

le Homme

Tle.
I. / 25
15. 8.

3. / 12

3. / 83
15. 8.

Morteaux-Couliboef

· 152

16. 8.

Versainville

Damblainville

16. 8.

Ante

Eraines

III. / 26

Fresné-la-Mère

Beaumais

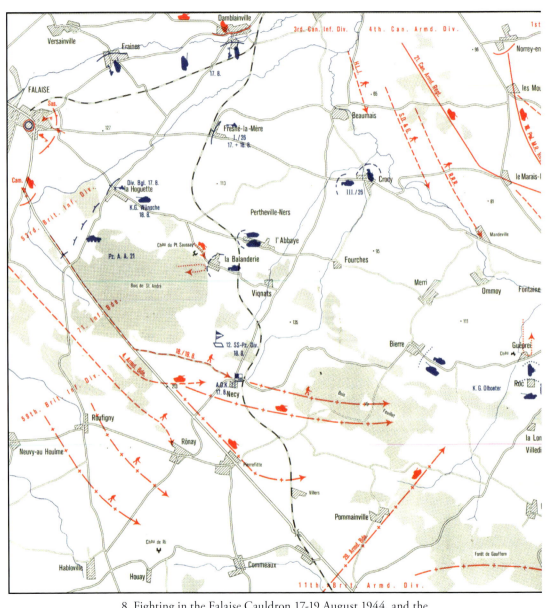

8. Fighting in the Falaise Cauldron 17-19 August 1944, and the
breakout from the Cauldron 19-20 August 1944

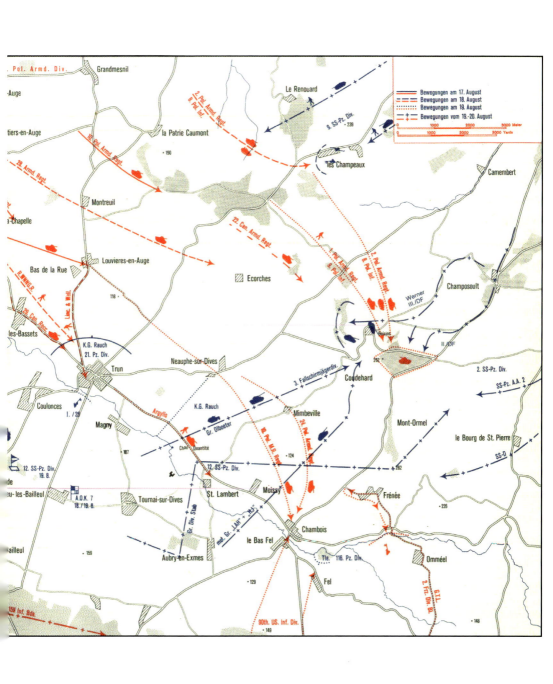

Pol. Armd. Div.
Grandmesnil
Le Renouard
-Auge
2. Pol. Armd. Regt.
la Patrie Caumont
R Pol. Inf.
9. SS-Pz. Div.
tiers-en-Auge
10. Pol. Armd. Regt.
· 190
· 239
les Champeaux
28. Armd. Regt.
Camembert
Montreuil
-Chapelle
22. Can. Armd. Regt.
2. Pol. Armd. Regt.
Bas de la Rue
Louvieres-en-Auge
R. Pol. Inf.
Werner
III./DF
Champsoult
Ecorches
116 ·
Goises
II./DF
les-Bassets
Linc. & Well.
K.G. Rauch
21. Pz. Div.
Trun
Neauphe-sur-Dives
2. SS-Pz. Div.
20. Can. Recc.
292 ·
SS-Pz. A.A. 2
Coulonces
1. / 25
K.G. Rauch
Argylls
3. Fallschirmjägerdiv.
Coudehard
Gr. Olboeter
Magny
Mont-Ormel
le Bourg de St. Pierre
· 187
Chât. Quantité
· 124
292 ·
SS-D
12. SS-Pz. Div.
19. 8.
12. SS-Pz. Div.
Mimbeville
St. Lambert
Moissy
de
-les-Bailleul
A.O.K. 7
18. / 19. 8.
Tournai-sur-Dives
Frênée
· 226
·Bailleul
· 159
Gr. Div. Stab
le Bas Fel
Chambois
Omméel
Aubry-en-Exmes
· 129
Tle. 116. Pz. Div.
Fel
159 Inf. Bde.
2. Fsj. Div. Bl.
6. T.I.
· 146
90th. US. Inf. Div.
· 149

A rare colour photo showing officers from *12.SS-Panzer Division*, Ardenne Abbey, Caen, early June 1944. The men are, left to right: *Obersturmbannführer* Heinz Milius (commander of *SS-Panzer-Grenadier-Regiment 25*); *Sturmbannführer* Hubert Meyer (*1.Generalstabsoffizier* (Ia) of the division); war correspondent Herbert Reinecker; *Obersturmführer* Bernhard Meitzel (at the time *Ordonnanz Offizier* (OI) on the divisional staff, later assigned to *II./SS-Panzer-Regiment 12*). Meitzel wears the Demyansk Shield on his upper left sleeve. (Bundesarchiv, Bild 164-14-136, photo: Wilfried Woscidlo).

*Sturmbannführer* Hubert Meyer was the only *1.Generalstabsoffizier* (Ia) of the *"Hitlerjugend"* Division (see Chapter 8 Footnote 24). (Mark C. Yerger)

The subordinated units report heavy German aircraft activity during the night of 29. 07. 1944.

1330 hours: the *Sicherungskompanie* arrested an enemy spy behind the positions. The spy is delivered to the *Ic-Abteilung* of the division[20].

1600 hours: heavy enemy artillery fire directly west of Argences. The day is spent without further notable events.

The quarters area of the *Stabskompanie, II./SS-Panzer Regiment 12,* is directly east of Ingouville. The quarters area of the *Versorgungskompanie* of the *II./SS-Panzer Regiment 12* is at Boissey, east of St. Pierre-sur-Dives.

2300 hours: at the command post of *Kampfgruppe "Prinz"* the commanders of the subordinated units are informed that *Sturmbannführer* Karl-Heinz Prinz has taken over the *Kampfgruppe*. Determination of the directives of coordination within the *Kampfgruppe*; defining the preparation and sending of the daily *Ia* reports[21].

Weather: dry, warm, slightly cloudy, ideal for fighter-bomber attacks.

---

20  This *Abteilung* of the *Divisionsstab* was concerned with intelligence gathering and its interpetation in the field was to include interrogation of prisoners.

21  These were daily reports describing operational/tactical events.

## 31 July 1944
### *I./SS-Panzer Regiment 12:*
Day without notable events. Repairs service and maintenance works at the *Kompanien*. At 2300 hours fire strike on the quarters area of the *Abteilung*, no losses.

### *II./SS-Panzer Regiment 12:*
The *8.Kompanie* reported the accomplishment of the withdrawal from the previous positions and the occupation of the new sector. The *Vierling Zug* of the *II.Abteilung* reported the changing of positions accomplished.

During the night hours the arrival of the units of the *Stabskompanie* and the *Versorgungskompanie* of the *II./SS-Panzer Regiment 12* to the sectors given in the order.

In the evening hours and during the night artillery harassing fire on the "Olboeter"[22] positions and in its vicinity. During the day artillery harassing fire on the crossroad 150 metres northeast of the train station at Moult and the positions of the *II.Abteilung*. Light aircraft activity over the sector of the *Kampfgruppe*.

### War Diary Appendix no. 13.

To *Kampfgruppe* "Prinz"
Because the tank assault positions in the woods near Navarve[23] were discovered by Allied forces, the armoured *Kompanie "Höfler"* is to regroup on the night of 31. 07. 1944 to the sector southwest of Valmeray. Pay attention to the trails! Leave gaps in the line! On 01. 08. 1944 makeshift dummy tanks are to be set up in the woods near Navarve.

1.Generalstabsoffizier
*12.SS-Panzer Division "HJ"*
signed
Meyer[24]

### War Diary Appendix. no. 14.

*12.SS-Panzer Division "Hitlerjugend"*
Abt. Ia Tgb. Nr. 912/44 g. Kdos.                                    *O.U.*, 31 July 1944

Copy!
Divisional Order

---

22  *Sturmbannführer* Erich Olboeter was commander of the *III./SS-Panzer-Grenadier-Regiment 26* equipped with armoured personnel carriers. See entry for 28 June 1944.
23  It has not been possible to establish this location.
24  Hubert Meyer was the only *1.Generalstabsoffizier* (Ia) of *„Hitlergugend"*. Graduated 1936 *Junkerschule* Bad Tölz, *Untersturmführer* November 9, 1938. Posted to *III./Leibstandarte* and later *Kompanie Chef* 12./Leibstandarte. After *„Leibstandarte"* brigade expanded to division commanded *III./SS-Panzer-Grenadier-Regiment 1* and awarded German Cross in Gold 6 May 1943. Attended General Staff training prior to posting with *„Hitlerjugend"*, promoted *Sturmbannführer* 20 April 1943 and *Obersturmbannführer* 9 November 1944. After Kurt Meyer's capture on 6 September 1944, Hubert Meyer also commanded the division until the arrival of *Standartenführer* Hugo Kraas in November. Meyer wrote the official *"Hitlerjugend"* division history and was also a senior speaker of HIAG.

1. On the night of 31. 07. 1944 the *II./SS-Panzer-Grenadier-Regiment 25* will be replaced in its positions by a *bataillon* of the *711.Infanterie Division*. The light infantry guns and the (vehicle-towed) 2cm anti-aircraft machine guns are to be left in the positions.

2. The *III./SS-Panzer-Grenadier-Regiment 26* (without its *Pak Zug*) will be placed under *Kampfgruppe "Wünsche"* (*Korpsreserve*) and on 31. 07., after nightfall, will regroup to the quarters area of *Kampfgruppe "Wünsche"*. The *Pak Zug* is to be left in the positions and is subordinated to the *II./SS-Panzer-Grenadier-Regiment 25*.

3. After the accomplishment of the replacement the *II./SS-Panzer-Grenadier-Regiment 25* will occupy the positions of the *III./SS-Panzer-Grenadier-Regiment 26* and will be subordinated to *Kampfgruppe "Prinz"*. The following are subordinated to the *II./SS-Panzer-Grenadier-Regiment 25*: the *Divisionsbegleitkompanie* and the *Pak Zug* of the *III./SS-Panzer-Grenadier-Regiment 26*.

4. The replacement to be carried out is to be reported to the division by 0600 hours on 01. 08. 1944.

*Erster Generalstabsoffizier*
*12.SS-Panzer Division "HJ"*
signed
Meyer

## 1 August 1944
### *I./SS-Panzer Regiment 12:*
Further maintenance work by the *Kompanien*. The day was spent calmly. Another fire strike of the enemy, no losses on our side.

### *II./SS-Panzer Regiment 12:*
The *III./SS-Panzer-Grenadier-Regiment 26* (without its *Pak Zug*) regrouped on the night of 31. 07. to the quarters area of *Kampfgruppe "Wünsche"*. Its subordination to *Kampfgruppe "Prinz"* ceased.

In the early morning hours of 01. 08. 1944 the *II./SS-Panzer-Grenadier-Regiment 25* occupied the positions of the *III./SS-Panzer-Grenadier-Regiment 26*. The *II./SS-Panzer-Grenadier-Regiment 25* was immediately subordinated to *Kampfgruppe "Prinz"*.

During the night of 31. 07. 1944 the *5./SS-Panzer Regiment 12* relocated to the south-western sector of Valmeray.

The *1./Sturmpanzer Abteilung 217* remained in its previous positions. The *8./SS-Panzer Regiment 12*, according to the given order, set up three dummy tanks in the woods near Navarve.

Artillery and rocket-launcher-harassing fire on the positions of the *5./SS-Panzer Regiment 12* and the *7./SS-Panzer Regiment 12*. Due to this, one killed, two severely wounded and two lightly wounded in the *II./SS-Panzer Regiment 12*.

Strong enemy aircraft formations flew over the sector of *Kampfgruppe "Prinz"*. Otherwise no notable events during the day.

The *9.Kompanie* was immediately renamed the *5.Kompanie*.

A destroyed British Universal (or Bren Gun) Carrier (on the left side of the photograph).
The open-topped 4.2 ton carrier had only 7.5-12mm armour. Its armament usually
consisted of only one light machine gun. It could carry two to four crew. It was
used mainly to carry out reconnaissance, communication, forward observation
and supply lift tasks (Hungarian Institute and Museum of Military History)

**War Diary Appendix. no. 15.**

*12.SS-Panzer Division "Hitlerjugend"*
Abt. Ia Tgb. Nr. 914/44 g. Kdos.                                   *O.U.*, 1 August 1944

Divisional order

1.  In spite of the disengagement of the enemy armoured divisions we should
    anticipate the renewal of enemy attacks, especially diversionary attacks and
    those with limited goals that engage our troops.
2.  The division will take over the sector of the *II./SS-Panzer-Grenadier-Regiment 2*
    as supplement. Left zone border: St. Sylvain (west)–La Hougue (east).
3.  On the night of 01. 08. the *II./Grenadier Regiment 731* will replace the *I./SS-
    Panzer-Grenadier-Regiment 26.* The *schwere Kompanie* of the *I.Bataillon, SS-
    Panzer-Grenadier-Regiment 26* will remain in position and will be subordinated to
    the *II./Grenadier-Regiment 731.* The *II./Grenadier-Regiment 731* is subordinated
    to *SS-Panzer-Grenadier-Regiment 26.* The *I./SS-Panzer-Grenadier-Regiment 26*
    will take over the positions of the *II./SS-Panzer-Grenadier-Regiment 25.*

The *Panzerjäger Zug*[25] of the *III./SS-Panzer-Grenadier-Regiment 26* is subordinated to the *I./SS-Panzer-Grenadier-Regiment 26*. The *I./SS-Panzer-Grenadier-Regiment 26*, as *Divisionsreserve*, is subordinated directly to the division.

The *Divisionsbegleitkompanie* is subordinated to *Kampfgruppe "Prinz"* and remains in its present positions.

4.  On the night of 01. 08. 1944 the *II./SS-Panzer-Grenadier-Regiment 25* replaces the *II./SS-Panzer-Grenadier-Regiment 2* in its positions held so far. The *leichte Infanteriegeschütz Zug* of the *II./SS-Panzer-Grenadier-Regiment 25* is again subordinated to it (without its two guns). Both platoons are to place fire in front of the sector of the *III./Grenadier-Regiment 731*.

The *9./SS-Panzer Regiment 12* is to be deployed as moving anti-tank instrument on the sector of the *II./SS-Panzer-Grenadier-Regiment 25*. The *II./SS-Panzer-Grenadier-Regiment 25* is subordinated to *SS-Panzer-Grenadier-Regiment 26*.

5.  A separate order will be sent in time for *SS-Panzer-Artillerie-Regiment 12* to deploy the artillery.

6.  The *14./SS-Panzer-Grenadier-Regiment 25*, *SS-Panzer-Grenadier-Regiment 26*, and the operational anti-aircraft gun platoons of the *Divisionsbegleitkompanie*, as light anti-aircraft batteries, with personnel, armament and vehicles are subordinated to *SS-Flak Abteilung 12*. Supply lift and deployment to be carried out by the commander of *SS-Flak Abteilung 12*, in agreement with the commander of *SS-Panzer-Grenadier-Regiment 26*. The supply lift is to be provided by the *14./SS-Panzer-Grenadier-Regiment 26* or the *Batterie* as supply unit.

The officers, NCOs and the enlisted men are reassigned to *SS-Flak Abteilung 12*; in case of reestablishment of the anti-aircraft *Kompanien* of the regiments, they are to return to these.

7.  Telephone and radio connection as before. SS-Panzer-Nachrichten-Abteilung 12 supports the requirements of SS-Panzer-Grenadier-Regiment 26.

8.  Divisional command post as before.

For accuracy:  Signed as draft by:

Meyer *Standartenführer* Meyer [26]

## 2 August 1944
### *I./SS-Panzer Regiment 12:*
Repairs service at the *Kompanien*. The day is spent calmly. At 1800 hours the *2. Kompanie*, commanded by *Obersturmführer* Gaede, together with elements of the *Bataillon "Olboeter"*[27], was deployed in the direction of Vire, in a reconnaissance mission against

---

25  The *Pak Zug* of the *Bataillon*.

26  *Standartenführer* Kurt Meyer was the *Divisionsführer* of the *12.SS-Panzer Division*. He won the Knight's Cross on 18 May 1941 as a *Sturmbannführer* commanding the *Aufklärungsabteilung* of the *„Leibstandarte"* and the Oakleaves 23 February 1943 commanding the same unit as an *Obersturmbannführer*. As commander of the *12.SS-Panzer Division „Hitlerjugend"* Meyer was awarded the Swords on 27 August 1944. He died in Hagen on 23 December 1961.

27  Reconnaissance *Kampfgruppe "Olboeter"* commanded by *Sturmbannführer* Erich Olboeter was formed on that day. The *2./SS-Panzer Regiment 12* with 13 Panthers, the *10./SS-Panzer-Grenadier-Regiment*

the enemy that had broken through. During the night the *Abteilung* sets up dummy tanks again.[28]

### II./SS-Panzer Regiment 12:

The subordination of the *II./SS-Panzer-Grenadier-Regiment 25* to *Kampfgruppe "Prinz"* ceased. The *II./SS-Panzer-Grenadier-Regiment 25* occupied the positions held so far by the *II./SS-Panzer-Grenadier-Regiment 2*[29] on the night of 01. 08. 1944.

The *5./SS-Panzer Regiment 12*[30] has been deployed as a mobile anti-tank unit on the frontline of the *II./SS-Panzer-Grenadier-Regiment 25*. The changing of positions was carried out on the night of 01. 08. 1944.

At 0400 hours the *5.Kompanie* occupied the positions given in the order (wooded area east of La Hougue) without any notable events.

The *Divisionsbegleitkompanie* has been subordinated to *Kampfgruppe "Prinz"*. The *Begleitkompanie* remains in its previous positions.

During the night hours heavy artillery and rocket-launcher fire on the positions of the *7./SS-Panzer Regiment 12*. Due to this, one man is wounded (remains with his unit).

Artillery direct hit on the anti-aircraft gun; the *Vierling* [quadruple] gun and the Fu5 [radio] is damaged.

Fighter–bomber attack on the car of the *Stabskompanie, II./SS-Panzer Regiment 12*, two are wounded (and carried to the central dressing-station).

Only weak enemy aircraft activity.

## 3 August 1944

### I./SS-Panzer Regiment 12:

Light enemy artillery harassing fire, no notable events.[31] Gaede's unit knocked out 5 Shermans and an armoured personnel carrier in the bolt position east of Vire[32].

### II./SS-Panzer Regiment 12:

The armoured *Kompanien* and the subordinated units remain in their positions of the day before. The command post of the *5./SS-Panzer Regiment 12* has been, together with the Schrott[33] command post, relocated to the north-western exit of Chicheboville.

---

26, the *1./SS-Panzer-Artillerie-Regiment 12* (with six "Wespe" self-propelled artillery pieces) and six armoured reconnaissance cars of the *1./SS-Panzer-Aufklärungsabteilung 1* with 80 watt radios were subordinated to the *Kampfgruppe*. It was subordinated to the *II.SS-Panzer Korps* and was regrouped in the sector east of Vire.

28  According to the KTB of *Panzergruppe "West"* (later *Panzerarmee 5*) altogether 65 dummy tanks were set up north and northwest of St. Sylvain.

29  This *bataillon* was part of the *1.SS-Panzer Division "Leibstandarte"*.

30  New designation for the former *9./SS-Panzer Regiment 12*.

31  According to the KTB of the *Panzergruppe "West"*, the *Flak Zug* of *SS-Panzer Regiment 12* shot down a P–47 Thunderbolt fighter-bomber southeast of Fierville around 1415 hours.

32  *Kampfgruppe "Olboeter"* and the independent *Pionier Bataillon 600* of the Army were active mostly around Chênedollé. The *2./SS-Panzer Regiment 12* occupied ambush positions on wide frontline south of the Vire–Vassy road, leaning on Viessoix with its left flank. Opposite to them stood most of the British 11th Armoured Division.

33  *Hauptsturmführer* Heinz Schrott was the *Bataillonsführer* of the *II./SS-Panzer-Grenadier-Regiment 25*. He was killed leading his command on 2 September 1944.

Heavy artillery and rocket-launcher fire all day and night on the positions of the *5.* and *7./SS-Panzer Regiment 12*. Harassing and destructive fire was laid on the positions of the *Divisionsbegleitkompanie*. Due to this, three were wounded, of which two remained with their units.

During the night hours heavy artillery fire on the quarters area of the *1./Sturmpanzer Abteilung 217*; due to this, one man badly wounded.

Aircraft activity: the night was calm, weak activity in the morning, in the afternoon intensive enemy fighter and reconnaissance activity. During the afternoon we observed the shooting down of a British fighter-bomber aircraft.

**War Diary Appendix. no. 16.**
*12.SS-Panzer Division "Hitlerjugend"*
Abt. Ia Tgb. Nr. 920/44 g. Kdos.                                                          *O.U.*, 3 August 1944

16 copies
5. copy
Copy

Divisional order

1.  Renewal of the enemy attacks on the frontline of the *I.SS-Panzer Korps"LSSAH"* is to be anticipated at all times.
2.  The division as *Korpsreserve* is assembling in the Bissières–St. Sylvain–Sassy–Escures sector and is ready for deployment towards northeast and northwest.
3.  In order to be able to carry out the above mentioned manoeuvre, during the night parts of the *272.Infanterie Division* will replace it on its frontline. *Kampfgruppe "Wünsche"* (with parts of the *1.SS-Panzer Division "LSSAH"*) has been subordinated to the division again. The *II.* and *III./Grenadier Regiment 731* are assigned to the *272.Infanterie Division*. Assignation of *schwere Artillerie Abteilung 555* has ceased, its new subordination is to be ordered in time.
4.  Regrouping:
    a.  *SS-Panzer-Grenadier-Regiment 26* (*Regimentsstab, I./SS-Panzer-Grenadier-Regiment 25* and *I./SS-Panzer-Grenadier-Regiment 26* with the subordinated regimental elements) after dark, and following replacement by parts of the *272.Infanterie Division* in the Cures (outside combat sector)–Magny la Campagne (outside combat sector)–Condé (outside combat sector)–Ernes (outside combat sector)–Sassy (inside combat sector) sector;
    b.  *Kampfgruppe "Wünsche"* (*Stab, SS-Panzer Regiment 12, I./SS-Panzer Regiment 12* without one of its *Kompanien, II./SS-Panzer Regiment 12* without one of its *Kompanien, III./SS-Panzer-Grenadier-Regiment 26* without its *Stab* and one of its *Kompanien*, and the *1.Sturmpanzer Abteilung 217* to the Condé-sur-Ifs (inside combat sector)–Vieux-Fumé (outside combat sector)–Bray-la-Campagne (inside combat sector)–St. Sylvain (inside combat sector)–Maizières (outside combat sector)–Ernes (inside combat sector) sector; (Until the night of 04. 08. 1944 the *5./SS-Panzer Regiment 12* will remain in its positions held. The *8.Kompanie* and

the *1./Sturmpanzer Abteilung 217* will regroup on 03. 08. 1944 after dark. Withdrawal of the *7./SS-Panzer Regiment 12* is to be effected on 04. 08. 1944 so that it will reach its new quarters area before dawn.)

c.  *Stab, SS-Panzer-Artillerie-Regiment 12*, the *1./SS-Panzer-Artillerie-Abteilung 12* (without its *1.* and *2.Batterien*) and *SS-Werfer Abteilung 12* to the wooded area 1.5 km Ouezy (inside combat sector)–Cauvigny (outside combat sector)–Vaux la Campagne (outside combat sector)–Magny la Campagne (inside combat sector)–Le Rouillis (outside combat sector) sector; (The *III.Abteilung* will remain in its positions. The *6.Batterie* will reture so that it can place fire in front of the previous division frontline. *SS-Panzer-Artillerie-Regiment 12* is to be ready at all times to support the defensive fight of the *272.Infanterie Division* on the previous frontline of the *12.SS-Panzer Division "Hitlerjugend"* if needed.)

d.  *SS-Panzerjäger Abteilung 12* (without its *1.Kompanie*) to the Maizières (inside combat sector)–Le Bû [-sur-Rouvres] (outside combat sector)–Rouvres (inside combat sector) sector; (The *1.Kompanie* is to be withdrawn from its previous positions on the night of 04. 08. 1944.)

e.  The *Divisionsbegleitkompanie* to the western part sector of Vieux-Fumé (its subordination to *Kampfgruppe "Prinz"* will cease immediately);

f.  *SS-Panzer-Nachrichten-Abteilung 12* to the eastern part sector of Vieux Fume.

5.  *SS-Panzer-Aufklärungs-Abteilung 12* and the *3./SS-Panzer-Pionier-Abteilung 12* will remain in their positions.

6.  *SS-Flak Abteilung 12* will remain in its anti-aircraft positions according to the instructions of the *Korps Flak Führer* of the *I.SS-Panzer Korps "LSSAH"*.

7.  The accomplishment of the replacements and exchange of command is to be reported by *SS-Panzer-Grenadier-Regiment 26* to the *Ia-Abteilung* of the division.

8.  The *9./SS-Panzer Regiment 12* and the *1./SS-Panzerjäger Abteilung 12* are ordered to cooperate with *Grenadier Regiment 982*, while remaining under direct subordination to the division.

9.  The cable connections towards the regiments, the independent *bataillons/Abteilungs*, the Stabsquartier and the *272.Infanterie Division* are to be reconditioned and maintained.

Radio alert!

10.  Division command post: Cauvigny (1 km southwest of Canon).

For accuracy: Signed as draft by:
signed: Meyer 1.Generalstabsoffizier *Standartenführer* Meyer

Addendum:

The *1.SS-Panzer Division* and parts of the *I.SS-Panzer Korps "LSSAH"* remain subordinated to *Kampfgruppe "Wünsche"* in their quarters area for now.

signed
Meyer

## 4 August 1944
*I./SS-Panzer Regiment 12:*
Repairs service at the *Kompanien*. No notable events.

### *II./SS-Panzer Regiment 12:*
By the order of the Division the *II./SS-Panzer Regiment 12* (without the *5.Kompanie*; with the assigned *1./Sturmpanzer Abteilung 217*) relocated on the night of 03. 08. 1944 to the Condé-sur-Ifs (outside combat sector)–Maizières (outside combat sector)–Ernes (outside combat sector) sector. The *5.Kompanie* remained in its previous position until the night of 04. 08. 1944.

The withdrawal of the *Kompanien* from their previous positions and the occupation of the new quarters area continued without any notable events.

The subordination of the *Divisionsbegleitkompanie* to *Kampfgruppe "Prinz"* has been suspended.

New command post of the *II.Abteilung* at the northern exit of Ernes (small mansion on the Condé–Ernes road).

Aircraft activity: our bomber formations were on missions at night from 0030 hours to 0500 hours. During the morning and in the afternoon occasional activity of the enemy air force.

Only weak harassing fire from the enemy artillery.

## 5 August 1944
*I./SS-Panzer Regiment 12:*
The *2.Kompanie* at Vire; repairs service and maintenance works at the other parts of the *Abteilung*. An enemy armoured fighting vehicle knocked out a Panzer V of the *2.Kompanie* which completely burnt out. The *Kompanie* knocked out a further four enemy (Sherman) tanks.

### *II./SS-Panzer Regiment 12:*
The *5.Kompanie* was withdrawn from its positions at La Hougue on the night of 04. 08. 1944 and was regrouped into the quarters area of the *II./SS-Panzer Regiment 12*. Regrouping accomplished without any notable events.

The *Stabskompanie* and the *7.* and *8.Kompanien* remain in the quarters area occupied two nights before. The day has been spent without notable events, with repairs service and cleaning of the armament.

Aircraft activity: occasional in the morning, nothing in the afternoon.

## 6 August 1944
*I./SS-Panzer Regiment 12:*
The *2.Kompanie* at Vire. Repairs service located at other parts of the *Abteilung*. At times fire strikes on the sector of the *Abteilung* from large calibre guns.

### *II./SS-Panzer Regiment 12:*
The *II./SS-Panzer Regiment 12* with the assigned *1./Sturmpanzer Abteilung 217* remained in the quarters area of the previous day.

The day has been spent repairing service [equipment], cleaning armament and medical examinations. The day was eventless. During the morning and in the afternoon enemy aircraft activity.

## 7 August 1944
### I./SS-Panzer Regiment 12:
By the order of the regiment, the regrouping of the *Abteilung* (*3.Kompanie, Nachrichtenzug, Kradschützen Aufklärungszug*, 3 tanks of the *2.Kompanie* and the vehicles of the *Stab*) 8 km southeast of Grimbosq. Departure from Fierville-Bray and Bray-la-Campagne at 0145 hours via St. Sylvain, Bretteville [-le Rabet], Grainville [Langannerie] and Monlatn[34]. Regrouping accomplished at 0430 hours.

The *3.Kompanie* with ten tanks, commanded by *Untersturmführer* Rudolf Alban, departed at 0500 hours with the task to report to a *bataillon* command post at Château-le-Montier[35] and in cooperation with the forces there, eliminate the enemy bridgehead[36] at Grimbosq, east of the Orne.

At 1030 hours parts of the *III./SS-Panzer-Grenadier-Regiment 26*, subordinated to the *Abteilung*, were assigned the task of marching to the area of Le Montier, securing the area and preparing for assault.

### II./SS-Panzer Regiment 12:
On the night of 06. 08. 1944 the *II./SS-Panzer Regiment 12* with the assigned *1./ Sturmpanzer Abteilung 217* carried out the regrouping as ordered, into the sector east of Thury Harcourt. Regrouping carried out without any notable events.

New *Abteilung* command post: Puant, east of Acqueville.

- *1./Sturmpanzer-Abteilung 217:* Fontaine-Halbout;
- *5.Kompanie*: at the La Motte mansion, south of Acqueville
- *7.Kompanie*: Acqueville
- *8.Kompanie*: Bois-Halbout
- *Stabskompanie*: Puant

Enemy reconnaissance and fighter-bomber aircraft activity all day.

---

34  There is no village with that mentioned name in Normandy, presumably a typing error.

35  This was probably the command post of the *I./SS-Panzer-Grenadier-Regiment 26*.

36  The bridgehead was held by two battalions of the 176th Infantry Brigade of the British 59th (Staffordshire) Infantry Division, and two Churchill companies of the battalion-sized 107th Royal Tank Regiment of the 34th Tank Brigade.

Swords holder *Brigadeführer* Theodor Wisch, commander of the
*1.SS-Panzer Division "Leibstandarte"* in Normandy until seriously
wounded during the Falaise fighting. (Mark C. Yerger)

## 8 August 1944[37]

*I./SS-Panzer Regiment 12:*

Heavy enemy artillery fire on the positions all night. At 0400 hours *Untersturmführer* Kurt Bogensperger replaced the 4 Tigers[38] standing at the western exit of Le Bas Brieux with 2 Panthers. A further Panther occupied position around 0700 hours in the crossroad directly east of Le Hout Brieux. *Untersturmführer* Matthis's [39] tank was knocked out by four anti-tank gun hits and he burned to death together with his gunner inside the tank.

*Untersturmführer* Bogensperger was given the task of taking over the positions of the Tigers in Le Hout Brieux, and preventing at all costs the further crossing of the enemy over the bridge thrown by them west of the village.

*Oberscharführer* Mende stood with his platoon northeast of Grimbosq. His task: to avert enemy attacks from Grimbosq in eastern and north-eastern directions. Heavy

---

37  Operation Totalize of the British–Canadian 21st Army Group began that day and lasted until 11 August 1944. The aim was to break through the German defences and to advance in the direction of Falaise. The Canadian II Corps formed the centre of the assault. Subordinated to this fought the Canadian 2nd and 3rd Infantry Divisions, the Canadian 2nd Armoured Brigade, the newly arrived Canadian 4th (Armoured) Division, the British 51st (Highland) Infantry Division, the British 33rd Armoured Brigade and also the fresh Polish 1st Armoured Division. Some of the supporting infantry followed the tanks on 'Kangaroo' armoured carrier vehicles that were created by disarming M7 Priest self-propelled guns.

38  Tiger I Ausf E heavy tanks of the *2. Kompanie*, a component of the *„Leibstandarte"*. See Wolfgang Schneider, *Tiger im Kampf* Band II, Uelzen: Schneider Armour Research, 2001, p.273.

39  *Untersturmführer* Peter Matthis was born in 1921 and had served with the *8./SS-Panzer-Grenadier-Regiment 26*.

The bomber planes deployed by the Allies for tactical reasons destroyed a number of towns in Normandy (above all, Caen). Most of the time, these attacks caused heavier losses to the French civilians and the attackers themselves than to the German defenders. (Hungarian Institute and Museum of Military History 55577-17)

enemy artillery fire all day, the first infantry positions were given up again and again by the local infantry commanders. The tanks of the *3.Kompanie* stood behind them as counter-bracing; this way the positions were held, often with the help of the personal intervention of the commanders.

At 1500 hours *Sturmbannführer* Arnold Jürgensen received the task from the *Regimentskommandeur* of holding the positions at Le Hout Brieux with a concentration of all tanks and armoured vehicles.

At noon the same day *Untersturmführer* Rudolf Alban, with the *"Mende" Zug*, supported one of the assaults of the Grenadiers, and advancing south of Grimbosq[40] smashed the counterattacks of the enemy with high explosive shells and machine guns. Now the assault could gain ground. One tank received an artillery hit, due to which its radio was damaged. On the way back it was driven into a large bomb crater in the heavy artillery fire. It was impossible to salvage the vehicle. After the main battle line was recaptured, following the detachment of the radio and the armament, the wrecked

---

40 The After Action Report attached to the KTB as Appendix no. 12 states that the tanks of the *3./SS-Panzer Regiment 12* advanced north of the village.

tank was blown up by orders of the commander. *Untersturmführer* Alban[41] was killed standing by the tank of *Oberscharführer* Mende, when he personally moved to forward a regimental order to the crew of the tank. *Untersturmführer* Kurt Bogensperger[42] was hit by an enemy tank and was killed.

In the evening orders for the *Abteilung* to relocate to the south-eastern sector of Cintheaux in order to repel the enemy that had broken through. Heavy enemy artillery fire during disengagement.

### II./SS-Panzer Regiment 12:

The *II./SS-Panzer Regiment 12* has been subordinated to *SS-Panzer-Grenadier-Regiment 26*. Regimental command post with the command post of *SS-Panzer-Grenadier-Regiment 26* in Urville.

Report regarding enemy movements: the enemy is advancing in the south-eastern direction with strong armoured forces. According to reports given by Wehrmacht soldiers the enemy has already reached Cintheaux and St. Sylvain.

0630 hours: departure of the *5.Kompanie* (with 5 Panzerkampfwagen IVs), the *7.Kompanie* (with 12 Panzerkampfwagen IVs)[43] and the assigned Tigers[44] of the *"Wittmann" Abteilung*[45] via Grainville and Hautmesnil towards Cintheaux.

At 0900 hours report from the Tiger *Kompanie* (*Hauptsturmführer* Franz Heurich[46]): "We have reached Cintheaux, no enemy in the village".

---

41  *Untersturmführer* Rudolf August Berthold Alban was born in 1922. His date of death is given as 7 August 1944 both by the history of the *12.SS-Panzer Division* and the database of the German War Graves Commission (Volksbund Deutsche Kriegsgräberfürsorge).

42  *Untersturmführer* Kurt Bogensperger was born in 1924 and came to *"Hitlerjugend"* having previously served with *SS-Panzer Regiment 1*.

43  This meant only 17 operational Panzer IV tanks altogether. In most works however – because the KTB of the *I./SS-Panzer Regiment 12* had not at that time been made available – the 39 operational Panzer IVs in the armoured-situation report of 6 August 1944 are taken as the number of tanks available and this number is given as the number of tanks still operational on 8 August 1944. For example see, among others: Patrick Agte, *Michael Wittmann und die Tiger der Leibstandarte SS Adolf Hitler*. Rosenheim: Deutsche Verlagsgesellschaft, 1995, p.258 (hereafter cited as Agte), and Reynolds, p.276.

44  Ten Tiger I Ausf E heavy tanks of the *3./SS-Panzer Abteilung 101* were subordinated to the *II./SS-Panzer Regiment 12* under command of *Hauptsturmführer* Franz Heurich. Only eight Tiger tanks set off on the actual mission together with the Panzer IVs.

45  *Kampfgruppe* of *schwere SS-Panzer Abteilung 101* commanded by *Hauptsturmführer* Michael Wittmann. He had served with the original *"Leibstandarte"* Sturmgeschütz *Batterie* in 1941 then the *13./SS-Panzer Regiment 1* of the same division. He then led the *2./schwere SS-Panzer Abteilung 101* before leading the *Abteilung*. Wittmann won the Knight's Cross on 14 January 1944, the Oakleaves on 30 January 1944, and the Swords on 22 June 1944. See throughout text for Normandy period details of this highest scoring Waffen-SS tank ace. Wittmann did not join the *Kommando* in his own Tiger (turret number 205, under repair) but in the 007 of the *Abteilungskommandeur*, around 1100 hours in the morning in Cintheaux. The *Abteilungsführer* of *schwere SS-Panzer Abteilung 101* at that time was *Obersturmbannführer* Heinz von Westernhagen. Previously the commander of *SS-Sturmgeschütz Abteilung 1* of the *„Leibstandarte"*, he later returned to command of *schwere SS-Panzer Abteilung 101* (later 501) and was killed on 20 March 1945 in Veszprém as an *Obersturmbannführer*.

46  In the original the name of the officer was mistyped as "Heurig".

The Panzer VI tanks[47] took up position on the northern outskirts of Cintheaux, adjacent to *Einheit "Gasch"*[48] on the right; no radio connection with *Einheit "Buettner"*[49]. *Einheit "Buettner"* had to occupy positions left of the Panzer VI *Kompanie*.

1045 hours: All quiet at *Kompanie "Heurich"* and *Kompanie "Gasch"*. Still no radio connection with Einheit *"Buettner"*. So far nothing notable had been reported about the enemy movements or its possible plans.

Around noon constant assaults from British four-engined bombers. Urville, Hautmesnil and Cauvicourt covered by carpet bombing.[50]

The radio connection with the *Kompanien* was interrupted. We collected the retreating infantry of the *Wehrmacht*[51], and they established securing positions south of Hautmesnil; 2 Panzer IVs and 5 Panzer Vs[52] also arrived here.

On the basis of the observation of the battlefield the enemy has slipped through from the northeast, between Cintheaux and Hautmesnil, thus there is imminent danger of the encirclement of the armoured *Kompanien*. Three Panzer VIs were able to retreat from Cintheaux in time.[53] No report about the Panzer IV *Kompanien*.[54]

---

47   In the original German text the tanks of the Tiger *Kompanie* were marked as Panzer IVs instead of Panzer VIs.

48   The *7.SS-Panzer Regiment 12*.

49   The *5./SS-Panzer Regiment 12*.

50   According to some sources, Kurt Meyer (promoted to *Oberführer* as of 1 August 1944) ordered the immediate launch of the attack otherwise scheduled for 1230 hours for *Kampfgruppe "Waldmüller"* (in it the Tigers of *schwere SS-Panzer Abteilung 101* and Panzer IVs as well as the subordinated Panthers of the *II./SS-Panzer Regiment 12*) before the air attack, because a lone Allied targeting bomber aircraft appeared in the air. He wanted to remove his forces from the area of the anticipated destruction. The plan of the attack was approved on the same morning by *General der Panzertruppen* Heinrich Eberbach, *Oberbefehlshaber* of *Panzerarmee 5* who arrived in Urville. See also Meyer, p.304.

51   Presumably parts of the *Grenadier Regiment 1055* of the *89.Infanterie Division*.

52   These tanks arrived back from the workshop *Kompanie* of *SS-Panzer Regiment 12* after having been repaired.

53   In the original German text the tanks of the Tiger *Kompanie* were marked again as Panzer IVs instead of Panzer VIs. These three Tigers remained from the eight, five of which, commanded by *Hauptsturmführer* Wittmann, ran into the ambush position of the parts of the British 33rd Armoured Brigade around 1239 hours. Between 1240 hours and 1252 hours a Firefly tank from 3rd Troop/A Squadron/1st Northamptonshire Yeomanry (an armoured regiment) with turret number 12 – according to some sources its name was "Velikye Luki" – knocked out three Tiger I Ausf Es from a distance of approximately 730-800 metres by fire directed towards their side armour. At the same time, the German heavy tanks were also attacked by the Firefly tanks of the British 144th Royal Tank Regiment (a battalion-sized unit) from Hill 122 (approximately 1,300 metres distance), and the Firefly tanks of the 27th Armoured Regiment (The Sherbrooke Fusiliers) of the Canadian 2nd Armoured Brigade from their firing positions west of the road to Cintheaux, in the area of Gaumesnil (from approximately 450 metres distance), through loopholes carved into a stone wall. See also Stephen A. Hart, *Sherman Firefly vs. Tiger, Normandy 1944*, Oxford, 2007, pp.62–63 (hereafter cited as S.A. Hart). At about 1300 hours the Firefly tanks of A Squadron 1st Northamptonshire Yeomanry hit two Panzer IVs of the *II./SS-Panzer Regiment 12*, not far from the Tigers that had already been knocked out. According to this, our opinion is that the Firefly tank in 3rd Troop, A Squadron, 1st Northamptonshire Yeomanry (turret number 12) knocked out three German Tigers, whilst two were knocked out by the Firefly tanks of the Canadian 27th Armoured Regiment. One of the latter two was probably Wittmann's "007" which was destroyed at 1248 hours and its turret blown off.

54   The remaining forces of *Panzergruppe "Prinz"*, subordinated to *Kampfgruppe "Waldmüller"* (altogether 20 Panzer IVs, Panthers and Jagdpanzer IVs, with the support of approximately 400 *SS-Panzergrenadiers*), engaged parts of the 1st Northamptonshire Yeomanry of the British 33rd Armoured Brigade at Le Petit

On the night of 08. 08. 1944 the *II./SS-Panzer Regiment 12* with the assigned Panzer VI (Tiger) tanks were withdrawn from their positions south of Hautmesnil in order to establish new positions eastwards at Soignolles.

2 km southeast of Soignolles the remnants of the *5.* and the *7.Kompanien* met parts of the *II./SS-Panzer Regiment 12* during the change of positions. The remnants of the *5.* and *7.Kompanien* succeeded in retreating under cover of darkness in a south-easterly direction, and in establishing communications with the *II.Abteilung*. During the night the armoured *Kompanien* were directed to establish positions on the northern outskirts of Soignolles.

New regimental command post in a small wooded area south of the Maizières–le Val road.

## 9 August 1944
### *I./SS-Panzer Regiment 12:*
On the night of 08. 08 regrouping accomplished with the full strength of the units[55]. The last five operational tanks were commanded by *Untersturmführer* Fritz Fiala. One tank remained to secure our positions, the others attacked the enemy tanks in the flank. The (lateral) countershaft on the tank of *Unterscharführer* Seifert was damaged due to a hit from an armoured fighting vehicle. Three tanks took positions far on the right flank. *Untersturmführer* Fiala attacked the enemy tanks from an advantageous firing position and destroyed the four Sherman tanks threatening the left flank, but after this an anti-tank gun on the right flank knocked his tank out. Four men were wounded, *Untersturmführer* Fiala was uninjured. The tank was towed away in the late evening.

The *Abteilung*, with the assigned Tigers, knocked out more than 30 tanks[56] of the enemy on this day. During the briefing of *Untersturmführer* Fritz Fiala, *Sturmbannführer* Arnold Jürgensen was wounded in his thigh on Hill 114 at Ouilly [-le-Tesson]. On the night of 09. 08. all fighting units were subordinated to the *2.Kompanie* arriving with four tanks from the Vire area, and the latter has been subordinated again to the *II.Abteilung*. The remaining parts of the *3.Kompanie*, the *Abteilungsstab*, the *Stabs* and *Versorgungskompanien* have been regrouped to the Le Neubourg area for reorganization, because the *1.* and *4.Kompanien* are still there.

---

Ravin, around 1255 hours. The battle went on until 1600 hours. According to British reports, 16 out of the attacking 20 German tanks were knocked out (of this, seven by Fireflies): seven Panzer IVs, four Panthers, and four Jagdpanzer IVs. The loss of the 1st Northamptonshire Yeomanry was 13 knocked out Shermans (from this number four were Firefly tanks). See also S.A. Hart, pp.67 and 72. Detailed description of the combat activity of the Jagdpanzer IVs taking part in the engagement can be found in this book, in the study concerning the combat activity of *SS-Panzerjäger Abteilung 12*.

55   According to the order given earlier, the regrouping was carried out in the south-eastern area of Cintheaux.

56   Eight Tiger I Ausf E heavy tanks from *schwere SS-Panzer Abteilung 101* and seven from *schwere SS-Panzer Abteilung 102* were deployed in the area. The German tanks knocked out 44 Shermans all together, two Stuarts and one Crusader; most of them belonged to the strength of the Canadian 28th Armoured Regiment. Most of the knocked out Allied tanks were destroyed by the heavy Tiger tanks. See Schneider, *Tiger im Kampf*, Band II, p.273.

### II./SS-Panzer Regiment 12:

During the night the *II. Abteilung* and its subordinated units relocated from the Bretteville [-le Rabet] area eastwards to the area of Soignolles.

The *"Buettner"* and *"Gasch" Kompanien*, which were almost encircled by the enemy south of St. Aignan-de-Cramesnil, were able to retreat with *Bataillon "Waldmüller"*[57] and reach the Soignolles area without further losses. The *Kompanien* are deployed on both sides of Soignolles. Command post 200 metres south-southwest of Point 111.

Positions given in the order occupied at 0600 hours. A quick surprise enemy attack in the early morning hours took the command post unawares, therefore it had to retreat westwards in order to retain connections with the units deployed.

The 3 Tigers and 7 Panthers assigned here were subordinated to the *Abteilung*,[58] and Hills 140[59] and 132 taken by the enemy were reoccupied with a counterstroke.

The units deployed at Soignolles were threatened from all sides, therefore they could only retreat in the direction of Le Bû [-sur-Rouvres]–Maizières during the night hours after having knocked out 56 tanks[60] and many infantrymen.

In the evening hours the enemy holding on at Point 111 was destroyed by two Tigers, two Panthers and two Panzer IVs, while we knocked out a further 22 tanks. We took a lot of prisoners of war (more than 200) who were led off by the infantry. Number of killed counted: 150.

We took a new system of positions with the remaining units and secured along the general line extending from the fringe of the wood north of Hill 140 as far as Point 111.

A further *bataillon*, Krause's, [61] *II./SS-Panzer-Grenadier-Regiment 25* was deployed during the night on our left flank.

Weather: dry, clear, warm.

Ammunition expenditure (together with 08. 08. '44): 450 high explosive shells, 190 armour-piercing shells, 7,000 [machine-gun rounds], 700 anti-aircraft high explosive shells, 500 anti-aircraft armour-piercing shells.

---

57  *Sturmbannführer* Hans Waldmüller was commander of the *I./SS-Panzer-Grenadier-Regiment 25*.

58  The *II./SS-Panzer Regiment 12* had ten operational Panzer IV tanks of its own on that evening. The subordinated *1./Sturmpanzer Abteilung 217* also had ten operational Sturmpanzer IVs. Eight Tiger I Ausf E heavy tanks from the *schwere SS-Panzer Abteilung 101* were also subordinated to the *Abteilung*.

59  Around Hill 140 parts of *SS-Panzer-Regiment 12* and the other armoured units subordinated to the *Regiment* encircled then totally destroyed the Worthington Force *Kampfgruppe* of the 28th Armored Regiment of the Canadian 4th (Armoured) Division that had broken through earlier. The Canadians lost some 250 killed, wounded or missing soldiers and 47 out of their 52 tanks were destroyed on that day, with a number of their armoured personnel carrier vehicles. In addition, Lieutenant-Colonel Dog G. Worthington, commander of the *Kampfgruppe*, and all his squadron leaders were killed.

60  These were partly the Sherman and Cromwell tanks of the Canadian 4th Armoured Division, partly the Polish 1st Armoured Division attacking towards Soignolles and la Croix. According to the operational report of the Polish Division it lost 656 soldiers altogether (of these, 121 killed and 36 missing) and 88 tanks between 7-12 August 1944. Furthermore, the Polish lost five tank destroyers and a self-propelled gun. The knocked out armoured fighting vehicles, apart from 10 tanks, were almost immediately replaced.

61  *Sturmbannführer* Bernhard Krause was commander of the *I./SS-Panzer-Grenadier-Regiment 26*. It is possible that he might have taken over the temporary command of the heavily abated *II./SS-Panzer-Grenadier-Regiment 25* within the framework of *Kampfgruppe "Krause"*.

## 10 August 1944
*I./SS-Panzer Regiment 12:*
March of the withdrawn units into the area determined. No notable events.

## War Diary Appendix no. 12.

| | |
|---|---|
| *12.SS-Panzer Division "Hitlerjugend"* | *O.U.*, 25 Sept. 1944 |
| *3. [Kompanie]/SS-Panzer Regiment 12* | |

Subject: After Action Report
Reference:
Date: 25 September 1944, 1800 hours
Attachment: –

To the *I./SS-Panzer Regiment 12 Ia*

06. 08. 1944:   The *Abteilung* was stationed in the area of Bray-la-Campagne as *Korpsreserve*. In the evening the regimental order arrived to relocate the *Abteilung* to the area of Grimbosq near the Orne in order to prevent the further eastwards advance of the enemy that had already crossed the Orne and with this to secure the left flank of our troops in the Cintheaux area.

07. 08. 1944:   During the night of 06. 08. 1944 the *Abteilung* marched with the *3.Kompanie* via St. Sylvain–Bretteville to Espins. The *3.Kompanie*, commanded by *Untersturmführer* Alban was deployed on both sides of Grimbosq in the following manner:
*Zug "Mende"* north of Grimbosq;
*Züge "Bogensperger"* and *"Matthis"* south of Grimbosq.

The frontline sector was under heavy enemy artillery fire. *Untersturmführer* Matthis was firing at enemy armoured fighting vehicles from a great distance. One enemy tank was hit and let off smoke but was still able to seek cover on its own in a dense fruit orchard.

08. 08. 1944:   In the evening the *Kompanie* had the task of launching an attack against the enemy from Grimbosq and destroying the enemy bridgehead at the Orne. During the counterstroke of *Bataillon "Krause"*[62], which was supported by Panthers and a Tiger, the tank of *Untersturmführer* Peter Matthis was hit and caught fire. The crew partly escaped. *Untersturmführer* Matthis burned in the tank.
*Untersturmführer* Bogensperger had the task of taking over the positions of the Tiger tanks in Le Hout Brieux; I personally briefed him on the field. The task of the *"Bogensperger" Zug* was the following: prevent at all costs the further crossing of tanks on the bridge built by the enemy over the Orne west of the village. *Oberscharführer* Mende stood with his *Zug* northeast of Grimbosq. His task was to prevent enemy attacks from Grimbosq towards the east and

---

62   The *I./SS-Panzer-Grenadier-Regiment 26.*

northeast. Extremely heavy enemy artillery fire was raging all day so the first infantry positions were given up again and again by the local infantry commanders. The tanks of the *3.Kompanie* stood behind them as counter-bracing, this way the positions were held, often with the help of the personal intervention of the commanders.

Around 1500 hours the commander of the *Abteilung* received the task from the *Regimentskommandeur* to hold the positions at Le Hout Brieux with the concentration of all tanks and armoured vehicles. At noon the same day *Untersturmführer* Alban with the *"Mende" Zug* supported one of the assaults of the Grenadiers, and advancing north of Grimbosq smashed the counterattacks of the enemy with high explosive shells and machine guns. Thus the assault could gain ground north of Grimbosq. One tank received an artillery hit, due to which its radio was damaged and could not be used. On its way back it drove into a large bomb crater in the heavy artillery fire because its on-board speakers could not be used, and it was impossible to salvage the vehicle for there was no towing equipment on the spot; it was not possible to prevent it from further bogging down and sinking in the soft ground. After the main battle line was recaptured, following the detachment of the radio and the armament, the wrecked tank was blown up on the orders of its commander. *Untersturmführer* Alban was killed by an artillery direct hit standing by the tank of *Oberscharführer* Mende, when he personally wanted to forward an *Abteilung* order to the crews of the tanks. *Untersturmführer* Kurt Bogensperger was hit by an enemy armoured fighting vehicle and was killed in his tank that afternoon at Le Hout Brieux.

*Unterscharführer* Freiberg from *Zug "Bogensperger"* destroyed two enemy anti-tank guns.

On the same morning *Unterscharführer* Freier destroyed two Churchills, one Sherman and two anti-tank guns near Le Hout Brieux.

In the evening order for the *Abteilung* to relocate to the southeastern sector of Cintheaux in order to repel the enemy advancing southwards.

| 09. 08. 1944: | On the night of 08. 08 regrouping was accomplished. The *Abteilung* took over the securing of Hill 114 north of Ouilly [-le-Tesson]. The *Abteilungskommandeur* was wounded.<br>On 09. 08. 1944, north of Ouilly [-le-Tesson]<br>*Unterscharführer* Freiberg destroyed two anti-tank guns,<br>*Unterscharführer* Freier destroyed two Churchills, one Sherman and an anti-tank gun, *Unterscharführer* Seifert destroyed two Shermans and an anti-tank gun. |
| 10. 08. 1944: | On the night of 09. 08. 1944 all fighting units of the *Abteilung* were subordinated to the *2.Kompanie,* and the latter was again subordinated |

to the *II./SS-Panzer Regiment 12*. The remaining parts of the *3.Kompanie*, the *Abteilungsstab*, the *Stabs* and *Versorgungskompanien* went back to Le Neubourg.

(Illegible name)
*Hauptsturmführer*[63] and *Kompanie Chef*

### II./SS-Panzer Regiment 12:

The line occupied during the night was held even against the enemy attack and it was strengthened with new forces directed here. Heavy artillery fire, constant fighter–bomber air raids.

We knocked out three enemy armoured fighting vehicles on the right flank north of Point 111.

*Kompanie "Buettner"* (*5.Kompanie*) and *Kompanie "Gasch"* (*7.Kompanie*) were concentrated because altogether only six of their tanks were operational.

The remaining parts of the *I.Abteilung* were subordinated to the *II.Abteilung*. Operational tanks on the evening of 10. 08. 1944: three Panzer VIs, nine Panzer Vs, seven Panzer IVs.

On the previous day *Kompanie "Höfler"* (*8.Kompanie*) with five tanks was deployed outside the force of the *Abteilung*, north of Point 195 and northwest of Fontaine-le-Pin.

## 11 August 1944

### I./SS-Panzer Regiment 12:

Command post of the *Abteilung* in St. Aubin. The *1.Kompanie* in Villez, the *3.Kompanie* and the *Ausbildungskompanie*[64] in Le Tremblay, the *4.Kompanie* in St. Aubin, the *Stabskompanie* in Quittebeuf, the *Versorgungskompanie* in Bernienville, the maintenance unit in Feuguerolles. The 17 crews of the *1.Kompanie* in Paris, the 8 crews of the *4.Kompanie* in Germany for tanks.

### II./SS-Panzer Regiment 12:

The *Kompanien* and the subordinated units remained in their previous day positions.

0730 hours: report from the regiment that the enemy had broken through the wooded area northwest of Le Bû [-sur-Rouvres]. The *Abteilung* had to use its three assigned Tigers so that they could prevent the breakthrough towards Le Bû [-sur-Rouvres]. Two Tigers were deployed. Further advance towards Le Bû [-sur-Rouvres] and the breakthrough did not take place.

The day was spent without any notable combat activity.

Heavy artillery fire on both sides. Heavy artillery fire on the command post of the *Abteilung*, which was in the château near Assy. Due to this considerable damage to the commander's command tank and to tank no. 784. Both tanks had to be brought to the workshop *Kompanie*.

---

63  Presumably the author of this After Action Report was *Hauptsturmführer* Kurt Brödel, *Chef* of the *3./ SS-Panzer Regiment 12*. Brödel was an Army transfer having previously served as an *Oberleutnant* with *Panzerjäger Abteilung 743*. He was killed on 18 December 1944 in Krinkelt.

64  Unfortunately there is no data concerning the origin of this *Kompanie* in the KTB. Presumably it was created for the training of the personnel that arrived as replacements during the reorganization of the exhausted *I./SS-Panzer Regiment 12*.

## 12 August 1944
### I./SS-Panzer Regiment 12:
The *Kompanien* are trained and reformed: the *4.Kompanie* will be operational in its full strength in a few days and received 15 new Panzer Vs, which have already partly arrived at the unit.

### II./SS-Panzer Regiment 12:
The command post of the *Abteilung* was relocated at 0900 hours on 12. 08. 1944. New command post in Sassy.

The subordination of *Einheit "Gaede"*[65] to *Kampfgruppe "Prinz"* ceased. The tanks of this *Kompanie* were withdrawn from their positions on the night of 11. 08. 1944. The strength of the tank destroyers assigned to the *Kampfgruppe* was strengthened during the night from three to five[66] under command of *Obersturmführer* Wachter. These five vehicles were commanded by *Obersturmführer* Erich Krauth following the drop out of *Obersturmführer* Wachter who was seriously wounded on the night of 11. 08.

At 1245 hours, following artillery preparation the enemy launched an attack against Le Bû [-sur-Rouvres] with two armoured fighting vehicles and infantry. The two armoured fighting vehicles were knocked out by one of the Panzer VIs of the *Einheit "Wendorff"*[67], upon which the attack against Le Bû [-sur-Rouvres] stuck.

Heavy artillery fire all day on both sides.

*Obersturmführer* Gaede was seriously wounded by a shell fragment in his arm at the command post.

Intensive enemy fighter-bomber activity.

Weather: dry, clear, warm.

Ammunition expenditure: 730 high explosive shells; 2,300 normal, 500 steel-core-tracer and 400 steel-core [machine gun ammunition rounds].

### War Diary Appendix no.17.
0730 hours
To *Kampfgruppe "Prinz"*

1. The enemy has penetrated the wooded area northwest of Le Bû [-sur-Rouvres].
2. *Kampfgruppe* "Prinz" immediately establishes communication with the right side neighbour via the *Ordonnanz Offizier* and asks for detailed report on the situation.
3. *Sturmbannführer* Prinz is to dispatch three Tigers drawn forward towards Assy so that the breakthrough towards Le Bû [-sur-Rouvres] can be prevented.
4. Until their arrival *Obersturmführer* Helmut Wendorff is to immediately depart for the sector of Point 83.

signed
Wünsche

65  Name of the *2./SS-Panzer Regiment 12*.
66  Jagdpanzer IVs of the *2./SS-Panzerjäger Abteilung 12*.
67  Helmut Wendorff was the *Kompanie Chef* of the *2./schwere SS-Panzer Abteilung 101*. Two days later he was killed. He came to the heavy (Tiger) *I.SS-Panzer Korps* unit having previously served in the „Leibstandarte" with *SS-Sturmgeschütz Abteilung 1* and then the *13./SS-Panzer Regiment 1*.

## 13, 14, 15, 16 August 1944
*I./SS-Panzer Regiment 12:*
Training and the reorganization of the *Kompanien* continued.

## 13 August 1944
*II./SS-Panzer Regiment 12:*
The *II.Abteilung* and the subordinated units have remained in their previous day positions. With three more Panzer VIs *Obersturmführer* Wendorff has advanced to the Tigers already in position; thus the *Kampfgruppe* consists of eight Tigers[68].

Heavy enemy artillery harassing fire during the day. Due to artillery direct hit, the car with telephone apparatus has been destroyed.

Intensive enemy fighter-bomber and bomber activity.

1545 hours: order from the regiment. *Kampfgruppe "Prinz"* (without its subordinated *Panzerjäger Kompanie*) regroups into the area of Potigny.

The new command post of the *Abteilung* foreseeably in Glatigny.

| | |
|---|---|
| Killed: | *Unterscharführer* Schlug. |
| Wounded: | *Oberscharführer* Witzel |
| | *Oberscharführer* Will |
| | *Sturmmann* Steinheimer |
| | *Sturmmann* Zeidler |
| | *Sturmmann* Ruske |
| | *Rottenführer* Fritsche (remained with the unit) |
| | *Oberschütze* Hau |

Weather: dry, clear, warm.
Ammunition expenditure: 15 8.8cm high explosive shells.

## 14 August 1944[69]
*II./SS-Panzer Regiment 12:*
Contraction of the command post of the *Abteilung* and the regiment in St. Quentin.

1230 hours: the commander[70] is killed at Le Torp due to artillery direct hit.

The remaining tanks of the *II./SS-Panzer Regiment 12* are commanded further by *Obersturmbannführer* Wünsche within *Kampfgruppe "Wünsche"*. The temporary command of the *II.Abteilung* has been assigned to *Hauptsturmführer* Hermann Tirschler, *Chef* of the 6.*Kompanie*.

During the night of 14. 08. 1944 retreat of *Kampfgruppe "Wünsche"* from Hills 160 and 165 southwards. New regimental command post between Vérsonville and Damblainville. The enemy is active with strong armoured forces. *Kampfgruppe "Wünsche"*

---

68  These heavy tanks were only subordinated to the *Abteilung*, they were not part of the strength of the unit.

69  Operation Tractable of the British-Canadian 21st Army Group began that day and lasted until 16 August 1944; it was launched in order to achieve the aims of the less successful Operation Totalize. The Canadian II Corps launched the new attack in the direction of Falaise with the same order of battle as it had possessed some days before.

70  *Sturmbannführer* Karl-Heinz Prinz, commander of the *II./SS-Panzer Regiment 12*. See award holders section.

heavily impedes the advance of these forces. The subsequent fighting has led to the encirclement of *Kampfgruppe "Wünsche"* with its command post in Fresné-la-Mère.

Before the encirclement was complete *Hauptsturmführer* Tirschler received the order to assemble its staff and at all costs arrange for the quickest possible despatch of those Panzer IV and V tanks of the *Kampfgruppe* under command to the spot.

Command post of the *II.Abteilung* was established in Friardel, on the Vimoutiers–Orbec road, in the quarters area of the *Versorgungskompanie* of the *II./SS-Panzer Regiment 12*.

In the meantime the circle around the *Kampfgruppe* has been closed. The *Kampfgruppe* tried to break through. As can be concluded from the accounts of those officers and men who were able to escape from the encirclement, the *Regimentskommandeur*, his *Adjutant* and the *Regimentsarzt* was captured by the British at Brieux.

*Hauptsturmführer* Tirschler tried to contract the remnants of the *I.* and *II. Abteilung* which are trying to prevent the enemy advancing in various battle groups.

## 15 and 16 August 1944
[Neither the *I.* nor the *II. Abteilung* had any entries.]

## 17 August 1944
### I./SS-Panzer Regiment 12:
The *4.Kompanie* received marching orders for Damville, in order to bar the enemy south of that sector advancing from the south, from the direction of Le Mans.

### II./SS-Panzer Regiment 12:
[No entry.]

## 18 August 1944
### I./SS-Panzer Regiment 12:
The *Kompanien* arranged for their march to reach the eastern bank of the Seine. The march of the *Ausbildungskompanie* commences.

### II./SS-Panzer Regiment 12:
[No entry.]

## 19 August 1944
### I./SS-Panzer Regiment 12:
The *4.Kompanie* in action (see the battle report attached!).

The *1.Kompanie* also relocated to the eastern bank of the Seine into the area of Etrepagny.

*Kampfgruppe "Mohnke"* has been created. The tanks of the *"Jürgensen" Kompanien*[71], 4 Panzer IVs and 3 Panzer Vs, are assigned here. Command post of the *Abteilung* in Acquigny–Louviers[72]. The tanks block the road from the south. They do not meet the enemy.

---

71  The operational tanks remaining from the original strength of *SS-Panzer Regiment 12* under the commander of the *I./SS-Panzer Regiment 12*.

72  Two different villages situated next to each other.

Having been created in the prewar *SS-Verfügungstruppe* period by *Hauptsturmführer Dr. Ing.* Wilhelm Brandt, camouflaged clothing and helmet covers issued to Waffen-SS troops gave them a decided advantage during the Normandy fighting. (Mark C. Yerger)

**War Diary Appendix no.13.**

*12.SS-Panzer Division "Hitlerjugend"*                                        O.U., 19 Sept. 1944
*4. [Kompanie]/SS-Panzer Regiment 12*

After Action Report from 19 Aug. 1944
The *Kompanie* secured south of Damville. Around 0300 hours a messenger brought orders according to which the *Kompanie* was to depart at once and reach Pacy [-sur-Eure-] via Damville–St. André [de l'Eure]. The former was anticipated to be occupied by the enemy. Furthermore, the order informed us that the enemy had cut the main road of Evreux–Mantes east of Pacy [-sur-Eure] and was advancing towards Vernon. The *Kompanie* was given the task of holding the enemy advancing in the north-western direction, and thus preventing encirclement. The fate of two armies depended on the quickest deployment of the *Kompanie*.

The *Kompanie* reached the village of Pacy [-sur-Eure] with ten Panzer Vs around noon; the village was under harassing artillery fire. There the *Kompanie* was given the task from *Kampfgruppe "Fick"* [73] of securing the north-eastern exit of Pacy [-sur-Eure].

73 The *Kampfgruppe* of the *17.SS-Panzer-Grenadier-Division "Götz von Berlichingen"* commanded by *Obersturmbannführer* Jakob Fick, commander of *SS-Panzer-Grenadier-Regiment 37*. Fick commanded the first *SS-Verfügungstruppe* anti-aircraft unit and won the Knight's Cross on 23 April 1943 as a

Jakob Fick as a *Hauptsturmführer* (see Chapter 8 Footnote 73). (Mark C. Yerger)

When the enemy noticed the deployment of armoured forces, it threw smoke shells over the area and retreated to the hills east of Pacy [-sur-Eure]. It was anticipated that the enemy had advanced further northwards via the Pacy [-sur-Eure]–Vernon road. Thus the *Kompanie* was assigned the task of advancing on the road to Vernon and establishing positions at La Heunière, which were to be held at all costs. Following preparatory reconnaissance the *Kompanie* reached the allocated positions around 1700 hours. The lead vehicle encountered light reconnaissance forces on the road. Upon reaching the allocated positions, seven Panzer Vs[74] of the *2.SS-Panzer Division "Das Reich"* were subordinated to the *Kompanie* as reinforcements. At 1900 hours the *Kompanie* received orders from the commander of the *Kampfgruppe* to launch a retaliatory attack[75] towards Blaru, because the terrorists[76] had engaged one of our reconnaissance units there. After the eager and well-paced attack was carried out the *Kompanie* reached the designated positions within the shortest time possible and advanced some 3 km further, thus it was stood directly at the Seine. The enemy was gathering its forces there and defended fiercely. Following the

---

*Sturmbannführer*. He assumed command of the former *I./Langemarck* of *"Das Reich"* in April 1943 just when that *Kradschützen Bataillon* was absorbed by the *Aufklärungsabteilung* of *"Das Reich"*. Fick transferred to *"Götz von Berlichingen"* when it first formed in command of *SS-Panzer-Grenadier-Regiment 37*. Promoted to *Obersturmbannführer* on 30 January 1944, he survived the war and died on 22 April 2004.

74  The tanks of the *2.SS-Panzer Division "Das Reich"*.
75  In the original: *"Vergeltungsangriff"*.
76  Members of the French national resistance movement. According to the KTB of *Panzerarmee 5*, *Kampfgruppe "Mohnke"* killed 41 "terrorists" (members of the resistance) in the area, between 20 and 24 August 1944. It is possible that the above mentioned mission of the *4./SS-Panzer Regiment 12* was partly in connection with this.

heaviest artillery, tank and anti-tank gun fire the *Kompanie* retreated towards Maulu. Here one of our tanks was knocked out and it has burnt out. Around 2100 hours the *Kompanie* reached the point of departure and was secured there from then on. Artillery harassing fire on our positions during the night.

> Scores: six trucks destroyed
> Losses: One killed, seven wounded
> Total loss: One Panzerkampfwagen V
> Other losses: none

Pohl
*Leutnant* and *Kompanieführer*

### II./SS-Panzer Regiment 12:
[No entry.]

## 20 August 1944
### I./SS-Panzer Regiment 12:

*Kampfgruppe "Mohnke"* is in its previous positions. During the late night hours the *Kampfgruppe* relocated to its new sector to Arambrai[77] near the Eure. All of the tanks are assigned to the armoured *Kampfgruppe "Jürgensen"*. Furthermore, three Jagdpanzer IVs[78] of the *116.Panzer Division*, three self-propelled 7.5cm anti-tank guns, four Panzer IVs of the *2.Panzer Division* and [?][79] Panzer Vs of the *9.Panzer Division* are also assigned to the *Kampfgruppe*. So far they have not met the enemy.

Battle report of the *4.Kompanie* about the combat activity in the Vernon–Pacy [sur-Eure] area [attached].

### War Diary Appendix no.14.

*12.SS-Panzer Division "Hitlerjugend"*         O.U., 19 Sept. 1944
*4. [Kompanie]/SS-Panzer Regiment 12*

After Action Report from 20 VIII. 1944

The *Kompanie* was securing at the north-eastern exit of the village of Le Heunière with 17 Panzerkampfwagen Vs with the task of holding the Pacy [-sur-Eure] – Vernon road at all costs. We knew that the enemy had advanced its tank and infantry forces 1,500 metres into the wooded area south of the road during the night. Constant harassing artillery fire on our positions. Around 0900 hours the enemy [80] tried to carry out a surprise attack and break through with tanks and mounted infantry. The attack was immediately discovered and was repulsed by the concentrated fire of the *Kompanie*, knocking out five enemy tanks[81]. Following this the *Kompanie* received the heaviest

---

77  There is no village with such name in the area.

78  In the original "Panzerjäger P. 4".

79  *II./Panzerjäger Regiment 33 (9.Panzer Division)* on 12 August 1944, had some 25 operational Panther tanks, which were fighting subordinated to the *116.Panzer Division* from this time until 20 August. From the text of the KTB we can assume that by that time only one operational Panther was subordinated to *Kampfgruppe "Mohnke"*.

80  Presumably parts of the 'A' Battle Group of the American 5th Armored Division.

81  During this time the 'A' Battle Group of the American 5th Armored Division lost three M4 (Sherman) tanks and three subordinated M10 tank destroyers.

artillery fire onto its uncovered positions. At the same time enemy tanks broke through the *Luftwaffe Feld Division*[82] on the right to get into the rear of the *Kompanie*. This assault was again discovered immediately and was repulsed by the *Reservezug* securing in the south-eastern direction by knocking out four tanks. The enemy assault aircraft[83] that discovered the engagement joined the action with bombs, machine gun and cannon fire so that three of our tanks were put out of action. The enemy attempted again and again to break through, but we repulsed them each time fighting fiercely and causing heavy losses. These engagements lasted until the evening.

The enemy succeeded in eliminating the Grenadiers deployed as support for the *Kompanie* with concentrated heavy artillery and fighter-bomber fire and weakened the *Kompanie* so much that three of our tanks were burnt out and a further four tanks were rendered out of action for engineering reasons. Despite this the next attack of the enemy was again repulsed under the fiercest of circumstances, knocking out a further three enemy tanks, two anti-tank guns, and a vehicle.

Around 1930 hours the enemy attacked the *Kompanie* in the rear from the west with strong tank forces. At the same time flanking manoeuvres were launched from the northeast, following a breakthrough on the left flank. Upon this the *Kompanie* followed the orders given to it and retreated via St. Vincent to St. Marcel, established a new defence line there and during the night retreated further towards St. Pierre.

Scores: 12 tanks, 2 anti-tank guns, 1 cross-country vehicle

Losses: 9 wounded

Total loss Panzerkampwagen V: 3

Other losses [Panzerkampwagen V]: 7

Pohl
*Leutnant* and *Kompanieführer*

### II./SS-Panzer Regiment 12:
[No entry.]

## 21 August 1944

### I./SS-Panzer Regiment 12:

**War Diary Appendix No.15.**
After Action Report of the deployment of the *2.* and *3.Kompanien* in the period 13–21 August 1944

I took over the parts of the *2.* and *3.Kompanien* contracted into one *Kompanie* from *Obersturmführer* Gaede, who suffered serious injuries the day before, on 13 August 1944[84]. This meant there were 15 tanks altogether.

The *Kompanie* stood, at this time, in attack positions, in a wooded area 2 km north of Ussy, assigned to the *Kampfgruppe* of *Sturmbannführer* Erich Olboeter.

---

82  Presumably parts of the *17.Feld Division* of the *Luftwaffe*.
83  Fighter-bomber aircraft of the Allied forces.
84  Although the battle report is unfortunately not signed, its author is presumably *Obersturmführer* Kurt Brödel, who was also *Kompanie Chef* of the *3./SS-Panzer Regiment 12* in September 1944 as a *Hauptsturmführer*.

*Standartenoberjunker* Ulrich Ahrens (*2.Kompanie*) and *Oberscharführer* Richard Mende (*3.Kompanie*) were available as *Zugführer*. All was quiet in the morning of 13. 08. '44; around noon Olboeter's command post began receiving alarming news that the Army units[85] assigned to *Kampfgruppe "Olboeter"* were not holding. Therefore, by order of the *Panzer Regiment*, around 1400 hours I deployed a *Zug* of three tanks, commanded by *Unterscharführer* Helmle, moving from Ussy, southwest of [Clair] Tizon for securing. Around 2000 hours I received an order from the regiment, according to which the *Kompanie* was to be deployed as follows: five tanks on both sides of Martainville, four tanks on the two sides of the village of La Val [Lègere], and the remaining parts of the *Kompanie* on both sides of the Ussy–[Clair] Tizon road, directly south of Point 170. The task of the *Kompanie* was as follows: "Prevention of the anticipated breakthrough of the enemy". After thorough reconnaissance during the night we occupied the positions for the *Züge*. At times we experienced heavy enemy artillery fire on the frontline sector. I instructed *Zug "Mende"* and with this I reconnoitred the extremely broken terrain.

14 August 1944

After this reconnaissance I personally effected communications with *Standartenoberjunker* Ulrich Ahrens in Martainville and I became familiar with the positions of the different tanks. Heavy artillery fire was lying on the frontline of the *Zug* of *Standartenoberjunker* Ahrens. The main battle line was occupied by the weak forces of *Bataillon "Olboeter"*[86]. Around 0700 hours I returned to Ussy and heard that the enemy was attacking with infantry in the sector of *Oberscharführer* Mende. However the attack was repulsed and the breakthrough of the enemy prevented. Around 0800 hours in the morning the enemy attacked with tanks and infantry south of the Ussy–[Clair] Tizon road, from [Clair] Tizon, while the Tigers positioned further to the south knocked out some armoured fighting vehicles. The tank of the *Kompanie Chef* destroyed an anti-tank gun, which was conducting flanking fire on the Tigers. Around 1100 hours the enemy attacked again with tanks and infantry forces in the sector of *Oberscharführer* Mende. The attack was repulsed as before. An infantry supported attack was launched immediately and it restored the main battle line lost by the infantry. *Unterscharführer* Seifert destroyed two enemy tanks here. *Oberscharführer* Mende's tank was damaged because of a tank round to its turret; also the tank of *Unterscharführer* Pietsch was rendered immobile because of a hit to its engine. Two of our tanks were holding the main battle line despite the confused terrain and they almost totally wiped out two attacking *Kompanien* with high explosive shells and machine gun fire. A unit which was deployed for the reinforcement of the sector and which was prepared again and again to abandon the frontline, was, on my orders, threatened with the necessary measures and was stopped by our tanks and they were forced to occupy the previous main battle line.

Around 1100 hours I was on the radio with *Standartenoberjunker* Ahrens who had connections again to *Unterscharführer* Helmle. From 1200 hours onwards there were no connections again with Ahrens, and, as it later turned out, the tank of *Standartenoberjunker* Ahrens received a direct hit from an artillery shell and its radio system was damaged. *Zug "Mende"* and the *Kompanie Chef*'s unit remained in the previous positions until 1400 hours, when I received an order from the regiment – delivered by an *Ordonnanz*

---

85  These were most probably parts of the *85.Infanterie Division*.
86  The *III./SS-Panzer-Grenadier-Regiment 26*.

## 16. 08. 1944

In the morning of 16. 08. 1944 the enemy covered our positions in heavy artillery fire, while continuing to move its tanks with the same strength as yesterday, though not in the direction of Falaise but eastwards, advancing north of Olendon. Around 1000 hours I received the order from the *Regimentskommandeur* which assigned me and my three tanks to (Tiger) *SS-schwere Panzer Abteilung 102*[91] (*Obersturmbannführer* Hans Weiss).[92] Two tanks remained on the road to secure approximately 1,200 metres south of Epancy, while the third tank was sent to Versainville, to the *Abteilung* command post of *Obersturmbannführer* Weiss. Heavy enemy artillery fire on our positions all day. Around 1800 hours I received the order from the *Regimentskommandeur* that the *Kompanie* was to change its positions immediately towards Les Croix and to hold and stop the enemy that was advancing in the afternoon north of Olendon via Jort–Tivos at the north-eastern exit of Beaumais[93]. The three tanks of the *Kompanie* departed at once and established positions before midnight in the sector of Hill 65 to prevent the enemy breakthrough towards the south at all costs.

## 17. 08. 1944

In the early morning hours the enemy advanced in front of our positions, approximately 3,000 metres away with strong forces from the northwest towards the southeast in the direction of Trun. During the manoeuvre the enemy covered its right flank with heavy artillery fire on our positions. We immediately engaged the individual armoured fighting vehicles that were pushing forward in the direction of our securing lines, and in this way set two Shermans and one armoured reconnaissance vehicle aflame during the day. We fired on another tank from 2,600–2,800 metres' distance and we hit it. The tank emitted smoke but was able to go into shelter in reverse, this way further observation became impossible. The enemy armoured echelons, armoured vehicles and trucks with mounted infantry were ceaselessly processing in front of us, approximately 3,500 metres away, towards Trun. Our right hand neighbour, the *Kompanie* of *Obersturmführer* Albert Gasch, knocked out some more armoured fighting vehicles during the day. The enemy turned westwards and tried to cut us off in the direction of Le[s] Moutiers [-en-Auge]; we prevented this by withdrawing *Obersturmführer* Gasch's forces and my tanks by order of the regiment during the night, and retreated to the positions on Hill 113, southeast of Fresné-la-Mère.

---

91  To *schwere SS-Panzer Abteilung 102*.

92  Hans Weiss commanded the *Stabskompanie* of *Regiment "Deutschland"* in the Polish Campaign and was then *Nachschubführer* of eventual *Division "Das Reich"* until April 1940. *Kompanie Chef* of the *4./Aufklärungsabteilung* in the 1940 French Campaign, in February 1942 he became commander of the *Kradschützen Bataillon*. He was deputy commander of *Kampfgruppe "SS-Reich"* in 1942 and then commander of the *"Das Reich" Aufklärungsabteilung* from June of that year. In mid-April 1943 he was commander *I./Panzer Regiment "Das Reich"* with the Knight's Cross awarded 6 April 1943. On 20 March 1944 he became commander *schwere SS-Panzer Abteilung 102*. Promoted *Sturmbannführer* 20 April 1943 he won the German Cross in Gold 23 April 1944. He was promoted to *Obersturmbannführer* 21 June 1944, captured seriously wounded on 19 August 1944 and died of a heart attack on 2 October 1978 while driving home from a veterans' reunion.

93  There is no village with the name of Tivos in Normandy.

18. 08. 1944

At dawn the positions were ready and we took over securing in the northern direction in order to hold and eliminate the enemy pushing after us. During the morning a further three tanks were assigned to the *Kompanie* that arrived from the repair station. The *Kompanie* then had six tanks available again. Around 1300 hours I received an order on the radio from the *Regimentskommandeur* that I was to occupy Hill 135 immediately with four tanks and repulse the enemy thrusting into the main battle line there. I departed at once with four tanks via Pertheville [-Ners] and reached the road at Hill 135 without meeting the enemy; there the *Regimentskommandeur* personally gave me a new attack order. On Hill 143 there was still a Luftwaffe *Kampfgruppe* containing four 8.8cm anti-aircraft guns and 12 2cm anti-aircraft guns, the crews of which had been partly lost, and had partly retreated from the attack of the enemy tanks and armoured vehicles via Hill 143 to the railway approximately 500 metres west of Pertheville [-Ners]. The *Regimentskommandeur*'s task for me was the following: "Occupy Hill 143 with four tanks, release our own *Kampfgruppe* on the Hill and with its armament lead it back to the new main battle line at the railway southwest of Pertheville". The attack against Hill 143 advanced well in spite of the enemy attempts to contain the manoeuvre from the flanks with armoured reconnaissance vehicles or anti-tank guns. The infantry and the escaped Flak crews were subordinated to me and so we reached Hill 143 where we met some of the men of the Flak *Kampfgruppe* of the Luftwaffe. Apart from two 8.8cm and two 2cm anti-aircraft guns all armament of the Flak *Kampfgruppe* was destroyed due either to enemy tanks or being blown up by the men themselves. Withdrawal of the small *Kampfgruppe* towards the railway was again disturbed by anti-tank gun and artillery fire. In spite of this the *Kampfgruppe* reached the assigned positions without suffering any losses; along the railway line the tanks also positioned themselves to secure. That night the *Kompanie* was ordered to change positions via Viqnats–St. Nikolas. The *Kompanie* marched as far as Bierre and established positions at Hill 117, northwest of Bierre.

19. 08. 1944

That morning the *Kompanie* received the news that the *Regimentskommandeur*, the *Regimentsadjutant* and the *Regimentsarzt* were missing and were presumably wounded and captured by the British.[94] *Sturmbannführer* Olboeter arrived at the command post of the *Kompanie* and reported that he had taken over the command of the regiment. In front of us, on our left and to our rear, heavy battle noise during the afternoon. The situation is extremely uncertain and the regiment also cannot provide any further information. At 2000 hours briefing at the regimental command post. The *Regimentsführer* informs us of the situation and the orders of the division, according to which during the night the division is preparing to break the encirclement at St. Lambert at dawn on 20 August and fight through the lines. Two codewords were given, that is, "if the units in front of us succeed in breaking through, the codeword 'Freiheit' [Freedom] is to be used, which

---

94  *Obersturmbannführer* Max Wünsche, commander of *SS-Panzer Regiment 12,* and *Hauptsturmführer* Dr. Rudolf Stiawa (the *Regimentsarzt*) were wounded. *Hauptsturmführer* Georg Isecke, *Adjutant* of *SS-Panzer Regiment 12,* was unharmed when captured by the Allied forces, though not on 19 August, but on 24 August, after days of hiding and attempts to get through the lines. Wünsche and Stiawa were captured by the Canadians, Isecke by the Americans.

means that we will take all elements of the regiment, including the wheeled vehicles". If the units marching in front of us cannot break through, the codeword 'Scheisse' [Shit] is to be used, which means that all non-armoured vehicles are to be blown up, and we have to attempt to fight with the armoured vehicles as far as it is possible considering the enemy situation and the available fuel. If, in case of heavier enemy resistance our weak armoured forces cannot break through, or, for any reason, the armoured fighting vehicles are rendered disabled, then these vehicles are also to be blown up, and the crews are to take as many weapons and ammunition with them as possible and are to break through the enemy lines at night or during the day until Rouen on the Seine, and reach the regrouping point of the division in Fleury, east of Rouen.

The armoured regiment assigned me to the following order of battle for the breakthrough: four tanks of my *Kompanie* will form the spearhead, behind them the *Flak Zug* of the regiment, the armoured personnel carrier *Bataillon*[95], the *Sturmpanzer Bataillon*[96], the *Panzerjäger Abteilung*,[97] and the Panzer IV *Kompanie*.

### 20. 08. 1944

Gathering of the Regiment accomplished at 0300 hours in the night. After the units emptied the fuel from the trucks of other units and from the other disabled vehicles, their own vehicles were filled up. Two tanks of the *Kompanie* were blown up, because we were unable to tow them with us; these were reported to the regiment the day before as being damaged and needing to be towed away. The *Kampfgruppe* of the regiment departed at 0500 hours under command of *Sturmbannführer* Olboeter via Bailleul – Tournai [-sur-Dives] towards St. Lambert, where we received heavy enemy defensive fire. The *Kampfgruppe* of the regiment, with three Panthers as the spearhead, together with our forces and those of other divisions following us pushed through St. Lambert to break through the enemy defence along the road leading to Coudehard. Directly northeast of St. Lambert extremely heavy tank–, anti-tank gun–, anti-aircraft-gun-, machine gun and artillery defensive fire hit us, because of this the attack did not succeed despite multiple attempts. During the fighting *Unterscharführer* Zwangsleitner knocked out a Sherman, but immediately after this he was knocked out by an enemy tank. His tank burnt out.

After this first unsuccessful breakthrough attempt, parts of the regiment regrouped and in a single force, with other SS, and Wehrmacht units, we reorganized ourselves for a renewed second attempt. That time we were able to break through the first enemy cordon. However, we met heavy enemy resistance on the Coudehard–La Coury de Bosy road where they had placed tanks in well-covered positions on a steeply ascending slope in order to prevent us breaking through. Some of the armoured fighting vehicles were disabled by the *Fallschirmjägers*[98] in close combat, so the advance could be continued on the steeply ascending and extremely broken terrain. Our tank drivers especially showed outstanding achievements on the narrow roads ascending steeply, these roads also being full of damaged vehicles. Not far from reaching the hill my tank received an artillery round to its side, though no damage was caused. Around 1700 hours we succeeded at

---

95  The *III./SS-Panzer-Grenadier-Regiment 26.*

96  Parts of *Sturmpanzer Abteilung 217.*

97  Parts of *SS-Panzerjäger Abteilung 12.*

98  *Kompanie*-strength group of the *3.Fallschirmjäger Division.*

last, our spearhead was over the enemy defence lines, and we reached the first securing forces of the *2.SS-Panzer Division "Das Reich"*[99].

The second tank of *Unterscharführer* Zund that had departed from St. Lambert was damaged during the advance and due to engine failure caught fire when mounting the steep slope. Because of an enemy infantry attack we were unable to extinguish the fire. The crew was able to get through the enemy securing lines at night and all reached the *Kompanie* in Le Neubourg. Only one of the four tanks taking part in the manoeuvre got through the enemy positions undamaged, and in the following days reached Le Neubourg via Orbec – Bernay and from there, through the Seine, the *I.Abteilung* at Poses.

**War Diary Appendix no. 16**
*12. SS-Panzer-Division. "Hitlerjugend"*                    O.U., 19 Sept. 1944
*4. [Kompanie]/SS-Panzer Regiment 12*

After Action Report from 21. VIII. 1944
Following the retrograde movement from Le Heunière the *Kompanie* was located in St. Pierre with seven operational and seven mechanically disabled Panzer Vs. Around 1200 hours *Sturmbannführer* Arnold Jürgensen led the *Kompanie* with seven Panzer Vs into new positions at Buisson, approximately 6 km south of Gaillon.

It was discovered that the enemy was advancing northwards from the south along the Seine and from La Chapelle into the direction of Gaillon.

The *Kompanie* secured on a 1.5 km wide line towards the south and southeast, in the direction of St. Pierre, with the task to hold and contain the enemy here, and abandon the position only when ordered. The day and night was spent without any notable events. The *Kompanie* met no enemy.

    Scores: none
    Losses: none
    Irrevocable tank losses: none
    Other losses: none

Pohl
*Leutnant* and *Kompanieführer*

*II./SS-Panzer Regiment 12:*
On 21. 08. 1944 the *II./SS-Panzer Regiment 12* had the following tanks:

- 6 Panzerkampfwagen IVs
- 3 Panzerkampfwagen Vs
- 1 anti-aircraft armoured fighting vehicle

These armoured fighting vehicles were subordinated to the *Kampfgruppe* of *Sturmbannführer* Gustav Knittel[100] for a mission against Fervaques. The *Kampfgruppe*

---

99 The *2.SS-Panzer Division "Das Reich"* was the early career unit for many officers who led units in conjunction with „*Hitlerjugend,*" including Jakob Fick and Hans Weiss.

100 *Sturmbannführer* Gustav Knittel was commander of *SS-Panzer-Aufklärungsabteilung 1* of the „*Leibstandarte*". He had previously served as *Kompanie Chef* of the *4.* and *3.Kompanien* of the same unit

was strengthened further by two assault guns. The tanks were directed to the place of the assault west of Cernay, under command of *Obersturmführer* Eggers.

1600 hours: relocation of the command post of the *Abteilung* to the estate 500 metres northeast of the church of Cernay.

1615 hours: the attack positions of the armoured *Kampfgruppe* are reached. *Hauptsturmführer* Tirschler, commander of the *II./SS-Panzer Regiment 12*, holds a briefing in the attack position. The armoured group has the mission of supporting the attack of the *12.SS-Panzer Division "Hitlerjugend"* and the Grenadiers and Engineers of the *21.Panzer Division*.

After a short artillery preparation, at 1630 hours launch of the attack against the enemy east of Fervaques. The enemy is pushed back to Fervaques. However we have difficulties in deploying the tanks because the terrain is extremely unsuitable for armoured vehicles.

At 2200 hours the *II./SS-Panzer Regiment 12* received the order to abandon its positions and move into the assembly positions of the *12.SS-Panzer Division "Hitlerjugend"* in La Barre-en-Ouche.

2230 hours: the disengagement of the *II./SS-Panzer Regiment 12* and the departure to La Barre-en-Ouche occurs. Parts of the *Stabskompanie* are sent forward to reconnoitre and place signposts on the road.

---

and was awarded the Knight's Cross as commander on 4 June 1944. He survived the war and died in Ulm on 30 June 1976.

# Fighting between Touques and the Seine, 22–29 August 1944

**22 August 1944**
*I./SS-Panzer Regiment 12:*

**War Diary Appendix no. 17**
*12.SS-Panzer Division "Hitlerjugend"*        *O.U.*, 19 Sept. 1944
*4. [Kompanie]/SS-Panzer Regiment 12*

After Action Report from 22. VIII. 1944
The *Kompanie* was assigned to *Kampfgruppe "Jürgensen"* and secured at Le Buisson[1] with seven Panzerkampfwagen Vs, with the task of holding and containing the enemy, abandoning its positions only when ordered.

It was discovered that the enemy was advancing northwards from the south in the direction of Gaillon. Around 0900 hours an enemy[2] armoured reconnaissance unit approached the *Kompanie*. With well-directed fire we knocked out three enemy tanks here and forced the others to turn away. After an hour six enemy tanks approached again, five of which were set aflame and the last one was rendered immobile. Because of this defeat the enemy brought anti-tank guns to the fringe of the forest and accurately engaged our tanks one by one. Thirty fighter–bomber aircraft have also been attacking our tanks alternately. During this time our position was under heavy artillery fire, due to which one tank was knocked out and another one was rendered immobile.

Around 1400 hours we discovered enemy tanks to the east which later proved to be a strong armoured force. Here the enemy attacked with an outflanking manoeuvre westwards and north-westwards with 70 tanks, 50 armoured personnel carriers and 100 trucks with mounted infantry. In the meantime the *Kompanie* was placed under ceaseless enemy artillery and fighter-bomber aircraft fire.

At 1430 hours the *Kompanie* received a further Panzerkampfwagen V as reinforcement.

In spite of the circumstances, in a short time we knocked out eight enemy tanks, five armoured personnel carriers and two trucks. Here the enemy suffered the bloodiest and heaviest losses. The fire of the enemy tanks, the artillery, anti-tank guns and fighter–bombers knocked out three of our own tanks and one was rendered immobile.

Now the *Kompanie* consisted of only two operational tanks, which were not able to hold the lines because they were fired at from all sides and the situation worsened with their encirclement. The supporting infantry had already retreated, thus further resistance was impossible.

---

1   There is no village with such name in the area of Gaillon.
2   Parts of a Combat Command from the American 5th Armored Division.

Martin Groß, the last commander of *SS-Panzer Regiment 12*, shown in
early and late war images (see Appendix II). (Mark C. Yerger)

In the evening the *Kompanie* established new positions with two newly assigned
Panzerkampfwagen Vs southwest of Heudebouville.

Scores: 16 tanks, 5 armoured personnel carriers, 2 trucks, approximately 50 killed

Losses: 1 killed, 8 wounded

Total losses in tanks: 6

Other losses: 1 Panzerkampfwagen V

Pohl

*Leutnant* and *Kompanieführer*

### II./SS-Panzer Regiment 12:

Arrival of the *Abteilungsstab* in La Barre-en-Ouche. Quarters prepared for the units of
the *II.Abteilung* in Thevray. The command post of the *Abteilung* is located in the château
near Thevray.

According to incoming reports the assembly positions of the *12.SS-Panzer Division
"Hitlerjugend"* can be found in Grancamps. *Hauptsturmführer* Tirschler personally went
to Grancamps, however he did not find the assembly positions there, nor any other
command of the *12.SS-Panzer Division "Hitlerjugend"*.

According to *Obersturmführer* Eggers, who has taken over the command of all the
tanks of the *Abteilung*, the enemy has already succeeded in breaking into Orbec. The
hills directly east of Orbec are held with weak securing forces.

Upon considering the situation the commander of the *II./SS-Panzer Regiment 12*
decided that the *II.Abteilung* is to relocate to its old quarters area in La Saussaye. The

reconnaissance platoon is immediately dispatched for reconnaissance and placement of signposts on the road. They are accompanied by the following:

- the *Versorgungskompanie* and the *Kampfstaffel*;
- the *Abteilungsstab* closes the line.

## 23 August 1944
### *I./SS-Panzer Regiment 12:*

**War Diary Appendix no. 18**
*12. SS-Panzer-Division. "Hitlerjugend"*            O.U., 19 Sept. 1944
*4. [Kompanie]/SS-Panzer Regiment 12*

After Action Report from 23. VIII. 1944
Last night the *Kompanie* established securing positions with four operational Panzerkampfwagen Vs southwest of Heudebouville. During the day the *Kompanie* received a further two Panzerkampfwagen Vs as reinforcements; this way the *Kompanie* secured the sector of 2 km width with six tanks. A *Pionier* unit[3] established positions approximately 300 metres in front of the *Kompanie*.

The enemy wanted to occupy the hill and the crossroad secured by the *Kompanie*. Position of the enemy was unknown.

Apart from short fire strikes by the enemy artillery the day was quiet. Around 2030 hours a messenger arrived running from the *Pioniers* and reported that the enemy was attacking with tanks. Shortly after this the enemy overran the *Pioniers* and approximately ten of their tanks were stood on the hill. Despite the darkness and the rain the *Kompanie* succeeded in knocking out four enemy tanks and repulsing the attack. The enemy did not renew the assault on this spot. Around midnight a courier delivered the orders of the *Abteilung* to retreat and to establish positions southwest of Vironvay, both of which were carried out during the night.

Scores: 4 tanks
Losses: none
Total losses in tanks: 1
Other losses: none

Pohl
*Leutnant* and *Kompanieführer*

### *II./SS-Panzer Regiment 12:*
Arrival of the *II.Abteilung* in La Saussaye in the early morning hours and in the morning.

Location: command post of the *Abteilung* at the quarters of the commander in La Saussaye, *Versorgungskompanie* and *Stabskompanie* in the old quarters of the former *Stabskompanie*, the combat units in Iville, between Amfreville and Le Neubourg.

At 1300 hours the following tank force was reported:

- 6 tanks reached Iville, of which 4 are only operational in a limited way;
- 3 tanks are being towed on the road to Iville.

---

3    Presumably parts of *SS-Panzer-Pionier-Bataillon 12*.

It was arranged immediately that all nine tanks were to be prepared to be fully operational within the shortest time possible.

*Hauptsturmführer* Siegel, who is commanding the base at La Saussaye, reported to the commander that the base had relocated to Le Thil [-Riberpré], east of the Seine and the intention was to relocate the base even further eastwards. The village of Rethel, northwest of Reims, is assigned for this. *Obersturmführer* Höfler was sent to reconnoitre the new base.

The *IIb-Abteilung* gathered data of the personnel of the *II./SS-Panzer Regiment 12*. According to this, officers, NCOs and enlisted men in the *II.Abteilung* as in the attached list[4].

1500 hours: *Hauptsturmführer* Tirschler went to the regimental command post in Louviers to bring further orders for the *Abteilung*.

At 1700 hours a report from *Hauptsturmführer* Walter Bormuth: according to two officers of the *LSSAH* the enemy tanks are already in Neubourg and Vernon, the enemy is advancing along the Le Neubourg–Iville road and is already firing at Iville.

A courier brought orders for *Obersturmführer* Eggers that he was to send the tanks in Iville into blocking positions and prevent the enemy from advancing further. Dispatch of a reconnaissance unit into the area of Iville–Vernon under command of *Untersturmführer* Gunnar Johnsson in order to determine the distance the enemy has taken forward.

At 1800 hours *Obersturmführer* Eggers reported that he had established securing positions even before the arrival of the report from the command post of the *Abteilung*. Four of the six tanks are operational, the guns of two tanks are damaged so they cannot be used. These latter two tanks were immediately withdrawn. During the engagement the enemy succeeded in knocking out three of our tanks. One tank took over the securing of the Le Neubourg–Elbeuf road.

1730 hours: order for the *Versorgungskompanie* and for all remaining parts of the *Abteilung* to immediately depart across the Seine to the base in Le Thil-en-Vexin.

At 1800 hours the first vehicles drove out of La Saussaye.

1900 hours: *Hauptsturmführer* Tirschler, who was escorted by *Untersturmführer* Walther, did not return until 1900 hours. Instead of him, shortly after 1900 hours, an *Obersturmführer* of the *LSSAH* reported and stated that *Hauptsturmführer* Tirschler and *Untersturmführer* Walther were engaged by the enemy in the area of La Vallee, between Elbeuf and Louviers and both were wounded. *Hauptsturmführer* Tirschler asked for a vehicle immediately. *Untersturmführer* Bock was dispatched at once to retrieve the wounded officers.

*Hauptsturmführer* Hans Siegel took over the command of the *Abteilung* in the afternoon, the commander of a Panzer V reported to the command post and said that his engine was not running perfectly and the tank was only partially mobile. By order of *Hauptsturmführer* Siegel this tank was dispatched to secure the Elbeuf–Louviers road at the northern exit of Louviers.

The last tank from Iville, and the 12 assault guns of *Einheit "Rettlinger"*[5] were withdrawn around 2300 hours to the southern outskirts of Elbeuf, to the railway

---

4    The list contains the names of 288 persons. The list of names is not published here.

5    *Sturmbannführer* Karl Rettlinger was the commander of *SS-Sturmgeschütz Abteilung 1* of the *"Leibstandarte"*. He was awarded the Knight's Cross as *Kompanie Chef* of the *3./SS-Sturmgeschütz Abteilung 1* on 20 December 1943 and the German Cross in Gold with the same unit on 28 March 1943. He died in Gunzenhausen on 14 June 1990.

crossing, in order to secure the Elbeuf–Le Neubourg road here. The *Abteilung* provided fuel for the assault guns of *Einheit "Rettlinger"*.

## 24 August 1944
### *I./SS-Panzer Regiment 12:*

**War Diary Appendix no. 19**

| | |
|---|---|
| 12. SS-Panzer-Division. "Hitlerjugend" | *O.U.*, 19 Sept. 1944 |
| 4. [Kompanie]/SS-Panzer Regiment 12 | |

After Action Report from 24. VIII. 1944

With four operational tanks the *Kompanie* established positions southwest of Vironvay as ordered. Two Panzerkampfwagen Vs and two Panzerkampfwagen IVs of the *Wehrmacht* were assigned to the *Kompanie*; these tanks also took up positions.

During the day the enemy occupied the village of Heudebouville previously abandoned by us, and slowly moved forward.

The day was spent quietly and without enemy attacks. One of our tanks ran over our own mine and following this, was knocked out by an enemy anti-tank gun.

Around 2200 hours an order was received to retreat and to cross the Seine, which was accomplished without any extraordinary events.

Scores: none[6]

Losses: 1 wounded

Total losses Panzerkampfwagen V: 1

[Other] losses: none

*Leutnant* and *Kompanieführer*


### *II./SS-Panzer Regiment 12:*

At 0200 hours *Hauptsturmführer* Hans Siegel assigned a Panzer IV and a Panzer V to the combat commander[7] to be used for deployment and supply.

During the day of 24. 08. 1944 the units of *II.Abteilung* crossed the Seine at Rouen and Poses, and assembled in Le Thil-en-Vexin. *Hauptsturmführer* Tirschler also arrived here. Despite the wound on his leg, he fought through the enemy lines until reaching the bridges on the Seine. Still no news of *Untersturmführer* Walther. According to *Hauptsturmführer* Tirschler, *Untersturmführer* Walther was presumably seriously wounded and captured by the British. *Hauptsturmführer* Tirschler knew nothing of *Untersturmführer* Bock and his Volkswagen.

In the afternoon, order for the *II.Abteilung* to regroup in the area of Conty during the day of 25. 08. 1944. The relocation began with the *Stabskompanie* on the night of 25. 08. 1944.

---

6   According to the KTB of *Panzerarmee 5*, *Kampfgruppe "Mohnke"* destroyed a total of 46 Shermans and one Churchill, 10 Universal Carrier armoured carrier vehicles, and three anti-tank guns between 20 and 24 August 1944. The Panthers of the *4./SS-Panzer Regiment 12* assigned to the *Kampfgruppe* knocked out 36 Allied armoured vehicles between 20 and 23 August 1944.

7   Presumably *Obersturmführer* Fritz Eggers.

## 25 August 1944
*I./SS-Panzer Regiment 12:*
[No entry.]


## II./SS-Panzer Regiment 12:
Arrival of the *Abteilung* into the area of Conty. Quarters:

- command post of the *Abteilung* in Louilley
- *Stabs-* and *Versorgungskompanie* in Louilley
- the *7.Kompanie* in Wailly
- the *Ausbildungskompanie* with the remains of the *5., 6.* and *8.Kompanien* in Forsemanant[8]


## 29 August 1944
*I./SS-Panzer Regiment 12:*

| | |
|---|---|
| *12.SS-Panzer Division "Hitlerjugend"* | O.U., 10. 09. '44 |
| *I./SS-Panzer Regiment 12* | |

After Action Report of *Panzergruppe "Berlin"* within *Kampfgruppe "Milius"* of *SS-Panzer-Grenadier-Regiment 25*

The seven Panzer Vs that were newly arrived to the regiment on 29. 08. '44 were assigned to me with incomplete crews in the quarters of the regiment in Vervins; they were to be immediately deployed. In order to restore their operational condition I had to obtain seven gunners, five loaders and three radio operators from the *1.Kompanie*.

On 29. 08. '44 around 1900 hours I reported to *Obersturmbannführer* Milius[9] for briefing. The tanks were distributed so that three tanks were assigned to the *III./SS-Panzer-Grenadier-Regiment 26*, the remaining four tanks were deployed in the zone of the *I./SS-Panzer-Grenadier-Regiment 25* in Montcornet and in its surroundings for securing the crossroads. On the other hand, the tanks within the *III./SS-Panzer-Grenadier-Regiment 26* were to secure the roads around Rozoy. On 29. 08. there was no sign of the enemy in this area.

Enemy presence in the Rozoy sector was discovered first in the hours around noon on 30. 08. The enemy was coming from the south in the direction of the securing units with tanks and armoured personnel carriers. Later enemy presence also in the sector on the right, at Montcornet, where tank *Keils* (wedges) arrived from the direction of Laon, advancing towards Montcornet to reach Hirson.

The enemy drew artillery and reinforcements forward during the night in Montcornet. As ordered by the *Kampfgruppe* commander, we established new securing positions during the night on the advantageous terrain, on the hills north of Montcornet. The tanks were located behind these positions in the centre as interventional reserves. During the morning of 30. 08., following artillery preparation, the breakthrough was

---

8   The last appendix to the KTB of the *II./SS-Panzer Regiment 12*, numbered 19, which details the relocation to the area appointed for refitting, is reproduced as Appendix XVII in this book.

9   *Obersturmbannführer* Karl-Heinz Milius was commander of the *III./SS-Panzer-Grenadier-Regiment 25*, around this time also led the *Kampfgruppe* based on *SS-Panzer-Grenadier-Regiment 25*. He later commanded *SS-Panzer-Grenadier-Regiment 25* and ended the war as a *Standartenführer*. Milius died on 31 March 1990.

launched towards Magny [-la Campagne], east of Montcornet. The tanks located here immediately stopped the advance on the undulating terrain intersected by water-courses and covered the retreat of the Grenadiers. We knocked out a Sherman here and an armoured personnel carrier. We did not have any losses, despite the fighter–bomber attacks. The running gear of a tank was damaged by the bomb from an aircraft.

By order of the division the *Kampfgruppe* retreated in the face of constantly strengthening pressure into the newly prepared blocking position at Plomion, on the sector of the [La] Brune river. The tanks were again deployed in securing the partly blown up, partly closed crossings on the Brune. The tanks succeeded in preventing the enemy from making a swift approach to the Brune and the crossing of the river. However, during the night, we received orders from the division to retreat to the line Buire–Hirson south, because the enemy had outflanked the *Kampfgruppe* on the right frontline sector, via the uncovered flank near Vervins.

During the morning hours of 01. 09. '44 each unit of the *Panzergruppe* reached the newly assigned sector. We immediately established securing positions, because the enemy was advancing in our rear even during the retreat at night. One tank secured the Vervins–Hirson main road. Two other tanks secured the open field southeast of Buire, one tank stood in front of the bridge in La Hérie to seal the crossing which was impossible to blow up because of a shortage of explosives.

During this time, at *Gruppe "Olboeter"*[10] one Panzerkampfwagen IV, which was assigned to me on 30. 08., and one Panzerkampfwagen V were knocked out. The Panzerkampfwagen IV was knocked out from an advantageous position, from a distance of 25 metres, because this tank allowed three Shermans to approach it to within 50 metres, and at that moment the loading of its gun was impeded. The Panzerkampfwagen V was knocked out in a battle against superior forces (tanks and armoured personnel carriers), after having knocked out two Shermans itself. Both tank crews were saved, leaving behind one soldier that was killed (the radio operator of the Panzerkampfwagen IV). The enemy, who pushed into Origny [en-Thiérache] during the afternoon, was repulsed with a counterstroke. Because the left-hand sector was threatened with the possibility of being flanked, two Panzerkampfwagen Vs under command of *Untersturmführer* Walter Blank had to take over the securing of the open left flank at the eastern exit of Hirson.

In order to prevent another outflanking and encirclement an order was issued to establish new positions in the area of Trélon. However these were replaced on the same night to move further backwards, to the southern sector of Beaumont. With this order the Panzergruppe was assigned to *Kampfgruppe "Siebken"*[11], which was already preparing passage lines at Liessies, at the river Helpe. After having reported, during the night I was escorted into the positions to the commander of the *II./SS-Panzer-Grenadier-Regiment 26* and I was able to escort the tanks into their positions at dawn. Now two tanks were securing the roads leading to Liessies from the south and west, and the three remaining tanks, those that provided the combat ready reserve of the *Kampfgruppe*, were securing westwards from the direction of Avesnelles, remaining near the command post at Felléries.

We were not able to contain the enemy on the open right flank, so another outflanking movement occurred as the *5./SS-Panzer-Grenadier-Regiment 26*, with a Tiger tank

---

10  The *Kampfgruppe* based on the *III./SS-Panzer-Grenadier-Regiment 26*.
11  *Sturmbannführer* Bernhard Siebken was commander of the *II./SS-Panzer-Grenadier-Regiment 26*.

assigned to me, was encircled by the enemy. The pressure of the enemy towards Felléries became stronger and stronger, and the situation was threatened by the encirclement of the *6.* and *8./SS-Panzer-Grenadier-Regiment 26*, so I deployed the reserve tanks to cover the retreat of the *Kompanien*. During the night two Panzerkampfwagen Vs were sent to the *Kompanie* from the maintenance unit. During the fighting we knocked out four Shermans while two of our Panzerkampfwagen Vs were damaged due to hits.

After having carried out the retreat, the *Kampfgruppe* was withdrawn to the positions prepared by *SS-Panzer-Grenadier-Regiment 25*, south of Phillippeville. One Panzerkampfwagen V (that of *Untersturmführer* Blank) had to be sent to the repair station because of a defect of its gearbox, so only one tank remained operational. The last tank that remained with *Kampfgruppe "Olboeter"* had to be blown up on the Mons–Beaumont road while making an attempt to tow it away as, due to enemy fire damaging its running gear and engine, it was rendered immobile; otherwise it would have been captured by the enemy advancing after us.

On 04. 09. '44 around 1400 hours new orders arrived with the task of retreating towards Philippeville. Whilst driving into the third firing position, when the enemy was closing in on three sides of the village, the lateral countershaft and the gearbox of the tank of *Unterscharführer* Voigt broke down and it was rendered immobile. Due to the immediate advance of the enemy the tank had to be blown up on the orders of *Obersturmbannführer* Karl-Heinz Milius. After this the order for a retreat at once through the Maas arrived, because parts of the *II./SS-Panzer-Grenadier-Regiment 26* and the *I./SS-Panzer-Grenadier-Regiment 26* were already encircled.

During these combats we knocked out ten Shermans and one armoured personnel carrier altogether while suffering seven total losses.

Berlin
*Hauptsturmführer*

Part II

# The Combat History of
# *SS-Panzerjäger Abteilung 12*
# in Normandy

# 1

# Organization, Equipment and Training of *SS-Panzerjäger Abteilung 12* (6 February–9 July 1944)

The initial negotiations concerning the *SS Division* to be created from the young members of the National Socialist youth organization, the Hitlerjugend, commenced in February 1943 between the representatives of the *Waffen-SS* and the organization. Upon their joint recommendation, on 24 June Adolf Hitler issued an order for the division to be set up in the Beverloo training facility north of Brussels.

The officers and NCOs for the new unit were reassigned from its patron division the *1.SS-Panzer-Grenadier-Division "Leibstandarte"*; the enlisted men consisted mainly of German young men born in the first half of 1926, who had received military training. Later, 50 officers were also reassigned to the division from the Army, some of these officers having been members of the Hitlerjugend.

The main body of the unit was formed by the Panzergrenadier system, and was composed of the *I.SS-Panzer Korps* together with the *"Leibstandarte"*. Because Hitler wanted the *Korps* to consist of two armoured (Panzer) divisions, at the end of October 1943 they began the reorganization of the *Divisions "Hitlerjugend"* and *"Leibstandarte"* into armoured divisions. At the beginning of January 1944, *"Hitlerjugend"* consisted mainly of young soldiers who had only completed 18 weeks of training.

On 6 February 1944, by the order of *Oberstgruppenführer und General der Waffen-SS* Josef (Sepp) Dietrich, *SS-Panzerjäger Abteilung 1* of the *"Leibstandarte"* separated from the strength of its army and was reassigned to the *12.SS-Panzer Division "Hitlerjugend"*. The unit of three officers, 39 NCOs, 83 enlisted men and 13 Eastern non-combatant personnel, commanded by *Obersturmführer* Karl aus der Wiesche, was loaded in at Volochisk railway station. The next day the train departed from the Eastern Front. The *Abteilungsführer* of the new *Panzerjäger Abteilung, Sturmbannführer* Jakob Hanreich, remained for the time being at the *Division "Leibstandarte"*.

The road led via Tarnopol, Lemberg, Krakow, Liegnitz, Dresden, Leipzig, Frankfurt, Koblenz, Trier and Metz to Leopoldsburg. Before reaching its destination, the train crashed on 12 February 1944 between Spincourt and Arrency, due to which two soldiers were killed, and eight were wounded (four of them were transported to hospital in Verdun). 17 trucks of the consignment were irrevocably damaged. The train could only continue its journey on 15 February, after two days of repairs.

The train arrived at Leopoldsburg on 16 February and unloaded. Following this, the soldiers marched to reach their assigned quarters. The *Abteilungsstab* was located in Merhout, the *1.Kompanie* in Qostham, the *2.Kompanie* in Quadmecheln, and the *3.Kompanie* in Gestel.[1]

On 20 February, 110 trainees of the tank destroyer NCO training course in Hilversum were reassigned to *SS-Panzerjäger Abteilung 12*. The trainees had previously been stationed with *SS-Panzer-Aufklärungsabteilung 12* as a *Panzerjäger-Lehr-Kompanie*.

The strength of the *Abteilung* was increased considerably when 315 enlisted men from *SS-Panzer Regiment 12*, 23 enlisted men from *SS-Panzer-Pionier-Bataillon 12* and 100 enlisted men from each of the two *Panzer-Grenadier-Regimenter* of the division arrived.

The table of order and equipment of the fighting *Kompanien* of *SS-Panzerjäger Abteilung 12* was, at that time, planned according to the directive no. 1148/b. (K.St.N. 1148b).[2] This system indicated three *Kompanien*, each equipped with 14 Nashorn self-propelled heavy anti-tank guns.

However, for the time being, the unit did not have any combat vehicles. In order to commence training as quickly as possible, two men were sent to Olmütz on 20 February to bring along two Marder III tank destroyers equipped with 7.5cm anti-tank guns. The two vehicles arrived at the *Abteilung* on 2 March.[3]

On 29 March *Sturmbannführer* Hanreich returned with eight enlisted men from the Eastern Front and took over the command on 4 April from the deputy commander, *Hauptsturmführer* Hermann Tirschler, who became *Chef* of the *2.Kompanie*.

Meanwhile on 30 March an order was received to relocate *SS-Panzerjäger Abteilung 12* into the area of Nogent-le-Roi. The troops departed on 2 April at 0545 hours by train to reach their new station via Brussels, Amiens, Rouen and Vernon, arriving on 5 April, at 2230 hours.

The command post of the *Stab* of the *Abteilung* was placed in Coulombs, the quarters of the *Stabskompanie* was in Nogent-le-Roi. Quarters area of the *1.Kompanie* was Villiers-le-Morhier, that of the *2.Kompanie* was Chaudon, and that of the *3.Kompanie* was Villemeux [-sur-Eure].[4]

On 14 April the last consignment arrived from the Eastern Front together with parts of the *Stab* and most of the *3.Kompanie*.

However, at the beginning of May *SS-Panzerjäger Abteilung 12* had to send off 367 of its enlisted men to the *1.SS-Panzer-Division*. With this, the number of personnel of the *Abteilung* was less than the 516 stated in the table of order and equipment, and the *3.Kompanie* had to be reduced to the level of a *Kompanienstab*.

There were also changes in the order of battle of the *Abteilung*. Now the unit planned to be equipped with Jagdpanzer IVs and towed 7.5cm anti-tank guns instead of the previously planned tank destroyers. The *1.* and *2.Kompanien* and the *Abteilungsstab* waited for 10-10 Jagdpanzers. The *3.Kompanie* became the *Unterabteilung*, and was equipped with towed anti-tank guns.

1    Vojenský Historický Archiv, Praha (Military History Archives, Prague), Tätigkeitsbericht der *SS-Panzer-Jäger-Abteilung* 12 "HJ" ab 6. Februar 1944, p.1.
2    Vojenský Historický Archiv, Praha (Military History Archives, Prague), Tätigkeitsbericht der *SS-Panzer-Jäger-Abteilung* 12 "HJ" ab 6. Februar 1944, p.3.
3    Vojenský Historický Archiv, Praha (Military History Archives, Prague), Tätigkeitsbericht der *SS-Panzer-Jäger-Abteilung* 12 "HJ" ab 6. Februar 1944, p.4.
4    Vojenský Historický Archiv, Praha (Military History Archives, Prague), Tätigkeitsbericht der *SS-Panzer-Jäger-Abteilung* 12 "HJ" ab 6. Februar 1944, p.6.

The strength of each of the Jagdpanzer *Kompanien* consisted of 3 officers, 44 NCOs and 72 enlisted men. Apart from the vehicles their armament consisted of 29 pistols, 59 rifles, 31 sub-machine guns and 2 machine guns. Each *Kompanie* was equipped with 26 vehicles and four motorcycles with sidecars.[5]

The prototype of the Jagdpanzer IV was finished in December 1943 in the assembly halls of the Vomag (Vogtländische Maschinen-Fabrik AG).

At the beginning of the standardized production, a 7.5cm PaK 39 gun with L/48 calibre barrel was built into the Jagdpanzer. Traverse ability of the gun was 20°, its elevation was -5° + 15°. 79 shells could be loaded for the primary weapon; its armament, besides the 7.5cm gun consisted of two 7.92 machine guns (with 600 rounds of ammunition altogether).

The weight of the vehicle was 24 tons with gun mantlet armour of 80mm thickness, 60mm sloped glacis plate armour and 30mm sloped side armour. The Jagdpanzer was able to move with a maximum speed of 40 km/h on road, meaning its operational range was 210 km.

The crew of a Jagdpanzer consisted of four men (commander, gunner, loader, and driver).

There were 769 Jagdpanzer IVs built between January and November 1944 along with 26 armoured recovery vehicle versions.[6]

The first Jagdpanzer IVs were sent to the *Panzerjäger Abteilung* of the *Panzer-Lehr-Division* in March 1944, and were deployed during the occupation of Hungary. However, the first real combat in which this type was deployed occurred in Italy, within the ranks of the *Panzer Division "Hermann Göring"*.

The first 10 Jagdpanzer IVs, assigned to *SS-Panzerjäger Abteilung 12* on 26 April 1944, arrived on 24 May, after four weeks of transport to the train station of Nogent-le-Roi. At that time, there were no muzzle-brakes on the guns and the Jagdpanzers were handed over without spare parts. One of the vehicles departing for the quarters area had its brake-system fail after unloading. It was repaired by *SS-Panzer Regiment 12* and took them three days.

Five of the ten Jagdpanzer were given to the *1.Kompanie* and five to the *2.Kompanie*. Because the division command ordered shooting practice to be held, special training was delayed.

There were also engineering problems with the new Jagdpanzer. On 3 June the Jagdpanzer IVs used for training the drivers were showing signs of constructional failures, as after having travelled 300 km it was impossible to change to third gear. This problem was, however, fixed by the *Panzerjäger Abteilung* workshop platoon.

One day later an *Unterscharführer* was sent to Plauen, to the Vomag factory manufacturing the Jagdpanzer, in order to bring equipment[7] necessary for modification of the vehicles.

At dawn on 6 June, at 0245 hours, *SS-Panzerjäger Abteilung 12* was informed by the division that from midnight on considerable airborne activity was going on in the

---

5    See K.St.N. 1149 (1.2.1944)

6    Peter Chamberlain and Hilary Doyle, *Encyclopedia of German Tanks of World War Two*, London: Arms & Armour Press, 1999[2] pp.102–103.

7    Vojenský Historický Archiv, Praha (Military History Archives, Prague), Tätigkeitsbericht der *SS-Panzer-Jäger-Abteilung 12 "HJ"* ab 6. Februar 1944, p.10.

sector of the *711.Infanterie Division*. At the same time alarms were raised and march alert was ordered for all units of the *12. SS-Panzer Division*. The Allied forces had launched Operation "Overlord".

At 1300 hours in the afternoon the *12.SS-Panzer Division* departed to its appointed deployment sector without, however, *SS-Panzerjäger Abteilung 12*, *SS-Werfer Abteilung 12* and *SS-Panzer-Feld-Ersatz-Bataillon 12*. These three units remained in their previous sectors and were securing there.[8]

While the division was engaged in heavy fighting around Caen, the *Panzerjäger Abteilung* resumed its training for the now inescapable deployment.

On 9 June the Jagdpanzers of the *2.Kompanie* (its new *Kompanie Chef* was *Obersturmführer* Johann Wachter) trained with tank guns and machine guns. The tank guns were not in operational condition, due to, after examination, to construction problems of the sighting optics or the improper adjustment of the guns.

The two Marder III tank destroyers that remained in the strength of the *Abteilung* were to be directed to the divisional command post on 16 June. En route, the two vehicles became out of order due to constructional problems, so two days later they returned to the unit. The workshop platoon repaired them; however, one of the two tank destroyers departing on 19 June was again rendered immobile.[9]

On 20 June the division ordered that *SS-Panzerjäger Abteilung 12* was to prepare one of its *Kompanien* for deployment and dispatch it to the fighting units. The commander of the *Abteilung*, *Sturmbannführer* Hans-Jakob Hanreich appointed the *1.Kompanie* for this task; at the same time, he ordered that shooting practice would be held for all Jagdpanzers on 22 June.

On 21 June ten men from the unit departed for Breslau to bring along the Jagdpanzer IVs assigned for the unit. Three men were sent to Magdeburg in order to take over an armoured recovery tank (Berge-Panzer).[10]

On 22 June the missing 11 Jagdpanzer IVs (from the 21 stated in the table of organization and equipment) were allocated at last to the *Abteilung*.[11]

The same day, the shooting practice for the vehicles was started again at 0930 hours. The Jagdpanzers were defective with high explosive shells, but they were excellent at shooting with armour-piercing shells.

The guns were still not equipped with muzzle-brakes. Officers of the *Panzerjäger Abteilung* were travelling in France to and fro to find these muzzle-brakes, and the necessary number of vehicles, fuel, ammunition and supplies for the coming deployment. So far they had not had much success. It was a comfort, though only small, that on 23 June the unit was informed that the equipment necessary for modifications to the Jagdpanzer IVs was at the *Panzerjäger Abteilung* of the *2.Panzer Division* in Bremoy.

In the evening of 26 June, the only Marder III tank destroyer (commander: *Unterscharführer* Elsässer) of the *Panzerjäger Abteilung* already at the frontline as reserve at the *Divisionsstab*, received orders to report to the *15./SS-Panzer-Grenadier-Regiment*

---

8   Vojenský Historický Archiv, Praha (Military History Archives, Prague), Tätigkeitsbericht der *SS-Panzer-Jäger-Abteilung 12 "HJ"* ab 6. Februar 1944, p.10.

9   Vojenský Historický Archiv, Praha (Military History Archives, Prague), Tätigkeitsbericht der *SS-Panzer-Jäger-Abteilung 12 "HJ"* ab 6. Februar 1944, p.11.

10  Vojenský Historický Archiv, Praha (Military History Archives, Prague), Tätigkeitsbericht der *SS-Panzer-Jäger-Abteilung 12 "HJ"* ab 6. Februar 1944, p.12.

11  Nevenkin, p.905.

25. However, the tank destroyer did not find the *Kompanie* because it had withdrawn in the meantime.

Thus the lone Marder III received new orders. Now it had to report to the *9./SS-Panzer Regiment 12*. The tank destroyer found the *Kompanie*, the right flank of which it was to secure. However, due to another engine failure it was again rendered immobile. The armoured *Kompanie* retreated because of the extremely heavy Allied artillery fire. The crew of the Marder had to follow them on foot. The Marder was eventually towed by a Panzer IV tank on 29 June to *SS-Panzerjäger Abteilung 12* to which the Marder was to be handed over as ordered by the division. The crew, apart from the missing driver, went back to *SS-Panzerjäger Abteilung 12*.

On 2 July the other Marder III, which had also been stationed as reserve at the divisional command post, was also reassigned to *SS-Panzer-Aufklärungs-Abteilung 12*, then its crew returned to their original unit.[12]

From 1030 hours on 6 July the *1./SS-Panzerjäger Abteilung 12* (*Kompanie Chef*: *Obersturmführer* Georg Hurdelbrink) was appointed for deployment again, and carried out shooting practice with six Jagdpanzer IVs. During the practice 30 high explosive shells were fired. The results were satisfactory as the guns were properly adjusted and the muzzle-brakes had also arrived at last.

At 2330 hours the orders of the division arrived, according to which the *1.Kompanie* was to go to the frontline.

During the morning of 1 July *Sturmbannführer* Hans-Jakob Hanreich discussed the details of departure and march with the *Kompanie Chef* of the *1.Kompanie*. The *Kompanie* could only move at night, or during the day when the sky was cloudy, this way reducing the possibility of meeting Allied fighter–bomber aircraft. The *Kompanie*'s first intermediary aim to reach was Acon on the Dreux–Verneuil road. Large distances were to be maintained between the Jagdpanzers in order to prevent concentration of the vehicles during an air raid.

The column, consisting of eight Jagdpanzer IVs and one fuel truck of the *1./SS-Panzerjäger Abteilung 12*, departed at 1500 hours towards the frontline.[13]

The next day four Jagdpanzers had already reached Acon, but three were stuck on the road because of minor failures. The eighth tank destroyer had to go to the workshop platoon.

On 9 July a Jagdpanzer IV (commander: *Untersturmführer* Helmut Zeiner) became out of order again. In the evening *Sturmbannführer* Hanreich followed the *1.Kompanie*, which he found after midnight, 4 km northwest of Falaise.[14]

12   Vojenský Historický Archiv, Praha (Military History Archives, Prague), Tätigkeitsbericht der SS-Panzer-Jäger-Abteilung 12 "HJ" ab 6. Februar 1944, pp.16–17.
13   Vojenský Historický Archiv, Praha (Military History Archives, Prague), Tätigkeitsbericht der SS-Panzer-Jäger-Abteilung 12 "HJ" ab 6. Februar 1944, p.18.
14   Vojenský Historický Archiv, Praha (Military History Archives, Prague), Tätigkeitsbericht der SS-Panzer-Jäger-Abteilung 12 "HJ" ab 6. Februar 1944, p.19.

# 2

# Combat of *SS-Panzerjäger Abteilung 12* in the Battle for Normandy, 10 July–26 August 1944

On 10 July the *Kompanie Chef* of the *1.Kompanie* received his mission at the command post of the *12.SS-Panzer Division "Hitlerjugend"* at Garcelles-Secqueville: his unit was subordinated to *SS-Panzer-Grenadier-Regiment 25* with his seven operational Jagdpanzer IVs, and was to secure the area of Ifs from the north. Until dark the Jagdpanzers occupied positions in the appointed area.[1]

However, the next day a new order was received. The *1.Kompanie* was withdrawn from the Ifs area and was directed to Conteville. It was only possible to carry out the relocation in the evening.[2]

On 12 July *SS-Panzerjäger Abteilung 12* – which was subordinated to *SS-Panzer Regiment 12* – received the news that another 11 Jagdpanzer IVs had arrived for them at Versailles. The Jagdpanzers were transported by train and were unloaded.

That day 5 officers and 50 SS soldiers were called out to Dreux where they had to force reluctant French civilians to work.[3]

On 13 July nine Jagdpanzers reached the *2.Kompanie* which had been, in the meantime, relocated to Villiers-le-Morhier. Two further vehicles became immobile on the way to the *2.Kompanie,* but they reached the quarters area on that day. These Jagdpanzers were already equipped with camouflage devices.

One day later, on 14 July, around 1300 hours one of the trucks of the *Abteilung* was attacked in Laroiullie by French the resistance. One SS soldier was killed by a headshot, another was wounded.[4]

On 17 July the *1.Kompanie* was stationed in the area of Renémesnil, 12 km south of Conteville. Its eight Jagdpanzers were operational, one further Jagdpanzer IV received a new engine. The *Divisionsstab* wanted to send a further Jagdpanzer to the *Kompanie* from the *Abteilung*, to backfill the unit to its full strength.[5]

The *1.Kompanie* was soon engaged by the Allied forces when on 19 July at Frénouville, as in-depth anti-tank reserve of the defence, a Jagdpanzer IV knocked out

---

1   Vojenský Historický Archiv, Praha (Military History Archives, Prague), KTB Nr. 1 der *SS-Panzer-Jäger-Abteilung 12*, 10. 7. 1944.

2   Vojenský Historický Archiv, Praha (Military History Archives, Prague), KTB Nr. 1 der *SS-Panzer-Jäger-Abteilung 12*, 11. 7. 1944.

3   Vojenský Historický Archiv, Praha (Military History Archives, Prague), KTB Nr. 1 der *SS-Panzer-Jäger-Abteilung 12*, 12. 7. 1944.

4   Vojenský Historický Archiv, Praha (Military History Archives, Prague), KTB Nr. 1 der *SS-Panzer-Jäger-Abteilung 12*, 14. 7. 1944.

5   Vojenský Historický Archiv, Praha (Military History Archives, Prague), KTB Nr. 1 der *SS-Panzer-Jäger-Abteilung 12*, 18. 7. 1944.

the first enemy tank in the history of *SS-Panzerjäger Abteilung 12*. The knocked out tank was presumably a Sherman of the British Guards Armoured Division.[6]

On 20 July a Jagdpanzer (its commander was *Oberscharführer* Kußmaul) was rendered immobile due to engine failure 6 km west of Dreux. The vehicle was repaired on the spot.[7]

On 21 July six 7.5cm Pak 40 towed anti-tank guns were allocated from the division to the *3.Kompanie*; they were towed with Maultier half-track trucks.

In the meantime the *1.Kompanie* was again relocated; this time it was stationed in the area of Mézidon, southeast of Caen. All of its eight Jagdpanzer IVs were operational. That day the *Kompanie* knocked out a further Allied tank and two trucks at Frénouville, which was occupied by the British Guards Armoured Division.

After 1900 hours in the evening two repaired Jagdpanzers (their commanders were *Oberscharführer* Kußmaul and *Unterscharführer* Pusch) departed to reach the *1.Kompanie*.[8]

On 22 July it was noted in the war diary of the unit that the written order for the reorganization of *SS-Panzerjäger Abteilung 12* according to the 1944-type battle order was ready.

On 23 July at 2100 hours part of the *3.Kompanie* (*Hauptsturmführer* Günther Wöst) departed to the frontline with Maultier vehicles – although without its allocated anti-tank guns.[9]

The next day, on 24 July, the *1.Kompanie* reported again from a new station in Vimont on the Caen–Lisieux road, 14 km southeast of Caen, that nine out of its ten Jagdpanzers were operational, and one was towed to the workshop *Kompanie* of *SS-Panzer Regiment 12* because of engine problems.

At dawn on 27 July the *1.Generalstabsoffizier* of the *12.SS-Panzer Division*, *Sturmbannführer* Hubert Meyer, informed the *Panzerjäger Abteilung* by a liaison officer that he wanted the *2.Kompanie,* still in training, to be operational in three days. That morning a truckload of spare parts for the Jagdpanzer IVs arrived from Breslau, and the chance of deployment of the *2.Kompanie* was increased.[10]

The *3.Kompanie* took over its anti-tank guns in Nécy, then, from midnight the next day, began to establish anti-tank positions between Argences and Moult.[11]

On the evening of 29 July there were 12 operational Jagdpanzer IVs in *SS-Panzerjäger Abteilung 12*.[12]

---

6  See Reynolds, p.214.

7  Vojenský Historický Archiv, Praha (Military History Archives, Prague), KTB Nr. 1 der *SS-Panzer-Jäger-Abteilung* 12, 20. 7. 1944.

8  Vojenský Historický Archiv, Praha (Military History Archives, Prague), KTB Nr. 1 der *SS-Panzer-Jäger-Abteilung* 12, 21. 7. 1944.

9  Vojenský Historický Archiv, Praha (Military History Archives, Prague), KTB Nr. 1 der *SS-Panzer-Jäger-Abteilung* 12, 23. 7. 1944.

10 Vojenský Historický Archiv, Praha (Military History Archives, Prague), KTB Nr. 1 der *SS-Panzer-Jäger-Abteilung* 12, 27. 7. 1944.

11 Vojenský Historický Archiv, Praha (Military History Archives, Prague), Anlagen zum KTB der *SS-Panzer-Jäger-Abteilung* 12 *"Hitlerjugend"*, Gefechtsberichte von Teilen der *3./SS-Pz.Jäg.Abt. 12 "HJ"*.

12 According to the daily report of the German *Panzergruppe "West"* (later *Panzerarmee 5*) from 29 July 1944.

Combat actions of the Jagdpanzer IVs from 2.*Kompanie/SS-Panzerjäger-Abteilung 12* in the region of Garcelles-Secqueville, 7-8 August 1944.

On 1 and 2 August the *Stab* of *SS-Panzerjäger Abteilung 12*, the *2.Kompanie,* and the important units of its *Versorgungskompanie* departed to the frontline. The *2.Kompanie* was given the task of replacing the armoured *Kompanie* fighting in the main battle line subordinated to *Kampfgruppe "Schrott"* (the *II./SS-Panzer-Grenadier-Regiment 25*) on the night of 4 August. During that night, the command post of the *Abteilung* had to be relocated to the northern outskirts of Beneauville.[13]

However, on 4 August all of the previously mentioned events were over. According to the new order *SS-Panzerjäger Abteilung 12* was to be quartered in the villages of Maizières and Rouvres, and the command post was to be set in Gauvigny. In the afternoon the *1.Kompanie* was instructed to come to this new quarters area (it arrived here the next morning). The *3.Kompanie*, equipped with anti-tank guns, was in Escures around that time.[14]

On 5 August the *2.Kompanie* was to be prepared for movement by order of the division. *Obersturmführer* Wachter's Jagdpanzers departed at midnight towards their new attack positions which were located northeast of Garcelles-Secqueville.

The *Kompanie* (with 6 operational Jagdpanzer IVs of the nine on its strength) reached the designated positions on 6 August at 0530 hours. However, *SS-Panzerjäger Abteilung 12* and the *Stab* of the *12.SS-Panzer Division* did not know the whereabouts of the *Kompanie* from midnight for 13½ hours because communications were temporarily severed.[15]

Until 0630 hours on the morning of 6 August the *2./SS-Panzerjäger Abteilung 12* held defensive positions in the north-eastern and north-western perimetres of Garcelles-Secqueville and established communication with *Hauptmann* Körner's *Grenadier Bataillon*[16]. Not long after 2300 hours a new order arrived from the *12.SS-Panzer Division*, according to which all units were to be prepared for relocation on the same night.[17]

The above-mentioned relocation was carried out on 7 August. The *Abteilungsstab* regrouped into Le-Hamel, the *1.* and *3.Kompanien* to the area of Villiers-le-Morhier. Apart from heavy artillery fire no other activity was experienced by the *Abteilung*.[18]

However, at 2200 hours the same day the heavy bombers of the Allied air forces carried out a 2½ hour-long carpet-bombing attack in the area of the positions of the *2.Kompanie* at Garcelles-Secqueville, and that was followed by heavy artillery fire.

Then on 8 August *SS-Panzerjäger Abteilung 12* found themselves in the middle of the fighting in Normandy. At 0130 hours Allied tanks set off towards Garcelles-Secqueville. The Jagdpanzer IVs of the *2./SS-Panzerjäger Abteilung 12* engaged them and knocked

---

13  The *Kampfgruppe* (and the *II.Bataillon*) were commanded by *Hauptsturmführer* Karl-Heinz Schrott who was killed on 2 September 1944. Vojenský Historický Archiv, Praha (Military History Archives, Prague), KTB Nr. 1 der *SS-Panzer-Jäger-Abteilung 12*, 3. 8. 1944.

14  Vojenský Historický Archiv, Praha (Military History Archives, Prague), KTB Nr. 1 der *SS-Panzer-Jäger-Abteilung 12*, 4. 8. 1944.

15  Vojenský Historický Archiv, Praha (Military History Archives, Prague), KTB Nr. 1 der *SS-Panzer-Jäger-Abteilung 12*, 5. 8. 1944.

16  This could be a *bataillon* of *Grenadier-Regiment 1055/89. Infanteriedivision* of the *Army*.

17  Vojenský Historický Archiv, Praha (Military History Archives, Prague), KTB Nr. 1 der *SS-Panzer-Jäger-Abteilung 12*, 6. 8. 1944.

18  Vojenský Historický Archiv, Praha (Military History Archives, Prague), KTB Nr. 1 der *SS-Panzer-Jäger-Abteilung 12*, 7. 8. 1944.

out nine Sherman tanks[19] while it was still dark. Despite this the Germans were not able to repulse the tank attack at night.

The battle continued until around noon on 8 August, when the encircled Jagdpanzer *Kompanie* managed to break out. The *2.Kompanie* reported at 1110 hours that until then altogether three of its Jagdpanzers had been knocked out, and these were irreparably damaged. The weary tank destroyers were gathering in Vieux-Pont.

At 0500 hours the *1.Generalstabsoffizier* of the division ordered the commander of *SS-Panzerjäger Abteilung 12* to immediately despatch the 10 Jagdpanzer IVs of the *1.Kompanie* to Garcelles-Secqueville, the anti-tank guns of the *3.Kompanie* were to depart for Hautmesnil.

The *1.Kompanie* was assembled at 0600 hours and after briefing was directed to Cintheaux from the area of St. Pierre–Potigny. The commander of the *89.Infanterie Division* had himself appointed the positions for the Jagdpanzers right of the Falaise–Caen highway.

At 0900 hours in the morning the *1.Kompanie* reported to *SS-Panzerjäger Abteilung 12* that it had established positions in Cintheaux from the crossroads to Hill 103.

The Jagdpanzers were previously subordinated directly to the *Begleitkompanie* of the *12.SS-Panzer Division*, which itself was subordinated to the *I./SS-Panzer-Grenadier-Regiment 25* (*Sturmbannführer* Hans Waldmüller). Their task originally was to advance via Estrées-la-Campagne and occupy the hill west of St. Sylvain.[20]

However, in the meantime the mission was changed. At 1130 hours the *1./SS-Panzerjäger Abteilung 12* was subordinated to *Sturmbannführer* Karl-Heinz Prinz, *Kampfgruppe "Prinz"*[21] under the command of the *II./SS-Panzer Regiment 12* equipped with Panzer IV tanks, and received the mission of advancing together with the tanks to occupy St. Aignan-de-Cramesnil and Garcelles-Secqueville. The main objective of the attack was to occupy Tilly-la-Campagne.

The Allied B–17 heavy bombers had been carpet-bombing the area when the German *Panzergruppe* commenced its attack at 1150 hours.

The *1./SS-Panzerjäger Abteilung 12* flanked the Le Mesnil-Robert farmstead from the right, then advancing fast, entering St. Aignan-de-Cramesnil village from the east. The Jagdpanzers reported having knocked out six Allied Sherman tanks. These were presumably tanks of C Squadron of the battalion–sized 1st Northamptonshire Yeomanry armoured unit from the British 33rd Armoured Brigade, equipped with Sherman tanks. According to the war diary of the British tank battalion the total loss for that day was 20 armoured fighting vehicles and 63 soldiers (the battalion commander was also wounded).[22]

---

19  These were presumably the tanks of the British 33rd Armoured Brigade. The battalion-size 1st Northamptonshire Yeomanry of the Brigade lost four Shermans from its complement of 59 tanks (of this 59, 12 were Fireflies) during the night engagement. Three were knocked out by the four Jagdpanzer IVs of the *2./SS-Panzerjäger Abteilung 12*, and one was destroyed by the German infantry with a Panzerfaust. In this engagement the Firefly tank named "8 Balaclava" fighting in 2nd Troop/A Squadron of the British unit destroyed two German Jagdpanzers. See also S.A. Hart, pp.58 and 72.

20  Meyer, p.302.

21  *Kampfgruppe "Prinz"* remained subordinated to *Kampfgruppe "Waldmüller"*.

22  See Reynolds, p.278. A Firefly tank from 3rd Troop/A Squadron of this British unit had knocked out three Tigers of *schwere SS-Panzer Abteilung 101* not long before.

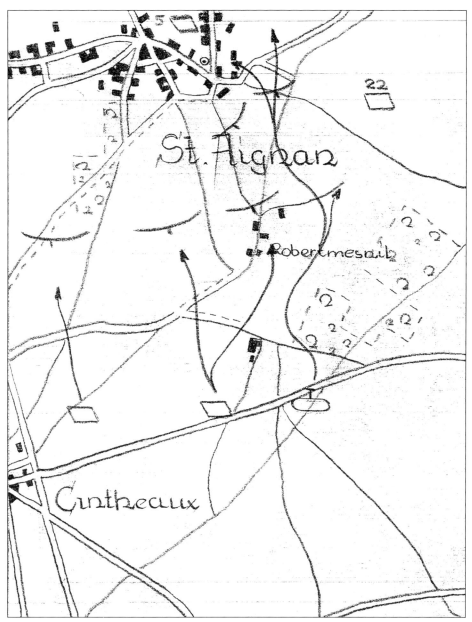

Combat actions of the 1.*Kompanie/SS-Panzerjäger-Abteilung 12*
near St. Aignan-de-Cramesnil, 8 August 1944.

Knight's Cross holder Rudolf Roy (see Appendix XVIII and main text). (Mark C. Yerger)

Not long after this the soldiers of the *1./SS-Panzerjäger Abteilung 12* discovered a group of enemy tanks (approximately 22) 1.5 km east of the village. The German Jagdpanzers engaged them from the nearby hill and from an area lower down, and soon reported to have destroyed 18 tanks. The remaining Allied tanks retreated quickly. These were presumably Polish tanks from the 2nd Armoured Regiment/1st Armoured Division. According to the war diary of the Polish Division the 2nd Armoured Regiment had been engaged by heavy fire at 1425 hours 2 km southeast of St. Aignan-de-Cramesnil.[23]

Two Jagdpanzer IVs of the *1.Kompanie* (commanded by the *Kompanie Chef*, *Obersturmführer* Georg Hurdelbrink and *Oberscharführer* Rudolf Roy (*Zugführer* of one of the platoons) advanced further through village. At the northern perimeter of the village Hurdelbrink knocked out a further five tanks, an armoured reconnaissance vehicle and two prime movers. Presumably these were also elements of the Polish 1st Armoured Division.[24]

The two SS Jagdpanzer held the northern perimetres of St. Aignan-de-Cramesnil until 2200 hours. The attacking Jagdpanzers were not supported by the infantry at all.

The Tiger and Panzer IV tanks attacking left of the *1./SS-Panzerjäger Abteilung 12* could not enter the village of St. Aignan-de-Cramesnil during the day due to heavy resistance from Allied forces. Because of this, the Jagdpanzers on their left received heavy

---

23  Reynolds, p.278.
24  The Polish 1st Armoured Division lost 40 tanks in just 15 minutes. See also Krzysztof Barbarski, *Polish Amour, 1939–1945*, London: Osprey, 1982, p.17 and S.A. Hart, p.75. Seven of the 40 Polish tanks knocked out were destroyed by the three Tigers of *schwere SS-Panzer Abteilung 101* east of St. Aignan-de-Cramesnil. See Schneider, *Tiger im Kampf,* Band II, p.273.

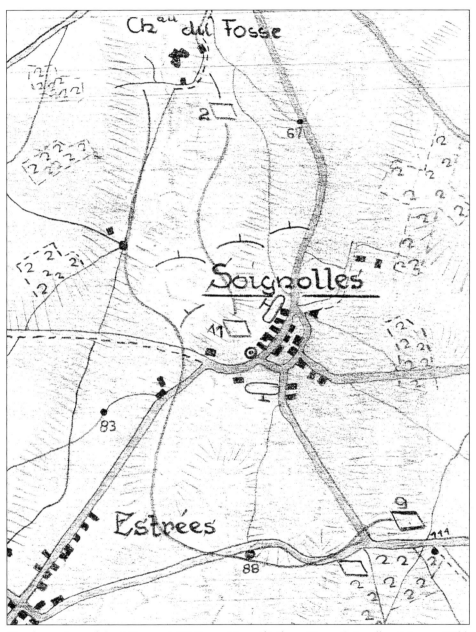

Combat actions of the *1.Kompanie/SS-Panzerjäger-Abteilung 12* near Soignolles, 9 August 1944.

Knight's Cross holder Fritz Eckstein (see Appendix XVIII). (Mark C. Yerger)

flanking fire from anti-tank guns and infantry weapons. There were also Allied tanks in the village. One of them knocked out one of the Jagdpanzer IVs of the *1.Kompanie*. At last, the *Kompanie*, together with the soldiers of the *I./SS-Panzer-Grenadier-Regiment 25*, brought their wounded and their vehicles out and withdrew to Soignolles.

The *1./SS-Panzerjäger Abteilung 12* knocked out 29 (mostly Polish) tanks, two prime movers, three trucks and one armoured reconnaissance vehicle altogether on that day. According to the reports, the gunner of Hurdelbrink's Jagdpanzer scored 11, Roy's eight[25], and *Untersturmführer* Theo Rabe's six of the total.[26] Losses of the *Kompanie* were, besides the knocked out Jagdpanzer IVs, three killed and 12 wounded.

The *3.Kompanie* occupied firing positions at 0900 hours in Hautmesnil, left of the Caen–Falaise highway, with projections towards the northeast, east and northwest.

The *Kompanie*, strengthened with two more anti-tank guns from *SS-Panzer-Aufklärungsabteilung 12*, was attacked in its anti-tank securing positions between 1230 hours and 1415 hours by approximately 300 Allied bomber aircraft that were attacking Daville and the German artillery and anti-aircraft positions in the area.

The *Kompanie* lost four killed and one wounded. Two anti-tank guns were damaged due to artillery hits; they had to be blown up. Two Maultiers were destroyed, two more were damaged.

---

25  In Roy's Jagdpanzer IV the gunner was *Rottenführer* Fritz Eckstein, who was awarded the Knight's Cross 1st Class for knocking out these eight tanks.

26  Vojenský Historický Archiv, Praha (Military History Archives, Prague), Anlagen zum KTB der *SS-Panzer-Jäger-Abteilung* 12 *"Hitlerjugend"*, Gefechtsbericht für 8. 8. 1944/1. *(schw.)/SS-Pz.Jäg.Abt.* 12 *"HJ"*.

Because of the loss of the half-track prime movers it was impossible to move the other anti-tank guns. The crews wanted to tow the guns from the positions at Cintheaux to Urville with borrowed armoured personnel carriers. At 2000 hours in the evening, two of the five remaining anti-tank guns were assigned to the *Begleitkompanie* of the *12.SS-Panzer Division* and two to the *Begleitkompanie* of the *I.SS-Panzer Korps*; the last one was directed on the next day to the *Versorgungskompanie* of *SS-Panzerjäger Abteilung 12*.[27]

On 9 August, around 0530 hours, the *1.Kompanie* – subordinated to the *I./SS-Panzer-Grenadier-Regiment 25* – inspected the hills south of Renémesnil in order to be able to appoint firing positions.

When the *SS-Panzergrenadiers* also moved off towards their appointed positions, they were attacked by the Sherman tanks of the Polish 1st Armoured Division. Some attacking tanks were destroyed by the infantry with close-combat anti-tank weapons; soon the Jagdpanzers of the *1./SS-Panzerjäger Abteilung 12* joined the fight.

It was already developing when nine Cromwell tanks of the 10th Armoured Reconnaissance Regiment (10th Mounted Rifles, Polish *10 Pulk Strzelcow Konnych*) got around the *I./SS-Panzer-Grenadier-Regiment 25* on the Maizières–Estrées-la-Campagne highway, cutting the supply lines of the unit with this manoeuvre. The gunner of *Oberscharführer* Roy's Jagdpanzer, *Rottenführer* Eckstein, destroyed all of these vehicles in a short time around Hill 111, thus allowing the re-supply of the Bataillon.

During the day heavy artillery, mortar and infantry fire on the German positions. The *I./SS-Panzer-Grenadier-Regiment 25* scheduled its retreat at 2200 hours, though the *1./SS-Panzerjäger Abteilung 12* ahd already began to withdraw at 2130 hours in the face of constantly increasing Allied fire.

In the middle of the disengagement manoeuvre the Sherman tanks of the Polish 1st Armoured Regiment[28] suddenly attacked the village of Soignolles. The Jagdpanzers of Hurdelbrink and Roy securing on the outskirts of the village took them in the flank and, apart from two, destroyed all of the enemy tanks. *Rottenführer* Fritz Eckstein, the gunner of Roy, again knocked out four tanks in this engagement.

After having smashed the Allied tank attacks, the SS Panzergrenadiers were able to continue their retreat because the enemy tanks did not advance further.

Soignolles was vacated around 2230 hours by the *1./SS-Panzerjäger Abteilung 12* who were acting as rearguard, and moved to Maizières during the night. That day the *Kompanie* knocked out 22 Polish Sherman and Cromwell tanks altogether. Of this number, Roy's Jagdpanzer IVs destroyed 13, Hurdelbrink's destroyed six tanks.[29] The armourer of the *1.Kompanie*, *Unterscharführer* Ortlep, knocked out two, and *Untersturmführer* Helmut Zeiner – a *Zugführer* from one of the platoons in the *Kompanie* – knocked out one tank.[30]

---

27  Vojenský Historický Archiv, Praha (Military History Archives, Prague), KTB Nr. 1 der *SS-Panzer-Jäger-Abteilung 12*, 8. 8. 1944, and Anlagen zum KTB der *SS-Panzer-Jäger-Abteilung 12 "Hitlerjugend"*, Gefechtsberichte von Teilen der *3./SS-Pz.Jäg.Abt. 12 "HJ"*.

28  Battalion-sized tank unit.

29  Vojenský Historický Archiv, Praha (Military History Archives, Prague), Anlagen zum KTB der *SS-Panzer-Jäger-Abteilung 12 "Hitlerjugend"*, Gefechtsbericht für 9. 8. 1944/1. *(schw.)/SS-Pz.Jäg.Abt. 12 "HJ"*. The war diary of the Polish 1st Armoured Division affirms the loss of the 22 tanks. See Reynolds, p.284 and note 38 on p.291. See also Appendix XVIII.

30  Meyer, pp.315–316. Meyer cites *Sturmführer* Walter Gömann in his work, who stated in 1974 that the victories at Ortlep took place on 10 August. According to the After-Action Report of the *1.Kompanie*

Two of the towed anti-tank guns of the *3./SS-Panzerjäger Abteilung 12* were in infantry positions on 9 August, together with the *Begleitkompanie* of the *I.SS-Panzer Korps* in Château du Fosse, two other guns were subordinated to the *Begleitkompanie* of the *12.SS-Panzer Division* between Château du Fosse and Soignolles. The two 7.5cm anti-tank guns of the *3.Kompanie* assigned to the *Begleitkompanie* of the *12.SS-Panzer Division* knocked out at least three tanks.[31]

At 1400 hours in the afternoon the positions of the *Kompanie* were attacked by Polish tanks and their supporting infantry. After half an hour, the tanks broke through the defence of the *I./SS-Panzer-Grenadier-Regiment 25* and its whole left flank was eliminated. The above mentioned tank battle was raging around the anti-tank gun positions. Around 1500 hours the Canadian tanks reached Château du Fosse. One gun was rendered disabled due to a high explosive shell hit, another was lost due to a direct hit. A third gun was blown away together with its Maultier prime mover after 1700 hours during the ordered retreat towards Rouvres. During the fighting on 8 and 9 August the *Kompanie* lost altogether five killed, six wounded and six missing.[32]

In the morning hours of 10 August, the *1./SS-Panzerjäger Abteilung 12* moved from Maizières via Potigny and Fontaine-le-Pin towards Hill 195, because enemy tanks were reported in that area. Reaching the crossroads 1.5 km north of Fontaine-le-Pin the *Kompanie* could not occupy its securing positions on the Hill northwards as ordered, because they saw Allied tanks there (presumably two tank squadrons of the battalion-sized Canadian 22nd Armoured Regiment (Canadian Grenadier Guards) and the forces of the 10th Infantry Brigade who were holding the Hill with 17-pounder and 6-pounder anti-tank guns).[33]

At 1130 hours the *1.Kompanie* subordinated to *SS-Panzer Regiment 12* was visited by *Obersturmbannführer* Max Wünsche, its commander, and who ordered Hill 195 to be immediately attacked.

The attack was carried out from 1155 hours by *Obersturmführer* Hurdelbrink's *1./SS-Panzerjäger Abteilung 12*, which was strengthened by a remote-controlled armoured *Kompanie*[34] (six Sturmgeschütz III assault guns and six B IV remote-controlled armoured demolition vehicles[35]).

The remote-controlled vehicles were at the spearhead of the battle order, behind them, on the left flank the assault guns, and the Jagdpanzers on the right flank.

The Germans reached the first hedgerow without the enemy firing at them. However the Jagdpanzers exploited the situation and from here knocked out three Shermans. At this the Allied artillery opened such a strong covering fire that any further frontal attack became impossible.

---

it was already fighting elsewhere on 10 August. Zeiner later became *Kompanie Chef* of the *1./SS-Panzerjäger Abteilung 12*.

31  Meyer, p.312.

32  Vojenský Historický Archiv, Praha (Military History Archives, Prague), Anlagen zum KTB der *SS-Panzer-Jäger-Abteilung* 12 *"Hitlerjugend"*, Gefechtsberichte von Teilen der *3./SS-Pz.Jäg.Abt. 12 "HJ"*.

33  See Reynolds, p.286.

34  Presumably the *4.Kompanie*/(remote-controlled) *Panzer-Abteilung 301* was subordinated to the *1./SS-Panzerjäger Abteilung 12*.

35  Reynolds, p.287, discusses Goliath remote-controlled „tanks" though this is inaccurate. The Type B IV was much larger than the Goliath. The 370 kg Goliath could carry 60 kg of explosives, while the 3.6 ton B IV could carry as much as 500 kg of explosives.

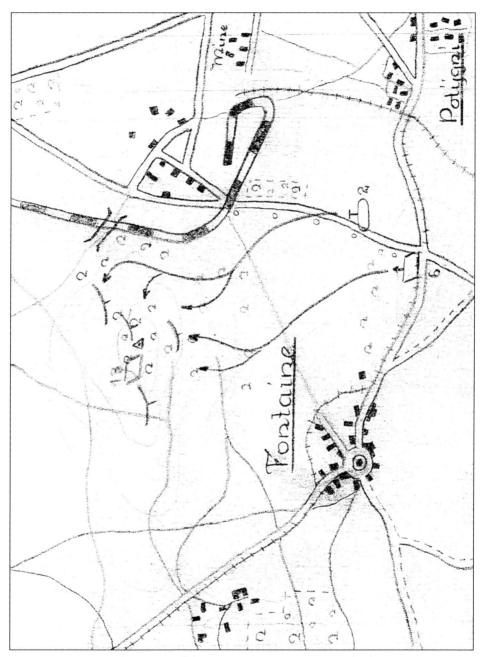

Combat actions of the *1.Kompanie/SS-Panzerjäger-Abteilung 12* near Fontaine-le-Pin, 10 August 1944.

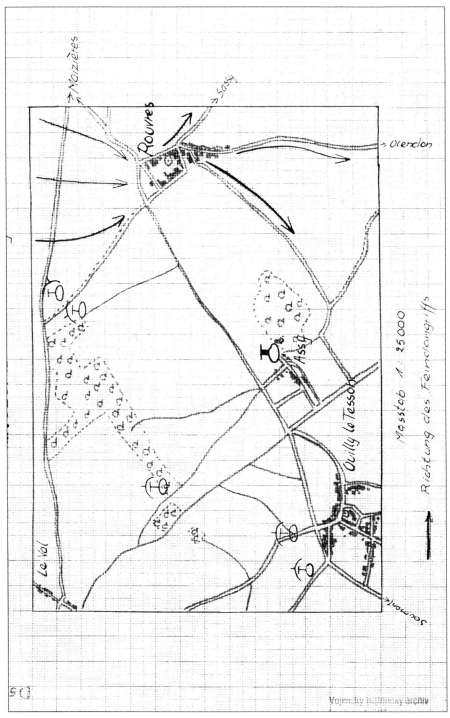

Combat actions of the *2.Kompanie/SS-Panzerjäger-Abteilung 12* near Assy, 14 August 1944.

Commander of the *Kampfgruppe, Obersturmführer* Hurdelbrink decided that the assault guns had to contain the enemy until two Jagdpanzer IVs (who else, other than Hurdelbrink and Roy?) got round on the right and pushed forward.

The two Jagdpanzers soon attacked the Allied tanks in the rear, the latter attempting to retreat. They did not succeed because the two Jagdpanzer IVs knocked out all of them. Hurdelbrink destroyed 10 Shermans, and Roy three in this tank battle.[36]

Around 1400 hours the Hill was again in German control. The hedgerow extending behind Hill 195 was held by considerable Allied (Canadian) infantry supported by 17-pounder and 6-pounder anti-tank guns. Therefore *Panzergruppe "Hurdelbrink"* could not continue its attack, and rather, prepared for the securing of the occupied area.

There were also Tiger heavy tanks fighting in the area from the *schwere SS-Panzer Abteilung 101* and *102*, besides the Jagdpanzer IVs of the *1.Kompanie*.

The *2./SS-Panzerjäger Abteilung 12* – with three operational Jagdpanzers – moved towards Assy around 1500 hours. According to the report sent at 2000 hours the *Kompanie* had already irrevocably lost its fourth Jagdpanzer; also, two vehicles and a motorcycle were damaged. Battle casualties were five seriously and one lightly wounded.[37]

According to the verbal order given by the commander of *SS-Panzer Regiment 12*, at dawn on 11 August the operational tanks of the *2.Kompanie* had to occupy positions north of Ouilly-le-Tesson and secure the road, with a projection towards the woods northwest of the village.

Infantry support for the Jagdpanzers were provided by *Obersturmbannführer* Bernhard Krause's *I./SS-Panzer-Grenadier-Regiment 26*. The further combat vehicles of the *2.Kompanie* still in motion had to gather in Assy. Around 1700 hours there were only two Jagdpanzer IVs in the positions assigned at Ouilly-le-Tesson.

During the night of 11 August the command of the *2.Kompanie* was taken over by *Obersturmführer* Erich Krauth because a shell fragment had wounded *Obersturmführer* Wachter's upper right arm. All of the remaining five Jagdpanzers of the *Kompanie* were in operational condition around 0500 hours.

In the evening of 13 August *Sturmbannführer* Hanreich ordered that the ten Jagdpanzer IVs under repair with the *Nachschubtruppen* of *SS-Panzerjäger Abteilung 12* in Nogent-le-Roi also had to be deployed. The tanks were led by *Obersturmführer* Günther Gornik towards the frontline.[38] These Jagdpanzers were placed into *Kampfgruppe "Wöst"* three days later.

On 14 August the Jagdpanzers of the *1.* and *2./SS-Panzerjäger Abteilung 12* (approximately ten operational Jagdpanzer IVs) occupied ambush positions in multiple units, north-northeast of Falaise on the north-western slopes of Monts d'Eraines and in the woods southeast of Epancy. These Jagdpanzer IVs provided armoured support for the Grenadiers of the *85.Infanterie Division* deployed here.

36  Vojenský Historický Archiv, Praha (Military History Archives, Prague), Anlagen zum KTB der *SS-Panzer-Jäger-Abteilung* 12 *"Hitlerjugend"*, Gefechtsbericht für 10. 8. 1944/1. *(schw.)/SS-Pz.Jäg.Abt. 12 "HJ"*. The Canadian and Polish units lost 142 of their armoured fighting vehicles in the area on 10 August 1944. See also Russell A. Hart, *Clash of Arms: How the Allies won in Normandy*, Boulder CO: Lynne Riener, 2001 (hereafter cited as R.A. Hart).

37  Vojenský Historický Archiv, Praha (Military History Archives, Prague), KTB Nr. 1 der *SS-Panzer-Jäger-Abteilung 12*, 10. 8. 1944.

38  Vojenský Historický Archiv, Praha (Military History Archives, Prague), KTB Nr. 1 der *SS-Panzer-Jäger-Abteilung 12*, 13. 8. 1944.

Tanks of *SS-Panzer Regiment 12* also occupied ambush positions on Hill 159, 3 km northeast of Falaise.[39]

During the morning hours the right flank of the *2./SS-Panzerjäger Abteilung 12* was attacked by Allied forces. The Jagdpanzers knocked out three Sherman tanks, and then in delaying combat they retreated together with *SS-Panzer Regiment 12*.

At 1340 hours the *Kompanie* reported that the Allies had broken through towards Assy, and continued the combat in the direction of Rouvres with 50 tanks and infantry.

By 1500 hours the enemy infantry had penetrated the German positions at Ouilly-le-Tesson also. All operational combat vehicles of *SS-Panzer Regiment 12* – including the Jagdpanzer IVs of the two *Kompanien* of *SS-Panzerjäger Abteilung 12* – fought around Hill 159. During this combat the *1.Kompanie* reported to have knocked out 12 Allied tanks, but one of the Jagdpanzers of the *Kompanie* (its commander: *Oberscharführer* Kußmaul) was also knocked out.

According to a report sent after 2000 hours the three Jagdpanzers of the *2.Kompanie* with parts of *SS-Panzer Regiment 12* were securing north-eastwards, 4 km northwest of Ouilly-le-Tesson, between the northern outskirts of the village and the woods lying northwest of the village. The Tiger tanks of *schwere SS-Panzer Abteilung 102* were fighting on the left flank of the *Kompanie*.[40]

From 1130 hours on 15 August the *1.Kompanie* was covering the Falaise–Jort highway in the area of Hill 120 by order of *Obersturmbannführer* Max Wünsche.

According to a report sent at 1400 hours the *2.Kompanie* with its four operational Jagdpanzer IVs was securing on the fringe of a wood southeast of Perrières. During the day both *Kompanien* were supplied with ammunition and fuel.[41]

On 16 August the *1.Kompanie* was regrouped to Versainville where the Jagdpanzer IVs securing with some infantry reported to have knocked out eight Sherman tanks from the Canadian 4th (Armoured) Division. With this they temporarily prevented the breakthrough of the Canadian tanks towards Damblainville.

Around midnight the *Kompanie* received new orders, according to which it was to occupy positions on Hill 95, approximately 2 km south of Damblainville.

Meanwhile the *2.Kompanie* retreated to the fringe of the Damblainville forest during the day.[42]

At dawn on 17 August the Jagdpanzer of the *Chef* of the *1.Kompanie* was rendered immobile due to a brake system failure, and went under maintenance in Fresné-la-Mère, near the church. *Hauptscharführer* Rautenbacher's Jagdpanzer remained behind during the retreat. Only the tank of *Unterscharführer* Rothaug reached Hill 95 around 0345 hours at dawn, where it occupied securing positions with a remote-controlled armoured vehicle. After 0400 hours Rautenbacher's Jagdpanzer IV tank also reached Hill 95.[43]

---

39   Meyer, p.324.

40   Vojenský Historický Archiv, Praha (Military History Archives, Prague), KTB Nr. 1 der *SS-Panzer-Jäger-Abteilung 12*, 14. 8. 1944.

41   Vojenský Historický Archiv, Praha (Military History Archives, Prague) KTB Nr. 1 der *SS-Panzer-Jäger-Abteilung 12*, 15. 8. 1944.

42   Vojenský Historický Archiv, Praha (Military History Archives, Prague) KTB Nr. 1 der *SS-Panzer-Jäger-Abteilung 12*, 16. 8. 1944.

43   Vojenský Historický Archiv, Praha (Military History Archives, Prague) KTB Nr. 1 der *SS-Panzer-Jäger-Abteilung 12*, 17. 8. 1944.

After this, the two Jagdpanzer IVs stood in readiness in the area of La Balanderie subordinated to the *Begleitkompanie* of the *12.SS-Panzer Division*. Apart from the Jagdpanzers the *Kompanie* only consisted of a combat strength of 15 men and two armoured personnel carriers.[44]

At 0300 hours at dawn on 18 August the *1.Kompanie* retreated west of the railway, to the wooded hill 2 km south of Fresné-la-Mère. At 1040 hours the *Kompanie* was redirected to the woodland west of Vignats, and the *Kompanie Chef* was called to report to the command post of the *Abteilung* together with its repaired Jagdpanzer.

The *2.Kompanie* changed positions at 0400 hours and secured on the hills northeast of Les-Creux. Around 1200 hours the *Kompanie* repulsed a tank attack, then an infantry assault in the evening. The Jagdpanzers knocked out one Sherman tank and three armoured carrier vehicles of the infantry.

At noon the same day there were only five operational Jagdpanzer IVs in *SS-Panzerjäger Abteilung 12*.[45]

At 0520 hours on 19 August *SS-Panzer Regiment 12* and the vehicle column of the *Stab* of *SS-Panzerjäger Abteilung 12* subordinated to *SS-Panzer Regiment 12* were advancing from Fourches to Bierre towards the railway when the Allies engaged the column. *Obersturmbannführer* Wünsche, commander of *SS-Panzer Regiment 12*, and *Sturmbannführer* Hans-Jakob Hanreich were missing in action (it later turned out that both were captured[46]); *Obersturmbannführer* Hans Weiss, commander of *schwere SS-Panzer Abteilung 102*, was captured seriously wounded.

Lastly, the *Stab* of the *Panzerjäger Abteilung* was led by *Untersturmführer* Hans-Egon Schmid, *Adjutant* to the *Abteilung* around 1130 hours, creating diversions southwest of Fresnay-le-Samson. Only a motorcycle and a 3-ton Opel truck were lost, which were damaged by artillery shells.

Around 1400 hours *Hauptscharführer* Rautenbacher's Jagdpanzer IV was hit by enemy artillery fire. The tank commander was wounded, and together with others, was transported to the dressing station by the armoured personnel carrier of the *1.Kompanie* via St. Lambert-sur-Dives. The crew of the Jagdpanzer brought back the vehicle from the frontline even in the absence of their commander.

In the evening *Sturmbannführer* Erich Olboeter, commander of the *III./SS-Panzer-Grenadier-Regiment 26*, took over the command of the remains of *Kampfgruppe "Wünsche"* (*SS-Panzer Regiment 12*, *SS-Panzerjäger Abteilung 12*, *SS-Panzer-Aufklärungsabteilung 12*, and the remaining Tigers of *schwere SS-Panzer Abteilung 101* and *102*), and ordered a breakout eastwards, between the extensive forest south of Dron and the town of Trun. The *3.Fallschirmjäger Division* attacked on the right, the weary units of the *1. SS-Panzer Division "Leibstandarte"* on the left side of the *Kampfgruppe*. What remained of the *12.SS-Panzer Division* followed them.

*Sturmbannführer* Olboeter ordered the following marching order for his *Kampfgruppe*: two Tiger heavy tanks and two Panthers were at the head of the column, followed by

44  Meyer, p.337.
45  Vojenský Historický Archiv, Praha (Military History Archives, Prague), KTB Nr. 1 der *SS-Panzer-Jäger-Abteilung 12*, 18. 8. 1944.
46  According to the British "many times the flagrant arrogance and annoying personal remarks of Hanreich almost led to his instant death", but in the end he was transported to a POW camp without any harm done to him. See Meyer, p.342.

two Hummel self-propelled howitzers, then the Jagdpanzers (at least three), behind them five self-propelled anti-aircraft guns, and at the rear the armoured personnel carriers and other vehicles were secured by at least six Panzer IVs. The breakout was scheduled at 0100 hours the next day, 20 August.

In the morning hours of 19 August the *2./SS-Panzerjäger Abteilung 12* changed its positions to an area 1 km south of Beaumais. Around 1500 hours an order was received that the Jagdpanzer IVs were to secure henceforth west of Crocy, on Hill 85. This was done until midnight when they departed to reach the hills 2 km south of Ommoy. They received the order there that remaining forces of the *12.SS-Panzer Division* were gathering south of Fresnay-le-Samson in order to break out of the Falaise Cauldron. The *2./SS-Panzerjäger Abteilung 12* – what remained of it – joined the gathering units.

On 20 August the breakout commenced with delays. At 0530 hours *Kampfgruppe "Olboeter"* led through Tournai-sur-Dives towards St. Lambert-sur-Dives. The units tried to get across the broken country north-eastwards, in the direction of Numberville, where they were engaged by Canadian infantry and anti-tank guns. As one of the soldiers of *SS-Panzer-Grenadier-Regiment 26* remembered:

"We speeded through the infantry positions of the Canadians, part of whom surrendered, and marched with us. The cover of the entrenched infantry and the anti-tank gun positions were simply blown away by the tank destroyers. Two hours later we broke through the enemy positions".*47*

Despite this the German *Kampfgruppe* lost a number of tanks and armoured personnel carriers, and the column collapsed.

During the battle the Jagdpanzer of the *Chef* of the *1.Kompanie, Obersturmführer* Hurdelbrink, was also knocked out, as was the Jagdpanzer IV of *Oberscharführer* Blum from the *2.Kompanie.*

Around 1100 hours the *Kampfgruppe* reached Numberville via a detour. The Allied artillery fired at the road leading from the north towards Coudehard, and this was also swept by tank- and machine-gun fire.

The *Kampfgruppe* was able to break through to the hill north of the village where they established communication with a number of remaining Panzer IV tanks of the *2.SS-Panzer-Division "Das Reich"*. *Kampfgruppe "Olboeter"* continued its way towards Bruyère-la-Fresnay where its units that had scattered during the night were gathering.[48]

At 0530 hours the next day, 21 August, the units that had already broken out departed to continue their way to the command post, 8 km south of Orbec, where other retreating forces of the *12.SS-Panzer Division* were gathering.[49] Those who had reached that point by 1000 hours in the morning successfully broke out of the Falaise Cauldron, and for them the battle in Normandy had reached its end. However, there were parts of *SS-Panzerjäger Abteilung 12* that had other hardships with which to contend.

47  Cited in Meyer, p.348.

48  Vojenský Historický Archiv, Praha (Military History Archives, Prague), KTB Nr. 1 der *SS-Panzer-Jäger-Abteilung 12*, 20. 8. 1944.

49  Vojenský Historický Archiv, Praha (Military History Archives, Prague), KTB Nr. 1 der *SS-Panzer-Jäger-Abteilung 12*, 21. 8. 1944.

## *Kampfgruppe "Wöst"*, 16–26 August 1944

On 16 August, parts of the *2.* and *3./SS-Panzerjäger Abteilung 12* that were still not deployed because of insufficient ammunition were stationed in Villiers-le-Morhier. *Obersturmführer* Günther Gornik had arrived here with eight Jagdpanzer IVs[50], which were brought from Nogent-le-Roi, but had been captured by the enemy in the meantime. Officers and NCOs from the *2.* and *3.Kompanien* took over the vehicles and formed a *Kampfgruppe* commanded by *Hauptsturmführer* Günther Wöst, commander of the *3.Kompanie.*

Around 1800 hours in the evening *Kampfgruppe "Wöst",* along with eight Jagdpanzers, departed from Villiers in an easterly direction, parallel to the highway leading to Condé. Around 2200 hours three Jagdpanzer IVs carried out a combat reconnaissance mission towards Nogent-le-Roi, although due to the darkness and the falling rain they could only determine that the village was controlled by the enemy and it was held by strong forces.

One of the Jagdpanzers (whose commander was *Unterscharführer* Preckner) had to be towed into Versailles because of engine failure.

On 17 August, at 0700 hours in the morning, *Kampfgruppe "Wöst"* was following in a parallel manner the enemy tanks going towards Faverolles, with the aim of taking them in the flank when they reached the hill by the village.

Around 0800 hours the advance guard of the German *Kampfgruppe* abruptly crashed into the British infantry moving along in the forest 3 km south of Faverolles. The Jagdpanzers launched the attack. Naturally the Allied tanks gathering south of the village also joined the fight.

Following a 45-minute battle *Kampfgruppe "Wöst"* retreated towards St. Leger. The Jagdpanzer IVs destroyed two Sherman tanks and a number of armoured trucks full of infantry, without suffering any losses themselves.

The *Kampfgruppe* drew fuel and ammunition rations in St. Leger, then a Jagdpanzer-*Zug* (three vehicles) carried out a reconnaissance towards Condé, then in a southerly direction as far as Faverolles. The reconnoitring Jagdpanzer IVs saw major tank forces gathering east of Faverolles.

This way *Kampfgruppe "Wöst"* moved to Condé where they secured westwards together with the tanks of the *Sturmgeschütz Brigade*[51] subordinated to *Kampfgruppe "Seidel"* (*Untersturmführer* Heinz Seidel).

At dawn on 18 August *Kampfgruppen "Wöst"* and *"Seidel"* moved to Houdan. The assault guns and *Kampfgruppe "Seidel"* secured the village, the Jagdpanzers of *Hauptsturmführer* Wöst acted as the reserve ready for action. After the supply trucks arrived the Jagdpanzer IVs had enough fuel and ammunition again, and the soldiers received rations.

At 1000 hours two Jagdpanzers carried out a reconnaissance towards the southwest. After moving 7 km they ran into Allied reconnaissance armoured cars which, upon being fired on by the Jagdpanzer IVs, retreated southwards. Following this the German vehicles returned to Houdan.

---

50  Gornik's group had ten Jagdpanzers at the beginning, but they most probably lost two Jagdpanzer IVs on the way.

51  In Normandy, the *Sturmgeschütz-Brigade 341* and *342* of the *Army* and the *Sturmgeschütz-Brigade 12* of the *Luftwaffe* had been deployed. For now we do not know which units were fighting in the area mentioned.

The Allied tanks, the infantry mounted on trucks and the armoured reconnaissance cars approached Houdan from the west around 1400 hours.

Due to this, after half an hour three Jagdpanzer IVs occupied securing positions 4 km southwest of the village. The advance guard of the Allied units retreated westwards from the Nebelwerfers of *Kampfgruppe "Seidel"*. This way the securing Jagdpanzers were also able to move into Houdan.

*Oberst* Seidel sent an order around midnight that the units were to retreat as far as La Queue, on the road leading to Paris.

On 19 August the Jagdpanzer IVs secured in La Queue westwards and southwards together with the *Sturmgeschütz Brigade*. Around 1500 hours the noise of battle could be heard 5 km east of the village, but again there was no engagement between the securing tanks and the Allied forces[52].

At 1700 hours the *Kampfgruppe* moved on via Gevanoires, Thoiry, Autouilett and Auteuil until they reached the Chambel farmstead. Two Jagdpanzers established securing positions on the road leading to Le Pontel. Most of the *Kampfgruppe* spent the night on the farmstead.

On 20 August the *Kampfgruppe* moved as far as Le Pontel, the western exit of which was secured by four Jagdpanzer IVs with supporting infantry. The securing group was engaged by artillery fire at 1230 hours. Two hours later one of the Jagdpanzers was hit by an anti-tank gun on its glacis plate. The shell did not pierce the armour; nevertheless the crew abandoned the tank. During the escape the driver was wounded on his shoulder by a shell fragment, and the gunner was hit in his right eye by a bullet. After this the securing Jagdpanzers were withdrawn.

Le Pontel was also fired on by German artillery. The *Kampfgruppe* counted 15-20 enemy tanks, which turned northwards 4 km before Le Pontel on the road leading to Paris.

Around 1700 hours enemy tanks were discovered in the forest, 100 metres in front of the railway bridge, and engaged the Jagdpanzers, upon which they retreated behind the railway embankment. However, from this position the Jagdpanzer IVs fired at the attacking tanks which were withdrawing in the direction of Neauphle-le-Château. Neither side suffered any losses.

At 1100 on 21 August hours a new order was received from *Kampfgruppe "Seidel"* according to which the units were to move further towards Pontchartrain. En route, two Jagdpanzer IVs established securing positions north of Brechell, and three Jagdpanzer IVs secured along the road leading to the village from the west. At 1800 hours the *Kampfgruppe* retreated via Trappes to Bois-d'Arcy, without combat activity. Three Jagdpanzers and a *Grenadier Bataillon* secured the village from the west against surprise attacks.

On 23 August at 1500 hours three Jagdpanzer IVs carried out reconnaissance towards Plaisir and confirmed that there were no enemy troops in the village. An order came after 2100 hours that two Jagdpanzers had to cover the western exit of Les-Gâtines with some infantry. Their left flank was strengthened by the three other Jagdpanzer IVs, together with the *Sturmgeschütz Brigade*.

---

52  According to the KTB of *SS-Panzerjäger Abteilung 12* the Jagdpanzers of *Kampfgruppe "Wöst"* nevertheless knocked out a Sherman tank on this day, 2 km north of Manfourt.

On 25 August at 1100 hours the two Jagdpanzers, together with their infantry support, moved into Bois-de-Arcy from Les-Gâtines. An hour later three Jagdpanzer IVs went to Versailles where *Kampfgruppe* "Seidel" had its command post, then the vehicles returned around 1500 hours. In the meantime, one of the Jagdpanzers had to be towed into Bois-d'Arcy because of engine failure.

According to an order from *Oberst* Seidel all combat vehicles of *Kampfgruppe* "Wöst" were to move into Versailles at 1630 hours.

The French resistance opened a heavy fire on the Jagdpanzers driving through the town. Upon reaching the command post of *Oberst* Seidel, the Jagdpanzer IVs were ordered to secure Versailles to the south with all of their combat vehicles. 1 km from the south-eastern exit of the town one of the Jagdpanzer IVs was knocked out by an Allied tank. The driver and the commander of the Jagdpanzer were wounded.

At 2200 hours *Kampfgruppe* "Wöst" was ordered to retreat to St. Germain. During the initial disengagement one of the Jagdpanzers had to be blown up 4 km north of Versailles because of technical problems.

At last the *Kampfgruppe* crossed the Seine on 26 August at 0530 hours. One Jagdpanzer IV had to be towed. This vehicle only crossed the bridge around 1130 hours. After this, *Kampfgruppe* "Wöst" moved to the northern outskirts of Paris, into Gorges.[53]

With this, the first operational service of the *Panzerjäger Abteilung* of the *12.SS-Panzer Division* ended.

---

53  Vojenský Historický Archiv, Praha (Military History Archives, Prague), Anlagen zum KTB der *SS-Panzer-Jäger-Abteilung* 12 *"Hitlerjugend"*, Gefechtsberichte von Teilen der *3./SS-Pz.Jäg.Abt. 12 "HJ"*.

# Conclusion

# The Effectiveness of the Armour of the *12.SS-Panzer Division "Hitlerjugend"* in Normandy

## SS-Panzer Regiment 12

*SS-Panzer Regiment 12* entered combat in Normandy equipped with 87 Panzer IV and 66 Panther tanks, 12 Flak-Panzer 38(t) anti-aircraft armoured vehicles and three self-propelled 2cm quadruple-barrelled anti-aircraft guns mounted on Panzer IV chassis. During the fighting it received a further 17 Panzer IVs and 35 Panthers as reinforcements. Thus there were 104 Panzer IVs and 101 Panthers, 205 tanks altogether, in the strength of the regiment between 6 June and 31 August 1944.

Unfortunately there are no contemporary summarized reports on the losses of the regiment in the surviving documents. According to the documents of the two *Abteilung*, a total loss of 65 Panthers and 59 Panzer IVs can be confirmed. However, the real total of the losses of armoured vehicles of *SS-Panzer Regiment 12* was certainly considerably larger. On 4 September 1944 the division was ordered to hand over all of its remaining tanks and Jagdpanzers – whether they were operational or repairable in 14 days – to other German units. This way the regiment was finally deprived of its last tanks salvaged from the fighting.

Most of the armoured vehicle losses of *SS-Panzer Regiment 12* in Normandy were combat losses. According to the written evidence only eight Panthers and one Panzer IV were destroyed by their crews. Most of the losses suffered during combat were caused by Allied anti-tank guns (among them tank-destroyers described as self-propelled anti-tank guns) and the guns of the field artillery. Allied tanks accounted for fewer. Despite the almost total dominance of the Allies in the air, in the case of the *12.SS-Panzer Division* only three Panthers and a Flak-Panzer 38(t) are likely to have been destroyed by Allied air raids (fighter-bomber aircraft).[1] The effective anti-aircraft defences of *SS-Panzer Regiment 12* contributed to this; the self-propelled 2cm guns of the three *Flak Züge* of the unit are documented to have shot down a total of 15 Allied aircraft during the fighting in Normandy.

At the beginning of October 1944, *SS-Panzer Regiment 12* summarized the number of Allied armoured combat vehicles knocked out by the tanks of the two *Abteilungen* in

---

1   Of the 110 German tanks captured and examined by the British in Normandy between 6 June and 7 August 1944, only 10 were rendered disabled by aircraft (seven by rockets and three by automatic cannon fire). During the examination carried out between 8 and 31 August 1944 again only 10 out of 223 captured German tanks were destroyed by aircraft (seven by rockets, two by automatic cannon fire and one by bombs). See Thomas L. Jentz, *Die deutsche Panzertruppe* Band 2, Wölfersheim-Berstadt: Podzun-Pallas Verlag, 1999, pp.189, 193 (hereafter cited as Jentz). According to this it can be stated that only 6% of the German armoured losses were caused by Allied aircraft in the British-Canadian sector.

Normandy[2]. According to this they knocked out 690 such vehicles during the fighting, of which 601 were tanks or tank destroyers. However, according to the war diaries of the two *Abteilungen*, 211 armoured fighting vehicles were knocked out by the Panthers, and 183 armoured fighting vehicles were knocked out by the Panzer IVs; a total of 394. This difference of more than 200 vehicles can be explained by the fact that in October 1944, scores by other German units temporarily subordinated to the regiment were also credited to the regiment (for example Tigers of *schwere SS-Panzer Abteilung 101*, the Panthers of the *1./Panzer Regiment 3* or the Jagdpanzer IVs of the *1./SS-Panzerjäger Abteilung 12*).

In the August 1944 issue of the *Nachrichtenblatt der Panzertruppe*, the journal issued by the chief inspector of the German *Panzertruppe*, the experiences of the armoured tactics in Normandy was summarized as follows:

[...]

III. Combat

1    The terrain is disadvantageous for tanks; therefore the concentrated deployment of the armoured forces, so effective otherwise, has to be abandoned. One should send the tanks into combat as tank destroyer commandos or armoured detachments!

2    These armoured detachments are to consist of a few tanks that stand directly behind the frontline. Their task is to immediately launch counterstrokes and to destroy the enemy that breaks through the lines.

3    The armoured detachments have to closely cooperate with the Panzergrenadiers and the Grenadiers, who shall direct them!

4    The interspaced battle order deprives the enemy of the ability to observe troop movements from the air. Camouflage of the vehicles will protect them from air raids. The tank commanders and gunners determine targets beforehand and prepare distance charts.

5    Changing positions shall be prepared for the tanks so they can serve in positions behind slopes (as defensive positions offering coverage from which the enemy can be defeated from short combat distances with surprise attacks). From these positions behind the slopes the enemy tanks that break through can be successfully attacked in the flank.

6    The enemy penetrability regarding close combat and flanking attacks shall be exploited with short counterstrokes, directly following the ceasing of artillery fire at the main battle line.

7    After the counterstroke has commenced the Grenadiers will defend the flanks of the tanks and fight directly with them.

Summary:

The strictest order to all troops and units is to exploit the possibilities presented by the terrain, the cover, entrenchments, strict observance of security instructions regarding radio and telephone contact. Civilians shall constantly be prevented from informing the enemy.

---

2    The tanks, tank destroyers, self-propelled guns, armoured reconnaissance cars and armoured personnel carriers were all reported as armoured combat vehicles.

The following experiences, acquired before, have now been confirmed:

1    The morale and training of our own tank crew is above that of the enemy. Dominance of the enemy can only be traced to the number of their tanks.
2    Morale of the British infantry is low. Due to this, until now we have only met British anti-tank units a few times.
3    Despite their thick armour the Tigers are forced to follow tactical regulations prescribed for light tank *Kompanien* (camouflage, exploitation of terrain, covered positions) due to enemy air superiority, well-directed artillery fire on identified targets and the 9.2cm anti-aircraft/anti-tank gun![3]

Because of the broken terrain in Normandy and the Allied dominance of the air *SS-Panzer Regiment 12* (the same as most of the German armoured regiments) had not been deployed in regimental force. For the same reasons the armoured *Kampfgruppe*s used on the Eastern Front (consisting of a *Panzer Abteilung*, a *Panzer-Grenadier-Bataillon* equipped with armoured personnel carriers, a self-propelled *Panzer-Artillerie-Abteilung* and a *Panzer-Pionier-Kompanie* mounted on armoured personnel carriers) were not successful either. Due to this the Germans soon ceased using this form of combat grouping.

After this, the tanks were mostly deployed (mostly in *Kompanie*-force) to support the *Panzergrenadier-Bataillone*. This way, the SS tanks fought with the attacking Allied tanks and tank destroyers as moving anti-tank reserves.

*Sturmbannführer* Jürgensen, who was awarded the Knight's Cross for his command of the *I./SS-Panzer Regiment 12* in Normandy (he was the only one in the *Abteilung* to receive the Knight's Cross), prepared the following report at the beginning of August 1944 of the experiences of the Panther tanks in his *Abteilung*[4]:

I./Panzer Regiment 12* was in battle from the third day of the invasion. During this time it was revealed that the battle fought by armoured forces in Normandy was very different from what was experienced in open country due to the undergrowth and the rugged terrain, and this prevented the normal deployment of panzers. Attack is extremely disadvantageous over terrain with the thick undergrowth of Normandy. The *Abteilung*-sized attack is very hard, if not entirely impossible, due to the undergrowth. The assault gun-like group deployment seems to be the most advantageous form of deployment, in close cooperation with the Panzergrenadiers. For this, good cooperation and extensive knowledge of the armoured units for at least the officers and NCOs of the Panzergrenadiers is essential. All experiences gathered so far have shown that the Grenadiers do not understand the battle deployment of tanks. On the one hand they require the impossible, on the other they fail to exploit even the most advantageous possibilities (firing positions).

Cooperation with the artillery is especially weak. During the whole campaign there was not a single example of at least an acceptable level of cooperation. The primary reasons are: the heavy radio equipment that is not mobile enough, and above all, is not sufficient or used adequately. Attacks with limited goals have failed

---

3    Cited in Jentz, pp.189–190.
4    The report constitutes Attachment no. 11 of the KTB for the *I./SS-Panzer Regiment 12*.

one by one, with extensive losses suffered, because the artillery were not ready, or were ready too late and even then it scarcely fired.

Both sides have to have knowledge and understanding of the armament and its functioning. Thorough preparation is essential at all times. It is better to depart half an hour later, following thorough preparations (briefing and discussion of the attack of the Grenadiers and the artillery) than to attack unprepared and scattered.

The advantages which the Panzer V (Panther) has, due to its optics or gun, cannot be exploited on terrain with thick undergrowth, as seen in Normandy, because of the short effective range and short lines of sight. The enemy anti-tank guns and tanks that are well-covered in the undergrowth and in the hollows at the outskirts of villages cannot be discovered, or only from a short distance by which time it is already too late: therefore the enemy anti-tank guns and tanks can easily knock out and disable the Panzer V (close cooperation of the tanks, Panzergrenadiers and the artillery).

The Panzerkampfwagen V has never failed regarding engineering, armament engineering and mechanical engineering, although engineering service was scarce and not sufficient. The exhausts glowing or flaming at night are extremely disadvantageous (they must be covered).

For the battle fought on the *Invasionfront* the tanks are best deployed as tank destroyers, well-camouflaged and covered, and directly behind the main battle line because of the dominance of enemy artillery and the extensive usage of enemy tanks.

Counterstrokes carried out by armoured units deployed in reserve were not effective again. Reasons: broken terrain with undergrowth, enemy artillery dominance, swiftly deployed anti-tank guns and tanks located on the outskirts of villages, behind bushes and hollows, in ambush positions, which let the counterstrokes come close then knocked out the armoured units at short range.

Battle tactics of the enemy tanks: avoiding the open field, stealth through valleys, hollows, ravines; camouflage and well-covered firing positions on the outskirts of villages, in the undergrowth, behind slopes and on the flanks; firing at long distances, extensive exploitation of smoke.

The experiences above could also have been echoed by *Hauptsturmführer* Michael Wittmann, the famous German Panzer ace. Although the tactical circumstances of the death of Wittmann and his comrades on 8 August 1944 do not constitute an essential part of the combat history of *SS-Panzer Regiment 12* in Normandy, we have to touch upon the subject, especially as the above mentioned event occurred subordinated to the *II./SS-Panzer Regiment 12*.

Before the catastrophic combat action is examined we would like to resolve quite an old ill-founded belief, which is that *Hauptsturmführer* Michael Wittmann was the most effective tank commander in the Second World War. Until 8 August 1944 the destruction of 138 enemy tanks was credited to Wittmann. On account of this he was probably the most effective German Panzer ace until his death. However the war raged

*Hauptsturmführer* Michael Wittmann, the highest scoring *Waffen-SS*
tank ace, receives his Swords to the Knight's Cross from Adolf Hitler
(see Chapter 8 Footnote 45 and main text). (Mark C. Yerger)

on in Europe for nine more months. During this time, three tank commanders of the Army[5] surpassed Wittmann, who was not able to increase his score any further.

On 8 August *Hauptsturmführer* Michael Wittmann did not depart on a mission, particularly because his heavy Tiger I Ausf E tank (turret number 205) was under repair. Some of the still operational Tigers of *schwere SS-Panzer Abteilung 101* (mostly from the *3.Kompanie*, commanded by *Hauptsturmführer* Franz Heurich) were assigned to the *II./ SS-Panzer Regiment 12* of *Sturmbannführer* Karl-Heinz Prinz.

As can be clearly seen from the war diary of the *II./SS-Panzer Regiment 12*, at 0630 hours that day the Tigers of Heurich were dispatched, together with the Panzer IVs of the *Abteilung*, via Grainville and Hautmesnil towards Cintheaux by the order of the *Abteilung* (that is, this was not done by order of Wittmann).

Wittmann was angry, offended that it was not he that had given orders to Heurich. The *Ordonnanz Offizier* of *schwere SS-Panzer Abteilung 101*, *Hauptscharführer* Josef Höflinger, was sent after Heurich's *3.Kompanie* to stop them and order him to wait for further orders. Wittmann drew up with Heurich's Tigers around 1100 hours in Cintheaux.[6] Considering the fact that the *Divisionsführer* of the *12.SS-Panzer Division*, *Oberführer* Kurt Meyer, discussed details of the planned attack with *Hauptsturmführer* Michael Wittmann and *Sturmbannführer* Hans Waldmüller, commander of the *I./SS-Panzer-Grenadier-Regiment 25*, Wittmann had surely taken over the command of the Tigers from Heurich by then.

*Oberführer* Meyer had earlier decided that the inevitable assault of the Canadian and Polish Armoured Divisions at the forefront of the Canadian II Corps would be anticipated with a sweep forward, and thus the unit should try to regain initiative.[7] To carry this out, around noon Meyer had eight Tiger I Ausf Es, five Panthers and nineteen Panzer IV tanks, plus ten Jagdpanzer IVs. This meant there were 42 operational German tanks altogether. Opposite them stood – taking only the Allied armoured units into consideration – two full armoured divisions (with 381 tanks in each) and two individual armoured brigades (with approximately 220 tanks). We can not apprehend how Meyer thought that he could regain initiative with his 42 tanks against 1,200 Allied tanks, even with the most advantageous circumstances?

In our opinion, it would have been more favourable, considering tactical aspects, if SS *Kampfgruppe "Waldmüller"*, strengthened with Tigers, had awaited the Allied tank assault in the southern-south-eastern area of Cintheaux, then, exploiting the temporary bafflement and organizational disturbances caused by the initial losses, had launched a counterstroke. In this case at least the exact enemy positions would have been known for all tank commanders taking part in the mission.

Instead of this, Meyer himself chose to attack, and sent *Kampfgruppe "Waldmüller"* into the 'unknown' without precise reconnaissance details. In our opinion Meyer would have sent his tanks into the assault even without the discovery of the Allied marker aircraft and his attempts to avoid the air raid, if just a little later. Incidentally Cintheaux

---

5   *Feldwebel* Kurt Knispel (*schwere Panzer Abteilung 503* then *"Feldherrnhalle"*) with 162 credited successes, *Oberleutnant* Otto Carius (*schwere Panzer Abteilung 502*) with 150 credited successes and *Hauptmann* Johannes Bölter (*schwere Panzer Abteilung 502*) with 144 credited successes.

6   Agte, p.258.

7   Meyer, p.304.

was not even listed among the targets to be bombed by the B-17s on that day.[8] The truth was, however, that Meyer did not know this for sure.

From then on, only Wittmann commanded the fight of the attacking Tigers, and in our opinion made a number of serious tactical mistakes.

First, he divided his already limited number of tanks, so three of the eight Tigers were left to strengthen the defence of Cintheaux, with the task of preventing the Canadian tanks from coming close. As there were already a number of German 8.8cm anti-aircraft guns and 2cm guns in firing positions around the village, we do not see the point of this action. The three Tigers could have been used for the covering of the unsecured flanks.

Second, although Wittmann had to launch an immediate attack in open terrain, without supporting *Panzergrenadier Infanterie*, in a totally unknown situation regarding the enemy's positions, he did not choose an appropriate formation for this. According to the war diary of the 1st Northamptonshire Yeomanry armoured regiment, his Tigers – baffling even the British – advanced towards the enemy in a column, behind each other. With this, they left their flanks and the weaker armoured sides of the heavy tanks exposed and defenceless. This formation was only used while in motion, and not at all before engagement with the enemy. In tactical situations like this, one platoon of tanks would form a *Keil* (wedge), in which two heavy tanks would drive to the front, besides each other in a line, and behind them, on the right and left sides, the other Tigers would have driven in echelon. According to some interpretations, Wittmann presumably anticipated enemy fire only from Hill 122 north of his position.[9] However this would not explain the improper tactical formation. It also cannot be excluded that the (successful) firefight with the Canadian tanks discovered north-westwards at a distance of 1,800 metres engaged his attention so much that his tanks were not able to watch their right flank.

Third, Wittmann could have secured the right flank of his tank group even better if he had waited for the Panzer IV tanks, Jagdpanzer IVs and the *SS-Panzergrenadiers* attacking eastwards to reach the orchard (where the ambush positions of the British tanks were hidden), and ordered the Tigers to attack in line with them in close cooperation. However, he acted differently, and led his heavy tanks directly in front of the British tank guns. The events that followed have become part of history.

In our opinion Wittmann was killed on 8 August 1944 due to the following causes and effects. At first, he unwarrantedly took over the command of the Tigers subordinated to the *II./SS-Panzer Regiment 12*, which were deployed by *Oberführer* Meyer in an unprepared 'rush'. Wittmann divided his forces and chose an improper tactical formation. Judging by the fact that he was rushing forward with his Tigers alone, we draw the conclusion that he misjudged the forces and abilities of both the enemy and the other units of *Kampfgruppe "Waldmüller"*.

---

8   Presumably because there were a number of German 8.8cm and 2cm anti-aircraft guns in firing positions around the village, which shot down nine B-17s. See Reynolds, p.277.

9   S.A. Hart, p.60.

## SS-Panzerjäger Abteilung 12

According to data from 1 October 1944, *SS-Panzerjäger Abteilung 12* only had two Jagdpanzer IVs (one in both the *1.* and *2. Kompanien*).[10] However this does not mean that 19 Jagdpanzers were lost in Normandy.

According to the original documents of the *Panzerjäger Abteilung* two Jagdpanzer were knocked out in the *1.Kompanie*, five in the *2.Kompanie,* and one in *Kampfgruppe "Wöst"* (eight altogether) by the Allies in combat. Apart from these, one Jagdpanzer IV was "missing" (that is, there was no information available as to the fate of the tank and its crew), and at least one was blown up by its own crew because of technical problems. Because the fate of only two of the eight Jagdpanzers of *Kampfgruppe "Wöst"* is known, and the group avoided the most dangerous sector of the breakout, it is possible that six of its tanks, towed or on their own, crossed the Seine at last. The remaining three Jagdpanzer IVs were presumably abandoned by their crews and/or were blown up during the breakout from the Falaise Cauldron.

During September 1944 *SS-Panzerjäger Abteilung 12* summarized the number of Allied tanks and other vehicles knocked out in the Normandy battles. The Jagdpanzer of the unit reported knocking out 102 tanks, one armoured carrier vehicle, one armoured reconnaissance car, four prime movers and five trucks. The towed 7.5cm anti-tank guns of the *3.Kompanie* knocked out at least a further three Allied tanks, however, because their crews had been killed or seriously wounded, there was no one to report these scores.

The Jagdpanzer IVs of the *1.Kompanie* reported destroying 86 Allied armoured fighting vehicles during seven days in combat. Could this amount be an exaggeration? Not so. The war diaries of the opposing Allied (British, Canadian and Polish) troops confirm this data, and they can be deduced from the tank scores of the other German units (for example the two *schwere SS-Panzer Abteilung* equipped with Tiger tanks) fighting in the same sector.

Therefore it is not a coincidence that three members of the *1./SS-Panzerjäger-Abteilung 12* were awarded the Knight's Cross because of their accomplishments in Normandy: *Obersturmführer* Georg Hurdelbrink, *Kompanie Chef* of the *1.Kompanie* and *Oberscharführer* Rudolf Roy, a *Zugführer* in the *1.Kompanie* on 16 October 1944, and *Rottenführer* Fritz Eckstein, the gunner of Roy's Jagdpanzer IV, on 18 November 1944.[11]

A number of books and internet websites describe *Oberscharführer* Rudolf Roy as one of the German "Panzer aces", having knocked out 36 armoured fighting vehicles.[12] Although Roy was an eminent Jagdpanzer *Zugführer* and tank commander beyond question, it was *Rottenführer* Eckstein behind the optical sight of the Jagdpanzer IV who provided a key element to Roy's success. Moreover, this Jagdpanzer knocked out only 26 Allied tanks in Normandy (all of them with Eckstein), and because Roy fell from a headshot on the second day of the Ardennes offensive, 17 December 1944, it is highly implausible for him to have knocked out ten more armoured fighting vehicles before his death.

10  Vojenský Historický Archiv, Praha (Military History Archives, Prague), Anlagen zum KTB der *SS-Panzer-Jäger-Abteilung* 12 *"Hitlerjugend"*, Kriegsgliederung Panzer-Jäger-*Abteilung* 12 "HJ" Stand: 1. 10. 1944.

11  Hurdelbrink and Eckstein survived the war. Roy was shot in the head by an American sniper on 17 December 1944 during the Ardennes offensive. See Appendix XVIII.

12  See, among others, S. Hart and R. Hart, *A Waffen-SS fegyverei és harceljárásai* [Weapons and Fighting Tactics of the Waffen-SS], Debrecen: Hajja, 1999, p.222.

At the same time, according to the combat reports of the *1.Kompanie*, Hurdelbrink had 36 confirmed armoured fighting vehicle scores before 16 August 1944. It is true however that he was also a tank commander and not a gunner when knocking out enemy tanks; despite this, Hurdelbrink is not usually featured on these "Panzer ace" lists.

The new commander of *SS-Panzerjäger Abteilung 12*, *Hauptsturmführer* Karl Brockschmidt, observed the following in 1977 in connection with the unit as it was reorganized before the Ardennes offensive in December 1944:

> The *Abteilung* as a *Panzerjäger Abteilung* fulfilled our expectations and was awarded high decorations. However this time the task was to form a *Sturmgeschütz Abteilung* from this *Panzerjäger Abteilung*. This meant that the approach of the tank destroyers (waiting, lying in ambush position, then knocking the armoured fighting vehicle out) was to be reformed into the dynamic tactics of a *Sturmgeschütz Abteilung*. The task of the *Abteilung* had to be to blow away everything from the centre and draw the infantry with them.[13]

However, Brockschmidt was only right in some respects. *SS-Panzerjäger Abteilung 12* only had two Marder III tank destroyers in Normandy, which had an open combat compartment at the top and at the back, and their armour was thin, therefore they waited for the enemy armoured fighting vehicles in ambush positions, and following direct fire had to change firing positions as quickly as possible. However, two *Kompanien* of the *Abteilung* were equipped with Jagdpanzer IVs and not with Marder III tank destroyers. These combat vehicles had closed combat compartments, thicker and sloped glacis plates and lower silhouettes. This meant they were not confined to the ambush positions and could take part actively in attacks as assault guns, under the protection of the infantry. Indeed the bold sweeps of Hurdelbrink and Roy exemplify that the Jagdpanzer IV was especially able for this kind of task even in the difficult terrain of Normandy.

Almost all hits of the German 7.5cm and the 8.8cm armour-piercing shells pierced the armour of the Sherman tanks, and in 62% of cases this also meant that the tank was knocked out.[14]

In the case of *SS-Panzer Regiment 12* both *Abteilungen* equipped with Panther and Panzer IV tanks reported to have knocked out 3.5 times more Allied tanks than their own losses in armoured fighting vehicles.[15] In most cases these losses are confirmed by the war diaries of the British, Canadian and Polish units. If we are trying to draw an exact picture of the efficiency of the regiment during the larger campaigns of the Allies in Normandy, with little margin of error we can state that all armoured fighting vehicles that were lost on the German side (regardless of the type) equalled three Allied tanks or tank destroyers lost. This rate is even more astonishing regarding the Jagdpanzer IVs of *SS-Panzerjäger Abteilung 12*: for each of their armoured fighting vehicles knocked out in combat 15 Allied armoured fighting vehicles were lost!

According to an Allied analysis the German gunners needed 1.63 armour-piercing shell hits to knock out a Sherman tank. The Allies, however, generally needed 2.55 hits in

---

13  Cited in Meyer, p.408.
14  John Buckley, *British Armour in the Normandy Campaign*, London, Frank Cass, 2004, p.125 (hereafter cited as Buckley).
15  See Appendix XIII.

the case of a Panther and 4.2 in the case of a Tiger to achieve the same result. According to another report, if a Sherman or a Cromwell tank was engaged from a distance of 500 yards (approximately 457 metres) or closer by German anti-tank guns, then the chance of the Allied tank surviving diminished by 50% every 6 seconds.[16]

The destruction ratio of the Sherman tanks was extremely high. A British examination discovered that 37 out of 45 Sherman tanks knocked out between 6 June and 10 July 1944 were burnt out (of these, 33 tanks were lost due to armour-piercing shell hits). 94 of the 166 tanks lost from the British 29th and 8th Armoured Brigades were burnt out. According to an American analysis 65% of their Sherman tanks knocked out by direct controlled gunfire were burnt out.[17]

Interestingly enough, despite the obstructed Normandy terrain – which was therefore extremely advantageous for tank destroying tactics – only 15% of the Allied losses in armoured fighting vehicles was caused by close combat. Within this figure only 6% of the total Allied losses were caused by Panzerfausts and Panzerschrecks. At the same time, almost half of the Allied armoured fighting vehicle losses in Normandy were caused by tanks, assault guns and Jagdpanzers.[18]

According to the remaining contemporary documents used in this work the tanks and Jagdpanzers of the *12.SS-Panzer Division* were not exceptions either; they knocked out almost 500 Allied armoured fighting vehicles altogether during the fighting in Normandy in 1944.

This, however, does not alter the fact that the *12.SS-Panzer Division* (with its *Panzer Regiment* and *Panzerjäger Abteilung*), similar to other German units, was defeated and almost completely destroyed in Normandy by the Allied troops.

16  Buckley, p.107.
17  Buckley, p.127.
18  Buckley, p.123.

# Table of Ranks

| SS | German Army (*Heer*) | US |
|---|---|---|
| *Oberst-Gruppenführer* | *Generaloberst* | Colonel General |
| *Obergruppenführer* | *General* | General |
| *Gruppenführer* | *Generalleutnant* | Lieutenant General |
| *Brigadeführer* | *Generalmajor* | Major General |
| *Oberführer* | no equivalent | Brigadier General |
| *Standartenführer* | *Oberst* | Colonel |
| *Obersturmbannführer* | *Oberstleutnant* | Lieutenant Colonel |
| *Sturmbannführer* | *Major* | Major |
| *Hauptsturmführer* | *Hauptmann/Rittmeister* | Captain |
| *Obersturmführer* | *Oberleutnant* | 1st Lieutenant |
| *Untersturmführer* | *Leutnant* | 2nd Lieutenant |
| *Sturmscharführer* | *Stabsfeldwebel* | Sergeant Major |
| *Stabsscharführer* | *Hauptfeldwebel* | Senior NCO post |
| *Hauptscharführer* | *Oberfeldwebel* | Master Sergeant |
| *Oberscharführer* | *Feldwebel/Wachtmeister* | Technical Sergeant |
| *Scharführer* | *Unterfeldwebel* | Staff Sergeant |
| *Unterscharführer* | *Unteroffizier* | Sergeant |
| *Rottenführer* | *Stabsgefreiter/Obergefreiter* | Corporal |
| *Sturmmann* | *Oberschütze* | Private 1st Class |
| *Mann* | *Schütze* | Private |

# Appendix II[1]

# Officers of *SS-Panzer Regiment 12*

T he primary known officers of *SS-Panzer Regiment 12* are listed below just prior to D-Day. As with all such personnel list completeness is impossible, both due to the standard record keeping of the day and shifting of positions. Less senior posts were often not listed, the *Regiment* having further men commanding at platoon (*Zug*) level. Those missing in action, for whom no fate is known – if indeed they survived the conflict – as well as those killed but never identified, further inhibits the completeness of such lists. Elsewhere in this appendix is a second list covering the same period through the end of the war, showing further losses during the Ardennes and late war combats before *"Hitlerjugend"* surrendered in 1945.

### *SS-Panzer Regiment 12*

| | |
|---|---|
| *Regimentskommandeur* | *Obersturmbannführer* Max Wünsche |
| *Adjutant* | *Hauptsturmführer* Georg Isecke |
| *Ordonnanz Offizier* | *Untersturmführer* Rudolf Nerlich |
| *Nachrichtenoffizier* | *Hauptsturmführer* Helmut Schlauß |
| *TFK I* | *Hauptsturmführer* Wilhelm Sammann |
| *Verwaltungsoffizier* | *Hauptsturmführer* Hermann Lütgert |
| *Regimentsarzt* | *Hauptsturmführer* Dr Rudolf Stiawa |
| *Zahnarzt* | *Hauptsturmführer* Dr. Heinrich Neinhardt |
| *Flak Zugführer* | *Untersturmführer* Walter Schaffert |
| *Werksttattkompanie Chef* | *Untersturmführer* Konrad Wörz |

### *I./SS-Panzer-Regiment 12* (Panther)

| | |
|---|---|
| *Abteilungskommandeur* | *Sturmbannführer* Arnold Jürgensen |
| *Adjutant* | *Untersturmführer* Heinz Hubertus Schröder |
| *Ordonnanz Offizier* | *Untersturmführer* Hans Hogrefe |
| *TFK* | *Untersturmführer* Helmuth Kloos |
| *TFW* | *Obersturmführer* Anton Stark |
| *Nachrichtenoffizier* | *Untersturmführer* Rolf Jauch |
| *Abteilungsarzt* | *Obersturmführer* Dr. Wilhelm Daniel |
| *Chef* of the *1.Kompanie* | *Hauptsturmführer* Kurt-Anton Berlin |
| *Chef* of the *2.Kompanie* | *Obersturmführer* Helmut Gaede |
| *Chef* of the *3.Kompanie* | *Obersturmführer* Rudolf von Ribbentrop |
| *Chef* of the *4.Kompanie* | *Hauptsturmführer* Hans Pfeiffer |
| *Werkstatt Zugführer* | *Untersturmführer* Robert Maier |

---

1   Award recommendation documents translated by Dr Frederick P. Steinhardt. This Appendix also includes biographical data relating to several award holders who were not officers.

2   In a *Waffen-SS Panzer Division* the repair *Kompanie Chef* was assigned to the staff with each *Abteilung* normally having a *Werkstattzug*.

**II./SS-Panzer Regiment 12 (Panzer IV)**

| | |
|---|---|
| *Abteilungskommandeur* | *Sturmbannführer* Karl-Heinz Prinz |
| *Adjutant* | *Obersturmführer* Friedrich Hartmann |
| *Ordonnanz Offizier* | *Untersturmführer* Herbert Walther |
| *Verwaltungsoffizier* | *Untersturmführer* Sebastian Schweiger |
| *TFK I* | *Obersturmführer* Dieter Müller |
| *TFK II* | *Untersturmführer* Karl Pucher |
| *Nachrichtenoffizier* | *Untersturmführer* Hermann Komadina |
| *Abteilungsarzt* | *Hauptsturmführer* Dr. Oskar Jordan |
| *Zahnarzt* | *Untersturmführer* Dr. Benno Hofer |
| *Chef* of the *5.Kompanie* | *Obersturmführer* Helmut Bando |
| *Chef* of the *6.Kompanie* | *Hauptsturmführer* Ludwig Ruckdeschel |
| *Chef* of the *7.Kompanie* | *Hauptsturmführer* Heinrich Bräcker |
| *Chef* of the *8.Kompanie* | *Obersturmführer* Hans Siegel |
| *Chef* of the *9.Kompanie*3 | *Hauptsturmführer* Wolf Buettner |
| *Werkstatt Zugführer* | *Obersturmführer* Dieter Müller |

## Knight's Cross Holders of *SS-Panzer Regiment 12*
### Oakleaves
| | |
|---|---|
| Max Wünsche | August 11, 1944, *Obersturmbannführer, Kommandeur, SS-Panzer Regiment 12* |

### Knight's Cross
| | |
|---|---|
| Arnold Jürgensen | October 16, 1944, *Sturmbannführer, Kommandeur, I./SS-Panzer Regiment 12* |
| Karl-Heinz Prinz | July 11, 1944, *Sturmbannführer, Kommandeur, II./SS-Panzer Regiment 12* |
| Richard Rudolf | November 18, 1944, *Oberscharführer, Zugführer, SS-Panzer Regiment 12* |
| Hans Siegel | August 23, 1944, *Hauptsturmführer, Kompanie Chef, 8./SS-Panzer Regiment 12* |

**Max Wünsche**: Born in Kittlitz on April 20, 1914 and joined SS start of October 1934. *Führeranwärter Lehrgang* (officer candidate course) in Jüterbog starting November 11, 1934 to April 24, 1935. Attends 2nd Class of cadets of *Junkerschule* Bad Tölz, then *Zugführer Lehrgang* (platoon leaders' course) in Dachau, *Standartenoberjunker* – February 25, 1936. April 28, 1936 made *Zugführer* in the *9./LSSAH*, then moved to *11.Kompanie* as *Zugführer*. October 10, 1938, becomes ordnance officer with the *Begleitkommando des Führers*. January 24, 1940, *Zugführer* in *15./LSSAH*. June 1940 returns to *Begleitkommando des Führers* as adjutant. December 5, 1940, becomes adjutant of *LSSAH*. February 1942 commander *Sturmgeschütz Abteilung LSSAH*. June 1 to August 31, 1942 attends *Generalstabslehrgang* (General Staff officers' course) at the Army *Kriegsschule* in Berlin September 1, 1942, returns as commander of *Sturmgeschütz Abteilung LSSAH*. October 22, 1942, appointed commander of *I.Abteilung, Panzer Regiment LSSAH*.

---

3   A *Versorgungskompanie*, it transported to the frontlines any supplies needed for the regiment's troops and vehicles.

Oakleaves recommendation cover for the eventual award to Max Wünsche, signed by
*"Hitlerjugend"* commander Kurt "Panzer" Meyer. Document appears courtesy of Mark C. Yerger.

Begründung und Stellungnahme der Zwischenvorgesetzten

In den harten Angriffs- und Abwehrkämpfen der 12. ϟϟ-Pz.Div. "Hitler-jugend" westlich Caen hat das ϟϟ-Panzer-Rgt. 12 unter Führung seines Kommandeurs ϟϟ-Obersturmbannführer Max W ü n s c h e bisher 219 Feindpanzer vernichtet. Dieser Erfolg ist lediglich auf die wendige Führung und Entschlußkraft seines Kommandeurs zurückzuführen. Unter rücksichtslosem Einsatz seiner eigenen Person hat er die schwierig-sten Lagen gemeistert. Durch den Einsatz des ϟϟ-Panzer-Rgt. 12 am 28./29. Juni 1944 südwestlich Caen wurde die feindliche Absicht, einen Brückenkopf bei Amayé und St. Andrée über die Orne zu bilden, vereitelt. Durch ständige Gegenangriffe und geschickt geführte Flankenstöße gelang es der Kampfgruppe Wünsche, die feindliche Panzerspitze zu zerschlagen. Ohne den Einsatz des ϟϟ-Panzer-Rgt.12 unter der Führung von ϟϟ-Obersturmbannführer Wünsche wäre es der Division nicht gelungen, die feindlichen Kräfte südwestlich Caen zu vernichten. Die Leistungen des ϟϟ-Panzer-Rgt.12 sind besonders hoch zu bewerten, weil es sich um ein junges Regiment mit einem sehr jungen Unterführerkorps und noch jüngeren Mannschaften handelt. Die eigenen Verluste des ϟϟ-Panzer-Rgt.12 stehen dabei in keinem Verhältnis zu den feindlichen Panzerverlusten. Im Nahkampf Mann gegen Mann wurde ϟϟ-Obersturmbannführer Wünsche bereits am 2. Tag verwundet. Trotzdem verblieb er bei seinem Regiment und führte es unter persönlichem tapferen Einsatz weiter.

Ich bitte, die persönliche Tapferkeit des Kommandeurs des ϟϟ-Panzer-Rgt.12, ϟϟ-Obersturmbannführer Max Wünsche und seine wendige Führung mit dem

Eichenlaub zum Ritterkreuz des Eisernen Kreuzes

auszeichnen zu wollen.

ϟϟ-Standartenführer
und Divisions-Kommandeur.

Recommendation of *Obersturmbannführer* Max Wünsche, *Kommandeur, SS-Panzer Regiment 12*, for the Oakleaves to the Knight's Cross. Document appears courtesy of Mark C. Yerger.

July 7, 1943, appointed commander of *Panzer Regiment "Hitlerjugend"* (also given as June 24, 1943, in a promotion recommendation dated November 28, 1943). July 28, to August 20, 1943, attends course for *Abteilung* commanders at Army *Panzertruppenschule* Wünsdorf. Wounded June 9, 1944, but remained with his command. *Untersturmführer,* April 20, 1936, *Obersturmführer,* November 9, 1938, *Hauptsturmführer,* May 25, 1940, *Sturmbannführer,* September 1, 1942, *Obersturmbannführer,* January 30, 1944. Iron Cross 2nd Class May 25, 1940, Iron Cross 1st Class June 20, 1940, Eastern Front Medal July 6, 1942, Wound Badge in Black 1940, Infantry Assault Badge in Bronze October 30, 1940, Wound Badge in Silver June 11, 1944, German Cross in Gold February 25, 1943, Knight's Cross February 28, 1943. Captured on August 19, 1944, during the Falaise pocket fighting after being wounded in the leg and a POW until 1948. Postwar manager of an industrial plant in Wuppertal and died on April 18, 1995, in Munich.

As commander of *SS-Panzer Regiment 12*, *Obersturmbannführer* Max Wünsche was recommended for the Oakleaves to the Knight's Cross by divisional commander Kurt Meyer. Submitted for approval in July and approved on 11 August 1944, Meyer's text reads as follows:[4]

In the intense offensive and defensive fighting of the *12.SS-Panzer Division "Hitlerjugend"* west of Caen, *SS-Panzer Regiment 12,* under its commander *Obersturmbannführer* Max Wünsche, has to date knocked out 219 enemy tanks. This success is entirely due to the flexible leadership and resolve of its commander. While recklessly exposing his own person he has mastered the most difficult situations. Thanks to the action of *SS-Panzer Regiment 12* on 28/29 June 1944, southwest of Caen, the enemy plan to build a bridgehead at Amayé and St. André was thwarted. By means of constant counterattacks and skillfully conducted flank attacks, *Kampfgruppe "Wünsche"* was able to smash the enemy armoured spearheads. Without the action of *SS-Panzer Regiment 12* and the leadership of *Obersturmbannführer* Wünsche, the division would have been unable to destroy the enemy forces southwest of Caen. The accomplishments of *SS-Panzer Regiment 12* deserve special recognition because it is a young regiment with an extremely young corps of non-commissioned officers and even younger enlisted men. The losses incurred by *SS-Panzer Regiment 12* bear no comparison with the enemy losses of armour. In hand-to-hand fighting *Obersturmbannführer* Wünsche was already wounded on the second day. Nevertheless, he remained with his regiment and continued to lead it with courageous personal commitment.

I request that the personal bravery of commander of *Obersturmbannführer* Max Wünsche and his flexible leadership be recognized with the award of the Oakleaves to
The Knight's Cross of the Iron Cross

(Signed) [Kurt] Meyer
*SS-Standartenführer* and Division Commander

**Arnold Jürgensen**: Born in Tellingstedt on May 17, 1910. Joined the SS on January 1, 1932, with the *2./I./53.SS-Standarte* and moved to the *"Leibstandarte"* on May 10,

---

4   Vorschlag Nr. 1 für die Verleihung des Ritterkreuzes des Eisernen Kreuzes mit Eichenlaub. See award proposal cover illustration.

Begründung und Stellungnahme der Zwischenvorgesetzten

ᛋᛋ-Sturmbannführer  J ü r g e n s e n  hat bisher an sämtlichen Feld-
zügen dieses Krieges teilgenommen. Er ist Kommandeur der I.(Panther)-
Abteilung des ᛋᛋ-Panzer-Rgt.12 der 12.ᛋᛋ-Pz.Div. "Hitlerjugend" und hat
sich als solcher in den Kämpfen an der Invasionsfront durch besondere
Tapferkeit und umsichtige Führung bewährt und ausgezeichnet. Die
Abteilung vernichtete unter seiner Führung in den Kämpfen an der
Invasionsfront 321 feindliche Panzer.

Besonders aber zeichnete sich ᛋᛋ-Stubaf. Jürgensen in den Kämpfen am
8.8.44 durch besondere Tapferkeit aus. Nachdem am Vortage, dem 7.8.44,
dem Feind der Durchbruch durch die Stellungen der 89.Inf.Div. im Abschnitt Garcelles - Laize-Mündung im Kampfraum südlich Caen gelungen
war, trat am 8.8.44 ᛋᛋ-Stubaf. Jürgensen mit wenigen eigenen Panzern
aus dem Abschnitt der linken Nachbardivision an, um sich zum Gegenangriff im Raum nördlich Rouvres bereitzustellen. In diesem Raum
wurde er jedoch von plötzlich auftretendem starken Panzerfeind von
etwa 60 Feindpanzern überrascht. ᛋᛋ-Stubaf. Jürgensen trat mit seinen
Panzern unverzüglich zum Angriff an, brachte die beherrschende Höhe
140 wieder in eigenen Besitz und brachte den Gegner zum Stehen. Hier-
durch wurde ermöglicht, daß die befohlenen geländemäßig günstigsten
Stellungen wieder eingenommen werden konnten. Dadurch aber wurde dem
Feind ein Durchbruch nach Falaise im Verlauf dieser Kampfhandlungen
unmöglich gemacht. Die von ᛋᛋ-Stubaf. Jürgensen geführten eigenen
Panzer konnten während dieser Kampfhandlungen 32 feindliche Panzer
vernichten. ᛋᛋ-Stubaf. Jürgensen selbst wurde hierbei verwundet, führte
aber seine Einheit bis zum Abschluß dieser Kämpfe weiter.

Der tatkräftigen, tapferen Führung des ᛋᛋ-Stubaf. Jürgensen ist es
zuzuschreiben, daß der Feind am 8.8.44 nicht bis Falaise durchstoßen
konnte. Der beispielhaften Tapferkeit ihres Kommandeurs ist es zuzuschreiben, daß die Panther-Abt. der 12.ᛋᛋ-Pz.Div. "Hitlerjugend" während des 10-wöchigen Kampfes an der Invasionsfront über 300 feindliche
Panzer vernichten konnte.

Ich halte den ᛋᛋ-Stubaf. Jürgensen für die Verleihung des

    Ritterkreuzes zum Eisernen Kreuz

würdig.

ᛋᛋ Oberführer
und Divisions-Kommandeur.

Recommendation of *Sturmbannführer* Arnold Jürgensen, *Kommandeur*, I./*SS-Panzer
Regiment 12*, for the Knight's Cross. Document appears courtesy of Mark C. Yerger.

1933. March 1935 became a *Zugführer* in the *8./LSSAH*, then a *Zugführer* with the *6./LSSAH* from August 1935. Mid-September 1939 Ordnance Officer *2./LSSAH* and then June 1940 *Kompanie Chef 11./LSSAH*. July 1940 *Kompanie Chef 13./LSSAH*. July 1942 infantry gun *Kompanie Chef* in *SS-Infanterie Regiment 1 "LSSAH"*. September 15, 1942, to *Panzer Abteilung LSSAH* and *1.Kompanie Chef*. German Cross in Gold as *Hauptsturmführer* and *Kompanie Chef, 1./SS-Panzer Abteilung 1 "Leibstandarte"*, May 6, 1943. November 15, 1943 to *"Hitlerjugend"* as commander *I./SS-Panzer Abteilung 12*, wounded August 9, 1944. *Untersturmführer* November 9, 1938, *Obersturmführer* January 30, 1940, *Hauptsturmführer* January 30, 1942, *Sturmbannführer* January 30, 1945. Iron Cross 2nd Class October 16, 1939, Iron Cross 1st Class July 22, 1940, Infantry Assault Badge in Bronze March 9, 1942, Eastern Front Medal August 25, 1942. Recommended for the Knight's Cross by Kurt "Panzer" Meyer on August 29, 1944. Severely wounded on December 21, 1944, he died in a field hospital in Büttgenbach two days later.

As a *Sturmbannführer* commanding the *I.Abteilung* of the *"Hitlerjugend" Panzer Regiment*, Arnold Jürgensen was recommended for the Knight's Cross by divisional commander Kurt Meyer. Meyer's proposal, submitted on 29 August 1944, reads as follows:[5]

*Sturmbannführer* Jürgensen has participated in all the previous campaigns of this war. He is the commander of the *I.(Panther)Abteilung* of *SS-Panzer Regiment 12* of the *12.SS-Panzer Division "Hitlerjugend"*. He has exhibited exceptional courage and circumspect leadership in the fighting on the Invasion Front. Under his leadership the *Abteilung* has destroyed 321 enemy tanks in the fighting on the Invasion Front.

*Sturmbannführer* Jürgensen was particularly conspicuous for exceptional bravery in the fighting on 8 August 1944. After the enemy had broken through the positions of the *89.Infanterie Division* on the previous day, 7 August 1944, in the Garcelles [-Secqueville] (mouth of the Laize River) sector in the combat area south of Caen, *Sturmbannführer* Jürgensen moved out with a few tanks on 8 August 1944. They went from the sector of the adjoining division to take position for a counterattack in the area north of Rouvres. In this area, however, he was surprised by the sudden appearance of a strong armoured force of about 60 enemy tanks. *Sturmbannführer* Jürgensen immediately attacked with his tanks, regained the commanding Hill 140 and brought the enemy to a halt. That made it possible to recapture, as ordered, the positions on the most favorable terrain. That, in turn, made it impossible for the enemy to break through to Falaise in the course of this combat operation. The tanks led by *Sturmbannführer* Jürgensen destroyed 32 enemy tanks during this action. *Sturmbannführer* Jürgensen was wounded in this action, but continued to lead his unit until the conclusion of this fighting.

The effective, courageous leadership of *Sturmbannführer* Jürgensen is the reason that the enemy could not break through to Falaise on 8 August 1944. Because of the exemplary courage of its commander, the *Panther Abteilung* of the *12.SS-Panzer Division "Hitlerjugend"* was able to destroy over 300 enemy tanks during the ten-week battle on the Invasion Front.

I recommend that *Sturmbannführer* Jürgensen be awarded

---

5   Vorschlag Nr. 7 für die Verleihung des Ritterkreuzes des Eisernen Kreuzes, with handwritten approval date of 16 October 1944.

The Knight's Cross of the Iron Cross.

(Signed) [Kurt] Meyer

*SS-Oberführer* and *Divisions-Kommandeur*

**Karl-Heinz Prinz**: Born on February 23, 1914, in Marburg and joined *Allgemeine-SS* February 1933. March 1935 joined *SS/VT* with *Regiment "Germania".* Attended 1936 class at *Junkerschule* Braunschweig April 1936 to end of January 1937. *Standartenjunker* September 28, 1936, *Standartenoberjunker* February 16, 1937. Served in *Totenkopfverbände* with *"Oberbayern"* after being commissioned. September 1939 to late March 1940 adjutant of *SS-Totenkopfstandarte 7.* Late March 1940 to *"Totenkopf"* *Division* as *Zugführer* in *14./SS-Totenkopf-Infanterie-Regiment 1.* June to late August 1940 *Kompanie Führer 14./Totenkopf-Infanterie-Regiment 1.* Transferred to *"Leibstandarte"* and self-propelled *Kompanie Chef 1./Panzerjäger Abteilung "LSSAH"*, German Cross in Gold March 28, 1943. To *"Hitlerjugend"* 1943 as commander *II./SS-Panzer Regiment 12.* Killed during an attack north of Falaise near le Torps on August 14, 1944. Promoted *Untersturmführer* April 20, 1937, *Obersturmführer* November 9, 1938, *Hauptsturmführer* April 20, 1941, and *Sturmbannführer* June 21, 1943. Iron Cross 2nd Class June 21, 1940, Iron Cross 1st Class September 24, 1941, Eastern Front Medal August 30, 1942, and Tank Assault Badge in Silver February 21, 1942.

*Panzer Regiment* commander Max Wünsche both proposed and formally submitted Karl-Heinz Prinz for the Knight's Cross for his commander of the *II. Abteilung*. Wünsche's recommendation, submitted on 20 June 1944, reads as follows:[6]

*SS-Sturmbannführer* Prinz has excelled in all the campaigns – Western, Balkan and Russian – and was awarded the German Cross in Gold. On 7 June 1944, as commander of the *II./Abteilung, Panzer Regiment 12* at Caen, with only a few tanks of his *Abteilung*, he opposed the attack of strong enemy forces that were already within 1500 meters of the Caen airfield. He repulsed the attack and thereby

1.) prevented the capture of the airfield and city of Caen, and

2.) established the prerequisites for a German counterattack.

Under extremely difficult circumstances, extremely heavy fire from enemy naval guns and in the face of numerous tanks and anti-tank guns, the attack brought the villages of Authie, Cussy, Buron and Contest into German hands. Despite the heavy enemy fire, Prinz fought his way forward with the *Abteilung* to Villons. In so doing he captured three English majors and one company, as well as destroying 14 enemy tanks.

At about 1800 hours, supported by the drumfire barrage of his naval artillery, the enemy renewed the attack with about 30 tanks. Thanks to the personal bravery and skilled leadership of *Sturmbannführer* Prinz, the enemy attack was repulsed and the attained line was held. In so doing, 16 enemy Sherman and General Lee tanks were knocked out.

On 11 June 1944, the enemy broke through with infantry and over 35 tanks via Le Mesnil-Patry toward the Tilly-Caen main road. On his own initiative, Prinz immediately launched a hasty counterattack. Through his skillful assault and bold

6    Vorschlag Nr. 1 für die Verleihung des Ritterkreuzes des Eisernen Kreuzes, with handwritten approval date of 11 July 1944.

Begründung und Stellungnahmen der Zwischenvorgesetzten

SS-Sturmbannführer Prinz, in allen Feldzügen - Westen, Balkan und Rußland -
aufs Höchste bewährt und dafür mit dem Deutschen Kreuz in Gold ausgezeichnet,
hat sich am 7.6.1944 als Kommandeur der II./SS-Pz.Rgt.12 bei C a e n  mit nur
wenigen Panzern seiner Abteilung dem Engländer entgegen-geworfen und den Angriff
starker Feindkräfte, die mit Panzern bereits 1500 m vor dem Flugplatz Caen stan-
den, abgewehrt und damit

  1.) die Wegnahme des Flugplatzes und der Stadt C a e n verhindert und
  2.) die Voraussetzungen für den eigenen Gegenangriff geschaffen.

Der unter schwierigsten Verhältnissen - schwerstem Feuer der feindl. Schiffs-Art.
und zahlreicher Panzer und Pak - vorgetragene Angriff, brachte die Ortschaften
A u t h i e , C u s s y , B u r o n und C o n t e s t  in eigene Hand. Trotz des
schweren Feindfeuers kämpfte sich Prinz mit der Abteilung weiter vorwärts und
stieß auf V i l l o n s  durch. Dabei gelang es ihm 3 engl. Majore und 1 Kompanie
gefangenzunehmen und 14 Feindpanzer abzuschießen.
Gegen 18.00 Uhr trat der Feind mit etwa 30 Panzern und durch das Trommelfeuer seiner
Schiffsartillerie unterstützt, erneut zum Angriff an. Der Feindangriff wurde durch
die persönliche Tapferkeit und die geschickte Führung des Sturmbannführer Prinz
abgeschlagen und die erreichte Linie gehalten. 16 Feindpanzer vom Typ Sherman
und General Lee wurden dabei abgeschossen.
Am 11.6.1944 brach der Feind mit Infanterie und über 35 Panzern über Le Mesnil-
Patry - Richtung Hauptstraße T i l l y - C a e n  - durch. P. trat aus eigenem
Entschluß sofort zum Gegenstoß an und vernichtete durch geschickten Ansatz und
schneidige Führung 21 Feindpanzer vom Typ Sherman und brachte Mesnil-Patry wieder
in eigene Hand und verhinderte den Durchbruch weiterer Feindkräfte von Norrey.
P. hat sich auch in den darauffolgenden Tagen immer wieder durch persönliche
Tapferkeit und Schneid hervorgetan. Er führte jeden Gegenangriff persönlich und
war seinen Männern ein leuchtendes Beispiel.
Mit seiner jungen Abteilung hat der Sturmbannführer Prinz in den nunmehr 15 tägi-
gen Kämpfen 73 Panzerkampfwagen vernichtet und 19 Flugzeuge abgeschossen und somit
an den Gesamterfolgen des Regimentes und der Division großen Anteil.

                              Der Kommandeur SS-Panzer-Regiment 12

                              SS-Obersturmbannführer

Recommendation of *Sturmbannführer* Karl-Heinz Prinz, *Kommandeur*, II./*SS-Panzer Regiment 12*, for the Knight's Cross. Document appears courtesy of Mark C. Yerger.

leadership, Prinz knocked out 21 enemy Sherman tanks, recaptured Mesnil-Patry, and prevented the breakthrough of additional enemy forces from Norrey.

In the ensuing days Prinz continued to excel in his personal bravery and zeal. He personally led every counterattack and was a shining example to his men. With his young *Abteilung, Sturmbannführer* Prinz has destroyed 73 enemy tanks and shot down 19 aircraft in what is now over 15 days of fighting, thereby contributing greatly to the overall success of the regiment and the division.

*Kommandeur, SS-Panzer Regiment 12*
(Signed) [Max] Wünsche
*Obersturmbannführer*

**Richard Rudolf**: Born April 16, 1923, in Hermsdorf/Sachsen and joined the *Waffen-SS* July 4, 1940. Posted to the *"Leibstandarte"* and promoted to *Unterscharführer* August 1, 1942. *Panzer Regiment "Leibstandarte"* as tank commander. To *"Hitlerjugend"* as a later NCO *Zugführer* in *SS-Panzer Regiment 12* and awarded the Knight's Cross. Iron Cross 2nd and 1st Class, Wound Badge in Silver, Tank Assault badge in Silver. Survived the war and died in Schönau on December 13, 2004.

**Hans Siegel**: Born in Böckau on July 25, 1918. Served in *15.SS-Totenkopfstandarte* before joining the *"Leibstandarte"* in 1938. In Poland he commanded a heavy mortar platoon with the *12./LSSAH*. Attended 2nd wartime cadet class at *Junkerschule* Bad Tölz, then *Zugführer* in *4./Ersatz Bataillon "Leibstandarte"*. 1941 became *1.Kompanie Chef*. December 1941 *I.Zugführer* in the *3.Batterie* of *Sturmgeschütz Abteilung "Leibstandarte"*. Autumn of 1943 with the *SS-Sturmgeschütz-Ausbildungs-und Ersatz Abteilung* at *Truppenübungsplatz "Heidelager"* near Krakow, Poland. January 10, 1944, to *12.SS-Panzer Division "Hitlerjugend"* as *8.Kompanie Chef, SS-Panzer Regiment 12*. Wounded June 27, 1944. Succeeded Karl-Heinz Prinz in command of *II./SS-Panzer Regiment 12* after Prinz was killed on August 15, 1944. When Herbert Kuhlmann became ill, Siegel given temporary command of *SS-Panzer Regiment 12* by divisional commander Hugo Kraas. When Martin Groß took command of *SS-Panzer Regiment 12* in 1945, Siegel then returned to command of its *II.Abteilung*. Seriously wounded on March 24, 1945, his ninth wartime wound. Captured May 8, 1945, his severe wounds resulting in an arm being amputated. *Untersturmführer* August 1, 1940, *Obersturmführer* November 9, 1942, *Hauptsturmführer* June 21, 1944. Iron Cross 2nd Class February 18, 1943, Iron Cross 1st Class June 14, 1944, Eastern Front Medal February 6, 1943, Wound Badge in Silver March 30, 1943, Tank Assault Badge in Silver March 30, 1943. Became an architect after the war and died on April 18, 2002, in Andernach.

As a *Hauptsturmführer* and *Kompanie Chef* of the *8./SS-Panzer Regiment 12*, Hans Siegel was recommended for the Knight's Cross on 1 July 1944. Panzer Regiment commander *Obersturmbannführer* Max Wünsche wrote and submitted the proposal that reads as follows:[7]

---

7    Vorschlag Nr. 4 für die Verleihung des Ritterkreuzes des Eisernen Kreuzes, with handwritten approval date of 23 August 1944. See elsewhere in this appendix for biographical data regarding Max Wünsche, as well as further references and photos throughout the main text.

Begründung und Stellungnahme der Zwischenvorgesetzten

SS-Hstuf. S i e g e l ist der Angriffsträger seiner Abteilung. Er hat in den wechselvollen Angriffs- und Abwehrkämpfen um C a e n als Kompanieführer, von 37 durch die Kompanie abgeschossenen Panzern, allein bisher 11 Feindpanzer vernichtet.

Am 11.6.1944 mußte er, weil zum vierten Male abgeschossen, bei dem Gegenangriff ostwärts T i l l y weit vor den eigenen Linien ausbooten und brachte dabei noch Gefangene ein.

Am 27.6.1944 brach der Engländer mit Panzern und SPW. von C h e u x auf G r a i n v i l l e und auf M o n e n durch. S. wurde aus schwersten Abwehrkämpfen, wobei Feindpanzer auf 30 m Entfernung abgeschossen wurden, herausgelöst und dem neuen Feind entgegengeworfen. Es gelang S. im Nachtangriff nach Norden Raum zu gewinnen und den Durchbruch der Feindpanzer über G r a i n v i l l e nach Süden zu verhindern. S. hielt seine Stellungen ohne jeden infantristischen Schutz und trotz schwersten Trommelfeuers.

Beim Ansetzen und Einweisen seiner Männer wurde er im Dunkel der Nacht von einem Feindspähtrupp überrascht und erlitt im Handgemenge einen Stich in die rechte Seite. Dennoch gelang es ihm, sich seiner Gegner zu erwehren und seine Stellung zu halten.

Am nächsten Morgen griff der Feind erneut an. S. kämpfte bis zum letzten seiner Panzer, wodurch er das Heranführen neuer Kräfte ermöglichte und einen entscheidenden Durchbruch des Engländers abermals verhinderte. S. wurde dabei zum fünften Male selbst abgeschossen und erlitt schwerste Verbrennungen.

SS – Obersturmbannführer
und Rgt.-Kommandeur

Ich halte SS-Hstuf. S i e g e l aufgrund seiner besonderen Tapferkeitstaten für die hohe Auszeichnung mit dem

Ritterkreuz des Eisernen Kreuzes

für würdig.

SS – Standartenführer
und Div.-Kommandeur.

Recommendation of *Hauptsturmführer* Hans Siegel, *Kompanie Chef, 8./SS-Panzer Regiment 12*, for the Knight's Cross. Document appears courtesy of Mark C. Yerger.

*Hauptsturmführer* Siegel is the soul of the fighting spirit of his *Abteilung*. In the eventful offensive and defensive fighting around Caen, as *Kompanie* commander, he knocked out 11 of the 37 enemy tanks destroyed by his company.

On 11 June, 1944, in the counterattack east of Tilly when his fourth tank was knocked out from under him, Siegel had to dismount far from friendly lines. He returned while also bringing in four prisoners.

On 27 June, 1944, the British broke through from Cheux to Grainville and Mouen. Siegel was withdrawn from the most extreme defensive fighting, where enemy tanks were knocked out at a range of 30 meters, and thrown into the fight against the new enemy attack. In a night attack, Siegel gained ground to the north and thwarted the advance of the enemy armour via Grainville to the south. Siegel held his positions without any infantry support and despite extremely heavy gunfire.

While positioning and briefing his men he was surprised in the dark of night by an enemy patrol. In the hand-to-hand fighting that resulted he was stabbed in the right side. Nevertheless, he was able to repulse the enemy and hold his position.

The next morning the enemy renewed their attack. Siegel fought with his tank to the last, making it possible to bring up new forces and thereby prevent a decisive British breakthrough. In so doing Siegel's tank was knocked out from under him for the fifth time and he suffered extremely severe burns.

(Signed) [Max] Wünsche
*Obersturmführer* and *Rgt.-Kommandeur*

Because of his extremely courageous actions I recommend *Hauptsturmführer* Siegel for this high award

The Knight's Cross of the Iron Cross

(Signed) [Kurt] Meyer
*SS-Standartenführer* and Division Commander

## German Cross in Gold Holders of *SS-Panzer Regiment 12*

| | |
|---|---|
| Ullrich Ahrens | August 25, 1944, *Standartenoberjunker, 2./SS-Panzer Regiment 12* |
| Kurt-Anton Berlin | confirmed award with date, *SS-Panzer Regiment 12* |
| Helmut Gaede | August 25, 1944, *Obersturmführer, 2./SS-Panzer Regiment 12* |
| Heinz Lehmann | August 25, 1944, *Hauptscharführer, 4./SS-Panzer Regiment 12* |
| Kurt Mühlhaus | August 19, 1944, *Standartenoberjunker, 6./SS-Panzer Regiment 12* |
| Erich Pohl | December 30, 1944, *Obersturmführer, 4./SS-Panzer Regiment 12* |
| Rudolf von Ribbentrop | August 25, 1944, *Obersturmführer, 3./SS-Panzer Regiment 12* Ludwig Ruckdeschel, August 19, 1944, *Hauptsturmführer, 6./SS-Panzer Regiment 12* |

**Ullrich Ahrens**: Saw combat in Poland, as an *Unterscharführer* with the *4./V./ LSSAH* in 1941. Attended *Junkerschule* for reserve officer candidates and killed as a *Standartenoberjunker d.R.* and *Zugführer* with the *2./SS-Panzer Regiment 12* on August

---

Begründung und Stellungnahme der Zwischenvorgesetzten.

---

A. nahm vom 1. 9. bis 28. 9. 1939 am Polenfeldzug, 6.4.1941 bis
14. 5. 1941 am Balkanfeldzug, vom 2. 7. 1941 bis 2.7.1942 am
Rußlandfeldzug und vom 1o.2. bis 15. 4. 1943 am Wintereinsatz
Charkow teil.

A. hat sich in allen Feldzügen durch sein kühnes, unerschrockenes
Handeln und vorbildliche Tapferkeit hervorragend bewährt.

Als Kommandant eines Tiger-Panzers stieß er während eines Angriffes
am 6. 3. 1943 im Kampf um Charkow auf eine starke feindl.Pak-Front.
Durch seinen persönlichen Einsatz und Unerschrockenheit vernichtet e
er sechs Pak ( 7,62 cm) und mehrere Infanteriewaffen. A. wurde bei
diesem Gefecht selbst abgeschossen, bootete aus und bekämpfte mit
der M. Pi. die in der Nähe befindliche feindl. Infanterie.

Bei den Kämpfen an der Invasionsfront zeigte A. bei einem Angriff
gegen Panzerfeind und Infanterie nördlich G r a i n v i l l e
wiederholt sein selbständiges zuverlässiges Handeln und besondere Tapferkeit .

Bei einem Gegenangriff auf dem Flugplatz C a e n bewies er erneut besonderen Schneid und Tapferkeit. Er vernichtete vier Feindpanzer mit folgender Infanterie und zerschlug damit den feindl.
Angriff.

Bei einem Gegenangriff am 9. 7. 1944 in M a l t o t zeichnete sich
A. durch Unerschrockenheit und Tapferkeit wiederholt aus. Im stärksten
Artillerie-Feuer vernichtete er 1 Karette und einen Feindpanzer vom
Typ " Sherman ".

A. ist auf Grund seiner mehrfach bewiesenen Tapferkeit würdig mit
dieser hohen Auszeichnung beliehen zu werden.

H – Sturmbannführer
und Abt.-Kommandeur

A. ist ein in allen Feldzügen bewährter Soldat, der auf Grund seiner
immer wieder besonderen Tapferkeit zum Offizier vorgeschlagen wurde und
den ich für würdig halte, mit dem Deutschen Kreuz in Gold ausgezeichnet
zu werden.

SS-Obersturmbannführer u.
Rgts.-Kommandeur.

Recommendation of *Standartenoberjunker* Ullrich Ahrens, *2./SS-Panzer Regiment 12*,
for the German Cross in Gold. Document appears courtesy of Mark C. Yerger.

14, 1944, in La Cambe. Iron Cross 2nd Class October 10, 1941, Iron Cross 1st Class December 24, 1941, Wound Badge in Black December 24, 1941, Tank Assault Badge in Silver March 1, 1943.

As a *Standartenoberjunker d.R.* and *Zugführer* with the *2./SS-Panzer Regiment 12*, Ullrich Ahrens was recommended for his award by *Sturmbannführer* Arnold Jürgensen. After being seconded by regimental commander Max Wünsche, the following proposal was submitted on 25 July 1944.[8]

> Ahrens participated in the Polish Campaign from 1 September to 28 September, the Balkan Campaign from 26 April 1941 to 14 May, 1941, the Russian Campaign from 2 July 1941 to 2 July 1942, and in winter action at Kharkov from 10 February to 15 April 1943.
>
> Ahrens has proven to be outstanding for his bold, fearless conduct and exemplary courage in all these campaigns.
>
> As commander of a Tiger tank he came up against a strong enemy anti-tank position during an attack on 6 March 1943 in the fighting around Kharkov. Thanks to his personal commitment and fearlessness, he destroyed six anti-tank guns (7.62cm) and several infantry weapons. Ahrens had his tank knocked out in this action, dismounted, and fought the enemy infantry in the area with his machine pistol.
>
> In the fighting on the Invasion Front Ahrens repeatedly demonstrated his independence, reliable conduct, and special bravery in an attack against enemy armour and infantry north of Grainville.
>
> In a counterattack on the Caen airfield he again displayed special zeal and courage. He destroyed four enemy tanks with their following infantry, thereby smashing the enemy attack.
>
> In a counterattack on 9 July 1944 in Maltot, he repeatedly excelled for fearlessness and bravery. Under extremely heavy artillery fire he destroyed one Bren Gun Carrier and an enemy Sherman tank.
>
> Because of his repeated demonstrations of courage I recommend him for this high award.
>
> (signed) [Arnold] Jürgensen<br>*Sturmbannführer* and *Abt.-Kommandeur*
>
> Ahrens is a soldier who has proven himself in all campaigns. Because of his repeatedly proven special bravery he is recommended for promotion to an officer, and I recommend him for the award of the German Cross in Gold.
>
> (signed) [Max] Wünsche<br>*Sturmbannführer* and *Rgts.-Kommandeur*

**Kurt-Anton Berlin:** Joined the SS at the start of 1932 and July 1933 to *"Leibstandarte"*. Attended 1938 class *Junkerschule* Bad Tölz then posted to *Totenkopfverbände* with *3./Thüringen* as *Zugführer* September 1938. May 1939 to *SS-Heimwehr Danzig*. July 1939 attached to Army *13./Infanterie Regiment 101* and with unit during combat in Poland. Assigned to *"Totenkopf" Division* November 1939 as *Zugführer* in *14./SS-Totenkopf-*

---

8   Vorschlag Nr. 16 für die Verleihung des Deutschen Kreuzes in Gold, with handwritten approval date from the Army Personnel Office dated 25 August 1944.

*Infanterie-Regiment 3*, May 1940 *14.Kompanie Chef*, August 1940 adjutant *SS-Totenkopf-Infanterie-Regiment 2*. Mid-November 1940 moved to *Einsatzstab "Wegner"* under *Reichskommissariat "Norwegen"*. Late March 1942 to *"Das Reich"* as *Stabskompanie Chef, Panzer Regiment*. Mid-November 1942 to *Panzer Abteilung "Leibstandarte"* until start of 1944. Assigned to *"Hitlerjugend" Panzer Regiment* January 1, 1944, and trained by Army on Panthers February 1944. *Kompanie Chef 1./SS-Panzer Regiment 12* until mid-January 1945. Transferred to *"Totenkopf" Division* as commander of *I.Abteilung, SS-Panzer Regiment 3*. Recipient Blood Order and German Cross in Gold without date. Iron Cross 1st and 2nd Classes, Tank Assault Badge in Silver. *Untersturmführer* November 9, 1938, *Obersturmführer* January 30, 1940, *Hauptsturmführer* January 30, 1942, *Sturmbannführer* January 30, 1945. Survived war and died on July 1, 1969.

**Helmut Gaede**: Joined SS 1938, to *Waffen-SS* September 22, 1939. Attended *Junkerschule* Bad Tölz May to September 1941 and posted to *"Leibstandarte"*. With *VII./Leibstandarte* and served with *Kampfgruppe "Schuldt"* (led by later Swords holder Hinrich Schuldt) in Don fighting to March 1943 when wounded. *SS-Panzer-Grenadier-Ausbildungs- und Ersatz Bataillon I* March to October 1943. Assigned to *"Hitlerjugend"* October 1943, led *2.*, then *1.Kompanie* of *SS-Panzer Regiment 12*. *Untersturmführer* January 30, 1942, *Obersturmführer* November 9, 1943. Iron Cross 2nd Class October 29, 1941, Iron Cross 1st Class March 21, 1942, Eastern Front Medal August 1, 1942, Wound Badge in Black March 5, 1943. He survived the war, eventual fate unknown.

Helmut Gaede was an *Obersturmführer* leading the *2./SS-Panzer Regiment 12* when recommended for the German Cross in Gold by Arnold Jürgensen. The proposal, seconded by *Panzer Regiment* commander Max Wünsche, was submitted on 25 July 1944 and reads as follows:[9]

Gaede took part in the Polish Campaign from 1 September to 16 September 1939.

From 18 September 1941 to July 1942 he took part in the Russian Campaign as leader of a machine gun platoon. There he repeatedly excelled through his coolness and personal commitment. On 28 October 1941 he completely destroyed an attacking Russian battalion with his machine gun platoon and gained mention in a division order for 29 October 1941 for his personal courage.

In the winter of 42/43 he repeatedly shone in the heavy defensive fighting in the Don Bend because of his courage and coolness.

Since the start of the fighting on the Invasion Front, he has repeatedly excelled through his personal commitment and daredevil actions.

On 29 June 1944 he repulsed several enemy attacks with his company due to his personal actions. In a counterattack on Hill 112, north of Esquay, he knocked out six enemy tanks.

During the time from 2 July 1944 to 8 July 1944 he repulsed heavy enemy attacks against the commanding heights of the Caen airfield, knocking out seven enemy Sherman tanks. In this he displayed personal courage in the face of the most difficult conditions.

---

9   Vorschlag Nr. 13 für die Verleihung des Deutschen Kreuzes in Gold, dated 25 July 1944 with handwritten approval date of 25 August 1944.

Begründung und Stellungnahme der Zwischenvorgesetzten

Gaede nahm am Polen-Feldzug vom 1.9. - 16.9.39 teil.

Vom 18. 9.41 - Juli 42 nahm er am Rußland-Feldzug als M.G.-zugführer teil. Hier hat er sich wiederholt durch besonderen Schneid und Kaltblütigkeit und persönlichen Einsatz hervorragend bewährt. Am 28.10.41 zerschlug er mit seinem M.G.-Zug ein angreifendes russisches Btl. und wurde wegen persönlicher Tapferkeit im Div.-Befehl vom 29.10.41 genannt.

Im Winter 42/43 hat er sich in den schweren Abwehr-Kämpfen im Don-Bogen wiederholt durch Mut und Kaltblütigkeit ausgezeichnet.

Seit Beginn der Kämpfe an der Invasions-Front hat er sich wiederholt durch persönlichen Einsatz und Draufgängertum hervorragend bewährt.

Am 29. 6.44 wehrte er mit seiner Kompanie durch persönlichen Einsatz mehrere Feindangriffe ab. Im Gegenangriff auf die Höhe 112 nördlich von E s q u a y schoß er 6 Feindpanzer ab.

In der Zeit vom 2. 7.44 - 8. 7.44 wehrte er starke Feindangriffe, unter Abschuß von 7 Feindpanzern vom Typ Sherman, gegen die beherrschende Höhe des Flugplatzes C a e n durch persönliche Tapferkeit unter schwersten Bedingungen ab.

Auf Grund der immer bewiesenen Tapferkeit ist G. würdig, diese hohe Auszeichnung zu erhalten.

ᛋᛋ - Sturmbannführer
und Abt.-Kommandeur

Abgesehen von den Einsätzen in Polen und Rußland , hat er sich während der Kämpfe an der Invasionsfront während des 6 wöchigen ununterbrochenen Einsatzes , mit seiner Kompanie fast ausschließlich in der HKL eingesetzt, in stärkstem feindl. Artilleriefeuer täglich aufs Neue bewährt. Ich halte ihn auf Grund seiner persönlichen Tapferkeit für würdig mit dieser hohen Auszeichnung beliehen zu werden.

SS-Obersturmbannführer u.
Rgts.-Kommandeur.

Recommendation of *Obersturmführer* Helmut Gaede, *2./SS-Panzer Regiment 12*, for the German Cross in Gold. Document appears courtesy of Mark C. Yerger.

Because of the repeated displays of courage, Gaede is recommended for this high award.

(Signed) [Arnold] Jürgensen
*SS-Sturmbannführer* and *Abt.-Kommandeur*

Aside from the actions in Poland and Russia, every day he has proven himself anew while his company has been committed almost exclusively in the main line of resistance. This six weeks of unbroken action was under extremely heavy enemy artillery fire. Because of his personal courage I recommend him for this high award,

(Signed) [Max] Wünsche
*SS-Obersturmbannführer* and *Rgts.-Kommandeur*

**Heinz Lehmann**: Joined *SS-Verfügungstruppe* November 1, 1938, with *5./Leibstandarte*. Trained with *"Das Reich"* and became NCO tank commander February 1942, with eventual *Panzer Abteilung "Leibstandarte"* when formed (*Oberscharführer* April 20, 1942). Transferred to *"Hitlerjugend"* and by July 1944 NCO *Zugführer* with *4./SS-Panzer Regiment 12* as a *Hauptscharführer*. Iron Cross 2nd Class October 3, 1940, Iron Cross 1st Class March 3, 1943, Tank Assault Badge in Silver April 1, 1943, Wound Badge in Black September 20, 1941, Wound Badge in Silver. *Untersturmführer* August 1, 1944 (field commission). Wounded July 14, 1941 (hospital until October 1941), February 15, 1943, and March 20, 1943. Killed August 23, 1944, in Champigny-St. André.

As a *Hauptscharführer* and *Zugführer* with the *4./SS-Panzer Regiment 12*, Heinz Lehmann was recommended for the German Cross in Gold on 25 July 1944. Proposed by *Sturmbannführer* Arnold Jürgensen, commander of the *I. Abteilung*, his recommendation text reads as follows:

During the bitter fighting in the winter of 1943 around Kharkov, Lehmann proved himself worthy of the highest recognition with his unusual courage.[10] On 16 February 1943 he stood out in the destruction of a Russian division with his conspicuously daredevil aggressiveness. As a tank commander, he unhesitatingly advanced toward the attacking Russian battalion and destroyed hundreds of Russians infantry through his reckless boldness.

He drove point in a breakthrough and, through circumspect action, destroyed two anti-tank guns in an anti-tank position.

Since the start of the fighting on the Invasion Front he has led his platoon with conspicuous bravery.

During a night attack on Rots-Bretteville, west of Caen, Lehmann shined brilliantly for his circumspect leadership and exemplary courage as platoon leader. He broke through the enemy anti-tank positions and reached his objective, destroying two enemy anti-tank guns and five Bren Gun Carriers.

In the same manner, on 11 June 1944 he inspired his men to charge in a hasty counterattack against a strong enemy penetration east of Tilly. Despite extremely heavy artillery fire, they destroyed four enemy tanks.

---

10  See Lehmann's personal data. Lehmann served with the *"Leibstandarte"* before being recommended for his award while serving in *"Hitlerjugend"*, as did several other award holders.

Lehmann hat sich während der harten Kämpfe im Winter 1943 um Charkow hervorragend als Panzerkommandant durch besondere Tapferkeit aufs Höchste bewährt. Am 16. 2.43 leistete er bei der Zerschlagung einer russischen Division durch sein Draufgängertum Hervorragendes. Er fuhr als Panzerkommandant mit seinem Panzer ohne zu zögern in ein angreifendes russisches Btl. und vernichtete durch sein kühnes Draufgängertum Hunderte von Russen.

Bei einem Einbruch fuhr er Spitze und vernichtete durch umsichtiges Handeln an einer Panzersperre 2 Pak-Geschütze.

Seit Beginn des Kampfes an der Invasions-Front hat er als Panzerzugführer durch beispielhafte Tapferkeit seinen Zug geführt.

Bei einem Nachtangriff gegen R o t s - B r e t t e v i l l e westlich C a e n hat sich L. durch umsichtige Führung und beispielhafte Tapferkeit als Zugführer hervorragend bewährt. Er durchbrach die feindliche Pak-Sperre und erreichte unter Vernichtung von 2 feindlichen Pak-Geschützen und 5 Kareten sein Angriffsziel.

In der gleichen Weise riss er seine Männer am 11. 6.44 im Gegenstoß gegen durchgebrochene Feindpanzer und am 25. 6.44 gegen einen starken feindlichen Einbruch ostwärts T i l l y trotz stärksten Artillerie-Feuers mit sich nach vorn und vernichtete 4 Feindpanzer.

L. hat sich in allen angeführten Einsätzen durch hervorragende persönliche Tapferkeit und umsichtige Führung seines Zuges besonders hervorgetan. - Ich halte L. für würdig, mit dieser hohen Auszeichnung beliehen zu werden.

⚡ = Sturmbannführer
und Abt.-Kommandeur

L. gehört zu den bewährtesten Unteroffizieren der Leibstandarte und zu den hervorragendsten Zugführern des Regiments, der sich in allen Feldzügen durch Tapferkeit und Schneid immer wieder bewährte und zur Beförderung zum Offizier vorgeschlagen ist. Ich halte ihn für würdig diese hohe Auszeichnung zu erhalten.

SS-Obersturmbannführer u.
Rgts.-Kommandeur.

Recommendation of *Hauptscharführer* Heinz Lehmann, *4./SS-Panzer Regiment 12*, for the German Cross in Gold. Document appears courtesy of Mark C. Yerger.

Lehmann has been especially remarkable for conspicuous personal bravery and circumspect leadership of his platoon in all of the actions which have taken place. I recommend him for this high award.

(Signed) [Arnold] Jürgensen
*SS-Sturmbannführer* and *Abt.-Kommandeur*

Lehmann is one of the most able non-commissioned officers of the *Leibstandarte* and one of the most outstanding platoon leaders of the regiment. He has repeatedly excelled in all campaigns for his courage and pluck and has been recommended for promotion to an officer. I recommend him for this high award.

(Signed) [Max] Wünsche
*SS-Obersturmbannführer* and *Regts.-Kommandeur*

**Kurt Mühlhaus**: Joined SS early 1938 and from April 1938 *"Leibstandarte"*. Start of war was motorcycle dispatch rider for an infantry company of *"Leibstandarte"* and *Unterscharführer* September 1, 1940. October 23, 1942, tank commander and *Truppführer* with *1./Panzer Regiment "Leibstandarte"*, *Oberscharführer* November 9, 1942. Attended *Junkerschule* as reserve officer candidate, to *SS-Panzer Regiment 12* as *Standartenoberjunker d.R.* and *Zugführer 6./SS-Panzer Regiment 12*. Iron Cross 2nd Class November 1, 1941, Iron Cross 1st Class March 3, 1943, Eastern Front Medal August 25, 1942, Infantry Assault Badge in Bronze September 22, 1943. Eventual fate unknown.

**Erich Pohl**: Promoted directly to Army *Leutnant* from *Gefreiter* after destroying 14 T-34s on August 18, 1941. Transferred to *"Hitlerjugend"* as a trained Panzer officer 1944, and *Kompanie Chef 4./SS-Panzer Regiment 12*. Given equal SS rank August 15, 1944, and promoted to *Obersturmführer* September 1, 1944. Both classes of Iron Cross August 18, 1941, Tank Assault Badge in Silver August 24, 1941, Wound Badge in Black September 15, 1941, Wound Badge in Silver September 15, 1944, Mentioned in *Wehrmacht* Daily Report August 21, 1941 (for August 18, 1941, combats), Roll of Honor Clasp February 5, 1945. Fate unknown.

Erich Pohl was recommended for the German Cross in Gold as a *Hauptsturmführer* and *Kompanie Chef* of the *4./SS-Panzer Regiment 12*. The proposal, written by Knight's Cross holder *Sturmbannführer* Arnold Jürgensen when commander of the *I./Panzer Regiment 12*, was submitted on 8 November 1944 and reads as follows:[11]

Pohl participated in the Russian campaign from 22 June to 19 August 1941 and again from 20 August 1942 to 1 May 1943.

There he repeatedly proved his pluck and courage. On 18 August 1941 he knocked out 14 T-34 tanks, for which he was awarded the Iron Cross 1st Class.[12] Pohl was mentioned in the *Wehrmacht* Daily Report for bravery and received a battlefield promotion from *Gefreiter* to *Leutnant*.

---

11  Vorschlag Nr. 31 für die Verleihung des Deutschen Kreuzes in Gold, dated 8 November 1944 with handwritten approval date of 30 December 1944.
12  Pohl received both classes of the Iron Cross on 18 August 1941.

Begründung und Stellungnahmen der Zwischenvorgesetzten

Pohl nahm vom 22.6.-19.8.41 und vom 20.8.42 bis 1.5.43 am Rußland-feldzug teil.

Er hat sich hier wiederholt durch persönlichen Schneid und Tapfer-keit bewährt. Am 18.8.1941 vernichtete er 14 Pz.Kpfw. vom Typ "T 34" und wurde dafür mit dem EKII ausgezeichnet, im Wehrmachts-bericht genannt und außerdem wegen Tapferkeit vor dem Feinde vom Gefreiten zum Leutnant befördert.

Bei den Kämpfen an der Invasionsfront bewährte er sich erneut gleich in den ersten Tagen durch besondere Tapferkeit und kühnes Handeln und schoß innerhalb zweier Tage mit seiner Kompanie 20 Feindpanzer vom Typ "Sherman", davon 4 persönlich ab.

Bei einem Angriff auf R o t s und B r e t t e v i l l e im Kampfraum C a e n gelang es ihm durch rücksichtslosen persönlichen Einsatz, von 8 angreifenden Feindpanzern 5 abzuschießen. Der An-griff wurde dadurch abgeschlagen.

Bei einem Nachtangriff auf C a r p i q u e t nordwestl. C a e n bewährte sich P. durch umsichtige klare Führung und persönlichen Einsatz auf das Höchste. Durch seinen schwungvollen Angriffsgeist gelang es ihm eine Artilleriestellung zu vernichten und dadurch der Infantrie spurbare Hilfe und Entlastung zu bringen.

Während der Kesselschlacht im Raume F a l a i s e war es wiederum P. der sich durch kühnes Handeln besonders hervortat. Bei den Ab-setzbewegungen nach der Kesselschlacht,bei C o n c h e s und V e r n e u i l , schoß er mit seiner noch aus 10 Wagen bestehenden Kompanie 12 "Sherman" ab und vereitelte damit den angestrebten schnellen Durchbruch der Amerikaner.

Am 21., 22., 23.8. schoß er mit seiner nun nur noch aus 6 Wagen bestehenden Kompanie im Raume V e r s o n /sur Seine, Pacy sur Eure und L o u v i e r s unter besonders schwierigen Verhält-nissen 20 Feindpanzer ab und trug damit erheblich zum Vereiteln des angestrebten Durchbruches bei.

Am 24., 25., 26.8. fühlte der Feind wiederholt erneut mit Panzer-spitzen vor, wurde aber durch die energische und tatkräftige Abwehr des SS-Ostuf. Pohl unter Abschuß von 5 Feindpanzer jedesmal abgewiesen

P. ist auf Grund seiner immer wieder bewiesenen Tapferkeit und um-sichtigen Führung würdig die hohe Auszeichnung zu tragen.

Befürwortet:
Rgt.Gef.Std., den 6.11.44

SS-Sturmbannführer
u. Rgt.-Kommandeur

SS - Sturmbannführer
und Abt.-Kommandeur

Recommendation of *Obersturmführer* Erich Pohl, *4./SS-Panzer Regiment 12*, for the German Cross in Gold. Document appears courtesy of Mark C. Yerger.

In the very first days of fighting on the Invasion Front he again demonstrated uncommon courage and bold action. In the first two days he and his *Kompanie* knocked out 20 enemy Sherman tanks, four of which he personally destroyed.

In a display of reckless personal commitment during an attack on Rots and Bretteville in the Caen combat area, he knocked out five out of eight attacking enemy tanks, thereby repulsing the attack.

In a night attack on Carpiquet, northwest of Caen, Pohl shined with clear, circumspect leadership and the highest level of personal commitment. Because of his bold, aggressive spirit he was able to destroy an artillery position, thereby bringing immediate perceptible aid and relief to the infantry.

During the Battle of the Falaise Pocket, Pohl again performed outstandingly bold actions. In the course of the withdrawal after the pocket battle at Conches and Verneuil, his *Kompanie*, which still had 10 tanks, knocked out 12 Sherman tanks. They thus thwarted the intended enemy breakthrough.

On 24, 25, and 26 August the enemy repeatedly probed with armoured spearheads. They were repulsed each time, with the loss of five enemy tanks, by the dynamic and effective defense of *Obersturmführer* Pohl.

Because of his repeatedly demonstrated courage and circumspect leadership, Pohl is recommended for this high award.

Endorsed:

Regimental Command Post, 6 November 1944

(Signed) [Willi] Hardieck     (Signed) [Arnold] Jürgensen

*SS-Sturmbannführer      SS-Sturmbannführer*

and *Rgts.-Kommandeur*     and *Abt.-Kommandeur*

**Rudolf von Ribbentrop**: Son of Foreign Minister Joachim von Ribbentrop, attended *NPEA* school in Ilfeld. Joined *Waffen-SS* September 1, 1939, with *11./Deutschland*. Attended 5th wartime cadet class at *Junkerschule* Braunschweig then attached to *Befehlshaber der Waffen-SS "Nord"*. June 1941 to *1./Aufklärungsabteilung SS-Kampfgruppe "Nord"* as *Zugführer*. Wounded September 1941 and after recovery in February 1942 to *Panzer Abteilung "Leibstandarte"*. *6.* then *7.Kompanie Chef, Panzer Regiment "Leibstandarte"*. To *"Hitlerjugend"* as *3.Kompanie Chef, SS-Panzer Regiment 12*. Wounded June 3, 1944. Following the injury of Jürgensen took command of *I.Abteilung, SS-Panzer Regiment 12* during Ardennes offensive. *Untersturmführer* April 20, 1941, *Obersturmführer* April 20, 1943, *Hauptsturmführer* January 30, 1945. Knight's Cross July 15, 1943, as *6.Kompanie Führer Panzer Regiment "Leibstandarte"*. Iron Cross 2nd Class June 19, 1940, Iron Cross 1st Class March 20, 1943, Infantry Assault Badge in Bronze April 1, 1941, Wound Badge in Black, Wound Bade in Silver April 1943. Living in retirement at time of writing.

Arnold Jürgensen recommended Rudolf von Ribbentrop for the German Cross in Gold for his command of the *3./SS-Panzer Regiment 12*, with his proposal then being seconded by regimental commander Max Wünsche. The 25 July 1944 recommendation was submitted by *"Hitlerjugend"* commander Kurt Meyer and reads as follows:

12. ⚡ – Panzer – Division
" Hitlerjugend "

(Vorschlagende Dienststelle)

Reichsführer-⚡ Perſönl. Stab.
Verb. Offz. b. OKH / PA /P 5

| Eingang | 10. Aug. 1944 | | |
| --- | --- | --- | --- |
| Tgb.Nr. 677/44⚡ | | | |

*224*

# Vorschlag Nr. 14

## für die Verleihung
## des Deutschen Kreuzes in · Gold

*Verliehen!  25. 8. 44*

Div.Gef.St. den  25. Juli  1944

(Unterschrift)

⚡-Standartenführer und Div.-Kommandeur.
(Dienstgrad und Dienststellung)

Folder for the German Cross in Gold proposal for *Obersturmführer* Rudolf von Ribbentrop
signed by Kurt "Panzer" Meyer. Document appears courtesy of Mark C. Yerger.

Begründung und Stellungnahmen der Zwischenvorgesetzten

v. Ribbentrop nahm vom 1o.5.bis 31.5.4o am Westfeldzug als Krad-
schütze teil. Ferner nahm er an der Sicherung Norwegens vom 25.4. bis
6. 6. 41 teil, sowie an der Sicherung Finnlands vom vor 7.5.bis 3o.6.41

Im Rußland-Einsatz(Charkow) Winter 42/43 hat er sich wiederholt als
Panzerzug-Führer durch hervorragende Tapferkeit und Kaltblütigkeit
besonders hervorgetan.

Er zeichnete sich durch besondere Tapferkeit,durch Schneid und Kaltblütigkeit am 12.7.43 in Rußland beim Angriff auf K u r s k aus.
Er schoß an einem Tage persönlich  14 Feindpanzer vom Typ" T 34 "
ab, außerdem gelang es ihm mit seiner Kompanie in wenigen Tagen
4o Feindpanzer zu vernichten.

An der Invasionsfront hat sich v. R.,obgleich er kurz vor Beginn der
Invasion durch Tiefflieger schwer verwundet worden war,durch Härte
gegen sich selbst und besonderen Schneid und Kaltblütigkeit besonders ausgezeichnet.

Am 8. 7. 44 wehrte er einen starken feindl. Durchbruch bei Buron
durch Gegenangriff unter persönlichem Einsatz,erfolgreich ab und
vernichtete mit seiner Kompanie 27 Feindpanzer vom Typ "Sherman",
8 Karetten und die aufgesessene Infanterie, sowie 2 Pak-Geschütze.

Auf Grund der immer wieder bewiesenen persönlichen Tapferkeit halte
ich v. R. für würdig mit dieser hohen Auszeichnung beliehen zu werden.

H - Sturmbannführer
und Abt.-Kommandeur

SS-Obersturmführer v. Ribbentrop ist trotz seiner mehrfachen Verwundungen
nicht von seiner Truppe weggegangen und hat in mehreren Fällen, noch nicht
voll genesen, sofort die Führung seiner Kompanie wieder übernommen und die
mit beispielhafter Tapferkeit und Umsicht geführt.
Ich schlage ihn infolge seiner stets aufs Neue gezeigten Tapferkeit für die
hohe Auszeichnung vor.

SS-Obersturmbannführer u.
Rgts.-Kommandeur.

Recommendation of *Obersturmführer* Rudolf von Ribbentrop, 3./*SS-Panzer Regiment
12*, for the German Cross in Gold. Document appears courtesy of Mark C. Yerger.

Von Ribbentrop participated in the Western Campaign from 10 May to 31 May 1940 as a motorcycle rifleman. He then took part in securing Norway from 25 April to 6 June 1941 as well as in securing Finland from 7 June to 30 June, 1941.

In the Russian Campaign (Kharkov) in the winter of 42/43 he repeatedly excelled as the leader of a *Panzer Zug* for outstanding bravery and coolness.

On 12 July 1943 he displayed special bravery, zeal, and coolness in Russia in the attack on Kursk. In a single day he personally knocked out 14 enemy T-34 tanks. In addition, with his *Kompanie*, he destroyed 40 enemy tanks in a few days.

On the Invasion Front von Ribbentrop particularly shined for self discipline and unusual zeal and coolness, even though he was severely wounded shortly before the start of the invasion by a low-flying enemy airplane.

On 8 July 1944, through personal commitment in a counterattack, he successfully thwarted an enemy breakthrough at Buron. With his *Kompanie*, he knocked out 27 enemy Sherman tanks, eight Bren Gun Carriers, mounted infantry, and two anti-tank guns.

Because of his unfailing display of personal bravery I recommend von Ribbentrop for this high award.

(Signed) [Arnold] Jürgensen
*Sturmbannführer* and *Abt.-Kommandeur*

Despite his repeated wounds, *Obersturmführer* von Ribbentrop has remained with his men. In several instances, though not fully healed, he immediately resumed command of his company and led it with exemplary courage and circumspection. Because of his constant display of fresh courage I recommend him for this high award.

(Signed) [Max] Wünsche
*Obersturmbannführer* and *Rgts.-Kommandeur*

**Ludwig Ruckdeschel**: October 1928 to September 1932 *Gau Geschäftsführer* and *Gau Propagandaleiter* for *Gau Oberfranken*. September 1932 deputy *Gauleiter* for Bayerische Ostmark. Joined SS October 1, 1934, retroactive September 1, 1934. *41.SS-Standarte* to November 1, 1935, then to *Abschnitt XXVIII* to April 1936. Staff officer same *Abschnitt* to November 9, 1941. Himmler's staff from then on, substitutes performing duties when with *Waffen-SS*. War Reporters' *Abteilung* November 1941 until assigned to replacements pool section of *Oberabschnitt "Main"*. May 1942 to *Panzer Abteilung "Leibstandarte"*, October to December 1942 platoon leader course at Army *Panzertruppenschule* Wünsdorf. Eventual *Zugführer* with *2./Panzer Regiment "Leibstandarte"*. May 1, 1943, to *SS-Panzer Regiment 12* as first *6.Kompanie Chef* of *SS-Panzer Regiment 12* until seriously wounded on June 26, 1944. To *SS-Panzer-Ausbildungs-und Ersatz Regiment*, fate afterwards unknown. *Allgemeine-SS*: *Sturmbannführer* November 9, 1934, *Standartenführer* January 1, 1936, *Oberführer* November 9, 1938, *Brigadeführer* November 9, 1941. *Waffen-SS*: *Untersturmführer d.R.* November 9, 1941, *Obersturmführer d.R.* April 20, 1943, *Hauptsturmführer d.R.* June 21, 1944, *Sturmbannführer d.R.* January 30, 1945. Iron Cross 2nd Class March 9, 1943, Iron Cross 1st Class March 17, 1943, Tank Assault Badge in Silver April 1, 1943, Wound Badge in Black April 1, 1943, Golden Party Badge.

SS-Hstuf. Ruckdeschel trat am 1.4.40 als SS-Mann in die Totenkopf-Division ein und wurde nach Besuch eines Unterführeranwärter-Lehrganges zum Gruppenführer ernannt und nahm als solcher bei der III./SS-T.Div. am Westfeldzug teil.
Am 28.6.1941 wurde er als Leiter einer Propaganda-Abteilung zur Heeresgruppe Süd versetzt. Nach seiner Beförderung zum SS-Untersturmführer am 1.12.1941 meldete er sich erneut zum Kampfeinsatz zum Panzer-Regiment der Leibstandarte SS Adolf Hitler. Als solcher nahm er an den Kämpfen um Charkow teil und wurde als Zugführer wegen seines vorbildlichen und überaus tapferen kämpferischen Einsatzes am 9.3.1943 mit dem E.K. II. und am 17.3.1943 bereits mit dem EK. I, am 1.4.1943 mit dem Verwundetenabzeichen in Schwarz, wegen Splitterverletzung am Kopf und Oberarm und am 1.4.43 mit dem Panzerkampfabzeichen in Silber ausgezeichnet.
Seit 7.6.1944 in der Schlacht um Caen mit seiner Panzer-Kompanie eingesetzt, hat er als Führer mit besonderer Bravour seine Kompanie geführt und nördlich Caen den ersten auftretenden englischen Panzergegner überzeugend geschlagen und am ersten Einsatztag 14 feindliche Kampfwagen, 3 Schützenpanzer und mehrere Pak vernichtet. Auch in den nachfolgenden Tagen hat R. bei den Kämpfen um die Höhe 102 ostwärts T i l l y im härtesten Kampf und stundenlangen Artillerie-Trommelfeuer dem Gegner empfindliche Verluste beigebracht und weitere 8 Kampfwagen und mehrere Pak abgeschossen. Immer wieder ist er es persönlich gewesen, der durch seine Standhaftigkeit, Unerschrockenheit seiner Kompanie ein hervorragender Vorkämpfer gewesen ist.
R. wurde im Osten 3-mal und am 7.6.1944 sowie am 17.6.1944 mit seinem Panzer abermals abgeschossen. Dabei hat er sich immer wieder beim Bergen seiner verwundeten Besatzungen hervorragend bewährt und sich trotz schwersten Artilleriefeuers und feindl. Panzereinwirkung in vorbildlicher Weise eingesetzt und hervorgetan.
Beim Durchbruch zahlreicher Feindpanzer im Raum C h e u x wurde er, vom Einsatz südlich T i l l y kommend, nach schwerstem Kampf mit Feindpanzern wieder abgeschossen und verlor dabei einen Arm.
Ich halte ihn für die Verleihung des Deutschen Kreuzes in Gold für würdig.

SS-Obersturmbannführer
und Rgts.-Kommandeur

Recommendation of *Hauptsturmführer* Ludwig Ruckdeschel, *6./SS-Panzer Regiment 12*, for the German Cross in Gold. Document appears courtesy of Mark C. Yerger.

Ludwig Ruckdeschel was a *Hauptsturmführer d.R.* leading the *6./Panzer Regiment* when recommended by Max Wünsche for the German Cross in Gold. Wünsche himself formally submitted the proposal that reads as follows:[13]

*Hauptsturmführer* Ruckdeschel joined the *"Totenkopf" Division* on 1 April 1940 as an *SS-Mann*. After attending an *Unterführeranwärter Lehrgang* [Non-commissioned officer candidate instruction course] he was promoted to *Gruppenführer* and took part in the Western Campaign as such in the *3rd Regiment*, *SS "Totenkopf" Division*.

On 28 June 1941 he was transferred to *Heeresgruppe "Süd"* as the leader of a Propaganda Detachment. Following his promotion to *Untersturmführer* on 1 December 1941, he reported anew for combat assignment to the *Panzer Regiment* of the *Leibstandarte SS "Adolf Hitler"*. As such he participated in the fighting around Kharkov and, as a platoon leader, on account of his exemplary and generally courageous action in combat, was awarded the Iron Cross 2nd Class, on 9 March 1943, the Iron Cross 1st Class on 17 March 1943, and the Wounded Badge in Black on 1 April 1943 for shrapnel wounds to the head and upper arm. On 1 April 1943 he was awarded the Tank Battle Badge in Silver.

Since 7 June 1944 he has been in action with his *Panzer Kompanie* in the battle for Caen, where he has shown unusual bravery in leading his *Kompanie*. North of Caen he convincingly smashed the first arriving English armoured opponent, destroying 14 English tanks, three troop carriers, and several anti-tank guns on his first day in action. In the ensuing days, during the fighting for Hill 102 east of Tilly, in extremely intense fighting and under hour-long artillery drumfire Ruckdeschel caused the enemy substantial losses. He knocked out eight more tanks and several anti-tank guns. He has repeatedly proven himself with his steadfastness and fearlessness as an outstanding front-line fighter in his *Kompanie*.

Ruckdeschel had his tank shot out from under him three times on the Eastern Front, again on 7 June 1944, and also on 17 June 1944. Each time he was outstanding in rescuing his wounded crew members. Despite extremely heavy artillery fire and involvement of enemy armour he has excelled and provided an outstanding example.

Returning from action south of Tilly, he came up against a breakthrough by numerous enemy tanks in the Cheux area. After an extremely intense fight with enemy armour his tank was again knocked out and he lost one arm.

I recommend him for the award of the German Cross in Gold.

(Signed) [Max] Wünsche
*Obersturmführer* and *Rgts.-Kommandeur*

## *SS-Panzer Regiment 12* 1944-1945

For reasons stated elsewhere in the appendix a complete listing of all officers of any late war formations such *"Hitlerjugend"* fighting in the West, especially in the final months of the war, is nigh-on impossible. Many having served with the *"Leibstandarte"*, the officer cadre of both units in this study suffered grievously in the less than a year between

---

13  Vorschlag Nr. 5 für die Verleihung des Deutschen Kreuzes in Gold, with handwritten approval date of 19 August 1944.

the start of the Normandy fighting and the end of the war. The following are known to have held the posts indicated and are in sequential order.

### SS-Panzer Regiment 12

| | | |
|---|---|---|
| Max Wünsche[14] | *Obersturmbannführer* | *Kommandeur* |
| Willi Hardieck[15] | *Obersturmbannführer* | *Kommandeur* |
| Hebert Kuhlmann[16] | *Obersturmbannführer* | *Kommandeur* |
| Hans Siegel[17] | *Sturmbannführer* | *Kommandeur* |
| Martin Groß | *Obersturmbannführer* | *Kommandeur* |
| George Iseke[18] | *Hauptsturmführer* | *Adjutant* |
| Dr. Wolfgang Rabe[19] | *Hauptsturmführer* | *Regimentsarzt* (IVb) |
| Dr. Rudolf Stiawa[20] | *Hauptsturmführer* | *Regimentsarzt* (IVb) |
| Heinrich Neinhardt[21] | *Hauptsturmführer* | *Zahnarzt* |
| Eduard Donaubauer | *Obersturmführer* | *Verwaltungsführer* (IVa) |
| Hermann Lütgert[22] | *Hauptsturmführer* | *Verwaltungsführer* (IVa) |
| Claus Müller | *Obersturmführer* | *Verwaltungsoffizier* (IVa) |
| Josef Breitenberger[23] | *Obersturmführer* | TFK (Technical Officer, Vehicles) |
| Wilhelm Sammann[24] | *Hauptsturmführer* | TFK (Technical Officer, Vehicles) |
| Josef Langreiter | *Obersturmführer* | TFK (Technical Officer, Vehicles) |
| Anton Stark | *Obersturmführer* | TFW (Technical Officer, Weapons) |
| Rudolf Nerlich[25] | *Untersturmführer* | *Ordonnanz Offizier* |
| Bernd Jungbluth[26] | *Obersturmführer* | *Ordonnanz Offizier* |
| Helmut Schlauß[27] | *Hauptsturmführer* | *Nachrichtenoffizier* |

---

14 Captured during the Falaise fighting on August 19, 1944, see Knight's Cross holders section of this appendix.
15 Killed on December 17, 1944.
16 Knight's Cross on February 13, 1944, and German Cross in Gold on November 8, 1944, as commander *I./Panzer Regiment "Leibstandarte"*. He became ill and was succeeded by Siegel. A graduate of the original 1935 *Führerschule* Braunschweig class, Kuhlmann also led *I./Panzer Regiment "Das Reich"*. Promoted to *Obersturmbannführer* on January 30, 1945. Survived the war and died in South America on November 9, 1995.
17 See Knight's Cross holders section in this appendix.
18 Born in Mangwitz on May 12, 1919, Isecke had served as an *Unterscharführer* with the *4./V./LSSAH* in 1941. Receiving a field commission, as an *Obersturmführer* he served as *Abteilungsadjutant* of the *I./ SS-Panzer Regiment 1 "Leibstandarte"* before moving to "Hitlerjugend." He was captured on August 24, 1944.
19 Died on March 2, 1992.
20 Previously the IVb of the *I.Abteilung* of SS-Panzer Regiment 1 "Leibstandarte", Stiawa was killed in action on August 18, 1944, in Brieux.
21 Previously with the *Sanitätsabteilung* of the *"Leibstandarte"*.
22 Previously the IVa of the *Freiwilligen Legion "Niederlande"*.
23 Died on May 2, 1998.
24 Previously *TFK* of the *I.Abteilung, Panzer Regiment "Leibstandarte"*.
25 Born in Breslau on January 13, 1920, he had served as an *Unterscharführer* with the *7.Kompanie* of SS-Panzer Regiment "Leibstandarte" before commissioned and was killed on June 9, 1944.
26 Died on January 14, 1966.
27 Born in Vienna on April 7, 1919. Schlauß joined the SS with the *Nachrichtenzug* of the *"Leibstandarte"* in 1937. Graduated with the 2nd wartime cadet class at *Junkerschule* Bad Tölz. *Untersturmführer* August 1, 1940, *Obersturmführer* November 9, 1942, *Hauptsturmführer* June 21, 1944. 1941 adjutant of the

| | | |
|---|---|---|
| Walter Schaffert[28] | *Untersturmführer* | *Flak Zugführer* |
| Helmut Post | *Untersturmführer* | *Versorgungskompanie Chef* |
| Paul Kändler[29] | *Untersturmführer* | *Kraderkundungs Zugführer* |
| Konrad Wörz | *Untersturmführer* | *Werksttattkompanie Chef*[30] |

### I./SS-Panzer Regiment 12

| | | |
|---|---|---|
| Thilo Beck[31] | *Hauptsturmführer* | *Kommandeur* (formation) |
| Arnold Jürgensen[32] | *Sturmbannführer* | *Kommandeur* |
| Rudolf von Ribbentrop[33] | *Hauptsturmführer* | *Kommandeur* |
| Heinz Kling[34] | *Sturmbannführer* | *Kommandeur* |
| Dietrich Minow[35] | *Hauptsturmführer* | *Kommandeur* |
| Hubertus Schröder[36] | *Untersturmführer* | *Adjutant* |
| Fritz Fiala[37] | *Obersturmführer* | *Adjutant* |
| Siegfried Nadler | *Untersturmführer* | *Adjutant* |
| Dr Wilhelm Daniel[38] | *Obersturmführer* | *Abteilungsarzt* (IVb) |
| Fritz Berger | *Obersturmführer* | *Verwaltungsführer* (IVa) |
| Hans Hogrefe[39] | *Untersturmführer* | *Ordonnanz Offizier* |
| Rudolf Walter | *Untersturmführer* | *Nachrichten Zugführer* |
| Rolf Jauch | *Obersturmführer* | *Nachrichten Zugführer* |
| Helmuth Kloos[40] | *Untersturmführer* | *TFK* |
| Hugo Surkow | *Obersturmführer* | *TFK* |
| Robert Maier[41] | *Obersturmführer* | *TFK* |
| Anton Stark[42] | *Obersturmführer* | *TFW* |

---

*"Leibstandarte" Nachrichtenabteilung*, then *Nachrichtenoffizier* for the *I./Panzer Regiment "Leibstandarte"*. Survived the war and died in Giesshübl on May 18, 2000.

28  Having served previously with the *"Leibstandarte" Panzer Regiment*, he was killed on June 10, 1944, while *Flak Zugführer* of *SS-Panzer Regiment 12*.

29  Killed on December 21, 1944.

30  In a *Waffen-SS Panzer Division* the repair *Kompanie Chef* was assigned to the staff with each *Abteilung* normally having a *Werkstattzug*. He coordinated the 2 platoons in conjunction with the *TFW*. His title was academic in the case of *"Hitlerjugend"* as there was no combined *Werkstatt Kompanie* per sé.

31  Died in 1984.

32  Wounded August 9, 1944, see Knight's Cross holders section in this appendix.

33  See German Cross in Gold holders section in this appendix. Wounded in the Ardennes after succeeding Jürgensen who had been injured in an accident.

34  Later commanded *sSS-Panzer Abteilung 501*. Died on September 30, 1951.

35  Killed on April 25, 1945.

36  Killed on June 25, 1944, near Fontenay.

37  Killed on October 12, 1944.

38  Daniel had served as a doctor with the *SS-Artillerie-Ausbildungs-und Ersatz Regiment* while an *Untersturmführer* in 1942. He came to the *I.Abteilung* having previously served as IVb for the *III./SS-Panzer-Grenadier-Regiment 9 "Germania"*. Daniel survived the war and died on August 28, 2002.

39  Survived the Normandy campaign and in 1945 was posted with the *SS-Panzer-Ausbildungs-und Ersatz Regiment*.

40  Held the post prior to D-Day. Survived the Normandy campaign and in 1945 was posted with *SS-Panzerjäger-Ausbildungs-und Ersatz Abteilung 2*.

41  Post Normandy fighting.

42  Previously *TFW* of *SS-Panzer Regiment 1 "Leibstandarte"*.

| | | |
|---|---|---|
| Waldemar Schütz[43] | *Hauptsturmführer* | *Versorgungskompanie*[44] |
| Walter Schmidt[45] | *Untersturmführer* | *Werkstattzugführer*[46] |

**1.Kompanie:**

| | | |
|---|---|---|
| Kurt-Anton Berlin[47] | *Hauptsturmführer* | *1.Kompanie Chef* |
| Bormuth, Walter | *Hauptsturmführer* | *1.Kompanie Chef* |
| Helmut Gaede[48] | *Obersturmführer* | *1.Kompanie Chef* |

**2.Kompanie**

| | | |
|---|---|---|
| Wilhelm Beck[49] | *Hauptsturmführer* | *2.Kompanie Chef* |
| Helmut Gaede[50] | *Obersturmführer* | *2.Kompanie Chef* |

**3.Kompanie**

| | | |
|---|---|---|
| Rudolf von Ribbentrop[51] | *Hauptsturmführer* | *3.Kompanie Chef* |
| Kurt Brödel[52] | *Hauptsturmführer* | *3.Kompanie Chef* |
| Walter Hils[53] | *Hauptmann* (Army) | *3.Kompanie Chef* |
| Dietrich Minow[54] | *Hauptsturmführer* | *3.Kompanie Chef* |
| Joachim-Carl Nölck | *Untersturmführer* | *3.Kompanie Chef* |

**4.Kompanie**

| | | |
|---|---|---|
| Hans Pfeiffer[55] | *Hauptsturmführer* | *4.Kompanie Chef* |
| Erich Pohl[56] | *Obersturmführer* | *4.Kompanie Chef* |

**II./SS-Panzer Regiment 12**

| | | |
|---|---|---|
| Karl-Heinz Prinz[57] | *Sturmbannführer* | *Kommandeur* |

---

43  Died September 9, 1999.
44  A *Versorgungskompanie* transported to the frontlines any supplies needed for the regiment's troops and vehicles. Although it is confirmed only that he was assigned to it, by rank Schütz was, in all probability, its *Kompanie Chef*.
45  Killed September 1, 1944
46  Repair platoon commander subordinated to the Werkstattkompanie *Chef* who was attached to the regimental staff. This was not a consolidated *Kompanie* but a platoon served with each *Abteilung*.
47  See German Cross in Gold holders section in this appendix.
48  See German Cross in Gold holders section in this appendix. From December 1944 and previously the *2.Kompanie Chef*.
49  Killed June 10, 1944.
50  See German Cross in Gold Holders section in this appendix.
51  Wounded June 3, 1944, see German Cross in Gold holders section in this appendix; later commanded the *I.Abteilung*.
52  Killed December 18, 1944.
53  Killed December 21, 1944.
54  In 1945 was *I.Abteilung Kommandeur*.
55  Joined SS with *Regiment "Germania"* in April 1935. Graduated 1936 cadet class of *Junkerschule* Braunschweig. *Untersturmführer* April 20, 1937, *Obersturmführer* January 30, 1939, *Hauptsturmführer* January 30, 1942. 1938 led *Panzerspäh Zug "Leibstandarte"*, became *6.Kompanie Chef* of *Panzer Regiment 1 "Leibstandarte"*. Killed on June 11, 1944, in Bretteville as *4.Kompanie Chef, SS-Panzer Regiment 12*.
56  See German Cross in Gold holders section in this appendix.
57  Killed on August 14, 1944, see Knight's Cross holders section in this appendix.

| Hermann Tirschler [58] | *Hauptsturmführer* | *Kommandeur* |
|---|---|---|
| Hans Siegel[59] | *Hauptsturmführer* | *Kommandeur* |
| Friedrich Hartmann[60] | *Obersturmführer* | *Adjutant* |
| Herbert Walther[61] | *Obersturmführer* | *Ordonnanz Offizier* |
| Dr. Oskar Jordan[62] | *Hauptsturmführer* | *Abteilungsarzt* (IVb) |
| Dr. Claus Müller | *Obersturmführer* | deputy *Abteilungsarzt* |
| Benno Hofner | *Untersturmführer* | *Zahnarzt* |
| Sebastian Schweiger | *Untersturmführer* | *Verwaltungsführer* (IVa) |
| Bruno Bierhold[63] | *Untersturmführer* | *TFK* |
| Dieter Müller[64] | *Obersturmführer* | *TFK* |
| Karl Pucher | *Untersturmführer* | *TFK* II |
| Herbert Walther | *Untersturmführer* | *Stabskompanie Chef* |
| Götz Großjohann | *Hauptsturmführer* | *Stabskompanie Chef*[65] |
| Götz Großjohann | *Hauptsturmführer* | *Versorgungskompanie Chef* |
| Karl-Wilhelm Krause[66] | *Untersturmführer* | *Flak Zugführer* |
| Hermann Komadina | *Untersturmführer* | *Nachrichten Zugführer* |
| Gunnar Johnsson[67] | *Untersturmführer* | *Nachrichten Zugführer* |

### 5.Kompanie

| Helmut Bando[68] | *Obersturmführer* | *5.Kompanie Chef* |
|---|---|---|
| Karl-Heinz Porsch | *Obersturmführer* | *5.Kompanie Chef* |
| Wolf Buettner[69] | *Hauptsturmführer* | *5.Kompanie Chef* |
| Eberhard Jeran[70] | *Untersturmführer* | *5.Kompanie Chef* |

### 6.Kompanie

| Ludwig Ruckdeschel[71] | *Hauptsturmführer* | *6.Kompanie Chef* |
|---|---|---|
| Helmut Buchwald[72] | *Untersturmführer* | *6.Kompanie Chef* |

---

58  Temporary until Siegel assumed command then resumed his post as *6.Kompanie Chef*. A graduate of the 5th Wartime cadet class at *Junkerschule* Braunschweig, prior to being posted to *"Hitlerjugend"* he had served as *Kompanie Chef* of the *2./Panzerjäger Abteilung "Leibstandarte"*.

59  Previously *8.Kompanie Chef*, see Knight's Cross holders section in this appendix.

60  Died in September 1995.

61  Wounded July 11, 1944. In 1943 served with the *4./SS Panzerjäger Abteilung 1 "Leibstandarte"* then with s*SS-Panzer Abteilung 101*. Survived Normandy and died on February 24, 2003.

62  Injured (broken leg) on June 20, 1944, and killed in February 1945 with *"Hitlerjugend"*.

63  Held the post before and during the initial Normandy campaign.

64  Held the post in July 1944 and was killed in August.

65  Normally listed as the *9.Kompanie* of the Regiment, *Hauptsturmführer* Wolf Buettner commanded that numbered *Kompanie* in the Ardennes. Not all the *Stabskompanie* commanders are known though all would have commanded the same elements. These elements included the *Pionier Zug* of each *Abteilung* after the original *Panzer-Pionier-Kompanie* was divided. The *Flak Zug* was a component as well as the platoons for signals, reconnaissance, and dispatch.

66  Died on May 6, 2001.

67  Held the post in July 1944 and later moved to the *8.Kompanie, SS-Panzer Regiment 12*.

68  Killed while *5.Kompanie Chef, SS-Panzer Regiment 12*, on June 27, 1944, in Cheux.

69  Still had the post during the Ardennes fighting.

70  Killed on March 11, 1945.

71  Seriously wounded on June 26, 1944, see German Cross in Gold holders section in this appendix.

72  Killed June 28, 1944.

| | | |
|---|---|---|
| Hermann Tirschler[73] | *Hauptsturmführer* | *6.Kompanie Chef* |
| Götz Großjohann[74] | *Hauptsturmführer* | *6.Kompanie Chef* |

**7.Kompanie**

| | | |
|---|---|---|
| Heinz John[75] | *Obersturmführer* | *7.Kompanie Chef* |
| Heinrich Bräcker[76] | *Hauptsturmführer* | *7.Kompanie Chef* |
| Albert Gasch[77] | *Obersturmführer* | *7.Kompanie Chef* |

**8.Kompanie**

| | | |
|---|---|---|
| Hans Siegel[78] | *Hauptsturmführer* | *8.Kompanie Chef* |
| Herbert Höfler[79] | *Obersturmführer* | *8.Kompanie Chef* |

---

73  Wounded July 10, 1944.
74  Previously *Stabskompanie Chef*, he led the *Kompanie* in the Ardennes and died on November 6, 1998.
75  Killed June 9, 1944.
76  Bräcker spent much of his career with the *1.SS-Infanterie Brigade (mot.)*. After serving as adjutant of the *I./SS-Infanterie Regiment 8* he acted as adjutant for the Brigade. In 1943 he became *3.Kompanie Chef* of *SS-Infanterie Regiment 10*. Bräcker had succeeded *Obersturmführer* Heinz John as *7.Kompanie Chef*. Heinrich Bräcker was killed while with *"Hitlerjugend"* on July 17, 1944, as *7.Kompanie Chef, SS-Panzer Regiment 12*.
77  Died November 1, 1983.
78  Wounded on June 27, 1944, see Knight's Cross holders in this appendix.
79  Succeeded Siegel when he took command of the *II.Abteilung*.

# Assignment of Tactical Numbers to *SS-Panzer Regiment 12*, January 1944

## Appendix II/4 to Action Report, *SS-Panzer Regiment 12*

Duplicate
*12.SS-Panzer-Division "Hitlerjugend"*                    O.U., 4 January 1944
*SS-Panzer-Regiment 12*

_____
*Ia Is / Schm. Br.Tgb.Nr.14/44 geh.*

Distribution: See draft
20 copies
17th copy

Re: Assignment of tactical numbers

Below are the tactical numbers for the tanks of the Regimental Staff, the *I.* and *II.Abteilungen*.

After the tanks are painted with new camouflage colours the numerals are to be applied according to the following specifications:

Dimensions: Height     35cm Width 22cm
Type of Numerals:      Numerals with the margins painted. Width of the margin 1cm, centre of the numeral open 4cm.[2]
Colour:                Black
Location:              Centre of each side of the turret and rear of turret.

**Tactical Numbers:**

| | | | | | | |
|---|---|---|---|---|---|---|
| | | | | *Nachr.Offz.* | | 153 |
| a) *Rgt.-Stab:* | *Rgt.-Kommandeur* | 055 | | *Aufklärungszug* | | 156-160 |
| | *Rgt.-Adjutant* | 054 | | | | |
| | *Ordonnanz-Offz.* | 053 | *1.Kp.:* | | | |
| | *Aufklärungszug* | 056-060 | *Kp.-Führer* | 105 | | |
| b) *I.Abteilung* | | | *Kp.-Truppfhr* | 104 | | |
| *Rgt.-Stab* | *Kommandeur* | 155 | *1.Zug/Zugf.* | 115 | | |
| | *Adjutant* | 154 | | 116-119 | | |

_____

1  Translated by Dr Frederick P. Steinhardt.
2  In other words, outline numerals with the outline 1cm wide and the interior (non-painted space) 4cm (total width of the numeral: 6cm: edge, space, edge).

| | | | |
|---|---|---|---|
| 2.Zug/Zugf. | 125 | | |
| | 126-129 | | |
| 3.Zug/Zugf. | 135 | | |
| | 136-139 | | |
| 4.Zug/Zugf. | 145 | | |
| | 146-149 | | |

**2.Kp.:**

| | |
|---|---|
| Kp.-Führer | 205 |
| Kp.-Truppfhr | 204 |
| 1.Zug/Zugf. | 215 |
| | 216-219 |
| 2.Zug/Zugf. | 225 |
| | 226-229 |
| 3.Zug/Zugf. | 235 |
| | 236-239 |
| 4.Zug/Zugf. | 245 |
| | 246-249 |

**3.Kp.:**

| | |
|---|---|
| Kp.-Führer | 305 |
| Kp.-Truppfhr | 304 |
| 1.Zug/Zugf. | 315 |
| | 316-319 |
| 2.Zug/Zugf. | 325 |
| | 326-329 |
| 3.Zug/Zugf. | 335 |
| | 336-339 |
| 4.Zug/Zugf. | 345 |
| | 346-349 |

**4.Kp.:**

| | |
|---|---|
| Kp.-Führer | 405 |
| Kp.-Truppfhr | 404 |
| 1.Zug/Zugf. | 415 |
| | 416-419 |
| 2.Zug/Zugf. | 425 |
| | 426-429 |
| 3.Zug/Zugf. | 435 |
| | 436-439 |
| 4.Zug/Zugf. | 445 |
| | 446-449 |

**II.Abteilung**

| | | |
|---|---|---|
| Rgt.-Stab | Kommandeur | 555 |
| | Adjutant | 554 |
| | Nachr.Offz. | 553 |
| | Aufklärungszug | 556-560 |

**5.Kp.:**

| | |
|---|---|
| Kp.-Führer | 505 |
| Kp.-Truppfhr | 504 |
| 1.Zug/Zugf. | 515 |
| | 516-519 |
| 2.Zug/Zugf. | 525 |
| | 526-529 |
| 3.Zug/Zugf. | 535 |
| | 536-539 |
| 4.Zug/Zugf. | 545 |
| | 546-549 |

**6.Kp.:**

| | |
|---|---|
| Kp.-Führer | 605 |
| Kp.-Truppfhr | 604 |
| 1.Zug/Zugf. | 615 |
| | 616-619 |
| 2.Zug/Zugf. | 625 |
| | 626-629 |
| 3.Zug/Zugf. | 635 |
| | 636-639 |
| 4.Zug/Zugf. | 645 |
| | 646-649 |

**7.Kp.:**

| | |
|---|---|
| Kp.-Führer | 705 |
| Kp.-Truppfhr | 704 |
| 1.Zug/Zugf. | 715 |
| | 716-719 |
| 2.Zug/Zugf. | 725 |
| | 726-729 |
| 3.Zug/Zugf. | 735 |
| | 736-739 |
| 4.Zug/Zugf. | 745 |
| | 746-749 |

*8.Kp.:*

| | |
|---|---|
| *Kp.-Führer* | 805 |
| *Kp.-Truppfhr* | 804 |
| *1.Zug/Zugf.* | 815 |
| | 816-819 |
| *2.Zug/Zugf.* | 825 |
| | 826-829 |
| *3.Zug/Zugf.* | 835 |
| | 836-839 |
| *4.Zug/Zugf.* | 845 |
| | 846-849 |

signed Prinz
*SS-Sturmbannführer* and
deputy *Rgt.-Kommandeur*

Anlage II/4   zum Tätigkeitsbericht ᛋᛋ-Panzer-Regiment 12
==========================================================

A b s c h r i f t
_____

12. ᛋᛋ-Panzer-Div. "Hitlerjugend"          O.U., den 4. Januar 1944
    ᛋᛋ-Panzer-Regiment 12
Ia Is/Schm. Br.Tgb.Nr. 14/44 geh.

                                    Verteiler: siehe Entwurf
                                    20. Ausfertigungen
                                    17. Ausfertigung


Betr.: Zuteilung von taktischen Nummern

Nachstehend werden dem Rgt.-Stab, I. und II. Abteilung die takt.
Nummern für die Pz.Kpfw. zugeteilt.
Die Beschriftung ist, nachdem die Pz. mit neuer Tarnfarbe ver-
sehen sind, nach den folgenden Massen durchzuführen:

    Masse: Höhe 35 cm     Breite 22 cm
    Art der Beschriftung: Zahlen nur mit Rand ausgeführt,
              Breite des Randes 1 cm, Mitte der Zahl frei 4 cm.
    Farbe: schwarz
    Anbringung: Mitte jeder Turmseite und Turmrückseite.

                T a k t i s c h e   N u m m e r n :

a) Rgt.-Stab:              Rgt.-Kommandeur    055
                          Rgt.-Adjutant      054
                          Ordonanz-Offz.     053
                          Aufklärungszug     056  - 060

b) I. Abteilung:
   Abt.-Stab              Kommandeur         155
                          Adjutant           154
                          Nachr.Offz.        153
                          Aufklärungszug     156  - 160

1.Kp.:                           2.Kp.:
Kp.-Führer     105               Kp.Fhr.      205
Kp.-Truppfhr 104                 Kp.Truppfnr204
1.Zug/Zugf.  115                 1.Zug/Zugf.215
             116 - 119                       216 - 219
2.Zug/Zugf.  125                 2.Zug/Zgf.  225
             126 - 129                       226 - 229
3.Zug/Zugf.  135                 3.Zug/Zgf.  235
             136 - 139                       236 - 239
4.Zug/Zugf.  145                 4.Zug/Zgf.  245
             146 - 149                       246 - 249

```
3. Kp.:                              4. Kp.:


Kp.-Führer      305                  Kp.-Führer      405
Kp.-Truppf.     304                  Kp.-Truppf.     404
1.Zug/Zugf.     315                  1.Zug/Zugf.     415
                316 - 319                            416 - 419
2.Zug/Zugf.     325                  2.Zug/Zugf.     425
                326 - 329                            426 - 429
3.Zug/Zugf.     335                  3.Zug/Zugf.     435
                336 - 339                            436 - 439
4.Zug/Zugf.     345                  4.Zug/Zugf.     445
                346 - 349                            446 - 449



II. Abteilung:

Abt.-Stab:            Kommandeur        555
                     Adjutant          554
                     Nachr.-Offz.      553
                     Aufklärungszug    556 - 560


5. Kp.:                              6. Kp.:           605

Kp.-Führer      505                  Kp.-Führer
Kp.-Truppf.     504                  Kp.-Truppf.     604
1.Zug/Zugf.     515                  1.Zug/Zugf.     615
                516 - 519                            616 - 619
2.Zug/Zugf.     525                  2.Zug/Zugf.     625
                526 - 529                            626 - 629
3.Zug/Zugf.     535                  3.Zug/Zugf.     635
                536 - 539                            636 - 639
4.Zug/Zugf.     545                  4. Zg/Zugf.     645
                546 - 549                            646 - 649



7. Kp.:                              8. Kp.:

Kp.-Führer      705                  Kp.-Führer      805
Kp.-Truppf.     704                  Kp.-Truppf.     804
1.Zug/Zugf.     715                  1.Zug/Zugf.     815
                716 - 719                            816 - 819
2.Zug/Zugf.     725                  2.Zug/Zugf.     825
                726 - 729                            826 - 829
3.Zug/Zugf.     735                  3.Zug/Zugf.     835
                736 - 739                            836 - 839
4.Zug/Zugf.     745                  4.Zug/Zugf.     845
                746 - 749                            846 - 849


                              gez.  P r i n z
                           SS-Sturmbannführer und
                           stellv. Rgt.-Kommandeur
```

# Appendix IV

# Tanks assigned to *SS-Panzer-Regiment 12* 1 January-30 April 1944

**Appendix ___ to Action Report** *SS-Panzer Regiment 12*

List
of tanks assigned to the Regiment during the period 1.1.1944 to 30.4.1944

|          | Type:                           | Gun:        | Quantity: |
|----------|---------------------------------|-------------|-----------|
| 4.1.44   | Pz.Kpfw.V Panther (Command)     | L 70        | 1         |
| 13.1.44  | Pz.Kpfw. IV long gun version    | L 48        | 20        |
| 19.1.44  | "                               | L 48        | 13        |
| 24.1.44  | "                               | L 48        | 15        |
| 25.1.44  | "                               | L 48        | 1         |
| 3.2.44   | "                               | L 48        | 1         |
| 7.2.44   | Pz.Kpfw.V Panther               | L 70        | 16        |
| 8.3.44   | Pz.Kpfw.V Panther (Command)     | L 70        | 2         |
| 2.4.44   | Pz.Kpfw.38t (self-propelled)    | 2cm Flak 38 | 12        |

Anlage _____ zum Tätigkeitsbericht SS-Panzer-Regiment 12

A u f s t e l l u n g

über die dem Regiment in der Zeit vom 1.1.1944
bis 30.4.1944 zugewiesenen Panzerkampfwagen:

| | Art: | Kanone: | Anzahl: |
|---|---|---|---|
| 4.1.44 | Pz.Kpfw.V "Panther" (Bef.Wg.) | L 70 | 1 |
| 13.1.44 | Pz.Kpfw. IV lang | L 48 | 20 |
| 19.1.44 | "    "    " | L 48 | 13 |
| 24.1.44 | "    "    " | L 48 | 15 |
| 25.1.44 | "    "    " | L 48 | 1 |
| 3.2.44 | "    "    " | L 48 | 1 |
| 7.2.44 | Pz.Kpfw.V "Panther" | L 70 | 16 |
| 8.3.44 | Pz.Kpfw.V "Panther" (Bef.Wg.) | L 70 | 2 |
| 2.4.44 | Pz.Kpfw. 38 t als SFL. | 2 cm Flak 38 | 12 |

# Appendix V

# Weapons inventory of *SS-Panzer Regiment 12* 30 April 1944

**Appendix \_\_\_\_ to Action Report of** *SS-Panzer Regiment 12*

Weapons inventory of the Regiment
Date:    30.4.1944

As of 30.4.44 the Regiment had the following inventory of weapons:

| Type: | Quantity: |
| --- | --- |
| KwK 30 (Pz.Kpfw. II) | 6 |
| KwK L/24 (Pz.Kpfw. IV short gun version) | 1 |
| KwK L/43 (Pz.Kpfw. IV long gun version) | 3 |
| KwK L/48 (Pz.Kpfw. IV long gun version) | 90 |
| KwK L/70 (Pz.Kpfw. V Panther) | 26 |
| 2cm Quadruple Flak | 3 |
| Flak 38 | 18 |
| Machine-guns | 326 |
| Submachine guns | 249 |
| Rifles | 1650 |
| 08 and 38 Pistols | 1496 |
| Bayonets | 919 |

Anlage _____ zum Tätigkeitsbericht SS-Panzer-Regiment 12

W a f f e n b e s t a n d  des  R e g i m e n t s

Stand:        30.4.1944

Mit Stand vom 30.4.44 verfügte das Rgt. über folgenden Waffenbestand:

| Art: | | | Anzahl: |
|---|---|---|---|
| KwK | 30 | (Pz.Kpfw. II) | 6 |
| " | L/24 | (Pz.Kpfw.IV kurz) | 1 |
| " | L/43 | (Pz.Kpfw.IV lang) | 3 |
| " | L/48 | (Pz.Kpfw.IV lang) | 90 |
| " | L/70 | (Pz.Kpfw.V"Panther") | 26 |
| Vierl.Flak 2 cm | | | 3 |
| Flak | 38 | | 18 |
| M.G. | | | 326 |
| M.Pi. | | | 249 |
| Gewehre | | | 1650 |
| Pistolen 08 u. 38 | | | 1496 |
| Seitengewehre | | | 919 |

# Appendix VI

# Allied aircraft shot down by the 2cm anti-aircraft guns of *SS-Panzer Regiment 12*, 10 May–3 August 1944

| Date | *Regimental Flak Zug/SS-Panzer Regiment 12* | *Flak Zug* of the *I./SS-Panzer Regiment 12* | *Flak Zug* of the *II./SS-Panzer Regiment 12* | Total |
|---|---|---|---|---|
| 10. 05. 1944 | – | – | 1 Thunderbolt | 1 |
| 13. 05. 1944 | 1 Thunderbolt | – | – | 1 |
| 25. 05. 1944 | 1 Thunderbolt | – | 2 Thunderbolts | 3 |
| 30. 05. 1944 | – | – | 3 Thunderbolts | 3 |
| **Total before the invasion** | **2** | **–** | **6** | **8** |
| 07. 06. 1944 | – | – | 5 fighter bomber aircraft | 5 |
| 13. 06. 1944 | – | – | 1 Hurricane 2 Thunderbolts | 3 |
| 14. 06. 1944 | – | 1 Thunderbolt | – | 1 |
| 16. 06. 1944 | – | 1 Thunderbolt | 1 Typhoon | 2 |
| 17. 06. 1944 | – | 1 Typhoon | 1 Typhoon | 2 |
| 18. 06. 1944 | – | – | 1 Auster IV | 1 |
| 03. 08. 1944 | 1 Thunderbolt | – | – | 1 |
| **Total following the invasion** | **1** | **3** | **11** | **15** |
| **Grand total** | **3** | **3** | **17** | **23** |

# Appendix VII

# Tank strength of
# *SS-Panzer Regiment 12*
# 1 June-11 August 1944[1]

| Date | Operational Panthers | Panthers repairable within two weeks | Panthers repairable more than two weeks | Total | Operational Panzer IVs | Panzer IVs repairable within two weeks | Panzer IVs repairable more than two weeks | Total |
|------|------|------|------|------|------|------|------|------|
| 01. 06. 1944 | 48 | 2 | 6 | 56 [1] | 91 | 7 | – | 98 |
| 16. 06. 1944 | 38 | No data | No data | 38 | 52 | No data | No data | 52 |
| 17. 06. 1944 | 38 | No data | No data | 38 | 46 | No data | No data | 46 |
| 18. 06. 1944 | 33 | No data | No data | 33 | 45 | No data | No data | 45 |
| 20. 06. 1944 | 42 | No data | No data | 42 | 59 | No data | No data | 59 |
| 22. 06. 1944 | 42 | No data | No data | 42 | 59 | No data | No data | 59 |
| 23. 06. 1944 | 43 | No data | No data | 43 | 55 | No data | No data | 55 |
| 24. 06. 1944 | 44 | No data | No data | 44 | 58 | No data | No data | 58 |
| 26. 06. 1944 | 37 [2] | 27 | | 64 | 60 | 12 | | 72 |
| 27. 06. 1944 | 24 | 16 | No data | 40 | 32 | 22 | No data | 54 |
| 02. 07. 1944 | 24 | No data | No data | 24 | 32 | No data | No data | 32 |
| 04. 07. 1944 | 24 | No data | No data | 24 | 37 | No data | No data | 37 |
| 05. 07. 1944 | 28 | 30 | | 58 | 30 | 24 | | 54 |
| 06. 07. 1944 | 28 | 10 | No data | 38 | 32 | No data | No data | 32 |
| 07. 07. 1944 | 39 | No data | No data | 39 | 40 | No data | No data | 40 |
| 09. 07. 1944 | 18 | 24 | 5 | 47 | 10 | 27 | 5 | 42 |

---

1    Zetterling, pp.360–361.

| Date | Operational Panthers | Panthers repairable within two weeks | Panthers repairable more than two weeks | Total | Operational Panzer IVs | Panzer IVs repairable within two weeks | Panzer IVs repairable more than two weeks | Total |
|---|---|---|---|---|---|---|---|---|
| 10. 07. 1944 | 18 | 24 | No data | 42 | 19 | No data | No data | 19 |
| 11: 07. 1944[3] | 18 | 24 | No data | 42 | 19 | 27 | No data | 46 |
| 16. 07. 1944 | 18 | No data | No data | 18 | 21 | No data | No data | 21 |
| 23. 07. 1944 | 21 | No data | No data | 21 | 37 | No data | No data | 37 |
| 24. 07. 1944 | 21 | No data | No data | 21 | 37 | No data | No data | 37 |
| 25. 07. 1944 | 21 | No data | No data | 21 | 37 | No data | No data | 37 |
| 27. 07. 1944 | 22 | No data | No data | 22 | 39 | No data | No data | 39 |
| 28. 07. 1944 | 22 | 11 | No data | 33 | 39 | 12 | No data | 51 |
| 29. 07. 1944 | 22 | 11 | No data | 33 | 39 | 12 | No data | 51 |
| 30. 07. 1944 | 22 | 11 | No data | 33 | 39 | 12 | No data | 51 |
| 01. 08. 1944[4] | 22 | 15 | No data | 37 | 39 | 15 | No data | 54 |
| 05. 08. 1944 | 9 | No data | No data | 9 | 37 | No data | No data | 37 |
| 06. 08. 1944 | 9 | No data | No data | 9 | 37 | No data | No data | 37 |
| 09. 08. 1944 | 5 | No data | No data | 5 | 10 | No data | No data | 10 |
| 10. 08. 1944 | 9 | No data | No data | 9 | 18 | No data | No data | 18 |
| 11. 08. 1944 | 7 | No data | No data | 7 | 17 | No data | No data | 17 |

## Notes

1   *SS-Panzer Regiment 12* had 26 Panthers on 20 April 1944, and a further 30 had arrived by 31 May. See also Vojenský Historický Archiv, Praha (Military History Archives, Prague) Tätigkeitsbericht des *SS-Panzer Regiments 12*, 1. Januar–4. Juni 1944, and Nevenkin, p.905. A further 10 Panthers had arrived by 10 June 1944.

2   That night only 17 Panthers were in operational condition. See Meyer, p.198.

3   Meyer, p.270.

4   Nevenkin, p.917.

# Appendix VIII

# Total losses of *I./SS-Panzer Regiment 12* in Panther tanks 7 June-4 September 1944

| Date | Cause of total loss | | | | | | |
|------|------|-------------------|-----------|------------------------------|---------------------|---------|-------|
|      | Tank | Anti-tank gun | Artillery | Fighter bomber aircraft | Destroyed by crew | Unknown | Total |
| 07. 06. 1944 | – | – | – | 1[1] | – | – | 1 |
| 08. 06. 1944 | – | 3 | – | – | – | – | 3 |
| 09. 06. 1944 | – | 6 | – | – | – | – | 6 |
| 25. 06. 1944 | – | 1 | – | – | – | 1 | 2 |
| 26. 06. 1944 | – | 2 | – | – | – | 3 | 5 |
| 27. 06. 1944 | – | – | – | – | – | 3 | 3 |
| 28. 06. 1944 | – | – | – | – | – | 1 | 1 |
| 05. 07. 1944 | – | 1 | – | – | – | 1 | 2 |
| 08. 07. 1944 | – | 5 | 2 | – | – | 2 | 9 |
| 11. 07. 1944 | – | 2 | 1 | – | – | – | 3 |
| 05. 08. 1944 | 1 | – | – | – | – | – | 1 |
| 08. 08. 1944 | 1 | 1 | – | – | 1 | – | 3 |
| 14. 08. 1944 | – | – | – | – | 2 | 1 | 3 |
| 19. 08. 1944 | – | – | – | – | – | 1 | 1 |
| 20. 08. 1944 | 1 | – | – | 3 | 3 | – | 7 |

| Date | Cause of total loss | | | | | | Total |
|------|------|------|------|------|------|------|------|
| | Tank | Anti-tank gun | Artillery | Fighter bomber aircraft | Destroyed by crew | Unknown | |
| 22. 08. 1944 | – | – | 2 | – | – | 4 | 6 |
| 23. 08. 1944 | 1 | – | – | – | – | – | 1 |
| 24. 08. 1944 | – | 1 | – | – | – | – | 1 |
| 01. 09. 1944 | 1 | – | – | – | 1 | 4 | 6 |
| 04. 09. 1944 | – | – | – | – | 1 | – | 1 |
| Total | 5 | 22 | 5 | 4 | 8 | 21 | 65 |

## Notes

1    This was not a Panther tank but a Flakpanzer 38(t) self-propelled anti-aircraft gun.

# Allied tanks knocked out by *II./SS-Panzer Regiment 12,* 7 June–9 August 1944

| Date | 5.Kompanie | 6.Kompanie | 7.Kompanie | 8.Kompanie | 9.Kompanie | Total |
|---|---|---|---|---|---|---|
| 07. 06. 1944 | 9 | 14 | 5 | 1 | – | 29 |
| 09. 06. 1944 | 5 | – | – | – | 3 | 8 |
| 11. 06. 1944 | – | – | – | 14 | 7 | 21 |
| 17. 06. 1944 | – | 4 | – | 2 | – | 6 |
| 18. 06. 1944 | – | 4 | – | – | – | 4 |
| 28. 06. 1944 | No *Kompanie*-level distribution | | | | | 14 |
| 08. 07. 1944 | 22 | 14 | | | 5 | 43[1] |
| 10. 07. 1944 | No *Kompanie*-level distribution | | | | | 34 |
| 09. 08. 1944 | 24 | | | | | 24[2] |
| Total | 36 | 22 | 5 | 17 | 15 | 183 |

## Notes

1 Of these, two Allied armoured fighting vehicles were knocked out by the Panzer IV tanks of the *Aufklärungszug/II./SS-Panzer Regiment 12.*

2 That day the *II./SS-Panzer Regiment 12* reported to have knocked out 78 Allied armoured fighting vehicles in its sector. These were knocked out not only by the Panzer IVs of the regiment but together with the three Tigers of *schwere SS-Panzer Abteilung 102* and the seven Panthers of the *3./SS-Panzer Regiment 12.* The former knocked out 44, the latter knocked out five Allied tanks.

# Battle casualties of the *Stab* of *SS-Panzer Regiment 12*, 7 June–27 September 1944[1]

| Killed | | | Wounded | | | Missing or captured | | | |
|---|---|---|---|---|---|---|---|---|---|
| Officers | NCOs | Enlisted Men | Officers | NCOs | Enlisted Men | Officers | NCOs | Enlisted Men | Total |
| 3 | 5 | 20 | 9 | 44 | 112 | 5 | 8 | 36 | 242 |

---

1   See Meyer, p.386.

# Appendix XI

# Battle casualties of *I./SS-Panzer Regiment 12*, 7 June–31 October 1944[1]

| Killed | | | Died | | | Wounded | | | Missing or captured | | | |
|---|---|---|---|---|---|---|---|---|---|---|---|---|
| Officers | NCOs | Enlisted Men | Officers | NCOs | Enlisted Men | Officers | NCOs | Enlisted Men | Officers | NCOs | Enlisted Men | Total |
| 11 | 12 | 60 | – | 2 | 3 | 16 | 75 | 242 | 3 | 16 | 141 | 581 |

---

1   See Meyer, p. 386.

## Appendix XII

# Battle casualties of *II./SS-Panzer Regiment 12,* 7 June–20 October 1944[1]

| Killed | | | Dead | | | Wounded | | | Missing or captured | | | |
|---|---|---|---|---|---|---|---|---|---|---|---|---|
| Officers | NCOs | Enlisted Men | Oficers | NCOs | Enlisted Men | Officers | NCOs | Enlisted Men | Officers | NCOs | Enlisted Men | Total |
| 9 | 30 | 115 | – | 1 | 1 | 28 | 68 | 296 | 6 | 6 | 144 | 704 |

1   See Meyer, p.386.

# Effectiveness of the armoured fighting vehicles of *12.SS-Panzer Division* related to Allied operations 7 June-16 August 1944

| Allied Operation | I./SS-Panzer Regiment 12 | | II./SS-Panzer Regiment 12 | | SS-Panzerjäger Abteilung 12 | |
|---|---|---|---|---|---|---|
| | Allied armoured fighting vehicles knocked out | Own total loss | Allied armoured fighting vehicles knocked out | Own total loss | Allied armoured fighting vehicles knocked out | Own total loss |
| Bridgehead battles (07-24. 06. 1944) | 27 | 10 | 68 | 23 | – | – |
| Epsom (25–30. 06. 1944) | 53 | 11 | 14 | 12 | – | – |
| Charnwood and Jupiter (08–11. 07. 1944) | 42 | 12 | 78 | 8 | – | – |
| Goodwood (18–20. 07. 1944) | 1 | – | – | – | 1 | – |
| Totalize (08–11. 08. 1944) | 8 | 3 | 24 | 11 | 70 | 4 |
| Tractable (14–16. 08. 1944) | 5 | 3 | – | – | 23 | 2 |
| Total (07.06.–16. 08. 1944) | 136 | 39 | 184 | 54 | 94 | 6 |

# Appendix XIV

# Summarised report of enemy tanks and other weapons knocked out by *SS-Panzer Regiment 12* 7 June-1 September 1944 (report dated 17 October 1944)

*12.SS-Panzer Division "Hitlerjugend"*　　　　　　　Regimental Command Post, 17.10.1944
*SS-Panzer Regiment 12*
*Ia Br.Tgb.Nr.　　/44*

Re. Number of victories
With reference to: *12.SS-Pz.Div. "HJ"* – Special instructions in relation to Ic (intelligence)
Nr 14 from 14.10.1944. Fig. 1
As of: 18.10.1944

To the
*12.SS-Pz.Div. "Hitlerjugend"*
*Abt. Ic*

[Publishers' note – for ease of reference the typed list has been reproduced in tabular form and totals added to calculate daily amounts and total amounts by type of vehicle/weapon.]

| Date | Sherman | Churchill | Cromwell | General Lee | Self-propelled guns | Unidentified tanks/AFVs | Armoured cars | Carriers | Armoured personnel carriers/half-tracks | Prime movers | Trucks | Anti-tank guns | Artillery pieces | Total |
|---|---|---|---|---|---|---|---|---|---|---|---|---|---|---|
| 7.6.1944 | 39 | 1 | - | - | - | - | - | 6 | 3 | - | - | 7 | - | 56 |
| 8.6.1944 | 3[1] | - | - | - | - | 1 | - | 1 | - | - | - | - | - | 5 |
| 9.6.1944 | 12 | - | - | - | - | 2 | - | - | - | - | - | 11 | - | 25 |
| 10.6.1944 | 2 | - | - | - | - | 1 | - | - | - | - | - | - | - | 3 |
| 11.6.1944 | 29 | 1 | - | 4 | - | 1 | - | - | - | - | - | 2 | - | 37 |
| 12.6.1944 | 2 | - | - | - | - | - | - | - | 4 | - | - | - | - | 6 |
| 13.6.1944 | - | - | 1[2] | - | - | - | - | - | - | - | - | - | - | 1 |
| 14.6.1944 | - | - | - | - | - | 1 | - | 2 | 5 | - | - | - | - | 8 |

| Date | Sherman | Churchill | Cromwell | General Lee | Self-propelled guns | Unidentified tanks/AFVs | Armoured cars | Carriers | Armoured personnel carriers/half-tracks | Prime movers | Trucks | Anti-tank guns | Artillery pieces | Total |
|---|---|---|---|---|---|---|---|---|---|---|---|---|---|---|
| 17.6.1944 | 5 | - | 1 | - | - | - | - | - | - | - | - | - | - | 6 |
| 18.6.1944 | 4 | - | - | - | - | - | - | - | - | - | - | - | - | 4 |
| 22.6.1944 | - | - | - | - | - | 2 | - | - | - | - | - | - | - | 2 |
| 25.6.1944 | 2 | - | - | - | - | 1 | - | - | - | - | - | 8 | - | 11 |
| 26.6.1944 | 54 | 1 | 4 | - | - | 13+1[3] | - | 3 | 3 | 2 | - | 14 | - | 95 |
| 27.6.1944 | 35 | 5 | - | 3 | - | - | - | - | 1 | 2 | 2 | 2 | - | 50 |
| 28.6.1944 | 14 | - | - | - | - | 5 | - | - | - | 1 | - | - | - | 20 |
| 29.6.1944 | 9 | - | - | - | - | - | 2 | 2 | - | 2 | - | 4 | - | 19 |
| 30.6.1944 | - | - | - | - | - | - | - | 3 | - | - | - | 2 | - | 5 |
| 2.7.1944 | - | - | - | 3 | - | - | - | - | - | - | - | - | - | 3 |
| 4.7.1944 | 6 | - | - | - | - | 2 | - | - | - | - | - | - | - | 8 |
| 5.7.1944 | 4 | 1 | - | 3 | - | - | - | - | - | - | - | 7 | 6 | 21 |
| 6.7.1944 | - | - | - | - | - | 6 | - | - | - | - | - | - | - | 6 |
| 8.7.1944 | 81 | - | - | - | - | - | - | - | 6 | - | - | 6 | - | 93 |
| 9.7.1944 | - | - | - | - | - | 7 | - | - | 6 | - | - | - | - | 13 |
| 10.7.1944 | 12 | 19 | 1 | - | 1 | 1 + 1[4] | - | - | 15 | - | - | 3 | - | 53 |
| 27.7.1944 | - | - | - | - | - | 1 | - | - | - | - | - | - | - | 1 |
| 28.7.1944 | - | - | - | - | - | 1 | - | - | - | - | - | - | - | 1 |
| 3.8.1944 | - | - | - | - | - | 5 | - | - | - | - | - | - | - | 5 |
| 4.8.1944 | - | - | - | - | - | 2 | - | - | - | - | - | - | - | 2 |
| 5.8.1944 | - | - | - | - | - | 5 | 3 | - | - | - | - | - | - | 8 |
| 6.8.1944 | - | - | - | - | - | - | - | - | - | - | - | 2 | - | 2 |
| 8.8.1944 | 40 | 1 | 1 | - | - | - | - | - | - | - | - | 1 | - | 43 |
| 9.8.1944 | 26 | - | - | - | - | 3 | - | - | - | - | 1 | - | - | 30 |
| 10.8.1944 | - | - | - | - | - | 1 | - | - | - | - | - | - | - | 1 |
| 11.8.1944 | 2 | - | - | - | - | - | - | - | - | - | - | - | - | 2 |
| 12.8.1944 | 8 | - | - | - | - | - | - | 1 | - | - | - | - | - | 9 |
| 13.8.1944 | 26 | - | - | - | - | - | - | 1 | 5 | 1 | 1 | 1 | 1 | 36 |
| 14.8.1944 | 10 | 1 | - | - | - | 3 | 1 | 1 | - | - | - | 2 | - | 18 |
| 15.8.1944 | 6 | 1 | - | - | - | 2 | - | - | - | - | - | 1 | - | 10 |
| 16.8.1944 | 1 | - | - | - | - | - | - | - | - | - | - | 1 | 1 | 3 |
| 17.8.1944 | 4 | 1 | - | - | - | 1 | 1 | - | - | - | - | - | - | 7 |
| 19.8.1944 | - | - | - | - | - | - | 5 | - | - | - | 1 | 1 | - | 7 |
| 20.8.1944 | 12 | - | - | - | - | - | - | - | - | - | - | 2 | - | 14 |
| 21.8.1944 | 1 | - | - | - | - | - | - | - | - | - | - | - | - | 1 |
| 22.8.1944 | 15 | - | - | - | - | 1[5] | 3 | - | 5 | - | 2 | - | - | 26 |
| 23.8.1944 | 2 | - | - | - | - | - | - | 1 | - | - | - | 5 | - | 8 |

| Date | Sherman | Churchill | Cromwell | General Lee | Self-propelled guns | Unidentified tanks/AFVs | Armoured cars | Carriers | Armoured personnel carriers/half-tracks | Prime movers | Trucks | Anti-tank guns | Artillery pieces | Total |
|------|---------|-----------|----------|-------------|---------------------|-------------------------|---------------|----------|------------------------------------------|--------------|--------|----------------|------------------|-------|
| 24.8.1944 | 1 | - | - | - | - | - | - | - | - | - | - | - | - | 1 |
| 25.8.1944 | 2 | - | - | - | - | - | - | - | - | - | - | - | - | 2 |
| 28.8.1944 | 4 | - | - | - | - | - | - | - | - | - | - | - | - | 4 |
| 29.8.1944 | 3 | - | - | - | - | - | - | - | - | - | 3 | - | - | 6 |
| 1.9.1944 | 3 | - | - | - | - | - | - | - | - | - | 3 | - | - | 6 |
| Totals | 479 | 32 | 8 | 13 | 1 | 70 | 15 | 21 | 53 | 8 | 13 | 82 | 8 | 803 |

**Notes**

1  Of which one was immobile.

2  Captured.

3  The list describes one 'Dreadnought' for this date, most likely a British Churchill with larger calibre gun.

4  Includes one flamethrower tank.

5  The list describes one 'Dreadnought' for this date, most likely a British Churchill with larger calibre gun.

12. ⚡-Pz.Div. "Hitlerjugend"                    Rgts.-Gef.Std. 17.1o.1944
⚡-Panzer-Regiment 12
Ia Br.Tgb.Nr.              /44


     Betr.: Erfolgszahlen
     Bezug: 12. ⚡-Pz.Div. "HJ" - Besondere Anordnungen für den Ic-Dienst
            Nr. 14 v. 14.10.1944. Ziff. 1.)
     Form.: 18.10.1944


     An die
     12. ⚡-Pz. Div. "Hitlerjugend"
     Abt. Ic
     =====================================


     Das Panzer-Regiment meldet zu o.a. Bezug:


     7.6.1944          39  Sherman
                        1  Churchill
                        7  Pak
                        6  Karetten
                        3  SPW

     8.6.1944           1  Panzer
                        2  Sherman
                        1  Sherman bewegungsunfähig
                        1  Karette

     9.6.1944           8  Kampfwagen
                       12  Sherman
                       11  Pak

     10.6.1944          1  Kampfwagen
                        2  Sherman

     11.6.1944          1  Kampfwagen
                       29  Sherman
                        1  Churchill
                        4  General Lee
                        2  Pak

     12.6.1944          2  Sherman
                        4  SPW.

     13.6.1944          1  Cromwell erbeutet

     14.6.1944          1  Kampfwagen
                        2  Karetten
                        5  SPW.

     17.6.1944          5  Sherman
                        1  Churchill

     18.6.1944          4  Sherman

     22.6.1944          2  Kampfwagen

- 2 -

| 25.6.1944 | 1 | Kampfwagen |
| | 2 | Sherman |
| | 8 | Pak |
| 26.6.1944 | 15 | Kampfwagen |
| | 54 | Sherman |
| | 1 | Churchill |
| | 4 | Cromwell |
| | 1 | Dreadnought |
| | 14 | Pak |
| | 3 | Karetten |
| | 3 | Spw. |
| | 2 | Zgkw. |
| 27.6.1944 | 35 | Sherman |
| | 3 | Churchill |
| | 3 | General Lee |
| | 2 | Pak |
| | 1 | Spw. |
| | 2 | Zgkw. |
| | 2 | Lkw. |
| 28.6.1944 | 5 | Panzerkampfwagen |
| | 14 | Sherman |
| | 1 | Lkw. |
| 29.6.1944 | 9 | Sherman |
| | 4 | Pak |
| | 2 | Panzerspähwagen |
| | 2 | Karetten |
| | 2 | Zgkw. |
| 30.6.1944 | 2 | Pak |
| | 3 | Karetten |
| 2.7.1944 | 3 | General Lee |
| 4.7.1944 | 2 | Panzerkampfwagen |
| | 6 | Sherman |
| 5.7.1944 | 4 | Sherman |
| | 1 | Churchill |
| | 3 | General Lee |
| | 7 | Pak |
| | 6 | Geschütze |
| 6.7.1944 | 6 | Panzerkampfwagen |

- 3 -

```
8.7.1944          81  Sherman
                   6  Pak
                   6  SPW

9.7.1944           7  Panzerkampfwagen
                   6  SPW

10.7.1944          1  Panzerkampfwagen
                  12  Sherman
                  19  Churchill
                   1  Flammenwerferpanzer
                   1  Cromwell
                   3  Pak
                   1  SPL
                  15  SPW.

27.7.1944          1  Panzerkampfwagen

28.7.1944          1  Panzerkampfwagen

3.8.1944           5  Panzerkampfwagen

4.8.1944           2  Panzerkampfwagen

5.8.1944           5  Panzerkampfwagen
                   3  Panzerspähwagen

6.8.1944           2  Pak

8.8.1944          40  Sherman
                   1  Churchill
                   1  Cromwell
                   1  Pak

9.8.1944           3  Panzerkampfwagen
                  26  Sherman
                   1  Lkw.

10.8.1944          1  Panzerkampfwagen

11.8.1944          2  Sherman

12.8.1944          8  Sherman
                   1  Karette

13.8.1944         26  Sherman
                   1  Pak
                   1  Geschütz
                   5  SPW
                   1  Zgkw.
                   1  Karette
                   1  Lkw.

                  - 4 -
```

| | | |
|---|---:|---|
| 14.8.1944 | 3 | Panzerkampfwagen |
| | 10 | Sherman |
| | 1 | Cromwell |
| | 1 | Panzerspähwagen |
| | 2 | Pak |
| | 1 | Karette |
| 15.8.1944 | 2 | Panzerkampfwagen |
| | 6 | Sherman |
| | 1 | Cromwell |
| | 1 | Pak |
| 16.8.1944 | 1 | Sherman |
| | 1 | Pak |
| | 1 | Geschütz |
| 17.8.1944 | 1 | Panzerkampfwagen |
| | 4 | Sherman |
| | 1 | Churchill |
| | 1 | Panzerspähwagen |
| 19.8.1944 | 5 | Panzerspähwagen |
| | 1 | Pak |
| | 6 | Lkw |
| 20.8.1944 | 12 | Sherman |
| | 2 | Pak |
| 21.8.1944 | 1 | Sherman |
| 22.8.1944 | 15 | Sherman |
| | 1 | Dreadnought |
| | 3 | Panzerspähwagen |
| | 2 | Lkw. |
| | 5 | Spw. |
| 23.8.1944 | 2 | Sherman |
| | 5 | Pak |
| | 1 | Karette |
| 24.8.1944 | 1 | Sherman |
| 25.8.1944 | 2 | Sherman |
| 28.8.1944 | 4 | Sherman |
| 29.8.1944 | 3 | Sherman |
| | 3 | Lkw. |
| 1.9.1944 | 3 | Sherman |
| | 3 | Lkw. |

# Appendix XV

# Allied tanks knocked out by the Panthers of *I./SS-Panzer Regiment 12* 8 June-1 September 1944

| Date | 1.Kompanie | 2.Kompanie | 3.Kompanie | 4. Kompanie | Total |
|---|---|---|---|---|---|
| 08. 06. 1944 | – | – | – | 1 | 1 |
| 09. 06. 1944 | – | 3 | 1 | 1 | 5 |
| 10. 06. 1944 | – | 1 | 1 | – | 2 |
| 11. 06. 1944 | 1 | 1 | – | 16[1] | 18 |
| 15. 06. 1944 | – | 1 | – | – | 1 |
| 25. 06. 1944 | – | 1 | – | – | 1 |
| 26. 06. 1944 | No *Kompanie*-level distribution | | | | 7 |
| 27. 06. 1944 | No *Kompanie*-level distribution | | | | 28[2] |
| 28. 06. 1944 | – | – | – | 6 | 6 |
| 29. 06. 1944 | 2 | 1 | – | 3 | 7[3] |
| 30. 06. 1944 | – | 1 | – | 3 | 4 |
| 04. 07. 1944 | 8 | 4 | – | – | 12 |
| 05. 07. 1944 | 5 | – | – | 1 | 6 |
| 08. 07. 1944 | 4 | 1 | 27 | – | 37[4] |
| 09. 07. 1944 | – | 4 | – | – | 4 |
| 11. 07. 1944 | No *Kompanie*-level distribution | | | | 1 |
| 20. 07. 1944 | – | 1 | – | – | 1 |
| 22. 07. 1944 | – | 1 | – | – | 1 |
| 03. 08. 1944 | – | 5 | – | – | 5 |
| 05. 08. 1944 | – | 4 | – | – | 4 |
| 07. 08. 1944 | – | – | 1 | – | 1 |
| 08. 08. 1944 | – | – | 3 | – | 3 |
| 09. 08. 1944 | – | – | 5 | – | 5 |
| 14. 08. 1944 | – | – | 2 | – | 2 |
| 15. 08. 1944 | – | – | 3 | – | 3 |
| 17. 08. 1944 | | | 3 | | 3 |

| Date | *1.Kompanie* | *2.Kompanie* | *3.Kompanie* | *4. Kompanie* | Total |
|------|------|------|------|------|------|
| 20. 08. 1944 | – | – | 1 | 12 | 13 |
| 22. 08. 1944 | – | – | – | 16 | 16 |
| 23. 08. 1944 | – | – | – | 4 | 4 |
| 30. 08. 1944 | 1 | – | – | – | 1 |
| 01. 09. 1944 | 9 | – | – | – | 9 |
| Total | 30 | 29 | 47 | 63 | 211 |

## Notes

1  Three of these were hit but not burnt out.

2  At least two of these were knocked out by the *2.Kompanie* and five by the *4.Kompanie*.

3  A further tank was knocked out by the tank of the *Nachrichtenoffizier* of the *Regimentsstab*.

4  Five of the 37 Allied tanks were destroyed by the Panthers of *I./SS-Panzer Regiment 12's Aufklärungszug*.

# Appendix XVI

# Supply of new tanks for *SS-Panzer Regiment 12* during the combat in Normandy 6 July-29 August 1944[1]

| Date of combat readiness | Unit | Number of new tanks received |
|---|---|---|
| 06. 07. 1944 | *3./SS-Panzer Regiment 12* | 13 + 1 Panthers[1] |
| 16. 07. 1944 | *7./SS-Panzer Regiment 12* | 17 Panzer IVs |
| 19. 08. 1944 | *4./SS-Panzer Regiment 12* | 14 Panthers |
| 29. 08. 1944 | *1./SS-Panzer Regiment 12* | 7 Panthers |
| | **Total** | 52 tanks |

**Notes**

1  Of these only 13 Panthers were new. The fourteenth tank was presumably a "used" tank handed in by *4.Kompanie/SS-Panzer Regiment 12.*

---

1  According to *SS-Panzer Regiment 12*'s own KTB.

# Movement orders for *12.SS-Panzer Division "Hitlerjugend"* and *SS-Panzer Regiment 12*, 26 August 1944

19. Appendix to War Diary No. : 3

*12.SS-Pz.Div. "Hitlerjugend"*
*SS-Panzer Regiment 12*                    Regimental Command Post, 26 August, 1944

Abstract from Division Order
from 26 August, 1944: War Diary No.: 1/44 , Secret, Confidential Military Document, 26 August, 1944

1.) The division, minus *Kampfgruppe "Mohnke"* and *Kampfgruppe "Waldmüller"* is to transfer for refitting to the area:
>  Montcornet (exclusive) – Vervins (exclusive) – La Capelle (exclusive) – Forêt de St. Michel (northeast of Hirson) – Aubenton – Bay (10 kilometers northeast of Rozoy)

2.) The formations are assigned to the following assembly areas:

>  *SS-Panzer Regiment 12 and SS-Panzerjäger Abteilung 12:*
>  Courteval – along the road to the north as far as Landouzy-la-Ville (inclusive) – La Herie (inclusive) Origny (exclusive) – La Bouteille (inclusive) – Themailles (exclusive) – Marigny (inclusive) – Jeantes (esclusive).

3.) In the evening of 26 August, 1944, the division is to reach the new assembly area by two days' marches. By early on 27 August, 1944, it is to cross the line Guiscard – Ham –Perones to the east. If the weather is clear, movement is only to be by night. Non-operational vehicles or issued equipment, which cannot be taken along, is to be shuttled to the new assembly area.

4.) Guide and main axis of movement is the Breteuil – Montdidier – Nesle – Ham – St. Quentin – Vervins – Landouzy-la-Ville highway. Movement on byroads is expedient.

---

1   Translated by Dr Frederick P. Steinhardt.

Local reconnaissance of roads and rest areas is to be conducted.
March sequence is:

Logistic elements, *III.Bataillon / SS-Panzer-Grenadier-Regiment 26, I.Bataillon /SS-Panzer-Grenadier-Regiment 26, Panzer-Aufklärungs-Abteilung 12, SS-Flak-Abteilung 12* on the southern road, which is to be independently reconnoitered.

Logistic elements, *SS-Panzer Regiment 12, SS-Panzer-Artillerie-Regiment 12, SS-Panzer-Grenadier-Regiment 25, SS-Panzer-Pionier-Bataillon 12* on the northern road, which is to be independently reconnoitered.

Signposting by *Panzer-Regiment 12* (Wünsche)
From : Vervins

Division staff, *SS-Panzer-Nachrichten-Abteilung 12, Divisionsbegleitkompanie* on above-named main road. During the course of the movement the formations are to maintain direct contact with one another.

5.) Every driver is to be familiarized with march objectives and routes. The division's advance message centre will be established by the Ia [operations officer] in Ham at the local commander's office [*Ortskommandantur*]. . Sign to be posted: *Meldekopf* Buchsein.

6.) Military police company is to control traffic through Montdidier – Roye – Ham – St. Quentin – and Origny.

7.) Division command headquarters will be in Sargus until 0500 hours on 27 August 1944. Effective 2000 hours on 27 August, 1944 in Hirson. Arrival of formations is to be reported immediately.

signed Meyer
*SS-Oberführer*

accuracy of above attested by:
signed Jürgensen
*SS-Sturmbannführer* and Commander
Supplement *Panzer-Regiment 12:*

1. The elements are to take care that all stragglers will be collected as rapidly as possible and the elements brought up.

2. The unit commanders are to be personally responsible for carrying this out.

3. Transfer:
The route of march, as given in the above order, is to be given to every driver in writing.

19. Anlage zum KTB Nr.: 3

12.SS-Pz.Div."Hitlerjugend"                    Rgt.Gef.Std.,den 26. 8.1944
SS-Panzer-Regiment 12

                    A b s c h r i f t  v. Div. Befehl
                    v. 26. 8.1944  :Tgb.Nr.: 1/44 g.Kdos. v.26.8.44

1.) Die Division ohne Kampfgruppe Mohnke und Kampfgruppe Waldmüller,
    verlegt zur Auffrischung in den Raum :
        MONTCORNEL(ausschl.-VERVINS (ausschl.) - La CAPELLE(ausschl.
        FORET DE ST.MICHEL (nordostw.HIRSON) - Aubenton - BAY (10 km
        nordostw. ROZOY)
2.) Den Verbänden werden folgende Unterkunfträume zugewiesen:
    SS-Panzer-Regiment 12 und SS-Panzer-Jäger-Abteilung 12:
        COUTENVAL - Verlauf der Straße nach Norden bis Landouzi la
        VILLE (einschl.) - LA HERIE(einschl.) ORIGNY(ausschl.) -
        LA BOUTEILLE (einschl.) - THENAILLES(ausschl.)-HAROIGNY
        (einschl.) - JEANTES (ausschl.)
3.) Die Division erreicht am 26. 8.44 abends antretend in zwei Tages-
    märschen den neuen Unterkunftsraum. Bis zum 27.August 1944 früh
    ist die Linie GUISCARD - HAM - PERONNE nach Osten zu überschreiten.
    Bei sonniger Wetterlage ist nur bei Nacht zu marschieren.
    Nicht fahrbereite Kfz. oder ausgelagertes Gerät , das nicht mitge-
    führt werden kann, sind staffelweise in den neuen Unterkunftsraum
    zu überführen.
4.) Anhalt und Hauptbewegungslinie ist die Strasse Breteuel -
    MONTDIDIER - NESLE - HAM - ST.QUENTIN - VERVINS - LANDOUZY LA VILL
    Marsch auf Nebenwegen ist zweckmässig.
    Es ist sofort Erkundung von Strassen und Raströumen durchzuführen.
    Reihenfolge des Abmarsches:
        Teile Versorgungstruppen, III./26, I/26, Pz.AA.12, SS-Flak.
        Abt.12 auf selbstständig zu erkundender Südstrasse.
        Teile Versorgungstruppen, SS-Pz.Rgt.12, SS-Pz.Art.Rgt. 12,
        SS-Pz.Gren.Rgt. 25 , SS-Pz.Pi.Btl.12 auf selbstständig zu
        erkundender Nordstrasse.
        Beschilderung Pz.Rgt. 12 (Wünsche)
        ab : V E R V I N S
        Div.Stab, SS-Pz.Nachr.Abt.12,Div.Begleitkompanie auf o.a.
        Hauptstrasse. Wegen des Ablaufes haben die Verbände direkt
        miteinander Verbindung aufzunehmen.
5.) Jedem Fahrer sind Marschziel und Marschweg bekanntzugeben.Meldekop
    der Division wird in HAM bei der Ortskommandantur durch Ib einge-
    richtet. Beschilderung: Meldekopf Buchsein.
6.) Feldgendarmerie-Kp. führt Verkehrsreglung in Montdidier - Roye -
    Ham - St.Quentin -und Origny durch.
7.) Div.Stabsquartier bis 27.8.1944 -05.00 Uhr - SARCUS - , ab 27.8.44
    -20.00 Uhr - HIRSON. Eintreffen der Verbände ist dorthin umgehend
    zu melden.

                                        gez. M e y e r
                                        SS-Oberführer

F.d.R.d.A.:
gez. J ü r g e n s e n
SS-Sturmbannführer u. Kdr.

The column commander is to take care that, during the movement, no new straggling takes place.

Special emphasis is to be placed on maintenance of discipline and proper uniform during the movement.

4.  All unit commanders are to be personally responsible to me for the smooth course of the movement. Arrival in the new area is immediately to be reported by the *Abteilungen* and regimental elements.

The Commander, *SS-Panzer Regiment 12*
signed Jürgensen
*SS-Sturmbannführer*

Zusatz  Panzer-Regiment 12:

1.  Die Einheiten tragen dafür Sorge, daß sämtliche Versprengten schnellstens zusammengesucht werden und den Einheiten zugeführt werden.

2.  Die Chefs haben sich persönlich hierfür einzusetzen.

3.) Verlegung:

Der Marschweg ist, wie im umstehenden Befehl angegeben, jedem Fahrer schriftlich mitzugeben.

Die Kolonnenführer haben dafür Sorge zu tragen, daß während der Verlegung nicht erneut Versprengte entstehen.

Auf Disziplin und Anzugsordnung während des Marsches ist besonderer Wert zu legen.

4.  Sämtliche Einheitsführer sind mir für reibungslosen Ablauf der Verlegung persönlich verantwortlich. Das Eintreffen im neuen Raum ist von den Abteilungen und Regimentseinheiten sofort zu melden.

Der Kommandeur SS-Panzer-Regiment 12

ges.: J ü r g e n s e n

SS-Sturmbannführer

# Appendix XVIII[1]

# Officers of
# *SS-Panzerjäger Abteilung 12*

T he primary known officers of *SS-Panzerjäger Abteilung 12* are listed below just prior to D-Day. As with all such personnel list completeness is impossible, both due to the standard record keeping of the day and shifting of positions. Less senior posts were often not listed, the *Abteilung* having further men commanding at platoon (*Zug*) level. Those missing in action, for whom no fate is known – if indeed they survived the conflict – as well as those killed but never identified, further inhibits the completeness of such lists. Elsewhere in this appendix is a second list covering the same period through the end of the war, showing further losses during the Ardennes and late war combats before *"Hitlerjugend"* surrendered in 1945.

## *SS-Panzerjäger Abteilung 12*

| | |
|---|---|
| *Abteilungskommandeur* | *Sturmbannführer* Hans-Jakob Hanreich |
| *Adjutant* | *Obersturmführer* Heinrich Winkler |
| *Nachrichtenoffizier* | *Obersturmführer* Gerd Siegert |
| 1.*Kompanie Chef* | *Obersturmführer* Georg Hurdelbrink |
| 2.*Kompanie Chef* | *Obersturmführer* Günther Gornik |
| 3.*Kompanie Chef* | *Hauptsturmführer* Günther Wöst |

## Knight's Cross Holders of *SS-Panzerjäger Abteilung 12*

Fritz Eckstein: November 18, 1944, *Rottenführer, Richtschütze, 1./SS-Panzerjäger Abteilung 12*

Georg Hurdelbrink: October 16, 1944, *Obersturmführer, Kompanie* Führer, *1./SS-Panzerjäger Abteilung 12*

Rudolf Roy: October 16, 1944, *Oberscharführer, Zugführer, 1./SS-Panzerjäger Abteilung 12*

**Fritz Eckstein**: Born in Schwaikheim on January 27, 1923, and joined the Hitler Youth in May 1933. Volunteered for the *Waffen-SS* in the spring of 1940 and assigned to *2./Der Führer* on June 6, 1940. Transferred to the *"Leibstandarte"* and became a *Sturmmann* on August 1, 1940, then a *Rottenführer* on June 1, 1942. After being wounded assigned to *SS-Panzerjäger Abteilung 1* of the *"Leibstandarte."* Assigned to *"Hitlerjugend"* with the heavy *1./SS-Panzerjäger Abteilung 12*. Eckstein served as the gunner in Knight's Cross holder Rudolf Roy's vehicle and destroyed a total of 26 enemy armoured vehicles in a five day period. Promoted to *Unterscharführer* on November 1, 1944, Eckstein was recommended for the German Cross in Gold by then *SS-Panzerjäger Abteilung 12*

---

1    Award recommendation documents translated by Dr Frederick P. Steinhardt. This Appendix also includes biographical data relating to several award holders who were not officers.

Eckstein　Fritz　Schwaich-
　　　　　　　　heim/Wttg.

SS-Rttf.　SS-Pz.Jg.Abt. 12

1.1.1941
8.11.1944

Richtschtz.
Soldat

SS-Pz.Jg.Abt. 12　　　　　　　　　　Abt.Gef.St., den 8.11.1944

SS-Rottenführer  E c k s t e i n  wurde am 8.8.44 das EK.1.Kl.
für seine hervorragende Tapferkeit bei dem Angriff auf einen
feindlichen Panzer-Verband bei St. Aignan verliehen, wo er allein
acht feindliche Panzer-Kampfwagen vernichtete.

Am Morgen des 8.8.44 waren feindliche Panzer-Kampfwagen durch
stützpunktartige HKL bei Soignolles in den Rücken der Kampfgruppe
Waldmüller eingedrungen und beherrschten von der Höhe E 111 alle
Nachschubwege.

Ein Panzerjäger 39 mit SS-Rottenführer Eckstein als Richtschütze
nahm den Kampf mit den zahlenmässig überlegenen Panzern des
Feindes auf. Trotz schwierigster Umstände schoss SS-Rttf. Eckstein innerhalb kurzer Zeit neun englische Panzer-Kampfwagen ab.
Dadurch war es möglich, dass der Nachschubverkehr für die Kampfgruppe wieder durchgeführt werden konnte.

Als in der Abenddämmerung ein feindlicher Panzerverband überraschend in die sich absetzende Kampfgruppe stiess, vernichtete

Recommendation of *Rottenführer* Fritz Eckstein, *1./SS-Panzerjäger Abteilung 12*,
for the Knight's Cross. Document appears courtesy of Mark C. Yerger.

commander *Hauptsturmführer* Günther Wöst on November 8, 1944. Eckstein died on April 4, 1979, in his home town.

The commander of *SS-Panzerjäger Abteilung 12* at the time, *Hauptsturmführer* Günther Wöst, wrote the proposal requesting the Knight's Cross be awarded to for Fritz Eckstein.[2] With Eckstein serving as a gunner, Wöst's 8 November 1944 recommendation reads as follows:

*SS-Panzerjäger Abteilung 12*       *Abteilung* Command Post, 8 November 1944

*Rottenführer* Eckstein was awarded the Iron Cross 1st Class for his outstanding courage in the attack on an enemy armoured formation at St. Aignan-de-Cramesnil. There he alone knocked out eight enemy tanks.

In the morning of 9 August, 1944, enemy tanks broke through the main line of resistance, held as a chain of strong points, into the rear of *Kampfgruppe* "Waldmüller."[3] *From Hill E 111 they controlled all supply routes.*

A *Panzerjäger 39*, with *Rottenführer* Eckstein as its gunner, engaged the numerically superior enemy armour. Despite the extremely difficult circumstances *Rottenführer* Eckstein knocked out nine English tanks. That made it possible for supplies to again be brought to the *Kampfgruppe*.

As dusk fell an enemy armoured formation attacked the withdrawing *Kampfgruppe* by surprise. Eckstein knocked out four of the attacking tanks. The *Kampfgruppe* was able to conduct the withdrawal without losses.

On this day *Rottenführer* Eckstein alone destroyed 13 enemy tanks. Within five days he raised his tally to 26 English tanks knocked out.

(Signed) [Günther] Wöst
*Hauptsturmführer* and *Abt.Kdr.*

*12.SS-Pz.Div. "Hitlerjugend"*
This recommendation is endorsed for the absent Division Commander

(Signed) [Hubert] Meyer
*Sturmbannführer* and General Staff Officer

*SS-Panzerarmeeoberkommando 6*      Army Headquarters, 8 November, 1944

This recommendation is forwarded

(Signed) [Josef] Dietrich
*SS-Oberstgruppenführer und Panzergeneraloberst der Waffen-SS*

**Georg Hurdelbrink**: Born in Altenmelle on October 6, 1919, and a member of the Hitler Youth during May 1933 to mid-November 1936. Joined the SS on November 15,

---

2    The proposal is a field typed document, the staff not having a normal pre-printed form and thus lacking a cover. It was approved by Hubert Meyer (*1.Generalstabsofficier*) and counter approved by *SS-Panzerarmeeoberkommando 6* commander Sepp Dietrich (also on 8 November 1944) before being forwarded to the Army's Personnel Office. Wöst's name is incorrectly typed as Woest in the original document.

3    See Chapter 8 Footnote 10 and photo for data on Knight's Cross holder Hans Waldmüller, the commander of the *Kampfgruppe*.

1936, with *SS-Totenkopfstandarte "Ostfriesland"* and in April 1939 attached to *SS-Schule* Wewelsburg. October 1939 moved to *"Totenkopf" Division* with an infantry regiment then in August 1940 transferred to the *"Leibstandarte"*. There served with the *3./V./ LSSAH* and took the 5th wartime reserve officer candidate class at *Junkerschule* Bad Tölz from November 1941 to January 30, 1942. Assigned to *SS-Panzerjäger Abteilung 1 "Leibstandarte"*, and commissioned *Untersturmführer d.R.* April 20, 1942. Promoted to *Obersturmführer d.R.* on November 9, 1943, moved to *"Hitlerjugend"* as *Kompanie Chef* of the heavy *1./SS-Panzerjäger Abteilung 12*. As an *Obersturmführer* was in command of *SS-Panzerjäger Abteilung 12* by January 1945. Recommended for the German Cross in Gold by *Hauptsturmführer* Günther Wöst, then commander of *SS-Panzerjäger Abteilung 12*. Iron Cross 2nd Class March 8, 1943, Iron Cross 1st Class August 11, 1944, Panzer Assault Badge March 23, 1943, War Merit Cross 2nd Class with Swords December 14, 1940. Survived the war and died on August 26, 2002.

The commander of *SS-Panzerjäger Abteilung 12*, *Hauptsturmführer* Günther Wöst, recommended George Hurdelbrink for his Knight's Cross. That proposal, seconded by temporary divisional commander Hubert Meyer and Josef "Sepp" Dietrich, was submitted on 2 September 1944 and reads as follows:[4]

On 8 August 1944, at 1130 hours, the *1.(schwere* [heavy] *Kompanie* of *Panzerjäger Abteilung 12 ("Hitlerjugend")*, under *Obersturmführer* Hurdelbrink, was attached by the commander of *Panzerjäger Abteilung 12* to *Kampfgruppe "Prinz"*, with the mission of advancing together with the tanks of the *Kampfgruppe*.

1st objective : St. Aignan.

2nd objective: Garcelles [-Secqueville].

The attack began at 11:50 hours. The company advanced rapidly, enveloping the Le Mesnil-Robert farmstead from the right and thrust into the village of St. Aignan from the east. Six enemy tanks were knocked out in so doing. During this time enemy armour assembled 1½ kilometers east of St. Aignan. As soon as it was identified, by order of *Obersturmführer* Hurdelbrink, it was successfully taken under fire from the hill and from the hollow, whereby 18 enemy tanks were destroyed. The remaining tanks fled. *Obersturmführer* Hurdelbrink and another *Panzerjäger* thrust on past the village, whereby *Obersturmführer* Hurdelbrink knocked out five more tanks at the northern edge of the village. The positions attained were held until 2200 hours. Enemy anti-tank and infantry fire from the left flank then became so intense that the *Kompanie* was forced to withdraw, bringing all its wounded, along with *Infanterie Bataillon "Waldmüller,"* via Sylvain-le Bû to Soignolles. On this day *Kompanie* Hurdelbrink knocked out 29 tanks, of which the company commander, *Obersturmführer* Hurdelbrink, destroyed 11.

9 August, 1944:

*Bataillon "Waldmüller"*, to which the *1.(schwere) Kompanie* of *Panzerjäger Abteilung 12 "Hitlerjugend"* was attached, was assigned the mission of taking position by 0550 hours on the high ground south of Renemesnil. Even before

---

4   Vorschlag Nr. 8 für die Verleihung des Ritterkreuzes des Eisernen Kreuzes, signed for submission by Meyer with approval date of 16 October 1944. Meyer, also the *1.Generalstabsoffizier* of the division, had been awarded the German Cross in Gold with the *"Leibstandarte"* on 6 May 1943.

Begründung und Stellungnahme der Zwischenvorgesetzten

Am 8.8.1944 um 11,30 Uhr wurde die 1.(schw.)/Pz.Jg.Abt.12 "HJ" unter
Führung von H-Ostuf. Hurdelbrink durch den Kommandeur Pz.Jg.Abt.12 "HJ"
der Kampfgruppe Prinz unterstellt, mit dem Auftrag, zugleich mit den
Panzern der Kampfgruppe vorzustoßen.
1.Angriffsziel:  ST. AIGNAN .
2.Angriffsziel:  GARCELLES .
Der Angriff begann 11,50 Uhr . Die Kompanie kam, das Gehöft ROBERTS MESNIL
rechts umfassend, rasch vorwärts und stieß von Osten in das Dorf
ST.AIGNAN. Dabei wurden 6 feindliche Panzer abgeschossen. Während dieser
Zeit stellten sich im Grund 1 1/2 km ostwärts ST.AIGNAN fdl. Panzer
bereit, die sofort nach Erkennen auf Befehl von H-Ostuf.Hurdelbrink
von der Höhe und aus der Senke erfolgreich unter Feuer genommen wurden.
Dabei wurden 18 Panzer vernichtet. Die restlichen Panzer entzogen sich
durch die Flucht. H-Ostuf. Hurdelbrink und noch 1 Panzerjäger stießen
an dem Dorf vorbei, dabei schoß H-Ostuf. Hurdelbrink am Nordrand
des Dorfes weiter 5 Panzer ab. Die nun erreichten Stellungen wurden
bis 22,00 Uhr gehalten, dann wurde das fdl. Pak- und Infanteriefeuer aus
der linken Flanke so stark, daß sich die Kompanie unter Mitnahme aller
Verwundeten, gleichzeitig mit dem Inf.Btl.Waldmüller über SYLVAIN-le-BUI
nach SOIGNOLLES absetzen mußte. Die Kompanie Hurdelbrink schoß an diesem
Tage 29 Pz.Kpfwg. ab. Davon der Kompanie-Führer H-Ostuf.Hurdelbrink
allein 11 Pz.Kpfwg.
9.8.1944:
Das Btl. Waldmüller, dem die 1.(schw.)/Pz.Jg.Abt.12 "HJ" unterstellt
war, hatte den Auftrag, gegen 05,30 Uhr Stellungen auf den Höhen südlich
RENEMESNIL zu beziehen. Bereits vor Erreichen der Stellungen wurde das
Btl. von fdl. Pz.Kpfwg. angegriffen. Die 1.Kompanie griff sofort in die
Abwehr ein und übernahm anschließend die Sicherung für das weitere Vor-
gehen des Btl. . Während des ganzen Tages war heftiges Artillerie -
Granatwerfer- und Infanteriefeuer auf den eigenen Stellungen. Gegen 20,00
Uhr beabsichtigte das Btl. Waldmüller sich vom Gegner abzusetzen. Mitten
in diese Absetzbewegung hinein, stießen überraschend fdl.Pz.Kpfwg. in
Richtung auf das Dorf SOIGNOLLES. Die Gefährdung des Btl. wurde von
H-Ostuf.Hurdelbrink sofort erkannt. Er konnte mit noch einem Panzerjäger
den Feind in der Flanke fassen und ihn bis auf 2 Pz.Kpfwg., die sich
durch die Flucht entziehen konnten, vernichten. An diesem Tage vernichtete
die Kompanie 22 Pz.Kpfwg. .
10.8.1944:
Die 1.(schw.)/Pz.Jg.Abt.12 "HJ" war dem Pz.Rgt.12 "HJ" unterstellt. Sie
erhielt den Auftrag, in den Morgenstunden bei MAIZIERES über POITGNY
nach Straßengabel 1,5 km ostwärts von FONTAINE zu verlegen. Von dort
aus erhielt sie den Befehl, auf der Höhe 195 zur Sicherung nach Norden
in Stellung zu gehen. Der Kompanie Hurdelbrink wurden dazu 6 Sturmgesch.
und 6 "P 4 " Fernlenkpanzer unterstellt. Nach Erreichen der Straßengabel
wird bereits festgestellt, daß die Höhe 195 bereits von fdl.Pz.Kpfwg.
besetzt ist. H-Ostubaf. Wünsche, Kdr.Pz.Rgt.12 "HJ", befiehlt danach
den sofortigen Angriff auf die Höhe. Die Kampfgruppe kommt zuerst ohne
fdl.Beschuß gut vorwärts. Plötzlich auftretendes starkes Artillerie-
sperrfeuer verhindert dann jegliches weitere frontale Vorgehen.
H-Obersturmführer Hurdelbrink kommt zu dem Entschluß: Die 6 Sturmgesch.
binden weiter frontal, 2 Panzerjäger 39, darunter H-Ostuf.Hurdelbrink,

_stoßen_

Recommendation of *Obersturmführer* Georg Hurdelbrink, *Kompanie* Führer, *1./SS-Panzerjäger Abteilung 12*, for the Knight's Cross. Document appears courtesy of Mark C. Yerger.

stoßen rechts umfassend weiter vor. Nach schnellem Vorstoß kommen
die beiden Panzerjäger dem sich langsam absetzenden Feind in die
Flanke und können alle fdl. Pz.Kpfwg. vernichten. Die Kampfgruppe
geht anschließend so in Stellung, daß die Höhe 195 gehalten werden
kann. Abschußergebnis der Kompanie an diesem Tage 13 Panzer. Davon
ⵏ-Ostuf. Hurdelbrink 10 Panzer.

Durch die hervorragende Führung der Kompanie durch ⵏ-Ostuf.Hurdelbrink
konnte die Kompanie vom 8.8.-16.8.1944 86 Panzerabschüsse erreichen.
An diesem Abschußergebnis war der ⵏ-Ostuf. Hurdelbrink mit 36 Abschüs-
sen beteiligt.

ⵏ-Hauptsturmführer<br>
u.Abt.Kdr.

Ich halte den ⵏ-Obersturmführer H u r d e l b r i n k aufgrund
seiner besonders tapferen Haltung und seiner hohen Abschußzahl
an Panzern für würdig, mit dem Ritterkreuz des Eisernen Kreuzes
ausgezeichnet zu werden.

Für den vermißten Div.-Kommandeur<br>
Der erste Generalstabsoffizier

ⵏ-Sturmbannführer

Der Oberbefehlshaber
Pz.A.O.K.6

Befürwortet:

O.U., den 28.September 1944

ⵏ-Oberstgruppenführer und<br>
Panzergeneraloberst der W.-ⵏ

Recommendation of *Obersturmführer* Georg Hurdelbrink, *Kompanie* Führer, *1./SS-Panzerjäger Abteilung 12*, for the Knight's Cross. Document appears courtesy of Mark C. Yerger.

reaching the position the battalion was attacked by enemy armour. The *1.Kompanie* immediately defended and then took over securing the further advance of the battalion. Throughout the entire day the positions were under heavy artillery, mortar and infantry fire. At about 2200 hours *Bataillon "Waldmüller"* intended to break contact with the enemy. In the midst of this withdrawal, enemy armour advanced by surprise toward the village of Soignolles. *Obersturmführer* Hurdelbrink immediately recognized the threat. Along with another *Panzerjäger*, he attacked the enemy in the flank and destroyed all but two of the enemy tanks. Those took flight and escaped. On that day the company destroyed 22 enemy tanks.

10 August, 1944:

The *1.(schwere) Kompanie* of *Panzerjäger Abteilung 12 "Hitlerjugend"* was attached to *Panzer Regiment 12 "Hitlerjugend"*. In the morning hours at Maizières it was assigned the mission of shifting via Potigny to the fork in the road 1.5 kilometres east of Fontaine [le Pin]. From there it was ordered to take position on Hill 195 to secure to the north. Six *Sturmgeschütze* and six *P 4 Fernlenkpanzer* (radio controlled tanks) were attached to *Kompanie* Hurdelbrink. After reaching the fork in the road it was determined that Hill 195 was already held by enemy armour. *Obersturmbannführer* Wünsche, commander of *Panzer Regiment 12 "Hitlerjugend"* thereupon ordered an immediate attack on the hill. Initially the *Kampfgruppe* made good forward progress without receiving enemy fire. The sudden onset of heavy enemy protective fire then prevented any further frontal advance. *Obersturmführer* Hurdelbrink decided to have the six *Sturmgeschütze* fix the enemy from the front, while two *Panzerjäger 39*, including *Obersturmführer* Hurdelbrink, advanced to envelop the enemy from the right. After a rapid advance the two *Panzerjäger* attacked the slowly withdrawing enemy in the flank and were able to destroy all the enemy tanks. The *Kampfgruppe* then went into position so that it was able to hold Hill 195. On this day the company knocked out 13 tanks, ten of which were destroyed by *Obersturmführer* Hurdelbrink.

Thanks to the outstanding leadership of the company by *Obersturmführer* Hurdelbrink, the company was able to destroy 86 tanks between 8 August and 16 August, 1944. *Obersturmführer* Hurdelbrink, himself, accounted for 36 of these.

(Signed) [Günther] Wöst
*Hauptsturmführer* and *Abt.Kdr.*

Because of his outstanding courage and large number of enemy tanks destroyed, I recommend that *Obersturmführer* Hurdelbrink be awarded the Knight's Cross of the Iron Cross.

(Signed) [Hubert] Meyer
For the absent Division Commander
the First General Staff Officer
*Sturmbannführer*

The Commander in Chief
*Panzerarmeeoberkommando 6*
Endorsed:
*O.U.*, 28 September, 1944

(Signed) [Josef] Dietrich
*Oberstgruppenführer* and
*Panzergeneraloberst der Waffen-SS*

**Rudolf Roy**: Born in Berlin August 15, 1920, and joined SS November 1938. With *1./Ersatz Bataillon "LSSAH"* then *Panzerjäger Kompanie* and finally *SS-Panzerjäger Abteilung 1 "LSSAH"*. Promoted *Unterscharführer* January 30, 1943, and *Oberscharführer* July 1, 1944. To *"Hitlerjugend"* as heavy self-propelled anti-tank commander in *1./SS-Panzerjäger Abteilung 12*. Received field commission as *Untersturmführer d.R.* November 9, 1944, and *Zugführer 1./SS-Panzerjäger Abteilung 12*. Iron Cross 2nd Class August 21, 1941, Iron Cross 1st Class September 16, 1943, Tank Assault Badge in Silver February 21, 1942, and Eastern Front Medal August 30, 1942. Killed in Hollerath on December 17, 1944.

As an *Oberscharführer* and vehicle commander with the *1./SS-Panzerjäger Abteilung 12*, Rudolf Roy was proposed for the Knight's Cross by *Hauptsturmführer* Günther Wöst. Hubert Meyer, Ia of the division and temporary divisional commander, seconded and then submitted the award on 2 September 1944. Their proposal text reads as follows:[5]

In the early dawn of 9 August 1944, enemy armour penetrated the line of strongpoints that constituted the main line of resistance at Soignolles into the rear of *Kampfgruppe "Waldmüller"* and controlled all supply routes from Hill 111.

*Oberscharführer* Roy was ordered to attack and destroy the enemy armour with his *Panzerjäger 39*. With nimble-minded zeal, Roy attacked the armour and, within a short time, knocked out nine English tanks. In so doing he provided the prerequisites for the withdrawal that was ordered for that evening.

As the *Kampfgruppe* started the withdrawal, as ordered, at about 2130 hours, enemy armour thrust by surprise into the midst of the *Kampfgruppe* from the village of Soignolles. On his own initiative, *Oberscharführer* Roy attacked them in the flank. Only two of the 15 attacking enemy tanks were able to escape in flight.

*Oberscharführer* Roy knocked out 13 enemy tanks that day. Within five days he knocked out 26, raising his total to 36 English and Russian tanks destroyed.

(signed) [Günther] Wöst
*Hauptsturmführer* and *Abt.Kdr.*

Because of his unusually courageous action and the large number of enemy tanks he has knocked out, I recommend *Oberscharführer* Roy for the award of the Knight's Cross of the Iron Cross.

For the absent Division Commander
the First General Staff Officer
(signed) [Hubert] Meyer
*Sturmbannführer*

## German Cross in Gold Holders of *SS-Panzerjäger Abteilung 12*
**Georg Mack**: November 18, 1944, *Hauptscharführer, SS-Panzerjäger Abteilung 12*

---

5    Vorschlag Nr. 9 für die Verleihung des Ritterkreuzes des Eisernen Kreuzes, with handwritten approval date of 16 October 1944.

Begründung und Stellungnahme der Zwischenvorgesetzten

In der Morgendämmerung des 9.8.1944 waren feindliche Panzer-
Kampfwagen durch die stützpunktartige H.K.L. bei SOIGNOLLES
in den Rücken der Kampfgruppe Waldmüller eingedrungen und
beherschten von der Höhe 111 alle Nachschubwege.

Der ᛋᛋ-Oberscharführer R o y erhielt den Befehl mit seinem
Panzerjäger 39 die Feindpanzer anzugreifen und zu vernichten.
Mit Schneid und Wendigkeit pirschte sich R. an die Panzer
heran und schoss innerhalb kurzer Zeit 9 englische Panzer-
Kampfwagen ab. Dadurch wurde die Voraussetzung für die für den
Abend befohlene Absetzbewegung geschaffen.

Als sich die Kampfgruppe um 21,30 Uhr infolge des ständig
anwachsenden feindlichen Feuers befehlsgemäss abzusetzen
begann, stiessen überraschend feindliche Panzerkampfwagen mitten
in die Kampfgruppe auf das Dorf SOIGNOLLES vor. Aus selbstständi
gem Entschluss fasste ᛋᛋ-Oberscharführer Roy die Panzer in der
Flanke. Von den 15 angreifenden Feindpanzern konnten nur
2 durch die Flucht entkommen.

ᛋᛋ-Oberscharführer R o y vernichtete an diesem Tage 13,
innerhalb von 5 Tagen 26 und erhöhte so seine Gesamtabschuss-
zahl auf 36 englische und russische Panzer-Kampfwagen.

ᛋᛋ-Hauptsturmführer
u.Abt.Kdr.

Ich halte ᛋᛋ-Oberscharführer R o y aufgrund seiner besonders
tapferen Haltung und seiner hohen Abschußzahl an Panzern für
würdig, mit dem Ritterkreuz des Eisernen Kreuzes ausgezeichnet
zu werden.

Für den vermißten Div.-Kommandeur
Der erste Generalstabsoffizier

ᛋᛋ-Sturmbannführer

Recommendation of *Oberscharführer* Rudolf Roy, 1./*SS-Panzerjäger Abteilung
12*, for the Knight's Cross. Document appears courtesy of Mark C. Yerger.

**Georg Mack**: Joined *SS-Verfügungstruppe* October 1, 1938, at age 19 with *Totenkopf-verbände* and assigned to *"Oberbayern"*. Prewar moved to *"Leibstandarte"* and with *Panzerjäger Kompanie* then *Panzerjäger Abteilung*. Moved to *"Hitlerjugend"* as a gun commander *SS-Panzerjäger Abteilung 12*, more than 20 kills by time of German Cross in Gold proposal. Iron Cross 2nd Class and Iron Cross 1st class. Eventual fate unknown.

As commander of the *1./SS-Panzerjäger Abteilung 12*, *Obersturmführer* Georg Hurdelbrink proposed Georg Mack for the German Cross in Gold. Submitted on 15 September 1944, its text was as follows:[6]

> *SS-Hauptscharführer* Mack was awarded the Iron Cross, 1st Class, on 8 March 1943, for his outstanding bravery in the defensive and offensive fighting in the Kharkov area from January to April 1943.
>
> In the fighting north of Belgorod, during the period from 6 to 16 July 1943, Mack supported the infantry that was breaking through the deeply organized Russian position with his platoon of 7.5cm anti-tank guns. As the result of his flexible leadership the platoon destroyed six T-34s north of Lutschki. Mack himself knocked out two enemy AFVs. Despite his wounds (shell fragments in the back) Mack chose to remain with the company throughout the fighting.
>
> When the *Leibstandarte SS "Adolf Hitler"* was in action in Italy in 1943, Mack was employed fighting partisans in Istria. As commander of a small *Kampfgruppe* he played an outstanding role in the destruction of numerous partisan bands and equipment. Frequently, and often alone, he consistently carried out the missions assigned. Once, when the *Kampfgruppe* was attacked by partisans as it moved forward on a sunken road, it was only thanks to the courageous and stalwart conduct of Mack that the partisans were repulsed and, for the most part, wiped out.
>
> In the fighting in the Zhitomir area from November to December 1943, Mack and his platoon were with *SS-Panzer-Grenadier Regiment 1, Leibstandarte SS "Adolf Hitler"*. Always advancing with the spearhead of the attack, Mach played a major part in making it possible to reach the Kiev-Zhitomir highway at Kotscherovo, thereby cutting off the Russian supply traffic. During this action Mack knocked out one T-34.
>
> In the attack east of Korosten, Mack knocked out two T-34s in extremely difficult conditions on 21 December 1943 at Peremoga. While overrunning an enemy trench he put two anti-tank rifles out of action at extremely close range.
>
> On 24 December 1943, under cover of dusk, enemy armoured spearheads penetrated into a locality where Mach and his platoon were quartered. Mack immediately pulled his men together, wiped out the mounted infantry in hand-to-hand fighting and attached a magnetic hollow-charge, which unfortunately failed to detonate, to a T-34. Two of the enemy tanks were destroyed.
>
> In the defensive fighting in the Berdichev area Mack was one of the last that were still in contact with the enemy. When the Russians repeatedly attacked Ossykova in regimental strength with armoured support on 1 and 2 January 1944, they were repeatedly repulsed by the steadfastness of Mack's platoon. Four T-34s were destroyed.

---

6   Vorschlag Nr. 27 für die Verleihung des Deutschen Kreuzes in Gold, signed for submission by Hubert Meyer with handwritten approval date of 28 November 1944.

---

Begründung und Stellungnahme der Zwischenvorgesetzten

---

Das E. K. 1. Kl. wurde dem SS-Hscha. Mack am 8.3. 1943 fuer seine hervor=
ragende Tapferkeit in Abwehr-u.-Angriffkaempfen im Raum um CHARKOW im
Januar bis April 1943 verliehen.

Jn den Kaempfen noerdl. BJELGOROD in der Zeit vom 6.bis 16.7.43 unter =
stuetzte M. mit seinem Zug 7,5 cm Pak Sf. die sich durch die tiefgeglie=
derten Stellungen der Russen schlagende Jnfaterie. Jnfolge der wendigen
Fuehrung konnte der Zug noerdl. LUTSCHKI  6 T 34 vernichten. Hiervon
schoss M. selbst 2 fdl. Pz.-Kpfwg. ab. Trotz Verwundung (Gr.-Spl.Ruecken)
verblieb M. waehrend der Dauer der Kaempfe auf eigenen Wunsch bei der Kom=
panie.

Jm Jtalieneinsatz der L.SS-A.H. 1943 wurde der Zug Mack in JSTRIEN zur
Bandenbekaempfung eingesetzt. Als Fuehrer einer kleineren Kampfgruppe be=
teiligte er sich hervorragend an der Vernichtung zahlreicher Banden und Ge=
raet. Sehr oft auf sich allein gestellt, fuehrte er seine Auftraege stets
befehlsgemaess durch. Als die Kampfgruppe einmal auf dem Vormarsch in ei=
nem Hohlweg von Banden angefallen wurde, war es nur der mutigen und stand=
haften Haltung von Mack zu danken, dass die Banden zurueckgeschlagen und
zum groessten Teil aufgerieben werden konnten.

Bei den Kaempfen im Raum um SHITOMIR im November bis Dezember 1943 befand
sich M. mit seinem Zug beim 1.Pz.Gren.Rgt., LSS-A.H.. Jmmer mit den Angriffs=
spitzen vorstossend, trug M. wesentlich dazu bei, dass die Rollbahn KIEW-
SHITOMIR bei KOTSCHEROWO erreicht werden konnte, und dadurch der Versor=
gungsverkehr der Russen unterbrochen wurde. Hierbei vernichtete M. 1 T 34.

Beim Angriff ostw. KOROSTEN schoss M. am 21.12.43 bei PEREMOGA 2 T 34
unter schwierigsten Bedingungen ab. Waehrend des Aufrollens eines fdl. Gra=
bens setzte er 2 Pz.-Buechsen auf naechste Entfernung ausser Gefecht.
Am 24.12.43 stiessen fdl. Pz.-Spitzen im Schutz der Daemmerung in einen Ort
in dem M. mit seinem Zug untergezogen war. Schnellstens fasste M. seine
Maenner zusammen, vernichtete im Nahkampf die aufsitzende Jnf. und brachte

Recommendation of *Hauptscharführer* Georg Mack, *SS-Panzerjäger Abteilung 12*, for the German Cross in Gold. Document appears courtesy of Mark C. Yerger.

BDC * THIS COPY HAS BEEN MADE AT BERLIN DOCUMENT CENTER * BDC

an einem T 34 eine Haftladung an, die leider nicht detonierte. 2 der fdl. Pz.-Kpfwg. wurden vernichtet.

Jn den Abwehrkaempfen im Raum um BERDITSCHEW gehoerte M. meist zu den Letz= ten, die am Feind waren. Als am 1. u. 2. Januar 44, als die Russen wiederholt bei OSSYKOWA in Rgt.-Staerke mit Pz.-Unterstuetzung angriffen, wurden diese durch die Standhaftigkeit des Zuges Mack immer wieder zurueckgeschlagen. 4 T 34 wurden vernichtet.

An der Jnvasionsfront zeichnete sich Mack bei CAEN durch Mut, Tapferkeit u. Umsicht hervorragend aus. Am 8.8.44 fuhr er als Spitzengeschuetz der Kp. vor= aus und stiess als Erster, nachdem er durch die fdl. Jnfanteriestellungen durchgestossen war, auf einen marschierenden fdl. Pz.-Verband in Staerke von etwa 30 Pz.-Kpfwg. M. meldete sofort die Feindpanzer und nahm den Kampf gegen die vielfache Uebermacht auf. Von einem in der Flanke stehenden fdl. Pz.-Kpfw wurde M. abgeschossen. Trotz eigener schwerster Verwundung rettete er seihem verwundeten Richtschuetzen aus dem sofort brennenden Pz.-Jaeger 39.

    SS-Hscha. Mack ist bisher vietmal mit seinem Pz.-Jaeger abgeschos= sen worden. Jmmer wieder ist er sofort auf ein anderes Geschuetz umgestiegen, um den Kampf seines Zuges weiter fuehren zu koennen. Durch seine beispielhaf= te selbstlose Haltung hat er seinen Zug immer wieder nach vorn gerissen, Kri= senlagen ueberwunden und allen Unteffuehrern und Maennern ein leuchtendes Vorbild seines immerwaehrenden Draufgaengertums und seiner aussergewoehn= lichen Einsatzbereitschaft gegeben.

    Der SS-Hscha. Mack vernichtete bisher mit seinem Zug 7,5 Pak Sf.

        21 fdl. Pz.-Kampfwagen.

                SS - Obersturmführer
                und Kompanie-Führer.

Recommendation of *Hauptscharführer* Georg Mack, *SS-Panzerjäger Abteilung 12*, for the German Cross in Gold. Document appears courtesy of Mark C. Yerger.

On the Invasion Front Mack excelled in his courage, bravery and circumspection. On 8 August 1944, as point-gun for the company, he led the advance. After thrusting through the enemy infantry positions, he was the first to run into an enemy armoured formation of about 30 tanks on the march. He immediately reported the enemy armour and engaged the manifold superior enemy armoured force. Mack's vehicle was knocked out by an enemy tank on his flank. Despite his own extremely serious wounds he saved his wounded gunner from the *Panzerjäger 39*, which immediately burst into flame.

*Hauptscharführer* Mack has had his *Panzerjäger* shot out from under him four times. He has always immediately climbed into another vehicle so that he could continue to lead his platoon in the battle. Thanks to his exemplary, unselfish conduct he has repeatedly carried his platoon forward, overcome crises and provided all the non-commissioned officers and men with a brilliant example as an unflagging daredevil with his extraordinary fighting spirit.

With his platoon of self-propelled 7.5cm anti-tank guns, *Hauptscharführer* Mack has , to date, destroyed 21 enemy tanks.

(signed) [Georg] Hurdelbrink
*Obersturmführer* and *Kompanie-Führer*

## *SS-Panzerjäger Abteilung 12* 1944-1945

For reasons stated elsewhere in the appendix a complete listing of all officers of any late war formations such *"Hitlerjugend"* fighting in the West, especially in the final months of the war, is nigh-on impossible. Many having served with the *"Leibstandarte"*, the officer cadre of both units in this study suffered grievously in the less than a year between the start of the Normandy fighting and the end of the war. The following are known to have held the posts indicated and are in sequential order.

| | | |
|---|---|---|
| Hans-Jakob Hanreich[7] | *Sturmbannführer* | *Kommandeur* |
| Günther Wöst[8] | *Hauptsturmführer* | *Kommandeur* |
| Karl Brockschmidt[9] | *Hauptsturmführer* | *Kommandeur* |
| Georg Hurdelbrink[10] | *Obersturmführer* | *Kommandeur* |
| Heinrich Winkler[11] | *Obersturmführer* | *Adjutant* |
| Hans-Egon Schmid[12] | *Untersturmführer* | *Adjutant* |
| Theo Rabe | *Obersturmführer* | *Adjutant* |
| Karl-Heinz Probst | *Untersturmführer* | *Adjutant* |
| Karl Roeseler[13] | *Obersturmführer* | *Verwaltungsführer* (IVa) |
| Dr. Karl Wotke | *Hauptsturmführer* | *Abteilungsarzt* (IVb) |
| Karl aus der Wiesche | *Obersturmführer* | *TFK* |

7   Captured in August 1944, died September 29, 1987.
8   He wrote Georg Hurdelbrink's German Cross proposal, confirming him as Hanreich's successor.
9   An Army transfer from the *Oberkommando des Heeres* and still in command during the Ardennes fighting.
10  See Knight's Cross holders section, previously *1.Kompanie Chef*.
11  Previously adjutant of *SS-Panzerjäger Abteilung 1 "Leibstandarte"*. *Adjutant* until August 1944 when he became *Stabskompanie Chef*.
12  Confirmed adjutant in August 1944 as Winkler's successor.
13  Killed on May 26, 1944.

| Bruno Gill | *Untersturmführer* | *TFW* |
| Heinrich Winkler[14] | *Obersturmführer* | *Stabskompanie Chef* |
| Gerd Siegert | *Hauptsturmführer* | *Nachrichten Zugführer* |
| Kuno Huber[15] | *Untersturmführer* | *Nachrichten Zugführer* |

**1.Kompanie**

| Georg Hurdelbrink[16] | *Obersturmführer* | *1.Kompanie Chef* |
| Helmut Zeiner | *Obersturmführer* | *1.Kompanie Chef* |

**2.Kompanie**

| Günther Gornik | *Obersturmführer* | *2.Kompanie Chef* |
| Johann Wachter[17] | *Obersturmführer* | *2.Kompanie Chef* |

**3.Kompanie**

| Günther Wöst[18] | *Hauptsturmführer* | *3.Kompanie Chef* |

---

14  Previously adjutant of *SS-Panzerjäger Abteilung 1 "Leibstandarte"*, later became *Stabskompanie Chef* of *SS-Panzerjäger Abteilung 12 "Hitlerjugend"*. The *Stabskompanie* controlled the reconnaissance, dispatch, anti-aircraft, engineer, and signals platoons though only the *Zugführer* for the latter has been found.

15  By September 1944.

16  Moved to command of *SS-Panzerjäger Abteilung 12*.

17  Wounded August 11, 1944, and killed on December 19, 1944.

18  In August 1944 became *Kommandeur* of *SS-Panzerjäger Abteilung 12*, it is unknown who directly succeeded him.

# Allied armoured fighting vehicles knocked out by the Jagdpanzer IVs of *SS-Panzerjäger Abteilung 12*[1]

| Unit | 19.07.–07.08. 1944 | 08.–14. 08. 1944 | 15.–21. 08. 1944 | 22.–28. 08. 1944 | Total |
|------|------|------|------|------|------|
| *1.Kompanie* | 2 | 76 | 8 | – | 86 |
| *2.Kompanie* | – | 12 | 1 | – | 13 |
| *3.Kompanie* | – | – | 3 | – | 3 |
| **Total** | 2 | 88 | 12 | – | 102 |

---

1 Vojenský Historický Archiv, Praha (Military History Archives, Prague), Anlagen zum KTB der *SS-Panzerjäger Abteilung 12 "Hitlerjugend"*, Panzer-Abschußlisten.

# Appendix XX

# Battle casualties of *SS-Panzerjäger Abteilung 12* in Normandy, August 1944

| Unit | 1.–7. 08. 1944 | | | 8.–14. 08. 1944 | | | 15.–21. 08. 1944 | | | 22.–28. 08. 1944 | | | Total | | |
|---|---|---|---|---|---|---|---|---|---|---|---|---|---|---|---|
| | Dead | Wounded | Missing | Dead | Wounded | Missing | Dead | Wounded | Missing | Dead | Wounded | Missing | Dead | Wounded | Missing |
| *Stabskompanie* | – | – | – | – | – | – | 2 | 4 | 3 | – | – | – | 2 | 4 | 3 |
| *1.Kompanie* | – | 4 | – | 3 | 15 | 3 | – | 7 | 9 | – | 3 | 6 | 3 | 29 | 18 |
| *2.Kompanie* | – | 1 | – | 6 | 2 | 1 | – | 1 | 2 | – | 2 | 3 | 6 | 6 | 6 |
| *3.Kompanie* | – | 3 | – | 5 | 8 | 3 | 1 | 6 | 5 | – | – | 1 | 6 | 17 | 9 |
| Total | – | 8 | – | 14 | 25 | 7 | 3 | 18 | 19 | – | 5 | 10 | 17 | 56 | 36 |

# Bibliography and Guide to Further Reading

## Unpublished sources

Vojenský Historický Archiv, Praha (Military History Archives, Prague):

Kriegstagebuch Nr.1. der I./*SS-Panzer Regiment 12*.
Kriegstagebuch Nr.3 der II./*SS-Panzer Regiment 12*.
Kriegstagebuch Nr. 1 der *SS-Panzer-Jäger-Abteilung 12*.
Tätigkeitsbericht der *SS-Panzer-Jäger-Abteilung 12 "HJ"*.

## Published sources

Agte, Patrick, *Michael Wittmann und die Tiger der Leibstandarte SS Adolf Hitler*, Rosenheim: Deutsche Verlagsgesellschaft, 1995.

Barbarski, Krzysztof, *Polish Amour, 1939–1945*, London: Osprey, 1982.

Buckley, John, *British Armour in the Normandy Campaign*. London: Frank Cass, 2004.

Chamberlain, Peter and Doyle, Hilary, *Encyclopedia of German Tanks of World War Two*. London: Arms & Armour Press, 1999.

Fellgiebel, Walther-Peer, *Die Träger des Ritterkreuzes des Eisernen Kreuzes 1939-1945*, Friedberg: Podzun-Pallas, 1993.

Hart, Russell A., *Clash of Arms: How the Allies won in Normandy*, Boulder CO: Lynne Riener, 2001.

Hart, Stephen A., *Sherman Firefly vs. Tiger, Normandy 1944*, Oxford: Osprey, 2007.

Hart, Stephen and Russell Hart, *A Waffen-SS fegyverei és harceljárásai* [Weapons and Fighting Tactics of the Waffen-SS], Debrecen: Hajja és Fiai Könyvkiadó, 1999.

Jentz, Thomas L., *Die deutsche Panzertruppe* Band 2, Wölfersheim-Berstadt: Podzun-Pallas Verlag, 1999.

Kortenhaus, Werner, *21. Panzerdivision, 1943–1945*. Uelzen: Schneider Armour Research, 2007.

Lehmann, Rudolf, *Die Leibstandarte* Band 1, Osnabrück: Munin Verlag, 1977.

Meyer, Hubert, *Kriegsgeschichte der 12. SS-Panzerdivision "Hitlerjugend"* 2 Bände, Osnabrück: Biblio Verlag, 1999, 4th edition.

Nevenkin, Kamen, *Fire Brigades – The Panzer Divisions 1943–1945*, Winnipeg: J.J. Fedorowicz, 2008.

Reynolds, Michael, *Steel Inferno: I SS Panzer Corps in Normandy. The Story of the 1st and 12th SS Panzer Divisions in the 1944 Normandy Campaign*, Staplehurst: Spellmount, 1999. The author used the Hungarian translation – *Acélpokol. Az I. SS-páncéloshadtest Normandiában*, Debrecen: Hajja és Fiai Könyvkiadó, 1999.

Schneider, Wolfgang, *Panzertaktik. German Small-Unit Armor Tactics*, Winnipeg: J.J. Fedorowicz, 2000.

Schneider, Wolfgang, *Tiger im Kampf* Band II. Uelzen: Schneider Armour Research, 2001.

Strauß, Franz Josef, *Geschichte der 2. (Wiener) Panzer-Division*. Eggolsheim: Dörfler, 2005.

*Wiking Ruf / Der Freiwillige*, Osnabrück: Munin Verlag, 1951-1990.

Yerger, Mark C.: *Waffen-SS Commanders, The Army, Corps, and Divisional Leaders of a Legend*, Atglen, PA: Schiffer, 1998-1999, 2 volumes.

Yerger, Mark C. *German Cross in Gold Holders of the SS and Police Volume 1: "Das Reich" – Heinz Lorenz to Herbert Zimmerman*, San Jose, CA: James Bender Publishing, 2005

Yerger, Mark C. *German Cross in Gold Holders of the SS and Police Volume 2: "Das Reich" – Kurt Almacher to Heinz Lorenz*, San Jose, CA: James Bender Publishing, 2004

Zetterling, Niklas, *Normandy 1944: German Military Organization, Combat Power and Organizational Effectiveness*, Winnipeg: J.J. Fedorowicz, 2000.

# Index

## Index of Places

## Index of German Military Units

Some units are referenced throughout the book or material relating to them is easy to locate – to save repetition and a profusion of page references, the following units are not included in this index:

> *12.SS-Panzer Division "Hitlerjugend"*
> *SS-Panzer Regiment 12* or any sub-units
> *SS-Panzerjäger Abteilung 12* or any sub-units

### Armies

### Corps

### Divisions

## Index of Allied Military Units

### Army Groups

### Corps

### Divisions

### Brigades

### Regiments

# Related titles published by Helion & Company

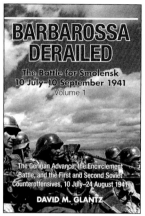

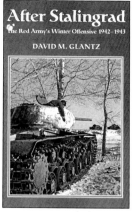

Barbarossa Derailed. The Battle for
Smolensk 10 July-10 September Volume 1.
The German Advance, the Encirclement
Battle, and the First and Second Soviet
Counteroffensives, 10 July-24 August 1941
David M. Glantz
656pp, photos, maps
Hardback
ISBN 978-1-906033-72-9

After Stalingrad. The Red Army's
Winter Offensive 1942-1943
David M. Glantz
536pp, photos, maps
Paperback
ISBN 978-1-907677-05-2

## A selection of forthcoming titles

**HELION & COMPANY**
26 Willow Road, Solihull, West Midlands B91 1UE, England
Telephone 0121 705 3393     Fax 0121 711 4075
Website: http://www.helion.co.uk